HITLER'S POLICE BATTALIONS

HITLER'S POLICE BATTALIONS

Enforcing Racial War in the East

Edward B. Westermann

Foreword by Dennis Showalter

University Press of Kansas

Published by the University Press of Kansas (Lawrence, Kansas 66049),
which was organized by the Kansas Board of Regents and is operated
and funded by Emporia State University, Fort Hays State University,
Kansas State University, Pittsburg State University, the University of
Kansas, and Wichita State University

Library of Congress Cataloging-in-Publication Data

Westermann, Edward B.
Hitler's police battalions : enforcing racial war in the East /
Edward B. Westermann ; foreword by Dennis Showalter.
    p.   cm. — (Modern war studies)
Includes bibliographical references and index.
ISBN 0-7006-1371-4 (cloth : alk. paper)
1. Nationalsozialistische Deutsche Arbeiter-Partei. Einsatzgruppen des
Sicherheitsdienstes und der Sicherheitspolizei.   2. World War,
1939–1945—Atrocities—Poland.   3. World War, 1939–1945—
Atrocities—Soviet Union.   I. Title.   II. Series.
D804.3.W445   2005
940.54´1343—dc22   2004026497

British Library Cataloguing-in-Publication Data is available.

Printed in the United States of America
10 9 8 7 6 5 4 3 2 1

The paper used in this publication meets the minimum requirements of
the American National Standard for Permanence of Paper for Printed
Library Materials Z39.48-1984.

FOR BRIGITTE, SARAH, AND MARLIES

CONTENTS

ILLUSTRATIONS

"Day of the German Police" in 1937 in Berlin.

Uniformed policemen clear out a hiding area used by Jews in
Lublin, Poland, in December 1940.

Himmler presents awards during the track and
field Police Championships held in June 1938 in Lübeck.

The German caption to this photograph reads: "On the
Soviet Front: police in combat against the partisans."

Captured Soviet partisans being guarded by policemen in
the vicinity of Zhitomir in September 1942.

Himmler leading the oath of Austrian policemen as they swear fealty to
Hitler in a ceremony at the "Square of Heroes" (Heldenplatz)
in Vienna on March 17, 1938.

Tables

Figures

ACKNOWLEDGMENTS

I have been researching and writing about the Ordnungspolizei since 1991. In the past thirteen years, I have received the generous assistance of numerous persons and organizations; all have greatly contributed to this work. As a graduate student pursuing a master's degree in European history at Florida State University, I received expert assistance from Alan Steinweis (my thesis adviser), Edward Wynot, and Peter Garretson as I began my inquiry into this subject. Likewise, Wolfgang Wippermann and Gerhard Baader supported my research during a stay at the Free University of Berlin as a Fulbright Fellow in 1994–1995. During my doctoral studies at the University of North Carolina, Chapel Hill, Gerhard Weinberg, Konrad Jarausch, and Christopher Browning generously looked at several different projects and provided expert suggestions and advice, even as I pursued a dissertation project unrelated to the German police. Gerhard Weinberg and Christopher Browning also looked at a draft of this manuscript and graciously provided their comments and insights.

While I was on a German Academic Exchange Service (DAAD) research fellowship in 2003–2004, Klaus-Michael Mallmann shared not just his hospitality but his thoughts and broad expertise, despite his own plans to publish a monograph on this topic. He also kindly allowed me to deliver a presentation on the Uniformed Police to his class at the University of Stuttgart and commented on a draft copy of the manuscript. The collegiality and friendship shown to a fellow scholar of the police are immensely appreciated. Likewise, I owe special thanks to Jürgen Matthäus for his friendship and assistance in the writing of this book. During my stay in Berlin, I also benefited from the insights of Andrej Angrick, Konrad Kwiet, and Ray Brandon. The last generously provided me with several copies of documents from his own collection.

I have also benefited from the support of several organizations, including the Fulbright Commission, the German Academic Exchange Service, and the U.S. Holocaust Memorial Museum. At the Holocaust Memorial Museum in the summer of 1999, Truman Anderson, Ray Brandon, Martin Dean, Isabel Heinemann, Wendy Lower, Dieter Pohl, and Helene Sinnreich contributed their valuable thoughts and suggestions to my research. In particular, Richard

Breitman graciously took time to discuss his views on the police over lunch during a sweltering July day in Washington, D.C.

A number of other people have played a key role in helping me pursue research or test my ideas about the police, including Don McKale, Omer Bartov, Thomas Pegelow, Alexander Rossino, John Dunn, Thomas Griffith Jr., and Donald Stoker. Special thanks are due to Dan Rogers, who allowed me to lecture on this topic to his classes at the University of South Alabama and read and commented on the manuscript for this project. I would also like to thank Mike Briggs, Susan Schott, Larisa Martin, and the entire team at the University Press of Kansas for their efforts in bringing this work to publication.

I have always received courteous and professional treatment from the staffs of the German Federal Archives in Berlin, Freiburg, Koblenz, and Ludwigsburg. I would especially like to thank Rainer Juchheim in Ludwigsburg and Martina Kaspers in Koblenz for their expert assistance during my last research visit to the Federal Republic in preparation for finishing the book manuscript. Likewise, the staff of the National Archives and Records Administration in College Park, Maryland, and the staff at the U.S. Holocaust Memorial Museum Archive provided expert assistance. Additionally, I want to express my appreciation for the support of the library staffs at Florida State University, the University of North Carolina, Chapel Hill, and the Air University library, especially Edith Williams from the interlibrary loan department of the last.

I am honored to have Dennis Showalter writing the foreword to this work. From my earliest experience in teaching the Holocaust and pursuing publication opportunities, his advice, friendship, and assistance have been invaluable. I am grateful for his assistance as a friend, mentor, and professional colleague. Likewise, I would like to thank Karl and Gisela Meyer for their gracious hospitality during my research visits to Berlin. Finally, I would like to thank my wife, Brigitte, for her encouragement, support, and proofreading efforts as I repeatedly decided to pursue "just one more project" on the police. As is apparent, I have benefited from the help of many talented and generous individuals, but any faults with this work are my responsibility alone.

FOREWORD

The National Socialist regime was both popular and populist. Its support steadily increased after it assumed power in 1933. It took pains to win the hearts and minds of the German people. It took further pains to keep them informed—especially about the ongoing war against social, political, and above all racial enemies. Perhaps the best evidence of the positive response is offered by the reliance of the security agencies on voluntary denunciations as the basis for most of their investigations.

Nor was this behavior compliance evoked by fear or by the often-alleged German submissiveness to authority no matter who exercises it. In *The Nazi Conscience*, Claudia Koonz demonstrates that the Third Reich successfully nurtured a powerful sense of right and wrong. Built around an ethnic community that excluded outsiders as a matter of principle, it inspired positive action from "ordinary people" in what is arguably best understood as a racial war with military elements that began in 1933 and ended only with the regime's annihilation in 1945.

No German institution illustrates this process better than the police battalions who served in the occupied East. Their taproot was the Ordnungspolizei, formed in most states of the Weimar Republic for internal security purposes. Brought under Reich control by Heinrich Himmler, the now-centralized police participated in the invasion of Austria and the occupation of the Sudetenland in 1938 and the absorption of the rump Czech state the next year. On the outbreak of war with Poland, they were organized into battalions that were used, not just for policing and internal security duties, but increasingly for the deportations and mass executions intrinsic to Nazi rule of Slavs and Jews.

In the war's first year, the number of police battalions increased to over a hundred. Once Himmler gained permission to accept volunteers, ranks originally limited to men too old for the field army were swelled by volunteers considering a permanent police career or simply hoping for a safe job. Levels of training varied, but, in *The Origins of the Final Solution*, Christopher Browning establishes two consistent points. One was militarization: establishing an organization with military capabilities while inculcating the Nazi conflation of military discipline and absolute obedience. The second was the growing integration of the Ordnungspolizei with the SS in terms of both

personnel and ideology, with the aim of infusing the institution with National
Socialist principles and values. The men who marched into Russia in 1941
were a long way from such familiar images of policemen as bringing home
village drunks and rescuing kittens from trees—or even, indeed, "interrogat-
ing" a recalcitrant suspect in the station basement with fists and rubber hoses.
Instead, they had become part of an organizational culture of genocide, with
Nazi racial ideology as its standard: "political soldiers" in a way foreign even
to a Waffen-SS whose focus was increasingly on frontline combat.

Edward B. Westermann brilliantly demonstrates the genesis and the consequences of that development. He synthesizes a broad spectrum of archival
research with comprehensive command of published sources in a definitive
presentation of one of the primary direct facilitators of genocide. He traces
the processes of creating a "new moral order," dominated by toughness, on
the one hand, and exclusion and enmity, on the other. The trail of atrocities
that the police battalions left in their wake was no mere manifestation of the
filth of war. It was part of a premeditated campaign of annihilation, ordered
from the Reich's summit, and privileged at all levels. Nor were the participants relative innocents, going with a flow that they could not master or
evade. The officers and senior enlisted men were usually professionals with
experience in the violent aspects of law enforcement. The junior ranks had
usually made an initial choice to serve in the police and usually knew in
advance what particular kind of "action" they would be performing. For
those unable to participate in murder, the usual penalty was, not instant execution, but extra duty—cleaning latrines, perhaps, or peeling potatoes,
accompanied by taunts from stronger-stomached comrades. Westermann
shows that there is not a single documented case of a policeman being shot or
imprisoned for refusing to kill Jews! Nor, among the thousands of pages of
records that Westermann has consulted, is there discussion at higher levels
of problems involving refusal to commit murder to order.

Negatives are not proof. The absence of evidence is nevertheless a strong
indication that the Uniformed Police made choices—not merely a one-time
Faustian bargain, but a plebiscite of everyday that consistently reaffirmed
their commitment to the National Socialist system. Persecution, exploitation,
and murder were positive behaviors in an organization whose institutionalized and internalized mission was serving the German people by annihilat-
ing its enemies.

In that context, Westermann's research also drives another spike—if one
is needed—into the "clean shield" mythology that depicts the Third Reich's
atrocities as the work of Party functionaries while the armed forces waged
war—admittedly hard war, but in the end war waged within generally
accepted parameters. Westermann's text depicts instead a close, virtually sym-

biotic relationship between the army and the police, a synergy in which missions were assigned and exchanged depending on circumstances. A police battalion might find itself in the front lines facing a Soviet offensive; it might be assigned to a "reprisal action" against purported guerrillas; or it might be given the job of shooting the Jewish population of a particular town. It was all in the day's work. And *Hitler's Police Battalions* extends our understanding of the ways in which men become murderers.

Dennis Showalter

INTRODUCTION

Christmas Eve 1941 was particularly cold for those serving on the Eastern Front, but, for the men of the Third Company of Police Battalion (PB) 322, the evening offered a chance to celebrate as a group indoors, away from the frigid weather. At the start of the evening's festivities, the men assembled around a Christmas tree, enjoying the soft light cast by the candles adorning the branches. A senior police sergeant began the festivities by reading a Christmas poem that he had composed expressly for this gathering of his comrades. After the poem was finished, the company commander, First Lieutenant Gerhard Riebel, moved forward to address the group.[1] The men probably expected their commander, a man who at one time had intentions of becoming a Protestant theologian, to offer a prayer or words of encouragement to bolster the spirits of a unit that had spent the last five months conducting operations in the East.[2] In fact, Riebel had prepared a "homily" for his men; however, his words did not highlight the virtues of charity, forgiveness, and redemption. Instead, he spoke of "the necessity of the battle between Germandom and Jewishdom" that justified the sacrifices made by men separated from their families in the "great contest between two [opposing] worldviews." Riebel's words apparently had the desired effect as the unit diarist made note of "the good spirits" of the men and the fact that the celebration lasted until the early hours of Christmas Day.[3]

Riebel's words concerning the battle between "Germandom" and "Jewishdom" were not simply the empty platitudes of a commander parroting the orders of his superiors or the propaganda slogans of the Third Reich. He and the men of his company had done much to translate words into action during their brief stay in the East. In fact, the senior leadership of the SS and police forces had paved the way for the actions of the entire Uniformed Police organization in the preceding eight years in both words and deeds, by creating an organizational culture within the police in which anti-Semitism and anti-Bolshevism emerged as institutional norms and expanded the boundaries of acceptable and desired behavior.

In the case of PB 322, the senior SS and police leadership provided clear instructions on their expectations prior to the unit's departure from Vienna. Already on April 15, 1941, an order from the Reich leader of the SS and chief of the German police, Heinrich Himmler, arrived at the battalion's headquarters, alerting the unit to an impending mission outside Germany with instructions that the battalion would be conducting operations under Himmler's "personal direction."[4] On June 7, Major General of the Police Retzlaff, the inspector of the Uniformed Police for Vienna, reminded the battalion of the importance of its mission and exhorted the policemen to "fulfill their duty." He also urged the men to "behave as racial superiors [*Herrenmenschen*] toward the Slavic peoples and to demonstrate that they were German."[5] Retzlaff ended his speech with an oath of allegiance to Hitler, and the gathered policemen joined him in the singing of the German national anthem and the National Socialist anthem, the Horst Wessel Song.[6]

On June 28, the battalion, now in Warsaw, assembled for an inspection by the higher SS and police leader (HSSPF) Erich von dem Bach-Zelewski and his Wehrmacht counterpart, Major General Max von Schenckendorff, in preparation for their imminent departure for operations in the Soviet Union. Schenckendorff praised the battalion and expressed his confidence that it would "completely fulfill the tasks at hand."[7] Later, Schenckendorff promised Bach "complete freedom" in the employment of the police forces within the rear areas of Army Group Center.[8]

As the policemen of PB 322 crossed into Russia, they wasted little time in translating racial theories into practice by forcibly enlisting over a hundred Jews to clean their accommodations in Bialystok. Two days later, on July 8, their activities took a more ominous turn as they conducted a surprise search of the Bialystok Jewish quarter, seizing some two thousand Jewish men, and executing "looters and weapons owners."[9] This first in what was to become a long line of "Jewish actions" happened to coincide with a visit by Himmler. In postwar testimony, one member of the battalion recalled Himmler's visit, noting that the Reich leader of the SS had complained that too few Jews had been rounded up and ordered the police leadership to increase their efforts.[10] Himmler's exhortation appeared to have the desired effect, as there is compelling evidence that policemen from PB 322 and PB 316 assisted Security Police forces in the murder of these Jewish men during that evening.[11] In this case, the two police battalions cooperated with the Wehrmacht's Field Command (Feldkommandantur) 539 as well as with members of the 221st Security Division and had received directions to remain in the city until the operation was finished.[12]

Himmler's visit was not coincidental, and his appearance at the Eastern Front in the early days of the campaign was undoubtedly part of an effort to observe, exhort, and, when necessary, direct the actions of SS and police units involved in a war of annihilation against the Third Reich's putative foe, the specter of Jewish-Bolshevism. In fact, only the day after Himmler's visit, the chief of the Uniformed Police, Kurt Daluege, inspected the members of

Police Regiment Center, arrayed in formation in a stadium near Bialystok. In hot and humid conditions, Daluege addressed the assembled policemen, delivering a clear and unambiguous message concerning their mission. He emphasized that the regiment could take pride in its role in the battle against Bolshevism, and he noted: "Bolshevism would be finally exterminated as a blessing [*Segen*] to Germany, Europe, and the entire world."[13]

The police battalions were not the only instruments of annihilation prepared by Himmler for the campaign to exterminate Bolshevism. The notorious Einsatzgruppen (Special Mission Groups) played a central role in Adolf Hitler's racial war in the East by acting as the vanguard of Heinrich Himmler's SS forces, tasked with the elimination of the Third Reich's putative racial enemies in the pursuit of living space (*Lebensraum*). Composed of members of the Security Police, including personnel from the Gestapo and the Criminal Police as well as members of the Security Service (SD), the Uniformed Police, and the Waffen-SS, the Einsatzgruppen entered the Soviet Union on a mission of conquest, exploitation, and extermination. By the end of 1942, they had murdered approximately 750,000 Jews and increasingly cooperated with German army forces in antipartisan operations in the East—operations aimed, not just at Jews, but at the entire spectrum of Nazi racial enemies.[14]

On July 10, Daluege, accompanied by Bach, visited the policemen of the Third Company as they guarded a prisoner-of-war (POW) transit camp. The company's war diary notes Daluege's visit but does not provide details of his words to the men. Still, it is reasonable to assume that he repeated his message of the previous day, an assumption made even more likely when one considers that the Third Company shot a total of 64 Jews "while trying to escape" in the period between July 10 and July 14.[15] In fact, PB 322 recorded the execution of 105 civilians and POWs for the period between July 6 and July 17. The battalion diary also noted that this total included 94 Jews and provided the rationale for these shootings as "looting or rather attempted escape."[16] The designation of Jewish victims as *looters* or *weapons owners* provided a thinly veiled justification for their murder, as did the ubiquitous use of the category *shot while trying to escape*. The executions of Jews and POWs, however, did not prevent the men of the Third Company from enjoying a "cozy get-together" around a campfire on the evening of July 26.[17]

July proved a deadly month for many who came into contact with the policemen of PB 322, but it was merely the sanguinary baptism of fire for a unit that would cut a bloody swath from Bialystok to Smolensk between July 1941 and May 1942, leaving at least eleven thousand men, women, and children dead in its wake, including nine thousand Jews.[18] On August 9, Riebel's company undertook an "evacuation action" of all Jews in the town of Bialowezie. The town's Jewish men between the ages of sixteen and forty-five

were placed in a temporary holding camp while the Jewish women and children and the remaining Jewish men were transported by truck to Kobryn with
only the possessions that they could fit into suitcases. Early the next morning, Riebel's men executed seventy-seven of the Jewish men in the holding
camp. Several men at a time were forced to lay facedown in a long ditch as
individual policemen stood over them and fired a round into the back of each
victim's head. The company then repeated this procedure, with new groups
forced to lie down on the bloody corpses of the group before them. Riebel
temporarily spared the lives of five tailors, four shoemakers, and one watch-
maker on the basis of the unit's "urgent need" for their services.[19] Only four
days later, the company embarked on another "Jewish action," this time
against the Jews of Narewka Mala. As in the case of Bialowezie, the unit gathered the Jewish women and children (259 and 162, respectively) for transport
to Kobryn; however, it broadened its charter by executing all the Jewish men,
who ranged in age from sixteen to sixty-five.[20] The evening following the executions, the company again assembled around a campfire and enjoyed a special ration of beer, an event once again described by the unit diarist as a "cozy
get-together" (*gemütliches Beisammensein*).[21]

Narewka Mala signaled an important escalation in the severity of the campaign aimed at local Jewish populations as the machinery of annihilation
expanded to encompass all adult males, even those of advanced age. The
escalatory spiral of brutality, however, was not at an end. Only two weeks
later, the company murdered 330 Jews from the Minsk ghetto, including 40
Jewish women. The ostensible reason for the inclusion of these women
involved their failure to display the yellow Star of David on their clothing.[22]
In any event, the inclusion of women as victims marked a further intensifi-
cation of brutality in the Third Reich's crusade in the East.

As the policemen of PB 322 celebrated Christmas, they had participated in
the full spectrum of security, pacification, atrocity, and reprisal actions conducted by German SS and police forces on the Eastern Front. Their victims
included almost the entire range of National Socialist racial, political, and
social enemies, including Jews, POWs, Communist functionaries, "vagrants,"
Russian civilians, partisans, and irregulars.[23] Senior SS leaders, including
Himmler and Daluege, had visited the battalion on several occasions to
emphasize the importance of its efforts, and Daluege himself sent at least one
congratulatory message to Police Regiment Center. Furthermore, the Wehrmacht leadership in the army rear areas became more and more reliant on
police assistance in support of their pacification efforts and even directly
requested the employment of police forces in actions aimed at Jews.[24] During
Hitler's "crusade" in the Soviet Union, Himmler's police emerged as one of
the primary instruments for the conduct of racial war, and the transforma-

tion of these men from civil servants into political soldiers offers a key insight into the nature of how men became murderers in support of an atavistic and malevolent campaign of destruction.

The Role and Function of Ideology

The role of ideology during the Third Reich remains an issue of continuing interest within the academic community even though almost sixty years have passed since the defeat of Nazi Germany. In many ways, questions concerning the relative importance of ideology often resemble eschatological or theological debates of little practical value. Those who choose to emphasize the importance of ideology are often accused of adopting a reductionist, or, even worse, a simplistic, Manichaean standard of evaluation. Certainly, there are differing interpretations concerning the utility and explanatory power of this concept. By privileging ideology, one runs the risk of disregarding the diversity of individual motivations in the search for a universalized explanation. Despite the risks inherent in oversimplification, the historian cannot afford to ignore or minimize the role of ideology in creating the environment that framed and even catalyzed the actions of individuals and specific organizations during the Nazi dictatorship. In short, ideology played a central role in the creation of the National Socialist racial state, which is not to say that every German embraced the most radical implications of the anti-Semitic and national chauvinistic images that confronted them daily in classrooms, workplaces, and theaters or in the print media or over the airwaves.[25]

In earlier studies tracing the effect of Nazi ideology, historians have examined the actions and motivations of a diverse array of organizations. For example, Christopher Browning found that Foreign Office personnel "were primarily motivated by considerations of careerism, not racial ideology or fanatical and blind obedience to higher authority" in the pursuit of "*Judenpolitik.*"[26] Similarly, Peter Hayes highlighted "amoral pragmatism and professionalism," not ideology, as the motive force guiding the actions of executives at IG Farben as German industry made its own contribution to the annihilation of the European Jews.[27] In a further example, according to Alfred Mierzejewski, as trains rolled toward Auschwitz, the leadership and operators of the German railway were motivated by professional competence and an "indifference" to the fate of the Jews trapped within Reichsbahn freight cars.[28]

If one accepts the premise that diplomats, businessmen, and railway personnel remained relatively immune to the poisonous influence of National Socialist ideology, can the same be said of the organizations of state control? In his work examining the motivations of the Security Police, Yaacov Lozowick reached the conclusion that these men were "a group of people completely aware of what they were doing, people with high ideological motivation, people of initiative and dexterity who contributed far beyond what was necessary. . . . [T]hey clearly understood that their deeds were not positive except in the value system of the Third Reich. They hated Jews and thought that getting rid of them would be to Germany's good."[29] Lozowick's contention is highly reminiscent of the explanation offered by Rudolf Höss, the commandant of the Auschwitz death camp, that the brutality of the SS concentration camp guards resulted from a "hate indoctrination" passed along from the senior leadership to the rank and file, a doctrine that was part and parcel of the National Socialist worldview.[30] Similarly, Michael Thad Allen's work on midlevel SS bureaucrats controlling the SS system of slave labor presents a picture of men with ideological commitment and not mechanical, amoral technocrats focused merely on the task at hand.[31]

Explaining the Behavior of the Uniformed Police

The recognition of the large-scale role of the Uniformed Police in the conduct of genocide has led to several competing explanations concerning the reasons why the men of the police battalions participated in the prosecution of racial war. In his innovative study of the activities of Reserve PB 101 in Poland, Christopher Browning paints a convincing portrait of "ordinary men" largely motivated by mundane concerns for acceptance and conformity within a larger group. According to Browning, the policemen of PB 101 were guided, not by ideological hatred or fanatical adherence to National Socialism, but by respect and deference to authority, concern for career advancement, and peer group pressure.[32] In contrast, the political scientist Daniel Goldhagen catalyzed an academic furor with the publication of *Hitler's Willing Executioners*. Although the actions of the police battalions were not the main focus of his work, Goldhagen devoted considerable attention to them, concluding: "The study of police battalions, finally, yields two fundamental facts: First, ordinary Germans easily became genocidal killers. Second, they did so even though they did not have to." For Goldhagen, what prepared German policemen for genocide was neither institutional affiliation nor professional background and experience but simply German culture itself with its existing atmosphere of "eliminationist anti-Semitism."[33] While Browning's explanation of police behavior minimizes the effect of ideology and indoctrination within the police, Goldhagen's model elevates ideology as the sine qua non of German social behavior.

More recently, the work of the German historian Klaus-Michael Mall-mann has provided important insights into the activities and motivations of the Uniformed Police.[34] Likewise, Jürgen Matthäus examined the effects of SS indoctrination efforts on the Uniformed Police with a specific focus on the portrayal of the "Jewish question" in SS and police literature. Matthäus recognized the importance of ideological indoctrination, especially within the circles of the senior SS leadership, and detailed the initiatives and themes pursued by the leadership as well as the practical effect of organized entertainment activities and professional and social get-togethers or "fellowship evenings" (*Kameradschaftsabende*) on police behavior. He argues that these efforts were "from the beginning directed at the internalization of an attitude; an attitude with regard to the methods to be used in the Jewish question that remained flexible and situational allowing for different practices [in application]."[35] Matthäus is correct in looking for the impulse for genocide among the ideological initiatives pursued by Himmler and the senior SS and police leadership; however, the ambition of these men extended beyond the conditioning of the police as convinced anti-Semites. Instead, Himmler, Daluege, and the HSSPFs sought to create an organizational culture within the police corps that glorified the concept of uniquely defined military identity married with the precepts of an SS ethic that embraced National Socialist racial philosophy and stressed the special obligations of membership in an exclusive and hallowed order. In fact, it was the acceptance by the Uniformed Police of this martial attitude in conjunction with Nazi racial ideology that resulted in the emergence of a police apparatus more suitable for the conduct of war and atrocity than public service.

Creating an Organizational Culture

The concept of organizational culture offers a useful framework for evaluating the institutional goals and standards established within the entire SS and police complex. For the purposes of this argument, Edgar H. Schein's pioneering work on organizational culture provides the foundation for relating this theoretical construct to the activities of the German Uniformed Police. Schein defines *organizational culture* as the "basic assumptions and beliefs that are shared by members of an organization, that operate unconsciously, and that define in a basic 'taken for granted' fashion an organization's view of itself and its environment."[36] In short, organizational culture sets the boundaries for accepted behavior, establishes institutional goals, and defines the standards of group membership.

The culture of an organization is formed and defined by the values, rituals, climate, and patterns of behavior of the organization's members; it is, however, leadership, according to Schein, that "embeds and transmits" culture to the organization's members and acts as the key mechanism in the creation of an institutional identity.[37] Contemporary research also demonstrates the key role of leadership in defining the organizational culture of law enforcement agencies. One study concerning police organizations described leadership as the glue holding all parts of the organization together through the propagation of a shared vision.[38] And, in fact, the leadership of the Uniformed Police played a key role in establishing an organizational climate within the police that established the precepts of National Socialist racial thought as the institutional standard.

The Facilitators of Genocide

Without a doubt, Heinrich Himmler and Kurt Daluege shared a vision of the police and expended substantial effort in promulgating this vision among the members of the organization. In the prewar years, and, especially, as Hitler embarked on his quest for an empire in the East, the Uniformed Police battalions became a special target of Himmler's and Daluege's efforts and a ready instrument for the conduct of annihilation. Indeed, two dominant characteristics within the organizational culture of the police offer strong evidence for explaining the actions of the police battalions on the Eastern Front.

First, the "militarization" of the police constituted a central objective of the Uniformed Police leadership from the initial National Socialist "seizure of power" until the ultimate collapse of Hitler's Thousand-Year Reich. The concept of militarization was not simply limited to the establishment of a hierarchical police organization with military capabilities but also encompassed a specific worldview (*Weltanschauung*) that married the concept of military duty with absolute obedience and the vision of a "higher purpose." Second, the police leadership increasingly pursued efforts to inculcate the "police soldier" with National Socialist values by "merging" (*verschmelzen*) the police in a psychological and physical sense with the SS. It is, of course, impossible, when dealing with a large organization, to achieve a homogeneous and unified body all members of which think and act completely alike in consonance with a shared corporate mind-set. However, it is equally clear that the dominant organizational culture of a particular institution plays a vital role in establishing the parameters of both desired and accepted behavior to guide the actions of individuals. Likewise, the dual initiatives of militarization and the merging of the police with the SS go far to explain the manner in which individual policemen and the police battalions were shaped into instruments of annihilation.

The SS and Police Complex

After the National Socialist seizure of power, Hitler and his paladins recognized the importance of gaining control of the Uniformed and Political Police forces of the independent state governments (*Länder*). Heinrich Himmler's plans for creating a national police force or "Reichspolizei" included, not only the men of the police, but also a fusion of state and party organizations, specifically the merging of the organizations of the SS with the police.[39]

The creation of the Security Police Main Office and the Uniformed Police Main Office in June 1936 under the command of Reinhard Heydrich and Kurt Daluege, respectively, went far toward achieving both goals.[40] The former encompassed the two branches of the Security Police, the Criminal Police and the secret state police or Gestapo, as well as the Party's intelligence branch, the Security Service. The Criminal Police (Kriminalpolizei) consisted of the Reich's plainclothes detective forces charged with the investigation of "nonpolitical" crimes. In contrast, the Gestapo investigated "political" crimes, including charges of treason, subversion, and, significantly, those dealing with the racial and political enemies of the Third Reich. The Security Service (SD) constituted the final element of the Security Police Main Office. Originally created as an intelligence-gathering network to support Party activities, the SD emerged as a key organization in the prosecution of Nazi racial policy in the occupied East, including the formation of the notorious Einsatzgruppen.[41]

The Uniformed Police Main Office under Kurt Daluege consisted of three branches of the police, including the Schutzpolizei (lit. "Protection Police"), the Gendarmerie, and the Gemeindepolizei (Community Police). The Schutzpolizei essentially resembled the beat cops of contemporary American society and were responsible for everyday law enforcement activities. The Gendarmerie, established on the French model in the first decade of the nineteenth century, conducted police duties in the countryside and in communities with fewer than two thousand inhabitants.[42] Finally, the men of the Gemeindepolizei with their motley collection of uniforms and rank insignia worked for the mayor in small towns and villages.[43]

In contrast to the police forces of the Reich, the SS under Himmler represented the soldiers of the Party. Established originally as an elite force charged with protecting Hitler, the black corps under Himmler emerged as the "ideological vanguard" of the National Socialist movement "invested with the responsibility for ensuring the racial renewal of the nation."[44] At the outbreak of World War II, the SS empire included the General SS (Allgemeine-SS), the SS Special Duty Troops (SS-Verfügungstruppe or SS-VT), and the SS Death's Head units (SS-Totenkopfverbände). The General SS provided the manpower base for the creation of the militarized SS units, including the SS-VT and the SS Death's Head formations. In turn, the garrisoned units of the SS-VT constituted the backbone of the Waffen-SS established in November 1939, while the Death's Head formations became infamous for their duties as the administrators and guards of the concentration camps.[45]

Hitler's selection on June 17, 1936, of Himmler to head this SS and police empire provided evidence of the Führer's desire to see the police merged with the "Party's soldiers," the SS, in both an organizational and a philosophical sense.[46] At the official ceremony to mark Himmler's appointment, Daluege made exactly this point by exclaiming: "We can be proud that at this moment a dream is coming true, something I dreamed of as an SS Leader before the [National Socialist] revolution, that is, the unification of the police of the movement [the SS] with the police of the state in the person of Reich Leader of the SS Himmler."[47] For his part, Himmler made his expectations for the police absolutely clear:

> We are a land in the heart of Europe, surrounded by open borders, surrounded in a world that is becoming more and more Bolshevized in which the Jew in his worst form increasingly takes control through the all-destructive tyranny of Bolshevism. . . . We have to expect that this battle will be a battle of the generations, the primeval contest between men and subhumans [that] in its contemporary form is the battle of the Aryan peoples against Jewry and its organizational manifestation, Bolshevism.[48]

Near the end of his speech, Himmler noted that he would need the loyalty and the commitment to duty of each individual within the "soldierly corps" (*soldatisches Korps*) of the police to achieve his vision.

Without doubt, Himmler intended to use his authority to set the tone and direction of the unified Reich-wide police force. In September 1936, the desire to inculcate a stronger military character among the police resulted in an order for "the official basic and continued professional training" of the entire German police to be based on a "military foundation."[49] In line with the second objective of the Nazi conversion strategy, Daluege embraced the "merging" of the SS and the police, declaring: "It can be only a question of time before the entire police coalesces with the SS corps into a permanent unit."[50]

Not only did Himmler's words present his expectations of the police under his command, but they also created an organizational culture within the

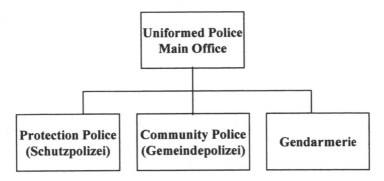

Figure 1. Organization of the Uniformed Police Main Office, 1936

Source: Created by the author from "Geschäftsverteilung u. Geschäftsverkehr d. Chefs der Deutschen Polizei im Reichsministerium des Innern, RdErl. des RFSSuChdDtPol. im RMdI v. 26.6.1936, O/S Nr. 3/36 [June 26, 1936]," T580, reel 95, NARA.

police in which anti-Semitism and anti-Bolshevism emerged as institutional norms. It is clear that not every policeman embraced the extreme implications of Himmler's rhetoric, but it is equally clear that the *Reichsführer*'s vision established an atmosphere promoting the development of a distinct institutional mind-set, one that saw the police as the ideal of a soldierly corps locked in an apocalyptic battle with "Jewish-Bolshevism." Himmler's efforts found similar expression in what Claudia Koonz has described as the "Nazi conscience" or a "secular ethos that extended reciprocity only to members of the Aryan community."[51] If the "Nazi conscience" established the principles of National Socialist "theology," then Himmler's SS and policemen acted as the protectors and guarantors of the new order, charged with the task of safeguarding and enforcing the dogma of racial superiority.

The men of the Uniformed Police experienced the same hate indoctrination as their counterparts in the Security Police and the SD did, and they did not prove immune to its effects. This process rapidly accelerated after June 1936 with Himmler's exercise of overlapping authority over the SS, the Security Police, and the Uniformed Police. From this point on, Himmler's control of all the institutions of internal state control guaranteed that all three would exist in a symbiotic relationship in which the Reich leader's goal of merging the SS with the police progressed in a physical and philosophical sense prior to 1939 and accelerated during the war years.

In fact, the entire SS and police complex existed as an interconnected and self-reflexive organization in which the initiatives taken by one affected the identity, attitudes, and actions of the whole. In fact, the patterns of influence in the SS and police complex operated in much the same way as the concentric rings produced by dropping a pebble into body of water. Initiatives pursued by Himmler with respect to the SS were bound to influence the behavior and actions of the Security and Uniformed Police through the mechanism of an intertwined leadership structure united in the persons of the HSSPFs as well as in the ranks of policemen holding SS membership. Likewise, the extensive collaboration between the Security Police and the Uniformed Police provided both an avenue for cooperation and an expression of an existing symbiotic relationship between the policemen in uniform and their plainclothes counterparts in the Gestapo, the Criminal Police, and the SD.

Ideology and Annihilation

In the prewar period, both Himmler and Daluege expended great effort to instill the Uniformed Police with a martial attitude and an SS ethic, and they brought this message to the police battalions during their repeated visits to the Eastern Front in 1941 in which they tasked these formations with the final annihilation of "Jewish-Bolshevism." The expression of anti-Semitism took several forms within the police, from the virulent to the taken for granted. In the case of the former, the police captain Erich Mehr, a company commander in Reserve PB 61, described by men in his unit after the war as a "fanatical Jew-hater," took delight in abusing Jews with his bayonet and randomly shooting at them in the Warsaw ghetto. Mehr told one of his platoon leaders: "The Führer said that the Jews must be exterminated, and I intend to see to it that the Jews will be exterminated."[52] In the case of the latter, another policeman, Kurt Möbius, provided an apt summary of the mindset of many of his colleagues during the war. Möbius reflected: "We police went by the phrase, 'Whatever serves the state is right, whatever harms the state is wrong.' . . . Although I am aware that it is the duty of the police to protect the innocent I was however at the time convinced that the Jewish people were not innocent but guilty." He continued: "I believed all the propaganda that Jews were criminals and subhuman. . . . The thought that one should oppose or evade the order to take part in the extermination of Jews never entered my head either."[53] This latter view was not unique or limited to the police. In her autobiography of life as a young woman in the Third Reich, Melita Maschmann recalled similarly taking for granted the depiction of Jews as the natural enemy of the Germans, a view that she held in spite of her close friendship with a Jewish girl.[54]

The words of Mehr and Möbius present two expressions of anti-Semitism within the police. Despite the degree of virulence separating the two, the practical manifestations of both were, in fact, the same, a belief in the necessity for the murder of Jews. Both men were, in fact, members of an institution whose leadership promoted an organizational culture that established anti-Semitism and anti-Bolshevism as organizational norms, a culture that extended the boundaries of desired and acceptable behavior within the ranks of the police, eventually facilitating countless acts of murder and atrocity throughout the occupied territories.

The effectiveness of these efforts can be seen in part in the responses of several of PB 322's members during a postwar criminal investigation into the unit's activities in Russia. One member of the battalion, Erich Holtzmeier (a pseudonym), provided the following response regarding the execution of defenseless persons: "Why the Jews? Because it was preached to us at every instructional period that one needed to exterminate this race. They [the Jews] were responsible for all the evil in the world and for the war." Concerning the Jews, another policeman from the unit stated: "Jews were in any event free game, and they were shot without mercy and without justification or the need to provide one."[55]

The open and frank statements of these policemen are somewhat unusual in the mass of postwar testimonies, in which, in the face of criminal prosecution, few men acknowledged that their units had conducted actions of atrocity and reprisal and even fewer admitted that they participated in these acts. The importance of these statements should not be minimized as they provide valuable insights into the mentality of the policemen and the unstated views and opinions of many of their colleagues both during their service and, in some cases, long after the end of the Second World War.

In addition to postwar testimony, policemen also gave vent to their feelings of anti-Semitism and anti-Bolshevism during their service in the East. For example, a policeman serving with a police regiment in Hungary in 1944 wrote a letter back to his colleagues in Flensburg contrasting the appearance of the Hungarian Jews with the Orthodox Jews (*Talmudjuden*) of the ghettos of the East. The writer noted his astonishment at the "marked Nordic characteristics" of the Hungarian Jews, an appearance that demonstrated the adaptability of these "parasites of humanity."[56]

Within the police, the use of anti-Bolshevist language complemented the message of anti-Semitism. Already in a speech in March 1933, Göring provided the police with marching orders in the "battle against Marxism" by promising the "extermination" of this "plague." He noted that this "battle of extermination" required, not only the forces of the police, but that of the "organized strength of the German people" as well.[57] Although targeted at the German parties of the political Left, Göring's and Himmler's words and those of the senior police leadership had, after the outbreak of war, implications for many living in the East. On his reassignment from the Ukrainian city of Zhitomir in 1943, Lieutenant Colonel of the Gendarmerie von Bredow thanked his men for their efforts in the "battle against the Bolshevist plague."[58] Likewise, the massacre of 705 "politically unreliable" persons, including 203 men, 372 women, and 130 children, by the men of PB 310 on September 23, 1942, in the Russian village of Borky provides but one manifestation of the practical effects of this message on the police.[59]

The manifestation of these prejudices also found expression in the personal and professional correspondence of the police. In his infamous speech to SS and Party leaders in October 1943, Himmler remarked: "Anti-Semitism is exactly the same as delousing. Getting rid of lice is not a question of ideology, it is a matter of cleanliness. In just the same way anti-Semitism for us has not been a question of ideology but a matter of cleanliness."[60] The metaphoric equation of Jews with filth, vermin, and disease also found expression in German theaters, where, in Fritz Hippler's *The Eternal Jew*, hordes of rats streaming across the movie screen symbolized the danger posed by Jews to the *Volk*.[61] The use of the terms *Pest* (plague) and *Seuche* (epidemic) within the police reports to describe both Jews and Bolshevists offers but one example. In this case, terms such as *ausrotten* (extermination) and *vernichten* (annihilation), used when the subject was the *Kampf* (combat) against a Jewish or Bolshevist *Pest* (pestilence), provided the perfect linguistic complement to this biologically prescribed threat.[62]

Despite Himmler's efforts, the actions of the police in dealing with the Jewish "danger" did not remain shrouded in secrecy. For example, a daily order issued by the commander of the Uniformed Police in Belorussia on August 14, 1943, cautioned: "In the public treatment of the Jewish question every discussion of a future total solution must cease. However, it can be stated that the Jews are being gathered together in groups for the purpose of work projects."[63] Even more direct was the letter of a police reservist stationed in Hungary published in a local police newsletter in 1944 comparing Germany with his present location: "Only here does one notice how beautiful our home [*Heimat*] is. Dirt and filth. A large percentage of the inhabitants are Jews. All the more urgent was the solution to the Jewish question. It [the solution to the Jewish question] is now being energetically driven forward from the Hungarian regime according to the German model."[64] In a final example, a senior SS and police commander castigated his policemen for discussing their activities, including executions, in a train filled with vacationers.[65] The discussion of the Final Solution on a train, in daily orders, and in hometown police newsletters indicates that the mass murder of the Jews was a matter of general knowledge within the police community, as do the multiple warnings issued to the police concerning the ban on photographing executions. The latter also provide indirect evidence of the desire of individual policemen to document their efforts in the prosecution of murder and atrocity.[66]

Instruments for Annihilation

The policemen of PB 322 were not unique in training or composition from the majority of the police battalions that served in the occupied territories. PB 322 was one of twenty-four police battalions participating in the initial phase of the assault against the Soviet Union, including a battalion that had been split up in order to support the Einsatzgruppen.[67] The police battalions that entered the Soviet Union in the summer of 1941 were, for the most part, led by officers and senior enlisted men from the ranks of career policemen[68]— a group of men whose backgrounds, demographics, and training, as well as the organizational culture within the police, had prepared them for a war of extermination in the East.

Of the nine police battalions placed directly at the disposal of the HSSPFs during the invasion of the Soviet Union, seven were regular battalions with numerical designations in the 300s. The enlisted ranks of these seven battalions consisted in large part of a pool of twenty thousand recruits mobilized from the 1909–1912 year groups. For example, the majority of the rank and file of PB 307 came from these year groups.[69] Likewise, the vast majority of the men of PB 310, another police battalion that cut a bloody path through the Soviet Union in 1942, came from the 1905–1915 year groups.[70] In his study of Party membership, Michael Kater found that National Socialism held its "greatest attraction" for those born between 1905 and 1912, precisely the age groups from which the 300-level battalions were drawn.[71] The relative youth of these policemen contrasts sharply with the age of the members of PB 101, who were, on average, thirty-nine years old.[72] Still, not all reserve police battalions followed this pattern, as the average age of thirty-one for the members of PB 61 demonstrates.[73] In fact, of the approximately one hundred police battalions mobilized during the Nazi dictatorship, only twenty came from the ranks of overage reservists.[74]

The "Other Policemen"

The men of the Uniformed Police serving with the police battalions and the Einsatzgruppen were not the only executors of racial policy within the ranks of the police. Their counterparts in Gendarmerie posts and individual duty posts throughout the East, assisted by indigenous auxiliaries (Schutzmann-schaften), provided another instrument for the murder of the putative enemies of the Third Reich. In the case of the former, small groups of four to five gendarmes operating in isolated rural locations in the East became themselves tools for liquidating Jewish ghettos and conducting "pacification" operations against suspected partisans.[75] In the case of the latter, companies and battalions of local auxiliaries under the command of German officers and senior enlisted personnel assisted in the annihilation of the Jews and antipartisan operations in support of their German masters.[76] In addition, precinct police (Schutzpolizei) departments throughout the Reich provided detachments of one officer and twelve enlisted men to guard trains carrying Jews to incarceration or annihilation in the East, a role that the police came to regard as a "regular function."[77]

The actions of small groups of gendarmes and local auxiliaries contributed in an important respect to German rule in the East, but it was the police battalions that served the role as *primus inter pares*. By the end of the war, Uniformed Police battalions had served from Norway in the north to Italy and Greece in the south and from Holland in the west to the Soviet Union in the east.[78] These battalions of approximately 540 men divided into a battalion staff, a signals platoon, a transportation detachment, and three companies of approximately 140 men each emerged as one of Himmler's most effective instruments in the prosecution of National Socialist racial policy.[79] These police battalions became, in fact, the sharp edge of a deadly sword wielded by Himmler and his HSSPFs in a war of annihilation against the enemies of the Third Reich.

The War against the Partisans as Racial War

If the police battalions acted as the spearhead for Himmler's racial war in the East, then the war against the partisans provided a convenient cover for the murderous activities of these SS and police units in the East. The historian Donald McKale aptly described the Third Reich's annihilation of the Jews as "Hitler's shadow war."[80] However, the shadow of this war in the East swallowed up several other groups as well, including the local Slavic population, the Sinti and Roma (Gypsies), and Soviet POWs. The conduct of war against the partisans also provided the pretext for the mass murder of women and children throughout the East, and the routine execution of the latter provides one of the clearest indications of the real intent behind German actions in the occupied territories. In fact, the war against the partisans in the East conducted by the SS, the police, and the Wehrmacht became a key mechanism for achieving the Third Reich's racial policies.

In a speech to the officer corps of the SS-Leibstandarte (Bodyguard Company) "Adolf Hitler" in September 1940, Himmler discussed the guerrilla war (*Bandenkrieg*) in Poland that was "more unpleasant than an open battle." For this reason, Himmler told his listeners that he needed "soldiers and formations that were ideologically dependable [*weltanschaulich klar*] to hold this occupied territory, whether the Czech Republic or Poland, in check." Himmler later revealed the extent of his definition of *guerrilla war* as he discussed the execution of "thousands of leading Poles" and the difficulty in "holding down a culturally backward, rebellious population," including conducting executions and the entire process of resettling populations. Significantly, Himmler chose this moment to emphasize the service of both the black-clad men of the SS and the green-uniformed men of the police as "equally valuable."[81]

If Himmler revealed the true nature of the partisan war in September 1940 to the Praetorian Guard of the Nazi messiah, then the opening of the campaign against the Soviet Union in June 1941 exposed the vast scope and scale of this effort. In a secret report of July 31, 1942, concerning "Combat of Partisans and Jewish Action in the White Russian District," Wilhelm Kube, the commissioner general for Belorussia, identified the Jews as the "primary bearers" of the partisan movement and laid out plans for their complete elimination. Kube remarked that, in the previous ten weeks alone, fifty-five thousand Jews had been "liquidated." He also noted plans for the pending execution of some twenty thousand more, plans that would end "the danger" of partisans receiving support from the Jews in his region.[82]

By the summer of 1942, not only had mass murder become standard operating procedure, but it had also been institutionalized and promoted at the highest levels. In fact, a Führer Order of August 18, 1942, identified the increasing importance attached to antipartisan measures. In the order, Hitler decried the "unbearable scope" of partisan activity and authorized the "extermination" of these forces through the combined use of the Wehrmacht, the SS, and the police.[83] Hitler's order became in many respects a "blank check" promoting the conduct of atrocity and offering institutional approval for these acts. In the fall of 1942, Himmler reported to Hitler that the war against the "partisans" in the Ukraine had resulted in the execution of 387,370 "gang helpers" and "suspected gangs," of which 363,211 were Jews.[84] The fact that almost 94 percent of the victims in the antipartisan war were Jews provides undeniable evidence of the true nature of these operations.

Himmler's intent to use antipartisan operations as a cover for annihilation did not go unnoticed by his policemen. For example, one member of PB 322 noted in his postwar testimony: "The expression 'combat of the partisans' is strictly speaking a complete misnomer. We didn't have a single battle with partisans after we left Mogilev. . . . The fact of the matter [was], that those [persons] found without valid identity cards, sufficed for their arrest and execution."[85] Another former policeman during his postwar interrogation associated "infantry training" and "field exercises" with actions aimed at the Jews.[86]

Wehrmacht and Police Cooperation

For its part, the attitude of the military leadership of the Wehrmacht moved from general resistance to the use of the police in antipartisan operations to a stance of enthusiastic and widespread acceptance of the employment of SS and police forces. Raul Hilberg observed: "The generals had eased themselves into this pose of cooperation through the pretense that the Jewish population was a group of Bolshevist diehards who instigated, encouraged, and abetted the partisan war behind the German lines." He continued: "The army thus had to protect itself against the partisan menace by striking at its presumable source—the Jews."[87] The postwar testimony of Walter Schellenberg confirmed Hilberg's assessment concerning the cooperation of the Wehrmacht with SS and police forces in the annihilation of Jewish-Bolshevism. Likewise, General Röttiger, reflecting in 1945 on the battle against the partisans, reluctantly admitted: "The ordering of the most severe measures for the prosecution of the war against the partisans [*Bandenkampf*] by the highest authorities possibly had the final purpose to exploit the military war against the partisans by the army in order to make possible the ruthless liquidation of the Jews and other undesirable elements."[88]

Hot-Blooded versus Cold-Blooded Atrocity

Without doubt, atrocity and reprisal have been a part of warfare since time immemorial. However, in the case of the actions of the SS and police forces on the Eastern Front, it is necessary to distinguish between "hot-blooded" and "cold-blooded" atrocity. The former occurs during actions in which a unit comes under hostile fire or experiences casualties. These combat situations have often spurred an orgy of blood lust involving the indefensible murder of civilians or the execution of prisoners. In contrast, the actions of the men of PB 322 and thousands of their police colleagues offer clear examples of cold-blooded atrocity. In this case, atrocity cannot be rationalized as a primal reaction to the deaths of comrades or the fear engendered by a unit's own experience. The actions of PB 322 demonstrate the acceptance of reprisal and atrocity as means of "signaling" the brutal consequences of actual or perceived opposition to German rule or simply membership in a group determined to pose a threat to the political, racial, or biological health of the German people. As the following chapters will show, the conduct of cold-blooded reprisal and atrocity by the Uniformed Police found repeated expression on the Eastern Front.

The Path to Genocide

The overwhelming evidence concerning the participation of the men of the Uniformed Police in the conduct of atrocity and genocide is but one part of this story. Inevitably, the historian must attempt to address, if not to explain, the motives for these actions. The chapters that follow present an analysis of the means by which civil servants charged with the preservation of public order became political soldiers of annihilation in support of a malevolent and atavistic racial regime. Chapter 1 examines the historical traditions of the German police prior to the National Socialist "seizure of power" and details the measures pursued by the National Socialist government to take control of the police. Chapter 2 analyzes the role of militarization within the police and examines the effects of a specific martial spirit in establishing the self-image and determining the actions of the police. Chapter 3 focuses on the initiatives pursued by the senior leadership of the SS and the police to instill an SS ethic within the green-clad corps of the Uniformed Police. Chapters 4 and 5 detail the way in which ideology was transformed from rhetoric and slogans into practice during the invasion and occupation of Poland and the Soviet Union. Finally, Chapter 6 focuses on the activities of the police during the occupation of the Eastern territories. Without doubt, Himmler and Daluege pursued a vision for the Uniformed Police, and the ultimate testament to their success in achieving this vision came in the actions of these men on the Eastern Front.

ONE

TAKING CHARGE
OF THE POLICE

A cleansing of the German police was required, as was a cleansing of all state
institutions of the Weimar Republic, in order to create the instrument that was suitable
for the honorable preservation of peace, order, and safety in the Reich of Adolf Hitler.
—Major General of the Police Rudolf Querner (September 1940)

From the moment of his appointment as chancellor, Hitler pursued measures
to ensure the success of the National Socialist "seizure of power" as well as
the "coordination" (*Gleichschaltung*) of the various official and semiofficial
nationalist organizations and, more important, the agencies and branches of
the Reich and individual state governments. This "creeping authoritarian-
ism" allowed the National Socialists to strengthen their hold on the institutions of state control and accelerate their program for the rebirth of a
Germany bound together by a mystical peoples' community.[1] Hitler and his
key lieutenants, including Hermann Göring and Heinrich Himmler, clearly
recognized that gaining control of the Uniformed and Political Police forces
of the individual state governments was a vital step in their plan for consolidating power. The tradition of regional particularism, the structural organization of the German state governments, and the relative autonomy of their
police institutions presented powerful counterweights to these efforts. However, not all historical factors impeded the National Socialist co-optation of
the police as some traditional attitudes and characteristics within the police
provided a solid foundation for this process.

Historical Traditions of the German Police

The drafting of the imperial constitution after the unification of the various
German states in 1871 highlighted the tension in the emerging nation-state
between desires for a federal state and demands for maintaining the rights of
the individual states in a confederation.[2] As a result, the framers of the constitution favored the prerogatives and sovereignty of the individual states, a

move that reinforced the tradition of autonomous police authorities. Despite some democratic trappings, imperial Germany remained an authoritarian state, the organization and conduct of the police reflecting this authoritarian style as well as a "passion for order" (*Ordnungslust*), and these attributes in turn shaping the attitudes and actions of local police authorities.[3]

Throughout the course of the *Kaiserreich*, the concept of protecting public order initiated a process whereby the scope and ambition of police authority expanded dramatically, especially with respect to political activities. In this case, policemen cleared streets of political protesters in order "to keep traffic flowing" and monitored the press, public assemblies, and club activities for signs of lèse-majesté. The emergence of a large working class, along with the rise of the Social Democratic Party (SPD) to represent its interests, had two effects. First, workers' strikes and protests catapulted the police into the front lines of an emerging struggle between existing authoritarian structures and demands for improved social conditions and increased political representation. Second, this conflict resulted in situations in which "almost every active Social Democrat had a similar [confrontational] experience with the police."[4]

One historian noted that the authoritarian attitude of the average Berlin policeman in the performance of his routine duties "would provoke a riot in two hours in Trafalgar Square." This same historian also remarked that the German policeman's capriciousness in the execution of his executive responsibilities "has bred a lively animosity particularly among the poorer classes. . . . To a large extent this is due to the fact that the police represent the imperial government, and thus the domination of the bureaucracy."[5] Whether viewed as the bureaucratic representatives of an authoritarian state (*Obrigkeitsstaat*) or as the protectors of the existing imperial social order, the policemen of the *Kaiserreich* evoked measures of resentment, fear, and respect from their fellow citizens.

Police confrontations with the advocates of social and political change were neither unique nor unprecedented. Already in the early nineteenth century, "everyday police work consisted of two tasks: firstly, the identification of 'dangerous persons,' and, secondly, their constant supervision and control." This in turn led to a situation supporting "arbitrary violence" where tolerance and caution on one day might be replaced by violent reaction on the next. For example, on August 31, 1830, the inspector of the police in the city of Cologne "quietly and calmly called on a large crowd of alley-lads and numerous onlookers to disperse"—with success. The reappearance of the crowd on the following day, however, triggered quite a different reaction. "There was no more talk of quiet, calm persuasion": "the crowd was charged with fixed bayonets and rifle butts" and chased by officers with drawn sabers.[6]

Likewise, the revolutionary events of 1848–1849 dramatized the somewhat schizophrenic nature of a civil police caught between support for popular democratic ideals and the maintenance of autocracy. Indeed, the reaction of individual policemen proved mixed, as in the case of Samuel Scheffler from Elberfeld, the only member of the municipal police who did not flee the city at the outbreak of revolution. Scheffler, a veteran of the Napoleonic wars, later explained his motive for offering his services to the committee of public safety, saying that he wanted to "protect Elberfeld's citizens from the outside insurgents, who were threatening their property and personal safety." In fact, other evidence indicates that he had sympathies for the democratic movement and especially the failed effort to place the imperial crown on the brow of Frederick William IV.[7] Scheffler's actions, however, proved to be the exception rather than the rule as the majority of civil police authorities joined with the military to squelch the revolution.[8]

The pervasive military inclination of late nineteenth- and early twentieth-century Germany significantly influenced the role and character of the German police in the period leading up to the National Socialist dictatorship. The historical reliance on the military as the last line of defense against internal unrest as well as the cooperation between the police and the military in quelling civil disturbances set a precedent for the handling of later events. The fact that the majority of policemen in this period were drawn from the former ranks of the army, combined with the creation of a police organization along the lines of a military hierarchy, helped shape the military orientation of the police.[9] Despite the use of the police in putting down civil unrest, the average imperial policeman, especially the policeman from a small community, seldom became involved in violent confrontations requiring the use of deadly force. It was only in the decade before World War I that policemen began to carry firearms in response to the presence of increasing numbers of armed criminals, especially in urban centers. For example, Hamburg's policemen were not issued service revolvers until January 1918. Even then, regulations limited the use of firearms to critical situations involving self-defense. In this respect, the police sword became the most visible symbol tying the policeman of the *Kaiserreich* to his military heritage.[10]

The purpose in drawing attention to the authoritarian traditions and military inclination of the German police is not to attempt to draw a straight line of continuity linking the *Kaiserreich* to the Third Reich, with Bismarck serving as a precursor to Hitler. But this review does show that the German police did not constitute a tabula rasa on which democratic and republican ideals might readily be written. Instead, there were important existing tendencies, attitudes, and organizational structures within the disparate state police organizations prior to the emergence of German democracy at the end of World War I. In turn, the existing mind-set and the predisposition of these policemen played a key role in the way in which they reacted to the parties of the Right whether nationalist or National Socialist during the final years of the Republic.

The Police under Weimar

The German defeat in the Great War and the resulting Treaty of Versailles affected both the size and the composition of the individual state police forces. Although most histories provide the limitation of the Reichswehr (German army) at 100,000, few mention that Article 162 of the treaty limited the size of state and local police forces to their 1913 levels and strictly prohibited policemen receiving "military training."[11] In response to fear of a "Communist victory in Germany," the Interallied Military Commission later agreed to increase the size of the Weimar police to a 157,000-member force, but the prohibition on military training remained in place.[12]

As the seat of government, Berlin and the state of Prussia played a key role in the life of Weimar. With a total of eighty-five thousand police civil servants, Prussia had also by far the largest police force in Weimar and serves as a fitting model for examining the Republic's police forces.[13] The Prussian Uniformed Police included the typical precinct forces found in most urban centers, the Protection Police (Schutzpolizei), a Landjägerei or Gendarmerie responsible for rural areas, a Community Police (Gemeindepolizei) for policing small villages, and a Landespolizei, consisting of large garrisoned police formations. Prussia's plainclothes policemen included the normal detective force or Criminal Police as well as the Political Police, the latter dedicated to identifying groups plotting against the government or seeking to bring down the government by nondemocratic means.[14]

The police forces of Weimar especially experienced the tension between national imperatives and individual state prerogatives. A system of decentralization and subordination to the various state governments of the German federation characterized the structure of the Uniformed Police.[15] In addition, the authority over the majority of police forces resided with the individual state; however, in some small villages and towns, communal authorities exercised control over their police forces.[16] The existence of seventeen separate state governments each with sole command of its own police forces arose from a desire by the states to maintain regional control of their police executives in the face of central government encroachment. The state of Bavaria's objection to the 1922 National Criminal Police Law provided one example of regional particularism at work. The law called for the "establishment of a national police force with its central office in Berlin, under the Minister of the Interior."[17] Despite the passage of the law by the German parliament, it remained a dead letter owing to the protests of the state governments.

The power of the purse provided one avenue for exerting central government control, and the Weimar government provided subsidies to the state police agencies. Still, the direct influence of the subsidies had significant limitations, allowing the states to maintain their stranglehold on recruitment, personnel selection, and operational control at the expense of accepting some administrative limitations as well as agreeing to a measure of standardization of the state police forces.[18]

In some respects, regional control proved a double-edged sword with respect to the police. On the one hand, lack of centralization and cross-jurisdictional cooperation and law enforcement mechanisms worked to the advantage of criminals and prevented federal authorities from standardizing qualifications, training, and procedures among the various state police agencies. On the other hand, regional control provided an important safeguard, preventing the co-optation of the police by a dominant national political party. In fact, the vice president of the Berlin police, Dr. Bernhard Weiss, warned of exactly this danger when he declared: "Every political party politician wants to capture the soul of the police."[19]

The soul of the police was not, however, completely shielded from partisan political manipulation. When invoked, Article 9 of the Weimar constitution empowered the central government to initiate legislation on a national level for the "protection of public order and safety," but attempts by the national government to enforce this provision proved generally unsuccessful.[20] In contrast, Article 48 of the Weimar constitution provided a method for direct control of the police by the central government in the event of the declaration of a state of emergency by the president of the Republic. The application of Article 48 and its enforcement during the summer of 1932 by the government of Franz von Papen constituted a fateful precedent for the Republic and served as the prelude to a Faustian bargain in which, not just the soul of the police, but that of the German people would be at stake.

The Character of the Weimar Police

As with the members of any large organization, the structure, composition, shared values, and attitudes of Weimar's policemen helped determine their character. The structure of the police in Weimar reflected the interplay of the antithetical forces of liberal socialism and the paramilitary police tradition. At one end of the spectrum was the garrisoned, military-style Landespolizei with large barracked formations, a heavily armed, quick-reaction force to be mobilized in the case of civil unrest. At the other end was the Community Police, which blended authoritarian and indulgent traits and acted as a veritable jack-of-all-trades in small villages, approaching in some respects the small-town American ideal expressed in Sheriff Andy Taylor of Mayberry.

The character of the average precinct policeman or *Schutzpolizist* balanced the extremes of the militarized *Landespolizist* and the semiprofessional, slightly comic figure of the community policeman. Still, Weimar's beat cops displayed a schizophrenic personality that found them rounding up married men from local bars on payday and escorting them home to their wives with their remaining money on one day and breaking in the windows of local bakers who ignored the nightly baking restrictions (*Backverbot*) on the next.[21] Excessive use of force and rough treatment of prisoners became an all-too-common occurrence, and even the most egregious cases of police brutality often failed to result in punishment for the offender as the judicial system favored police testimony over medical reports and eyewitness testimony. In the case of the industrialized Ruhr area, newspapers of the Left and the Left-liberal persuasion often criticized the behavior of the police as "out of proportion and without feeling for the existing situation."[22] In the end, spiraling rightist and leftist political agitation, especially within the larger metropolitan areas such as Berlin in the late 1920s and early 1930s, confronted these precinct policemen with escalating violence and forced them into the front lines of innumerable street battles, with the fate of Weimar democracy hanging in the balance.[23]

Soldiers in Police Uniform?

In the early years of the Weimar Republic, the Prussian police and its state counterparts were faced with a variety of challenges, including several "threats" from the Left. The widespread dissolution of the workers' and soldiers' councils through the combined efforts of the police and semiofficial paramilitary forces—in some cases with Allied assistance—ended the initial efforts of the far Left to establish the direction of the nascent government.[24] The paramilitary groups, the Freikorps or Free Corps, carried the "main burden of fighting" and played a key role in assisting the police in crushing the Spartacist Revolt in Berlin as well as in toppling the short-lived Munich Soviet in 1919.[25]

The combined actions of the police, the military, and the Free Corps against the forces of the extreme Left in the early days of the Republic were important in several respects. First, many of the men from the Free Corps subsequently found employment in the ranks of the police, and their attitudes

helped shape that of the rank and file in the early 1920s, creating a mentality that divided the world into the black and white of "friend" and "enemy."[26]
Second, the ideal of the Prussian authoritarian state dominated the worldview
of the police officer corps, a mind-set that viewed democracy as "weak" and
"un-German."[27] For example, the Prussian Police Officers' Association, count-
ing the membership of almost 90 percent of the state's police officer corps,
took great pride in the "traditional Prussian sense of duty and officialdom"
and remained throughout its existence under the cloud of "lingering suspicion
of political opposition" to the Republic.[28] Not surprisingly, the Reichswehr
also shared this view and rejected democracy, liberalism, and socialism.[29]
Third, the fear of revolution from the Left further shaped the way in which
the police viewed Weimar's political landscape. Disdain for democracy and
the distrust of republican ideals, coupled with a deep-seated suspicion of the
Left, did not make policemen committed National Socialists, but it did align
them in many respects with the parties and causes of the Right, whether reac-
tionary or "revolutionary."

Meeting the Threat in the Streets

In March 1921, the police forces from across Germany, including Berlin and
Hannover, were mobilized to suppress a large-scale Communist uprising, this
time in the German state of Saxony in the industrial area near Merseburg.
The primary fighting between the workers of the "Red Army" and company-
sized units of the Uniformed Police took place in the battle for control of the
Leuna works, but violent confrontations occurred throughout Saxony. By
the end of March, the major fighting was over, and, by the end of July, the
police forces from neighboring states returned to their garrisons. During the
conflict, the police captured or arrested 3,470 persons and confiscated 1,346
rifles, 10 pistols, and 34 machine guns. Police casualties included 35 killed
and 53 wounded, compared to 145 persons killed (either revolutionaries or
those caught in the cross fire) and an indeterminate number wounded.[30] Similarly, a Communist uprising in the city of Hamburg directed at gaining control of the city's police stations in October 1923 once again led to armed
violence as police forces crushed the revolt at the cost of 17 policemen killed
and 62 wounded, with losses for the revolutionaries estimated at 61 killed,
267 wounded, and almost 1,000 arrested.[31]

The instances of violence in Saxony and Hamburg offer but two of the
most dramatic examples of confrontations between police and militant forces
of the Left in the early years of the Republic. These confrontations were
important in several respects. First, the violent confrontation between the

police and workers reinforced a specter of revolution from the Left that served as both the real and the imagined bogeyman for many in the German middle class, including the civil service, throughout the life of the Republic.[32] Second, the police, not the army, emerged as the guarantor of domestic order.[33] Third, the casualties experienced by the police and the revolutionaries alike in these actions radicalized the atmosphere and upped the stakes of future skirmishes. Finally, the employment of the police in large formations set the precedent for the creation and maintenance of a Landespolizei modeled along military lines; however, this military influence did not stop and start at the gates of the police garrisons but became a crucial part of the entire police training curriculum.[34]

Training Weimar's Policemen

The basic training of the police candidate in Prussia embraced many of the elements made famous in Stanley Kubrick's portrayal of the authoritarian marine drill sergeant in *Full Metal Jacket*. In addition to emphasizing physical fitness, the training used repetitive and seemingly nonsensical exercises and barked commands to socialize the new recruit. Willi Lemke, a Prussian police recruit, described his experience: "From the first hour we were left in no doubt as to the manner in which we would be treated. . . . [W]e were made to practice roll call . . . repeated a dozen times . . . accompanied by the inevitable screams of the instructors. . . . I guess the idea was to break our individual will right from the beginning."[35]

Sometimes this training crossed the line, moving beyond simple harassment into the realm of physical and psychological torment. On August 18, 1928, a newspaper in Königsberg broke the story of the alleged abuse of police recruits at the police academy in Sensburg. Charges of excessive physical abuse included the practice of forcing recruits to raise and lower their rifles (*Karabinerpumpen*) repeatedly until reaching the point of exhaustion. Additionally, a police major allegedly screamed at a police recruit that the answer to the question "What are you?" was, not a "police recruit," but a "pig." After investigating the charges, the Prussian Interior Ministry found that it could not dismiss the offending civil servant as he had over twelve years of service, but the ministry did order his transfer. Likewise, a police first lieutenant accused of attempting to intimidate recruits and keep them from making statements in the case received a disciplinary transfer. In the latter case, the civilian leadership found out that almost the entire training cadre and the police academy's band escorted the transferred man to the train station on the day of his departure.[36] The picture of a disciplined officer cheered by his colleagues and marching to music at the event of his transfer offers a strong indication of the support for the existing training methods— at least at this police school—as well as the open disdain for the ministry's decision.

Whether all police schools embraced the same harsh training regimens is not certain; however, the strongly military character of the training at police academies throughout Prussia is undeniable. In the wake of the March 1921 unrest in Saxony, the "main effort" of the training curricula at the Prussian police academies focused on the employment of large formations of policemen. This training was similar to company-sized training of the army in infantry tactics with an increasing emphasis on procedures for the "suppression of [domestic] unrest." One description of police training at the academy in Münster noted: "Police training in part resembles that of the infantryman and in part the cavalryman." The fact that instructors drawn largely from the former ranks of the military would emphasize military training, even going so far as to use copies of army field manuals, should not be surprising, but it did establish a distinctly martial environment within the police academies and did promote a distinct organizational culture that exalted military traditions and values. Likewise, the injection of a discussion of the Treaty of Versailles as part of training curricula offers another insight into the mind-set of the training officers. Little imagination is needed to envision the tone and content of such a discussion as presented by former officers of the Kaiser's army.[37]

The Political Inclination of the Police

One historian argued that, by 1933, the Weimar police had reached a major crossroads, caught between the current of a preexisting military identity and the tide of modernization that offered the hope for a professionalization of the police.[38] However, the events of the summer of 1932, when combined with the surprisingly rapid coordination of the Uniformed Police in support of the political and social policies of the National Socialist regime, seem to indicate that years of traveling along the same path had not prepared the police to switch direction away from their authoritarian and martial predilections.

The transformation of the police into a partisan political instrument of the state occurred for two reasons. First, the demographic composition of the police, including the high proportion of veterans of the Great War, made that institution a ready target for a nationalistic philosophy that laid the blame for the "shame of Versailles" at the feet of leftists and Jews. In turn, this image of "treasonous" leftists and Jews helped shape the personal and political beliefs of many policemen throughout the interwar period. This does not necessarily mean, of course, that the policemen of Weimar were simply waiting for Hitler to appear in order to release their frustrations against the "November Republic." Rather, it simply means that many of these men shared the dogma of the radical Right, with anti-internationalism, antiliberalism, and anti-Semitism forming the touchstones of their belief system. However, the NSDAP (National Socialist German Workers' Party) was but one of many potential choices.[39]

Second, the actions of the police during the Weimar period demonstrated the tenuous hold of republican ideals within this organ of state control. The ultranationalist Freikorps played a key role in suppressing leftist "revolts" and "uprisings" during the interwar period. In turn, many from these groups flocked to Hitler's movement in 1923.[40] Likewise, unable to find a place in the Reichswehr owing to Versailles restrictions, a large number of the demobilized members of these groups entered the ranks of the Uniformed Police.[41] The activities of July 1932 and the use of the police as an instrument of the von Papen government and the political Right perhaps more than any other event demonstrated the real sympathies of the police.

The "Papen Putsch"

The Prussian state elections of April 24, 1932, marked an important turning point for Germany's largest state government, the National Socialists garnering 36.3 percent of the vote, the existing government coalition receiving a bare plurality, 38 percent. Although the National Socialists were unable to form a ruling coalition, their electoral success heralded a dramatic strengthening in support for the far Right and seemed an ill omen for the "Prussian bastion" of the Republic. An open melee between Communist and National Socialist representatives during the second day of the opening session on the floor of the parliament left eight persons seriously injured and provided an apt demonstration that the political violence of the streets had found its way into the halls of government. Fearing a possible Nazi co-optation of the Prussian police, the Reichswehr leadership considered plans for the subordination of the police to military control even before the National Socialist electoral success.[42]

That electoral success was not, however, without influence on the behavior of the ministerial bureaucracy within Prussia as Prussian higher civil servants anticipated a move to the Right and adjusted their bureaucratic behavior accordingly. For example, the Police Section of the Interior Ministry forwarded a draft proposal to Carl Severing, the Prussian minister of the interior, calling for the prohibition of partisan political newspapers. Significantly, this draft included only newspapers from the Social Democratic and Communist Parties, not those of the Right.[43] Whether as a result of pragmatic political calculation or political affinity alone, or a combination of both, this shift demonstrated, at least on the surface, a willingness by these civil servants to move toward the Right if conditions allowed.

On July 20, 1932, Reich Chancellor Franz von Papen, under President Paul von Hindenburg's authority, invoked a state of emergency, thereby subordinating the Prussian government to the Reich. Significantly, this measure included the subordination of the Prussian police apparatus to the Reich Ministry of the Interior. The "Papen Putsch" proceeded under the pretext of the collapse of order within Prussia and resulted in the immediate dismissal of Prussian Minister of the Interior Severing, Berlin's police president Albert Grzesinski, Berlin's police vice president Bernhard Weiss, and the commander of the police Colonel Magnus Heimannsberg. In all, Papen's seizure of control led to the removal of 94 of 588 of the state's political appointees in the police, mostly from the Left. In addition, Hindenburg signed a second emergency decree placing Berlin's and Brandenburg's Uniformed Police forces under the authority of the commander of Military District III, General Gerd von Rundstedt.[44]

On the one hand, the putsch demonstrated the ability of von Papen's right-wing government to subvert democratic processes through executive fiat. On the other hand, it also illustrated the willingness of Germany's largest state police force to accept a purge of its own leadership in support of the objectives of the political Right. In his study of the Prussian Schutzpolizei, Eric Kohler concluded: "The evidence presented here indicates that the Schupo [Schutzpolizei] officers were never very reliable defenders of the Republic. . . . Given the ease with which this force was transformed into a reliable instrument of the totalitarian state after 1933, . . . one may even legitimately question whether it was ever a dependable servant of Weimar democracy at all."[45] In the end, the absence of a police officer corps grounded in a belief in republican and democratic ideals proved a critical weakness in protecting Weimar democracy. While the right-wing and military leanings of the police certainly were not the only factors in facilitating the success of the subversion of democracy in Prussia, both these elements played a key role in shaping the reaction of the police to the crisis and their view of the world.[46]

In one respect, the events of July 20 placed the Prussian police between a rock and a hard place. Opposition by the police to the Reich government's declaration of a state of emergency threatened to ignite an internal conflict of loyalty within a police corps ostensibly committed to upholding the Weimar constitution. Paradoxically, Papen's putsch presented the police with the choice

of upholding either the "law" or the true spirit of the republican and democratic ideal. In the end, Severing did not force the police to make this choice.
This seems to have been a wise decision as evidence indicates that many within
the police were sympathetic to Papen's coup and would not have opposed the
Reichswehr in order to preserve the Social Democratic government.[47]

National Socialists in Police Uniform?

The role of the police in the actions against the Social Democrats in July
1932 certainly provided one clear inference concerning the political sympathies of the Weimar police in the state of Prussia. The majority of the Weimar
police certainly were not closet Nazis merely waiting for Hitler to achieve
power before revealing their true colors; however, the military experiences
and political sympathies of the police made them a prime and attentive audience for the Nazi message after January 30, 1933.[48] For instance, one study
of German voting patterns in the 1930s found that, prior to September 1,
1930, German civil servants as a group were already overrepresented within
the Nazi Party. More specifically, the study remarked on a trend showing
increased "sympathy" for National Socialism within the ranks of police officials.[49] Evidence indicates that the National Socialists made inroads into the
police prior to 1933 in spite of the prohibition on civil servants holding membership in the Party or its organizations and warnings from the Weimar government to civil servants, including the police, against membership and even
participation in the organizations of the NSDAP.

In the effort to prevent civil servants from joining the NSDAP, several state
governments joined the central administration by issuing their own prohibitions concerning Party membership. The Hamburg senate issued a directive
on November 3, 1930, threatening administrative action against any civil
servant supporting or promoting organizations calling for the violent over-
throw of the state, specifically identifying the NSDAP and the German Communist Party (KPD). Later, after the lifting of the prohibition in the Hansa
city in October 1932, the senate passed another statute preventing regular
policemen from joining "political cells," a prohibition directly aimed at police
members of the NSDAP.[50] The importance of the prohibitions should not be
overlooked for they clearly highlighted a contemporary fear among the political leadership that the National Socialists had made inroads into the police
or were threatening to do so. If this were not the case, then there would not
have been any pressing rationale for enacting these bans.

The threat of expulsion from the police did not keep many policemen from
joining the Party. For example, Hermann Franz clandestinely joined the

NSDAP in October 1929 before he officially entered the Party in December 1931, and he entered the SS in 1940.[51] Franz provides the perfect illustration of the "political soldier." He joined the imperial army as an enlisted soldier in 1909 and fought at the front in World War I, where he was wounded and won the Iron Cross, second-class. After the war, he joined the Saxon police but continued to describe himself as a "career soldier" (*Berufssoldat*). From June 1933 until August 1938, Franz served as the police director in Plauen and participated in the occupation of the Sudetenland before commanding a police battalion in the Polish campaign and a police regiment in the Soviet Union. The actions of his regiment during the invasion of the Soviet Union would demonstrate his commitment to the prosecution of the Third Reich's racial policies.[52]

Franz was not the only member of the police in Saxony with ties to the NSDAP. In response to a query from the Munich Party headquarters concerning the political allegiance of the various police unions in Saxony, the Party office in Saxony responded: "We are happy [to report] that a large part of the Saxon police are on our side and we have a considerable number of members within the police."[53] The most interesting aspects of the response include the assertion of the number of members of the NSDAP within the ranks of the Uniformed Police and the fact that this letter was written on June 28, 1932, a full seven months before Hitler's appointment as chancellor. In one respect, the strong showing of the Nazis in Saxony might be expected owing to the strength of the Party in this state in general. Still, the apparent penetration of the police provides strong circumstantial evidence of their general sympathies.

In other German states, the National Socialists did not need to wait for Hitler's appointment as chancellor to initiate their program for co-opting the police. In the Thuringian state election of December 8, 1929, the National Socialists for the first time in their history received over 10 percent of the votes cast and were invited to join a coalition government. In exchange for Nazi participation, Hitler demanded the posts of the minister of the interior and the minister of education. The former provided the lever for control of the civil service and, most important, the police, while the latter presented an opportunity for bringing the National Socialist message into the state's schools and universities. Hitler remarked: "He who controls both these ministries and ruthlessly and persistently exploits his power in them can achieve extraordinary things." Foreshadowing a later strategy with respect to the Nazi "seizure of power," Wilhelm Frick received the appointment to both positions and began the process of "purging the civil service, police, and teachers of revolutionary, Marxist, and democratic tendencies."[54] In another example, the success of the National Socialists in the June 1932 state par-

liament elections in Mecklenburg-Schwerin resulted in the appointment of a
new commander of the police by the newly elected Nazi minister-president,
Walter Granzow.[55]

Even in the Hansa city of Hamburg, a bastion of the KPD with its large
pool of blue-collar workers, there are indications that the NSDAP made
headway in the police. Alf Krüger, a Hamburg policeman, formed an association of National Socialist colleagues that numbered between 112 and 165
members in the period between 1925 and 1929. Furthermore, the results of
a local election on September 27, 1931, in three districts that each included
garrisoned police forces provided strong, if only inferential, evidence of a
National Socialist bent among the police civil servants. In the election, the
NSDAP received 1,076 of 3,421, or 31 percent, of the votes cast. This surprisingly strong showing, combined with the presence of 947 civil servants
in these districts, with most of these coming from the garrisoned police
forces, led the *Völkischer Beobachter* to claim an "absolute National Socialist majority" within the police barracks.[56] With respect to the issue of civil
servant voting patterns, one study found that, in the case of an urban context, "the percentage of civil servants among eligible voters definitely had
the ability to exert a noticeable influence on the election success of the
NSDAP."[57]

In the case of Hamburg, after the lifting of the restriction on membership
in the NSDAP in August 1932, over 10 percent of the city's senior police
leadership (*Oberbeamten*) joined the Party.[58] In a final example, the NSDAP
district office for Berlin forwarded a report to the Munich headquarters on
January 24, 1933, concerning a request by the "Reich Association of Former Police Civil Servants" to be recognized as an official organization of the
National Socialist movement. The report noted that the association operated
strictly along "National Socialist principles" and had remained in "close contact" with the Party's office in Berlin since its creation. In addition, it emphasized that these former policemen had been extremely active on the side of
the NSDAP in previous elections, especially in organizing mass assemblies
and in propagandizing former and active members of the Uniformed Police.[59]
The fact that the district office forwarded this request less than a week before
Hitler's appointment should not obscure the fact that these former policemen clearly had been active during the previous months or years on behalf
of the NSDAP.

In a similar vein, a former Prussian policeman contacted Himmler in July
1931 on behalf of the "Local Group Groß-Essen of Former Prussian Policemen" with a question concerning the future role of the SS. The writer, a Herr
Pauls, expressed the general dissatisfaction of his group with the government
of Weimar and their hope for a National Socialist regime. In this event, he

calculated that a pool of up to forty thousand former policemen existed who would be willing to rejoin the police. Obviously a perceptive observer of the Party, the writer asked Himmler whether the SS was intended to become the police of the Third Reich, and, if so, he requested that his group be allowed to join. Himmler responded with alacrity to the letter and made trips to the Ruhr and Berlin to discuss the offer.[60] Although Pauls's letter does not provide definitive proof of the general political orientation of the police and its former members, it does, when combined with the other examples, offer strong circumstantial evidence concerning the sympathies of the police in the last years of the Republic.

In the end, efforts to remold the Prussian police into a republican and democratic force seemed to be based more on hope than reality, as the events of July 1932–January 1933 demonstrated. After July 20, the Reich commissar chosen to run the Prussian Ministry of the Interior, Franz Bracht, pursued a policy that led to "the favoring of the NSDAP and special consideration for the SA [Storm Troops]." Bracht's lifting on July 27, 1932, of the June 1930 prohibition on police membership in the NSDAP provided one manifestation of the changed atmosphere. The attendance of fifty policemen in uniform at a special NSDAP-sponsored event for the police in Cologne on July 29 offered another visible sign of open sympathy with the far Right.

"Day of the National Uprising"

On January 22, 1933, some fourteen hundred policemen blockaded the Berlin headquarters of the KPD in support of an SA memorial march in honor of Horst Wessel, National Socialism's most famous martyr, providing a portentous dress rehearsal to the torchlit SA and SS procession that nine days later marched through the Brandenburg Gate in review for the new Reich chancellor.[61] From the moment of his appointment as chancellor on January 30, 1933, Hitler pursued a series of measures designed to increase the new administration's grip on the reins of power and to "coordinate" the official agencies and branches of the Reich government. Hitler and his cohorts in the Party recognized that control over the police executives of the state governments was vital to the consolidation of their power. It is, there-fore, significant that the only National Socialist members in Hitler's cabinet, Wilhelm Frick and Hermann Göring, occupied positions from which control over the police could be exercised.

Frick had gained valuable experience in purging the civil service and police as interior minister in Thuringia and was a natural choice for implementing the same strategy at the national level, even if the Reich minister of the interior held a position from which nominal influence could be exerted over the various state police authorities. In contrast, the selection of Göring as Reich minister without portfolio and Prussian minister of the interior provided a means for the direct control of the entire Prussian state police, both uniformed and plainclothes. A secondary and by no means unimportant appointment involved Göring's choice of Kurt Daluege as commissioner for special duty, in charge of the Police Section within the Prussian Ministry of the Interior.[62] Likewise, Himmler's stock rose rapidly in the first months of the regime as he maneuvered for control of the Political Police executives of several states in his quest to create a unified Reich police force as the "strongest linchpin" of the State.[63]

Hitler chose well in the selection of his agents for the reshaping and coordination of the police, and he wasted little time in proceeding with the consolidation of this power base. After only five days in office, he issued his first emergency degree, the "Decree of the Reich President for the Protection of the German People." This measure limited the freedom of the press and the right of assembly and provided specific authorities to the Reich minister of the interior and the police to prohibit and control public gatherings.[64] The burning of the Reichstag building on the night of February 27 led to the declaration of a general state of emergency entitled the "Decree of the Reich President for the Protection of People and State," more commonly referred to as the "Reichstag Fire Decree," of February 28, 1933. This decree effectively suspended the constitutional rights and basic civil liberties of all German citizens and provided the mechanism for the suppression of opposition political parties in the scheduled March election.

As Hitler tightened his grip on the government, Göring took another step in the co-optation of the Prussian police with the promulgation of an order for the "Advancement of the National Movement," or "Shooting Directive," calling for direct assistance to and protection of "national organizations," including the SA, the SS, and the Stahlhelm (Steel Helmet), on February 17, 1933. Aimed at "enemies of the state" and specifically at "Communist acts of terror and assaults," the directive stated: "Police officials who use their weapons in the conduct of their duties will be covered by me without regard to the consequences of using their weapons." Göring's directive also contained a subtle warning to those who might favor restraint by noting: "Whoever misguidedly fails in this duty can expect disciplinary action."[65] Later that year, Göring broadened the limits for the use of deadly force by ordering the "ruthless use of weapons" against those distributing political pamphlets in the event they tried to flee from police.[66] Not only did Göring's orders pave the way for a "shoot first, ask questions later" mentality, but they also established this attitude as the organizational standard of action within the Prussian police.

"Cleansing" the Ranks of the Police

Admittedly, much of the evidence presented concerning the penetration of the NSDAP into the ranks of the Uniformed Police prior to 1933, whether in Hamburg, Berlin, Saxony, or Prussia, is circumstantial, and the prohibition on police membership in the NSDAP until the summer of 1932 and the continued threat of career repercussions after that time make it difficult to gain an empirical overview of the political sympathies of the police. Still, the measures taken in the initial months of 1933 to "coordinate" the police provide indications of the success of the Party in co-opting the police.

During a speech in October 1935, Daluege described the "transformation" of the police in the first two years after the Nazi seizure of power as "one of the most urgent tasks" faced by the new government.[67] The "coordination" of the Prussian police followed a dual strategy of subordinating the police executive to National Socialist political authority while undertaking steps for the replacement of police officials deemed either "uncooperative" or "politically unreliable." In the case of the latter, the Nazi government forced thirteen police presidents, including the two remaining Social Democratic police presidents who escaped dismissal during the events of July 1932, into retirement on February 13, 1933.[68] Three weeks later, on March 8, Frick increased the National Socialist stranglehold on the police with the appointment of Reich commissioners for the police in the states of Baden, Württemberg, Saxony, and Schaumburg-Lippe. This measure resulted in the subordination of the police forces of every state to either a National Socialist state government or a National Socialist Reich commissioner for the police, with the notable exception of Bavaria.[69] The circle of police control closed the following day, March 9, with the selection of Adolf Wagner as Bavarian minister of the interior and the subsequent naming of Himmler as Bavarian police president.[70]

Stacking the Deck

During the purge of the police, the Prussian government dismissed 826 enlisted policemen and 200 police officers, including 22 of 32 police colonels, amounting to 7 percent of the police officer corps and 2 percent of the enlisted force.[71] In the case of Prussia, it is important to remember that this "housecleaning" followed on the heels of that done by von Papen the summer before and is, therefore, skewed by the prior removal of many police officials affiliated with the Social Democratic Party. The dismissals of early 1933 extended, not only to the ranks of the police, but also, and even more importantly, to the higher civil servants exercising authority over state, regional, and even communal police forces. On February 14, 1933, the *Völkischer Beobachter* announced Göring's dismissal of three district presidents, three district vice presidents, and twelve police presidents in the state of Prussia alone.[72] This move involved the dismissal of district presidents in Wiesbaden, Kassel, and Arnsberg as well as police presidents in almost all major urban centers, including Frankfurt am Main, Koblenz, Dortmund, Hannover, Breslau, and Bochum.[73] In the state of Thuringia, the National Socialists went one step further by suspending all Social Democratic mayors who exercised police authority and placing this authority in the hands of "dependable nationally inclined civil servants."[74]

The process of removing civil servants and political authorities who were not "nationally inclined" accelerated in the coming months as Hitler sought to increase the National Socialists' hold on the reins of political and police authority. On February 17, a newspaper story announced the appointments of Party "old fighters" to fill the positions in Prussia, including (retired) Admiral Magnus von Levetzow as the new police president of Berlin, Wilhelm Schepmann as the police president in Dortmund, and Viktor Lutze as the police president in Hannover.[75] All three men were veterans of the Great War and members of the Party, and Schepmann and Lutze held senior positions in the SA. In a diary entry, Josef Goebbels, the Party's propagandist, recorded Göring's effort with approval and delight: "Göring's cleaning out the rubbish."[76] In March, the purge of the civil service continued as SA Leader Wolf Graf von Helldorf was appointed as the police president in Potsdam, SA Leader Edmund Heines took charge of the police presidency in Breslau, and Paul Hinkler, a National Socialist member of the state parliament, became the police president in Gladbach-Rheydt. In the following months, SS and SA leaders received appointment as police presidents in Koblenz, Kassel, Essen, and Erfurt.[77]

In addition to filling the ranks of the senior police leadership with Party loyalists, Göring, in his position as the Prussian minister of the interior, released a directive on February 28, 1933, ordering that National Socialist candidates receive "primary consideration" for entry into the ranks of the police. Furthermore, the directive called for consultation on applicants between the leaders of the Party, the SA, the SS, and the Stahlhelm as well as the requirement that senior police administrative officials consult directly with the commanders of the police schools to ensure the choice of the appropriate candidates.[78]

Daluege later boasted about the decision to fill officer and enlisted positions made available by dismissals or forced retirements with "the oldest National Socialists."[79] One manifestation of this strategy included a proposal for the accession of some 60 SA and 25 SS men who were intended to take over leadership roles in the Prussian police at the rank of captain and above, after the completion of a short training course. According to Daluege, this initiative would "bestow the suitable expression of the close ties between the state instruments of power [i.e., the police] and the SA and SS."[80]

In a report to Göring in January 1934, Daluege stressed his efforts and success in finding positions for "old Party comrades" within the Prussian police. He listed the presence of 200 SS men, 891 SA men, and 335 Stahlhelm men as well as 201 additional Party members within the ranks of the police civil service (*Beamte*). In addition, he highlighted the presence of 307 SS men, 786 SA men, 7 Stahlhelm men, and 43 male and 20 female Party members in non–civil service positions (*Angestellte*) within the police.[81] In a related measure, Frick issued a directive in July 1934 prohibiting the promotion of police officers who had previously belonged to the "system parties" during Weimar, placing additional obstacles in the paths of non-NSDAP or other nationalist party members.[82]

In Bavaria, Himmler followed a strategy similar to the Prussian model by mobilizing SA and SS men into the police. In an interview, he remarked that this practice had proved extremely valuable as these men "knew exactly the hideouts of the Marxist organizations" better than the police owing to their "long years of tough battles against Marxism."[83] The incorporation of SA and SS men into the police leadership allowed the Party to make direct inroads into the police in the early phase of the National Socialist consolidation of power, providing an instrument for direct action against the regime's political and racial foes as well as a mechanism for influencing the organizational climate within the precincts and garrisons.

The Police and the Party

In December 1935, Martin Bormann, the chief of staff in the office of the deputy to the Führer, sent Daluege a personal letter in which he addressed the cooperation between the police and the various agencies of the NSDAP. Bormann argued that "the maintenance of domestic security and the battle against enemies of the state" demanded the closest cooperation between Party and police officials, not only at the state level, but also at the local level.[84] In his response, Daluege informed Bormann that, in Prussia alone, every police presidency and police directorate was in the hands of the "oldest National Socialists" and that there were only two men among these police officials who were not SA or SS leaders as well. Daluege remarked that these were not the type of men who would allow personnel decisions to be made at the local level that did not conform to the objectives of the Party. He also observed: "Here, I want to again emphasize that, statistically speaking, over 20 percent of the German police civil servants are at present Party members, including 3,000 'old fighters.'" Daluege continued with a hint of acerbity: "I don't know whether any other organizations or branches of the civil service can show this degree of penetration with National Socialists."[85] Daluege's point was, in fact, well taken as civil servants as a group composed 13 percent of the Party's membership in January 1935.[86]

The Road to a Reich Police

The National Socialist usurpation of state government authority accelerated with the enactment of the first and second "Coordination Laws" on March 31 and April 7, 1933, respectively. The former established the applicability of Reich government legislative measures with respect to the state governments, but it did not mandate structural changes in the state administrations. In contrast, the "Second Law for Coordination with the Reich" redefined the relation between the Reich and the states by vesting ultimate authority within the latter in the person of a National Socialist Reich governor (*Reichsstaathalter*). The Reich governor essentially had the responsibility for ensuring the "observation of the political principles laid down by the Reich chancellor."[87] The appointment of Reich governors effectively supported the earlier selection of the Reich commissioners of the police by seizing control of the state administrations from the top down.

However, Frick's plans for the police extended beyond merely consolidating National Socialist control over the state police forces. In separate letters in May 1933, Frick informed Göring of his plans for the future of the Reich's police forces. On May 12, he notified the Prussian minister of the interior that he was "extraordinarily interested" in plans concerning the unification and centralization of the Reich's political police. He requested that Göring refrain from making any decisions until he had time to finalize his own position on the subject.[88] In a subsequent letter on May 24, Frick informed Göring of his intent to centralize the states' political and criminal police organizations under Reich control while "preserving the police sovereignty of the states."[89] In this letter, Frick gave vent to his frustration at the reluctance of the states to subordinate their efforts to the national government; however, the solution to this problem presented itself less than a year later.

On January 30, 1934, the "Law Concerning the Restructuring of the Reich" finalized the "coordination" of the state governments as they transferred their sovereignty to the Reich.[90] In a decree of February 19, Frick informed the Reich governors that he now exercised "direct command authority over all state police forces in the German Reich." However, Göring resisted Frick's attempt to establish direct control over a Reich-wide police, countering the move by subordinating the head of the Police Section of the Prussian Ministry of the Interior to himself, thereby depriving Frick of more than half the Reich's police forces. In late March, Göring reluctantly relented, and the Prussian Ministry of the Interior began discussions with its Reich counterpart concerning the incorporation of the various state ministries into the central government. During these negotiations, Himmler garnered the post of inspector of the Gestapo in Prussia, while Kurt Daluege moved into a position to influence the Uniformed Police of the entire Reich.[91] Despite the need for further negotiations concerning budgetary authority between the states and the Reich in preparation for the transfer of the police to the central government, a crucial step in the centralization of the Uniformed Police had been taken.[92]

A View from the Opposition

The Social Democratic opposition to Hitler's regime addressed the Nazi "cleansing" (*Säuberung*) of the police in the November/December 1934 edition of its underground reports smuggled out of Germany. The report warned: "The police is probably the administrative branch in which the personnel and administrative policy of National Socialism has been most active." It continued: "Extensive organizational changes have resulted, and work on the creation of a national police administration is proceeding with enthusiasm."[93] In a later speech to the Party leadership, Daluege confirmed this assessment: "Certainly no other part of the general German civil service had as great a percentage of members removed from its ranks as the police."[94] The report listed the numbers of police officers forced to retire or removed from the ranks as 7.3 percent of the precinct (Schutzpolizei) officer corps, 13.5 percent of the rural (Gendarmerie) officer corps, and 15 percent of the Community Police (Gemeindepolizei) officer corps.[95]

Removal from the ranks for some policemen proved to be a traumatic experience. In one case, a policeman in Braunschweig was called out before his comrades and declared to be "a scoundrel and informer" for allegedly providing information to the SPD. As a result, the police commander confiscated the man's headgear and weapon before tearing off his epaulets and sending him to jail.[96]

Some states were harder hit than others, Hessen, for example, losing 50 percent of its officer corps and over 5 percent of its Landespolizei members. A breakdown of the "cleansing" in Hessen revealed the ousting of over 16 percent of the precinct police, almost 8 percent of the Gendarmerie, and almost 17 percent of the Community Police as well as 11 percent of police administrative officials.[97] The explanation for the sweeping changes in Hessen was the opposition initially faced by the National Socialists from the state interior minister Wilhelm Leuschner after Hitler's appointment as Reich chancellor and the generally prorepublican orientation of the Hessian police. After Nazi gains in the March election of 1933 and the naming of Jacob Sprenger as the Reich governor in May, the "cleansing" of the Hessian state police accelerated with the naming of Party members to key positions within the police apparatus.[98]

The Social Democratic reports offer two insights into the Nazi co-optation of the police. First, the high proportion of dismissals and forced retirements from the Community Police clearly was linked to a general dissatisfaction with the qualifications of these men as expressed by Himmler and Daluege on several occasions.[99] In this respect, the German equivalent of the prototypical American law enforcement characters of Andy Taylor and Barney Fife did not fit Himmler's or Daluege's vision for the Community Police. Second, one would expect some regional disparities in the purge of the police on the basis of social and confessional demographics leading to differences in political voting patterns, as the Hessian case indicates.

The Hilfspolizei Experiment

In his desire to carry the battle to the parties of the Left, on February 22, 1933, Göring mobilized fifty thousand men from the SA, the SS, and the Stahlhelm as auxiliary policemen to assist the Prussian police in their duties.[100] The creation of the Prussian Hilfspolizei, or Auxiliary Police, enabled Göring to undertake a campaign of terror directed against members of the Communist Party as well as the leadership and the rank and file of the Social Democratic Party in advance of the national elections on March 5. In Prussia alone, police authorities placed some twenty-five thousand persons in "protective custody" in March and April.[101] In numerous cases, members of the KPD and SPD simply disappeared, vanishing into improvised concentration camps run by the SA and the SS.[102]

The establishment of the Hilfspolizei represented an important initial step in binding the police with the organizations of the Party in both a symbolic and a substantive sense. In Hessen, Werner Best, a leading Nazi jurist, worked enthusiastically to enlist thousands of auxiliary policemen as a method by which to create a "bond of the active forces of the movement" with the police for the fulfillment of Party objectives and to ease the transition of the state into the National Socialist camp.[103] On April 4, the chief of staff of the SA, Ernst Röhm, followed the Prussian lead by proposing the creation of a Bavarian Hilfspolizei with a strength of up to 40 percent of the existing Schutzpolizei in the areas under state police administration. In this case, Röhm, like Göring, recognized the potential advantages of using the Party's paramilitary forces in concert with the police as a potential lever to augment his own power and as a mechanism by which to gain increased influence over the Bavarian police.[104]

A brief examination of Hilfspolizei activities provides a clear picture of the broad powers and brutish efficacy enjoyed by this particular instrument of coordination. For example, auxiliary policemen in Upper Silesia confiscated records from the city of Hindenburg's financial administration department as part of an investigation of property tax levies.[105] The Hilfspolizei in the state of Württemberg operated a concentration camp at Heuberg, incarcerating fifteen hundred political detainees.[106] In Saxony, a raid conducted by the police with the assistance of the Hilfspolizei resulted in the arrest of seventy persons on charges of suspected involvement in a Communist courier ring, and, in the East Prussian city of Riesenburg, SS auxiliaries arrested five "Communist leaders," thirty-five SPD and KPD "functionaries," and "several Jewish businessmen" in March 1933.[107] In a paradoxical turn of events, police auxiliaries participated in dispersing SA men attempting to block access to Jewish-owned department stores and businesses in Berlin and Essen in early March.[108] This last example—in which we see auxiliaries enforcing police directives against their SA and SS compatriots—confirmed the ultimate command authority of the regular police and demonstrated the Nazi leadership's opposition to independent initiatives that might affect commerce.

In general, the augmentation of the Uniformed Police with the Hilfspolizei served two functions. First, it publicly legitimized the men of the SA and SS who enlisted as auxiliaries as well as their acts of political and racial violence. In this respect, the image of brawling "brown shirts" and "black shirts" transformed into paramilitary protectors of public order provided one avenue for legitimizing the past actions of these groups in their pursuit of a "national revolution." Second, it provided members of the SA and SS with an improved opportunity for recruitment into the ranks of the regular police. A letter from Göring's office in the Prussian Ministry of the Interior to the presidents of the Prussian administrative districts in May 1933 high-lighted the degree to which the thinking and methods of the SA and SS had penetrated the police. According to the letter, experience had shown that the questioning of those suspected of political offenses by the regular police "had not achieved the success that could be obtained by members of the SA and the SS in the interrogation of the same suspects." It was then suggested that, in "suitable cases," the police could hand over suspects to the Hilfspolizei for interrogation, reassuming custody after the completion of questioning.[109] In an order of June 15, 1933, Daluege, in his position as head of the Police Section of the Prussian Ministry of the Interior, noted his conviction that the majority of police officers "unreservedly" served the interests of the National Socialist state. Nevertheless, he remarked on his intention to accelerate and supplement the "assimilation" of proven SA and SS leaders into the Prussian police in order to lend appropriate expression to the "close relationship" between "the power center of the state" and the SA and SS.[110]

Recognizing that the Prussian auxiliary policemen had served their pur-pose in the Nazi consolidation of power, Göring disbanded the force on August 2, 1933.[111] He made an exception for the SA Group Berlin-Branden-burg, which was reconstituted as the Feldjägerkorps (Field Security Corps) on October 1, 1933.[112] In contrast, Röhm's influence allowed the Bavarian auxiliaries to remain in existence until December 31, 1933, at which point they too were disbanded.[113]

In the final analysis, the Hilfspolizei experiment allowed for the mobi-lization of National Socialist "true believers" into the ranks of the Uniformed Police during a crucial period for the nascent regime. The contact between the police and the SA and SS contributed to a progressive radicalization of the organizational culture of the police, a process that became more pro-nounced with the enlistment of former auxiliaries into the police. The Ger-man political scientist Karl Dietrich Bracher aptly observed: "The directive of February 22 meant no less than the entrustment of police functions to the National Socialist Party's paramilitary forces, a particularly important step in the process of coordination and the one-sided employment of state author-ity through National Socialist leadership."[114]

Creating an Organizational Culture

On April 7, 1933, the "Law for the Restoration of the Civil Service" came into force, giving the Reich carte blanche with regard to the dismissal of civil servants. The entire civil service, including the police, now faced removal or summary demotion on political, racial, or ideological grounds. One Nazi pub-

lication proclaimed that the Civil Service Law provided "the National Socialist revolution with the possibility of cleansing the civil service of politically
and racially unacceptable elements."[115] At the end of June 1933, an additional
decree allowed for the dismissal or forced retirement of civil servants for the
"simplification" of administration or "in the interests of the service."[116] At
the same time, Daluege called for the "acceleration" of efforts to incorporate
"tried and tested SA and SS leaders" into the Prussian police.[117]

The recruitment of these true believers into the institution offered one of
the key methods for perpetuating culture within the organization.[118] The
purging of the police of "politically and racially unacceptable elements,"
combined with the appointment of Party and other like-minded nationalists
to positions of leadership within the officer corps and in the ranks, went far
in creating the foundation for an organizational culture in which the racial
and ideological precepts of the Party provided the direction for careerists and
true believers alike.

A New Image for the Police

Soon after Hitler's appointment as chancellor, the new government embarked
on a public relations campaign aimed at creating a new image of the police as
"friend and helper." In some respects, this campaign was not wholly new, as
Severing had attempted to remold the authoritarian image of the average
policeman and to gain public respect and trust for the police through such
measures as the Great Police Exhibition of 1926 under the motto "Please,
come closer."[119] The intent of the 1926 exhibition was to "demonstrate the
rapprochement of police and public" and to dispel the image of the police
as "an inconvenient authority, here only to admonish and tutor." The success of these efforts in Prussia proved mixed. On the one hand, Berlin's toy
stores for the first time offered police dolls during the 1926 Christmas sea-
son. On the other hand, the refusal to issue policemen identification numbers for their uniforms provides an apt illustration of the continuing cleft
between those tasked to preserve public order and their fellow citizens.[120]

In contrast, the National Socialist ambitions for the police extended
beyond a simple rapprochement toward a union of the police with the *Volk*.
In their public pronouncements, the leadership of the police emphasized the
emergence of a police whose bond of allegiance to a monarchical or constitutional state was replaced by a bond of service to the German people.
Göring's March 1933 decision to abolish the requirement for the carrying of
the police baton (*Gummiknüppel*) was intended as one visible expression of
the changed nature of the relationship between the police and the people.[121]

The baton had become under Weimar a symbol for the role of the police in the bloody street fighting and was, therefore, disliked by policemen and feared by the public. An article in *The German Police,* the professional journal of the police, heralded the decision to collect and recycle the rubber-based police batons as the end to an "infamous chapter" in German history, specifically the Republic.[122]

As part of the public relations campaign, the concept of the policeman as "friend and helper" became a ubiquitous theme in both the police literature and the mass media. For example, a newspaper article of August 1, 1933, entitled "Berlin's New Police" discussed the increased efforts of the police to "cleanse" the city's streets of the "unpleasant manifestations" (*unerfreuliche Erscheinungen*) of prostitution and homosexuality. The article then turned to a discussion of the special effort directed against career criminals as well as the "exceptionally strong impression" made on criminals by the execution of death sentences, progress made possible by increased cooperation with the Ministry of Justice. In conclusion, the article presented the police president's goals that "the citizen of Berlin should see a friend and helper in the policeman" as well as the transformation of the city's police into a "people's police" (*Volkspolizei*) similar to the London bobby.[123]

Choosing the London bobby as the model for Berlin's policemen proved an ambitious goal. Still, it was not just Berlin's policemen that were to be remade but the entire German police. Daluege made exactly this point in a speech to Uniformed Police commanders in April 1935 in which he declared that, in order to instill pride in his title on the part of the policeman and respect from the *Volk,* "the police will and must be bound to the people."[124] The process of establishing a bond of trust between the people and the police extended beyond mere rhetoric to include the use of ceremony, demonstrations, and exhibitions.

The Use of Ceremony and the Day of the German Police

In October 1933, Göring ordered the entire Prussian police to participate in activities designed to collect money for the less fortunate, activities that included recommended "voluntary" contributions from each policeman's paycheck depending on rank.[125] This effort found subsequent expression with the creation of a national "Day of the German Police" (Tag der Deutschen Polizei) in 1934. The Day of the German Police provides an excellent example of the use of ceremony in an effort to improve the public image of the police and to demonstrate the new bond between the people and the National Socialist police.

In his decree designating December 18 and 19, 1934, as the Day of the German Police, Frick noted that the purpose of the day was twofold. First, the events and activities were meant to demonstrate the bond between the people and the police. Second, the police dedicated the day to the collection of contributions for the winter welfare drive (*Winterhilfswerk*) to benefit the less fortunate.[126] Photographs of the day's events reinforced this image by showing policemen eating lunch at tables with young children and senior citizens as well as instructing a young girl how to use a camera and giving rides to children on police horses.[127]

In addition, a small paperback entitled *The Police: Your Friend and Your Helper* and aimed at young readers was published in 1936 with its cover displaying a drawing of two prototypical "Aryan" males, a worker and a policeman, shaking hands below an oversized police crest. One chapter covers the dos and don'ts of traffic regulation, with photographs of children playing in a busy street and holding on to passing carts while riding their scooters and scooters with improperly affixed reflectors, all don'ts. Another chapter shows a lost toddler at the precinct house having a tea party with the policemen. When the mother is finally located, she promises to bring the child back the next day to visit the good "Uncle Police Sergeant." Although generally downplayed, ideology too makes an appearance, with drawings of young boys using the "Hitler greeting" to salute policemen. Still, in a chapter devoted to policemen who lost their lives in the line of duty, the young reader learns: "The number of casualties in the police was especially high in those years in which the Bolshevist murderous arsonists plunged our Fatherland into misery and want."[128] In this narrative, police sacrifice and German misery are laid squarely at the feet of the Communists.

After his appointment as Reich leader of the SS and chief of the German police in June 1936, Himmler reinforced the bond between the police and the people in his foreword to a short book designed to accompany the Day of the German Police: "Unlike in earlier decades, the German National Socialist police is not the police servant of an absolutist or constitutional state directed against the people but rather a police coming from the people [and] for the German people."[129] In conjunction with the 1937 celebration, one newspaper showed a picture of a traffic policeman helping two young girls cross the street. The photograph appeared over a poem entitled "The Good 'Uncle Schupo,'" a four-stanza celebration of the virtuous "Uncle Schupo" and his efforts to safeguard "little Marie" (Mariechen) and "little Margret" (Margretchen) on their daily walk to school. Posters from the 1939 celebration continued this theme by showing a traffic cop with a young girl in one arm and an elderly woman on the other crossing a busy street, a bicyclist and a double-decker bus with the destination "Adolf Hitler–Platz" visible above its windshield waiting in the background for instructions to proceed.[130]

Not all themes were as treacly as that of the friendly traffic cop. For example, press coverage of the 1937 event carried a speech by Himmler under the heading "Enemy of the Criminal—Friend of the People" as well as an article by Göring under the motto "Police Duty on a Soldierly Foundation." At the Nuremberg Party rally in 1937, Hitler too emphasized the dual character of the police as a representative of the state and as the "best friend of the people" while remaining the "pitiless agent of the peoples' community" against criminals.[131]

Similarly, Daluege informed his listeners at the Reich press conference in July 1935 that the "new police" were concentrating on making it impossible for "asocial elements" to disrupt the peace. In an address entitled "The Jew and Criminal Statistics," he explicitly identified the Jews as these "asocial elements," presenting statistical data indicating that Jews were responsible for almost 30 percent of the international drug trade, 42 percent of illegal gambling and con games, and 42 percent of cases involving pickpockets. Daluege exclaimed that these numbers demonstrated the "danger of Jewishdom for the German people."[132] The portrayal of the Jew as criminal transgressor by the chief of the Uniformed Police in front of the national media provided a powerful image for both the average person in the street and the cop on the beat.

The image of the heroic policeman placed in positions of danger in his role as protector of the people also found expression in police literature. For example, a poster from the 1939 Day of the German Police depicts two plainclothes detectives, presumably from the Criminal Police, engaged in a gun battle with several robbers. One of the detectives is seen clutching his chest in an effort to staunch the bleeding caused by a gunshot wound. In this picture, the placement of the detective's wound directs the viewer's attention to a Party badge worn on his tie, at once underlining the danger faced by the police in their protection of the people and evoking the cult of sacrifice whereby another member of the movement joins the ranks of the Party martyrs.[133]

The portrayal of the policeman as the guardian of young children and the elderly may appear mundane to today's reader, but it is important to note that the dedicated effort to establish a relationship between the people and the police was fundamentally new for Germans of the early twentieth century. If Heinrich Mann could fantasize about Berlin's imperial police hacking their way through a café with drawn sabers at the turn of the century, then this itself provided tangible evidence of the distance between the men and women in the street and the protectors of public order.[134] However, the

Nazi emphasis on the shared bond between the police and the German people reflected a perverted and malevolent relationship in which putative racial and biological characteristics determined membership in this "peoples' community." In the "racial state" of Hitler's Reich, the police were not the friends and helpers of Jews, Sinti and Roma ("Gypsies"), homosexuals, or the mentally and physically handicapped or of those whose behavior was deemed harmful to the *Volk*.

A New Concept of Crime

The National Socialist ascension to power and the consolidation of control over the various state police organizations precipitated a decisive change in the definition of crime itself. Under a regime in which the police became the trusted agents for ensuring the "health of the body of the German folk," the nature and character of crime expanded to include any act, either political or criminal, injuring or weakening the social and political fabric of this constructed community.[135] It is in this respect that one must understand the efforts to establish a centralized police apparatus and create a "Protective Corps" (Staatsschutzkorps) binding all organs of the Political, Criminal, and Uniformed Police together in a common cause to protect the racial, biological, and social health of the peoples' community. Himmler's declaration in early 1937 concerning the importance of police powers to ensure the security of the "life force and institutions" of the German people offers one example of the initiative for expanding cooperation between all institutions of state control.[136] This in turn led to a situation in which, not only political opposition, but also social conduct became the focus of a police complex whose raison d'être centered on ensuring the health of a metaphoric German corpus. This effort included preventing the introduction of such "diseases" as alternate political philosophies and, eventually, purging the "germs" and "parasites" most visibly represented in National Socialist ideology in the form of the Jew.[137]

Cooperating with the Gestapo

The purge of the civil service and the accession of Party loyalists into the ranks constituted specific structural initiatives aimed at reshaping the police in support of the National Socialist consolidation of power. The efforts of the Nazi leadership, however, did not stop there. If actions speak louder than words, then Göring, Himmler, and Daluege wasted little time in translating organizational initiatives into concrete measures in the realm of daily policing. Without a doubt, the Security Police (the Gestapo and the Criminal Police) received the primary task of leading the battle against the Reich's putative political and racial enemies. Still, as the historian Robert Gellately demonstrated, the Gestapo "did not possess the omnipotence often attributed to it, but relied upon the collaboration of a whole host of organizations and institutions." In truth, the personnel of the Security Police, especially the Gestapo, were stretched thin across Germany and were forced to rely on the population for denunciations and information. In their turn, the men of the Uniformed Police "dutifully checked" denunciations and complaints of all kinds made by their fellow Germans.[138]

Besides informants, the Gestapo also relied heavily on the cooperation of all branches of the Uniformed Police.[139] The "First Gestapo Law" of April 1933 directed *all* Prussian police authorities to support the Gestapo in its investigations.[140] Two months later, in a letter of June 26, 1933, marked "extremely urgent" and restricted to hand-to-hand transfer only, Daluege made the requirement for members of the Prussian Uniformed Police to assist the Gestapo explicit. The letter referenced the decree of April giving the Gestapo responsibility for the investigation and combat of all seditious activities. Daluege noted that it was absolutely clear from this decree alone that all local police authorities, including the police presidents, were bound to "carry out the instructions" of the Gestapo in support of their investigations.[141]

One study commented on the importance of cooperation between the uniformed policemen and the Gestapo, arguing: "Effective law enforcement, especially as it pertained to political 'crimes,' subversive activities, and sabotage, could not have been achieved without the extensive Orpo [Ordnungspolizei] network and the constant cooperation between the uniformed regular police and the agents of the political police."[142] Admittedly, this close cooperation between uniformed policemen and their plainclothes counterparts in the Political and Criminal Police had its precedent during the Weimar period; however, after 1933, these close working relationships emerged as a routine fact of daily operations.[143] The practical manifestations of this cooperative relationship ranged from the mundane to the sinister. For example, the Gestapo enlisted the assistance of the Franconian police in the gathering together of unit flags from the Stahlhelm for a permanent display in Magdeburg's "old Nicholas Church."[144] In the Cologne area, the Gestapo office asked for the assistance of rural police posts with the confiscation of books, periodicals, and printed flyers as well as the surveillance of meetings by a Catholic youth organization.[145] In another case, the Gestapo tasked the police with the responsibility of canvassing local shop owners to investigate cases of "hoarding" three weeks after the outbreak of war.[146]

Police assistance to the Gestapo included, however, a more ominous side. For example, uniformed policemen, acting alone or in cooperation with the Political Police, raided the homes, meeting places, and headquarters of the Communist Party and its members and participated in the roundup of political enemies of the Reich as well as their incarceration in concentration camps.[147] On March 2, 1933, police raids in numerous cities throughout the Rhineland and Westphalia led to the arrest of over two thousand "Communists."[148] In addition, uniformed policemen guarded concentration camps in north Germany, and a police major served for a time as the commandant at the concentration camp in Papenburg. Uniformed policemen also conducted duties at the Wittmoor concentration camp near Hamburg.[149] In short, the involvement of the police in the repression of the parties of the Left emerged as a routine part of their duties under the new regime.

In July 1933, the Cologne Gestapo office ordered rural police stations to dedicate themselves with "complete energy and zeal" to "the combat of Communist and Marxist endeavors" in their jurisdictions.[150] In Prussia, on July 25, 1933, the Secret Police office (*Gestapa*) directed the activities of the entire Uniformed Police and Hilfspolizei in a statewide series of identity checkpoints along railroads and major highways, resulting in the arrest of suspected enemies of the state.[151] In October, Gestapo headquarters in Berlin sent a letter to the local Uniformed Police officials in the north German coastal city of Kiel with instructions on the treatment of "followers and low-level functionaries of Marxist parties" recently released from concentration camps in the area. The letter highlighted the requirement that former inmates of the camps report to their local police three times a week. It also stressed that the police should maintain surveillance of the former inmates and, if necessary, enlist the support of Party organizations, including the SA and SS, in this task.[152] The cooperation of the Uniformed Police with Party organizations extended beyond the mere surveillance of "suspect elements" to include the provision of information on the political reliability of citizens within their jurisdictions.[153]

In one respect, the cooperation with Party organizations against the enemies of the Left set a precedent for later cooperative efforts, including the persecution of foreign forced laborers within the Reich during the war.[154] In addition, the Uniformed Police also adopted a key role in the prosecution of racial policies. For example, the task of registering Germans designated as medically or physically handicapped (*erbkrank*) in preparation for forced sterilization fell to the Uniformed Police.[155] In these cases, the police not only served as the escorts for those designated to be sterilized or incarcerated in psychiatric institutions for observation; they also occasionally provided information on and recommendations regarding the mental health of these individuals to support the diagnosis of the medical board charged with making a determination. For example, one Gendarmerie station reported on an individual under investigation: "His empty expression alone shows that [one] is dealing with a sick person. Sterilization would certainly be appropriate." Another Gendarmerie report noted that the individual in question must be an "eccentric" (*Sonderling*) as he wore his wool jacket while working in the summer heat.[156] Furthermore, the police used "protective custody" to incarcerate, not only political enemies of the Reich, but the mentally and physically handicapped as well. This practice led to complaints from Göring's office and the reminder that the limited space in the existing concentration camps was reserved for "enemies of the state."[157]

In the case of Germany's Jewish population, it is important to note, not just what the police did, but also what they failed to do. For example, the boycott of Jewish businesses in April 1933 and the November 1938 pogrom that saw little or no police interference provide their own indictments of the sin of omission.[158] In a sin of commission, many times precinct policemen or Gendarmerie members made the initial arrest of Jews before their transfer to the Gestapo for incarceration in concentration camps.[159] The regular police also played an important role in enforcing discriminatory ordinances and statutes aimed at the Jews, including the enforcement of the provisions of the "Nuremberg Laws" of 1935. In this case, local police officials reviewed and remarked on paperwork documenting "Aryan" ancestry and helped enforce the many supplementary laws aimed at normalizing discrimination against Jews and their exclusion from German society.[160]

Tightening the Bond

With the "Third Gestapo Law" of February 10, 1936, Reich Minister of the Interior Frick broadened the responsibility of the Gestapo and increased the limits of cooperation between regular police authorities and the Gestapo, a measure that once again reinforced the symbiotic relationship between the Security and the Uniformed Police and demonstrated the patterns of concentric influence between the two organizations.[161] From a procedural perspective, several memoranda and letters from Gestapo headquarters commented on the process and importance of identifying directives for the Political Police that also needed to be made available to the regular police authorities.[162] In his book *The German Police*, Werner Best, a senior SS leader and leading Nazi jurist, also emphasized the obligation of "all SS and police organizations" to provide "mutual support in the fulfillment of their individual tasks."[163] Another important aspect of the "Third Gestapo Law" was that it laid the foundation for the subsequent fusion of the Security Police apparatus with Himmler's SS.[164]

The transfer of uniformed policemen into the Security Police provided an additional mechanism for strengthening the bond between the two organizations. In June 1937, Daluege wrote to Reinhard Heydrich, chief of the Security Police and Security Service (SD), to discuss the issue of uniformed policemen chosen for transfer into the Criminal Police. Reacting to a proposal to reduce these numbers, Daluege reminded Heydrich: "A large portion of your men in the Secret State Police [Gestapo] are sergeants in the [Uniformed] Police. . . . I believe 1,300 sergeants in the Reich." He then remarked: "The Uniformed Police is in a position to provide good men for your purposes and needs . . . now and in the future."[165] Daluege's apprehension with the proposed reductions involved his concern about having to find billets for these men to remain within the police and the resultant cascading effect on promotions and manning throughout the organization. Despite differences on the numbers of transfers, uniformed policemen continued to move into the ranks of the Security Police with an agreement in July 1937 that the Uniformed Police would supply 80 percent of Criminal Police and 50 percent of Gestapo replacements from a pool of policemen who had finished eight years of service.[166]

Although the Gestapo laws and subsequent directives established a basis for cooperation between the regional and the local offices of the Security Police and the Uniformed Police, such was not always the case between the main offices of the two organizations. In a letter to Heydrich on December 7, 1937, Daluege protested the SD's practice of enlisting uniformed policemen to provide political evaluations of their police superiors. In principle, Daluege did not object to policemen providing information to the SD—so long as the information did not pertain to their police duties or their colleagues.[167] In late 1940, Daluege again became embroiled in a discussion of the respective authority of the Uniformed Police and the Security Police in Luxembourg and the occupied East. In response to a charge by Heydrich, Daluege adamantly denied that he was attempting to manipulate issues related to legal jurisdiction in these areas. Daluege closed his letter by reaffirming his commitment to working with Heydrich and the Security Police Main Office before the implementation of any police decrees, and he called for a meeting between all concerned parties.[168]

Despite the friction between Heydrich and Daluege, the Gestapo made extensive use of the cooperation of all branches of the Uniformed Police. Reports from rural Gendarmerie stations in the vicinity of Würzburg between 1936 and 1938 demonstrate the importance of the gendarmes in assisting their counterparts in the Security Police. For example, a March 1936 report from the head of the Gendarmerie station in the town of Münnerstadt offered an evaluation of the political reliability of members of the local Augustinian order.[169] Similarly, in 1938, the Gendarmerie post in the village of Ebenhausen compiled two reports on the local Protestant pastor and his successor.[170] In the former case, the requests for information from the Gestapo headquarters in Würzburg concerning political reliability went through the local city and police authorities and even involved searching for potentially scandalous material, including an order in 1937 for local police authorities to determine whether any of the Catholic priests in the region had fathered children.[171] In another case, at the request of the SD, the Gendarmerie stations in the vicinity of Bad Kissingen compiled a list of children in the surrounding villages who were preparing for their first communion.[172]

The activities of the Gendarmerie stations clearly went beyond simply making reports. In March 1938, the Gestapo directed local authorities to confiscate copies of the magazines *German Freedom* and *Breakthrough,* a task passed along to the local Gendarmerie.[173] Additionally, local policemen participated in efforts to find and appropriate copies of books described as "inferior entertainment literature" (*minderwertiges Unterhaltungsschrifttum*), leading to the confiscation of over fifteen hundred copies of fourteen different works.[174] The participation of the Gendarmerie in these activities demonstrates that even the smallest and most remote of the Uniformed Police posts had ample opportunity to participate in the enforcement of the political and social policies of the Third Reich. However, the Uniformed Police also continued to play a key role in the prosecution of racial policy prior to the war.

The "Night of Broken Glass" and the Police

One of the clearest manifestations of the change of the organizational norms and values of the Uniformed Police involved their actions with respect to Germany's Jews. In a speech to a Party gathering in Essen in March 1933, Göring exclaimed that the police were not a security force for the protection of "Jewish department stores."[175] It is, therefore, not surprising that, three weeks later, a lack of police intervention allowed the members of the SA and the SS free rein for their tactics of intimidation and exclusion during the April 1, 1933, boycott of Jewish businesses. In one case, a policeman who witnessed the posting of anti-Jewish posters simply accepted the words of the miscreants that it did not concern him and continued on his way without intervening.[176] In another case, the local police in Rüdesheim simply looked the other way during the destruction of the synagogue and the physical abuse of the town's Jews in November 1938.[177] In response to protests from Jewish citizens and organizations, the police adopted the attitude that they were "powerless" to oppose the actions of a citizenry expressing their beliefs, even when these convictions crossed the line from words to actions, as they did so graphically in November 1938.[178]

Kristallnacht, or the Night of Broken Glass, is, in many respects, emblematic of the increased radicalization of racial policies aimed at Germany's Jewish population during the course of National Socialist rule. Reich Propaganda Minister Josef Goebbels sent the signal for the start of the countrywide pogrom during a speech on the night of November 9, 1938, to the "old fighters" of the Party commemorating the failed putsch of 1923. Members of Nazi Party organizations, including the SS, SA, and Hitler Youth, subsequently murdered Jews, arrested and confined some twenty-six thousand in concentration camps, destroyed over seven thousand businesses, and set fire to almost two hundred synagogues.[179] In addition to Party organizations, the Security Police and the Uniformed Police proved instrumental as willing accomplices in the death and destruction visited on Germany's Jewish population. For example, Heydrich issued instructions to all regional and subregional Gestapo offices in the early hours of November 10 in which he underlined Himmler's order for "the closest cooperation" between the Gestapo, the Uniformed Police, and the fire-fighting service in support of the pogrom. In the case of the last, local fire departments received the responsibility to ensure that fires in Jewish businesses or synagogues did not spread to surrounding "Aryan" property. In comparison, members of the Security Police, both the Gestapo and the Criminal Police, were to prevent looting, while their counterparts in the Uniformed Police had the task of sealing and securing apartments and businesses destroyed during the violence as well as preventing the plundering of these sites.[180]

The stories of bystanders and victims provide graphic illustration of the role, or the lack thereof, of the police in the events. Frederic Zeller, a young Jewish boy living in Berlin, attempted to help prevent the store of a family friend from being looted by clearing out the merchandise in the store's front window. Subsequently, a beat cop with the "icy eyes of a fat policeman" ordered him to climb down from the storefront and clean up the mess made by the shattered glass along the pavement. Zeller also remarked that, as the scale of the violence throughout Germany became apparent, his mother stopped asking the question: "'Where are the police?'"[181] Zeller's mother was not the only person asking this question. In another case, a Jewish doctor sought refuge with a non-Jewish German friend, telling her: "They're hunting us down like rabbits. . . . They made me run halfway down the Kurfürstendamm, and yelled after me, 'Jewish swine, mass murderer, drop dead you stinker!'" The friend responded: "And the police?" The reply: "The police just looked on. They let anything that's on fire burn, and anyone get killed who's supposed to be killed."[182]

Despite orders from above, some policemen attempted to fulfill their duty to protect the public order. Bernt Engelmann remarked on the actions of a policeman who assisted an old Jewish man to a nearby hospital after he had been beaten. Interestingly, Engelmann reflected less on this small act of kindness and more on the fact that the policeman "was terrified that he might be punished" for it.[183] In another example, a Jewish woman brought her husband's handgun and permit to a police sergeant, a friend of the family, hidden in a cigar box underneath a layer of cigars. The policeman in this case took out a cigar and lit it with the gun license and then disposed of the handgun in the wastebasket, but not before he told the woman to hurry home "before you give me a heart attack!" The act of putting a handgun in a wastebasket appears somewhat odd, but the policeman's reaction again confirms the perceived risk associated with helping Jews, even in the case of the voluntary turning in of a legally registered firearm.[184]

In the end, small acts of kindness or looking the other way could not outweigh the general attitude and orientation of the police that allowed the streets of Germany to become the playground for the regime's racial and ideological bullies. Without a doubt, the violence and destruction associated with the November pogrom could never have achieved the scope and scale that it did without the willingness of the police forces to stand by and allow these acts to occur. The tacit acceptance and passive involvement of the police also sent a very clear message to the organization's membership concerning the appropriate treatment of Jews, a message that contributed further to shaping the worldview of these policemen.

Raised Expectations

Hitler's appointment of Himmler as Reich leader of the SS and chief of the German police in the Reich Ministry of the Interior on June 17, 1936, resulted in the "unified concentration of the entire police apparatus . . . [and] the administrative concentration of the police forces of the entire Reich."[185] Hitler tasked Himmler with "the direction and execution of all police matters within the competence of the Reich and Prussian ministries of the interior" but placed him "personally and directly subordinate to the Reich and Prussian minister of the interior."[186] In the original draft, Himmler favored the term *personal subordination,* while Frick demanded the less ambiguous wording *direct subordination.* Hitler's inability to decide, or calculated resolution not to decide, led to the inclusion of both terms.[187] In the end, Hitler's indecision proved of little consequence as Himmler skillfully outmaneuvered and bypassed Frick until his appointment as Reich minister of the interior in August 1943.

In June 1936, Himmler had already gained the upper hand in his struggle with Frick for control of the police, but it was not until May 1937 that the Reich minister of the interior conceded partial defeat by withdrawing from the battlefield and granting Himmler the authority to issue "ministerial decisions."[188] Despite personal rivalry, on June 18, 1936, Frick could still endorse the Führer's decision to appoint Himmler, exclaiming: "This is the first time in the thousand-year history of Germany that a unified police leadership for the entire Reich has been established. One leader of the entire German police, who is to answer for the unification of the [police] executive."[189] The subsequent creation of a "main office" (*Hauptamt*) for both the Uniformed and the Security Police under the leadership of Daluege and Heydrich, respectively, provided the foundation for the expansion of Himmler's SS and police empire.

Daluege's appointment reconfirmed his selection in 1934 as head of all the Reich Uniformed Police executives. For his part, Daluege established the basic organizational structure of the Uniformed Police Main Office in directives of June 30 and September 1, 1936. The Main Office consisted of the chief of the Uniformed Police with his adjutant and personal office staff, an administrative and legal department, an operations department, an inspec-

Figure 2. Security Police and Uniformed Police Structure, 1936

Source: Created by the author from "Geschäftsverteilung u. Geschäftsverkehr d. Chefs der Deutschen Polizei im Reichsministerium des Innern, RdErl. des RFSSuChdDtPol. im RMdI v. 26.6.1936, O/S Nr. 3/36 [June 26, 1936]," T580, reel 95, NARA.

tor general for the Protection Police (Schutzpolizei), an inspector general for the Gendarmerie and the Community Police, and, finally, an inspector general for the police schools.[190]

By 1936, the expanding organizational structure and increasing span of authority of the Uniformed Police outpaced the ability of the police to recruit and maintain adequate reserves, a problem of escalating concern to the senior police leadership throughout the late 1930s. In 1933, the Uniformed Police numbered approximately 126,000; however, the loss of the 56,000-man Landespolizei to the Wehrmacht resulted in a decrease to 83,000 by the spring of 1935. By the end of 1935, the total strength of the Uniformed Police included 49,610 Schutzpolizei, 16,759 Gendarmerie, and 16,420 Community Police.[191] Three years later, the manpower situation had improved somewhat, with 62,300 men in the Schutzpolizei, 21,000 in the Gendarmerie, and 16,500 in the Community Police. But the problem of insufficient personnel would plague the organization throughout the existence of the Third Reich, especially after the outbreak of war.[192]

In a June 1939 speech to the Reich governors, Daluege noted several reasons for the inability of the Uniformed Police to meet its personnel goals, including substandard pay, the lack of service-sponsored housing, and ever-increasing responsibilities both within the Reich and in extraterritorial operations. More important, as war approached, the Wehrmacht emerged as a major competitor for both recruits and men already within the ranks of the police. In the case of the latter, the Uniformed Police lost almost fourteen thousand men to the armed forces at the outbreak of the war.[193] The creation of a ninety-five-thousand-man Police Reserve (Verstärkter Polizeischutz) drawn from the 1901–1909 year groups provided one potential solution, allowing citizens with basic military training and rudimentary practical police training to be mobilized for duty within their hometowns in order to protect sites important to the war effort.[194] The men of the Police Reserve came in part from the middle class and in part from the SA reserves in areas where the local police president was also a member of the SA. In the course of the war, these men increasingly became involved in precinct duties or individual duties.[195]

Between 1933 and 1939, the National Socialist regime pursued numerous organizational and institutional measures aimed at bringing the Uniformed Police firmly under its control. Throughout this period, Himmler, assisted by his paladins Heydrich and Daluege, emerged as the architect for the coordination and centralization of the police and the merging of the police with his SS empire. Furthermore, Himmler's and Daluege's efforts in creating a martial spirit within and instilling an SS ethic in the police provided the foundation on which these men eventually marched into war, a foundation that proved crucial in preparing civil servants for the conduct of racial war.

TWO

BUILDING A MARTIAL
IDENTITY

In the event of war, a great deal depends on the Uniformed Police. . . . I am engaged in a battle so that the police officers corps will not become a second-class officers corps.
—Heinrich Himmler (January 1937)

The dominant thrust of National Socialist ideology revolved around the two ideas of race and space. Gerhard Weinberg noted: "Racial vitality and spatial expansion were directly related."[1] In the case of the former, the concept of anti-Semitism, based on a corruption of Social Darwinism and the idea of the survival of the fittest, constituted the central pillar of Hitler's worldview. In turn, Hitler blamed the German defeat in World War I on the "Jews and their Marxist fighting organization" that had stabbed the German people in the back.[2] Hitler's conflation of the Jews with Bolshevism provided the foundation on which the genocide of the European Jews would be built. In the case of space, Hitler repeatedly advocated, according to Weinberg, "the adjustment of space to population by the conquest of additional land areas whose native population would be expelled or exterminated, not assimilated."[3]

One of the unavoidable implications of this ideology included the need for conquest and a German population steeled to the hard realities of struggle and discipline. During a speech celebrating the sixth anniversary of the National Socialist rise to power, Hitler made exactly this point: "It is complete nonsense to presume that obedience and discipline are useful only to soldiers and that they have no further application in the life of people beyond this. To the contrary: a *Volksgemeinschaft* [community of the people] instilled with discipline and obedience can far more easily mobilize the forces necessary to secure the survival of its own people."[4]

In truth, Hitler's appeal to soldierly virtues and his exhortation to the German people to prepare themselves for war benefited from an existing trend in literature and film beginning in 1929 that witnessed a "boom" in military tendencies and military ideologies, a trend exploited by the National Socialist leadership in the creation of an attitude of "latent war readiness" within the general populace by 1939.[5] According to one historian: "There was a fateful overflow of military concepts, in fact of a war mentality, into civilian life."[6] Similarly, the German historian Wolfram Wette noted: "Military and war fatalistic ideologies were at least as widespread as those antidemocratic ideas that decisively contributed to the destruction of the [Weimar] Republic."[7] Without doubt, the Nazis proved adept at taking full advantage of the changing tide of public opinion with respect to military ideals and shaping it to their own purposes.

The Militarization of German Society

The police certainly were not the sole objects of a campaign designed to promote martial values. Indeed, National Socialist leaders embarked on a propaganda campaign aimed at the whole of German society, a campaign whose object included the praise of military virtue and the glorification of national sacrifice at the altar of Mars.[8] In his biography of Hermann Göring, Richard Overy described this effort: "For Nazis, military endeavour was a reflection of the spirit of the race, a sign of a healthy people, aware of the historical necessity for struggle and willing to fight for its rewards. . . . From the outset the tone of military life under Nazism became more aggressive, while the population was bombarded with propaganda on the virtues of military duty and sacrifice. The revival of German military life became closely associated in the popular mind with the party rather than with the old military elite."[9]

Overy makes a crucial point by highlighting the National Socialist view of military virtues as being inextricably intertwined with the Party and its own worldview (*Weltanschauung*). It is in this respect that one should understand Gregor Strasser's boast in the summer of 1932 that the Party had created "a political soldier, a totally new phenomenon in history . . . a preacher with a soldierly bearing and outlook."[10] Strasser's fusion of the martial with the political using religious imagery mirrored perfectly the Nazi ideal for German society.

This march toward "social militarization" did not go unnoticed by contemporary observers. In a diary entry of September 10, 1934, William Shirer, an American radio correspondent in Berlin at the time, reflected that militarism "is something deeply ingrained in all Germans."[11] Similarly, the American ambassador to Germany and president of the American Historical Association William E. Dodd reflected in his diary on July 13, 1934, on the part played by the Prussian tradition of "military brutalism" in preparing the path for the National Socialist "reign of terror."[12] With respect to the police, the French delegation at disarmament talks in Geneva in 1932 complained of the military training and organization of the German police as well as the creation of a "military character" within their ranks.[13]

The "Political Youth Generation"

With regard to German society in general, it can be argued that, in the pursuit of a "militarized society," the reach of National Socialist ambition exceeded its grasp; however, such was not the case when it came to specific groups within German society. Youth groups proved especially susceptible to the siren song of martial values and the myth of Langemarck, the blood sacrifice of German youth in World War I. In fact, in an interview on October 18, 1933, Ward Price, a correspondent for the *Daily Mail*, raised concerns directly with Hitler concerning the training of German youth in military discipline and the "fear in France, and in part, in England that development of a military spirit in young Germans could . . . be put to practical use." In response, Hitler denied that German youth were receiving "military knowledge" and instead described this training as a form of social education.[14]

Despite Hitler's protestation to the contrary, the Wehrmacht already in 1933 began cooperating with the Hitler Youth and the SA in a secret program of military training.[15] One historian of the Hitler Youth noted: "The concept of 'the soldier' became the yardstick of German post-war youth movements, as did military forms of organization."[16] Martin Koller, a member of a youth group under Weimar, recalled: "The combat soldier was an ideological symbol for us." He continued: "Even then the Hitler Youth was in existence, and the *Jungstahlhelm* (Young Steel Helmets), soldiers' kids who wore field-gray uniforms. All of these groups were military-oriented."[17] Similarly, Günter de Bruyn, a teenage boy in 1933 living in Berlin who later became a celebrated writer, reflected on the influence of military values during his youth. De Bruyn admitted that his age cohort was "infected with a prevailing ideology," but he argued that this ideology rested, not on the cult of Germandom or anti-Semitism, but rather on the imperial tradition of the "martial spirit" (*soldatischer Geist*).[18] Young women were not immune to the siren call of militarism, as demonstrated by the response of those within the women's Labor Service as legions of *Arbeitsmaiden* mobilized for potential colonization duties in the East on the outbreak of war.[19]

The co-optation of German youth was, in fact, critical to Hitler's plans for conquest, and it is important to remember that many of these youths socialized in the prewar period provided a ready pool for service with the Wehrmacht, the Waffen-SS, and police formations during the war.[20] Not surprisingly, German educators played a key role in this effort with their adoption of "the political soldier as the personification of the ideal German. . . . [and] the model for character development." One educator described the essence of this process as embodying, "not Weimar, not the Paul's Church of Frankfurt with its poets, philosophers and learned men, . . . but the spirit of Prussian militarism, the spirit of manliness, armed strength, breeding, honor, [and] loyalty."[21] Similarly, Peter Merkl noted: "Whole generations of Weimar youth had been politically mobilized without developing a democratic political consciousness. Not a few million of innocents mistook the *Fuehrer* for the political Messiah."[22] These were the young men who answered Hitler's call to be "quick like greyhounds, tough like leather, and hard like Krupp steel."[23]

The Front Generation

In contrast to the millions of German youths preparing their minds and bodies for the austere demands of military life, another generation existed that had weathered the "storms of steel" during World War I in the trenches of the Western Front and on the battlefields throughout Europe. The so-called front generation emerged from the war scarred by the death and destruction that they had faced but also "purified" by the heat of battle. They saw themselves as "singular men of steel, who had survived the bloodiest, wildest and most brutal of all wars in the trenches . . . because in their blind rage they had been able to stand the final test of manhood in killing and offering up their lives for a sacred cause."[24] In the case of the police, the National Socialist government honored the memory of their sacrifice in words and deeds, including the building of a monument to fallen Prussian gendarmes from the Great War in August 1939.[25]

During the interwar period, the almost half-million-man strong right-wing paramilitary Stahlhelm organization expounded a version of the "front soldier ideology" that sought the creation of a state based on the Führer principle in which former front soldiers would assume the positions of the social and political elite. In addition, these men all found common cause in their "vehement rejection of the military provisions of the Versailles Treaty."[26] The ideas espoused by the men of the Stahlhelm were not unique to them but shared by their former comrades in arms within the SA and the SS, a point that Hitler would later make explicit in his mobilization of these "coreligionists" into the ranks of the police. Similarly, in a speech to the Fraternal Order of German Policemen (Kameradschaftsbund Deutscher Polizeibeamten) in August 1937, Daluege emphasized the special role that the former front soldiers played in the SS movement. He then asked that their demonstrated values of comradeship and attachment to German "blood and soil" provide the basis for the education of the police.[27]

The Freikorps

The end of the *Kaiserreich* in 1918, resulting as it did in the disintegration of much of the German army, witnessed the growth of a number of politically radicalized and paramilitary groups, known collectively as the Freikorps. Not only did the ranks of the Freikorps provide the men of the front generation with an opportunity to continue their military service, but it also offered several younger year groups who had missed out on the Great War their baptism by fire in the struggle against the forces of the Left. Although not a recognized police authority, these groups assumed the mantle of a quasi police force operating under the aegis of an ultranationalistic ideology. Described by Göring as "the first soldiers of the Reich," these men were characterized by one historian as the prophets of "nihilism and destruction," a movement, not cemented together by a common political program, but united by a common understanding of what they did not want and what they hated. In the words of Franz Seldte, the head of the Stahlhelm: "We must fight to get the men into power who will depend on us front soldiers for support—men who will call upon us to smash once and for all these damned revolutionary rats and choke them by sticking their heads into their own shit."[28]

The memoirs of another Freikorps member published in 1931, before the Nazi seizure of power, demonstrated the mentality and the motivation of many within this group. Peter von Heydebreck, a former officer in the Kaiser's army who lost an arm during the Great War, joined the Freikorps after the war and remained a member until their dissolution in 1923. After being forced to retire from the army, Heydebreck continued to see himself as a soldier, and his political sympathies clearly lay with the Right, including the Nazi Party. He perfectly encapsulated his belief in the soldier charged with a political mission in his declaration: "So you men of the Free Corps, you last soldiers of the front, shall be at the same time the first combatants of the coming Reich."[29]

Although, institutionally, the Freikorps proved a transitory phenomenon, one historian argued: "Hitler needed the Freebooters and without their help it is highly probable that the Nazi movement would not have come to power."[30] In return, the SA became the home for many of these men, even if the new government failed to fulfill their grandiose visions of their place in the Third Reich. In comparison, the effect of the movement on the ranks of the Security and Uniformed Police should not be underestimated as many of the former Freikorps members attained senior leadership positions in both organizations, including Heinrich Himmler, Reinhard Heydrich, Kurt Daluege, and Wolf Heinrich Graf von Helldorf.[31] In an April 1937 speech, Daluege glorified the men of the Freikorps, who, along with the police, had, he said, played a key role in the "battle of annihilation" against the "Bolshevist plague."[32] The migration of these men to the organizations of state control contributed to the further radicalization of the organizational culture within the police by moving values, behaviors, and political affiliations further to the Right, replete with the ultranationalist and racial and political prejudices implied in this shift.

The "Political Soldier"

The interwar period in Germany witnessed a process whereby youths emerged as a politically conscious generation and proved a ready audience for the message of militarization. Additionally, veterans of the front generation emerged with a decided penchant for right-wing ideologies and organizations. Finally, Nazi Party organizations existed that were poised to take advantage of the human resources to be found in both groups. For example, one study of the SA found that "nearly all the SA men of 1933" had been members of a youth group by the time they reached the age of twenty-five. In turn, the majority of the youth groups to which these SA men belonged were either quasi-military groups or affiliated with National Socialism or right-wing folkish (*völkisch*) thought.[33] It is, therefore, not surprising that another study found that the highest leaders of the SA "were the true and original political soldiers of the Nazi Party": "They were the ones who combined military expertise and experience in paramilitary groups with a singular political radicalism and commitment to völkisch ideology. . . . They were both soldiers and politicians, and they were equally at home in ideology and in formation."[34] This marriage of military character with a right-wing political inclination was by no means limited to the SA in the interwar period.

Like the SA, the various German police forces under Weimar were strongly influenced by military standards and ideals. Indeed, the pervasive military inclination of late nineteenth- and early twentieth-century Germany significantly influenced the role and character of the German police in the period leading up to the National Socialist dictatorship. The German historian Hans-Ulrich Wehler argued: "The militarization of Prussian society since the eighteenth century . . . led to military norms, patterns of behavior and ways of thinking taking an increasing hold over bourgeois society."[35] The Prussian police, by far the largest of the German police forces, particularly experienced the pervasive effects of militarism as the majority of recruits were retired military noncommissioned officers who tended to set the everyday tone of the organization. This trend continued into the twentieth century with over half the 2,350-man officer corps of the Prussian police in 1931 coming from the ranks of former military members.[36]

Similarly, the vast majority of the police personnel in the first years of the Weimar Republic consisted of former soldiers and those who had served in the First World War. As previously noted, Richard Bessel has argued that the Weimar police forces struggled to balance an older military identity and a new professional identity.[37] The nationalistic philosophy and the military ideals of the police made them, much like the SA membership, susceptible to the "stab in the back" myth in which Germany's defeat in the war could be laid at the feet of profiteers, leftists, and Jews.[38] In fact, the idea of the "humiliation" or "shame" of Versailles emerged as a consistent and powerful theme in National Socialist police literature.[39] In turn, this image of "treasonous" leftists and Jews helped shape the personal and political beliefs of many policemen throughout the interwar period.

The National Socialist Ideal

In one of his works on National Socialism, the German historian Detlev Peukert reflected on the martial influences apparent in the many autobiographical documents and memoirs of the Freikorps, the SA, and the prewar generation that exalted the ideal of "the 'soldierly' man, with an inner hardness which . . . finds its fulfillment in acts of terror and mass slaughter."[40] It was this image that Himmler and the senior Party and police leadership sought to reinforce within the ranks of the "new" police, and it was an image that found ready soil in which to grow.

National Socialist leaders wasted little time in bringing their message to the police. On February 7, 1933, Göring, the new Prussian minister of the interior, spoke to the uniformed officers and men of the Prussian police (Schutzpolizei). Göring opened his speech by exclaiming: "Comrades! With special joy I greet you as the uniformed members of the police. For the most part, the honored field gray uniform of the German soldier unites us. Therefore we belong together." He then declared his intention that the police should be, not only the best civil servants, but the best soldiers as well. Significantly, Göring warned that, in the coming months, the police would again face a "battle at the front" and that they should "not hesitate" to use their weapons in the fight against "criminals and [the] leftist rabble [*Verbrechertum und internationales Gesindel*]."[41]

The description of the pending National Socialist offensive against the parties of the Left, combined with the Great War imagery of a battle at the front lines, once again illustrated the importance of this comparison in the minds of the senior Nazi leadership. Furthermore, they believed that this theme would resonate with the men of the police, whom they expected to accept the idea that actions against the parties of the Left were simply an extension of a soldierly conflict stretching from the battle against the soldiers' and workers' councils of the November Republic to the Weimar system itself. This imagery would also play a key role in the preparation of the police for the campaigns in the East during the Second World War. In another example, in an address to the Pomeranian league of farmers in March 1933, Göring emphasized the role of the police in a "battle of extermination" (*Ausrottungskampf*) against the Marxist "pestilence" within Germany.[42] For Göring, the shared honor of military service united these men with him and, ultimately, with the ambitions and the philosophy of the Nazi Party.

Symbols and Manifestations of Unity

A decree of April 19, 1933, mandating the exchange of salutes between military and police members constituted but one outward sign of the elevation of the status of the police and their symbolic union with the military.[43] National Socialist leaders did not limit their actions to symbolic gestures alone. Already on February 28, Göring had issued a decree that members of the Party and its sister organizations were to receive priority as applicants for the Ordnungspolizei.[44] Göring's words were not empty rhetoric as the creation of the Feldpolizei (Field Police) and the Hilfspolizei in early 1933 showed. Furthermore, in the wake of the April 1933 purging of the civil service of "politically and racially unacceptable elements," the Nazi leadership opened the door for the entry of the political soldiers of the movement into the ranks of the police.[45]

In an April 1934 press release entitled "The Solidarity of the SA and the Police," Daluege affirmed that the civil service law created an opportunity for the Prussian police "in its entire organization . . . to be infused with long-serving and proven SA, SS, and Stahlhelm members." He continued: "The politically schooled soldiers of the movement are the guarantors that the National Socialist ideology [*Ideenwelt*] would become the common property of the Prussian police."[46] Throughout the first year of the regime, Daluege remained focused on achieving the objective of a National Socialist–oriented police.

Daluege's emphasis on the political and soldierly characteristics of this group once again demonstrated the fusion of the Party ideal with a military character, an expression of Hitler's own vision for the pillars of state control. In fact, Hitler later justified this policy in a speech to the Reichstag by announcing: "In assigning men to posts of leadership in State and Party, attitude and character are to be valued more highly than so-called purely scientific or supposed mental qualifications."[47]

In June 1933, in his role as chief of the Prussian police, Kurt Daluege composed a secret memorandum describing the state of the police and his plans for the future of Germany's largest police force. He described the Uniformed Police as "the strongest domestic instrument of power" with the exception of the Wehrmacht. Daluege observed that, as the training and buildup of the police increasingly assumed a "military point of view," the importance of finding appropriate leaders would continue to increase. He therefore suggested a short training course for SA and SS men who were intended to take over leadership roles in the Prussian police at the rank of captain and above.[48]

The infusion of the "political soldiers" of the movement from the SA, the SS, and the Stahlhelm helped reinforce both the military character of the Uniformed Police and their political commitment to Hitler's government. In this respect, the incorporation of members from the Party's paramilitary organizations served the twofold purpose of reinforcing the militarization of the police and strengthening the organization's identification with the political and racial views of National Socialism. More significantly, the leadership and men of the SA numbered some of the most willing instruments of anti-Semitic activities in the prewar years.[49] Daluege matched his rhetoric with action, and ten thousand members of the SA and SS had joined the ranks of the police and police administration in the state of Prussia alone by November 1934.[50]

The Police and the "Night of the Long Knives"

It was not coincidental that the most militarized branch of the German Uniformed Police during the early years of the National Socialist regime, the garrisoned Landespolizei, was chosen by Hitler to assist in the emasculation of the SA and its leadership during the "Röhm affair," or the "Night of Long Knives," on June 30, 1934. The question of whether these forces would participate in the suppression of the SA elite was swiftly and decisively answered. Göring's mobilization of the Prussian Landespolizei proceeded without incident as the entire force was placed on a state of alert. The directive placing the Landespolizei on alert emphasized the close relationship between SS and police forces and ordered: "As a rule arrests are to be undertaken by the SS, but requests by the SS for police support are to be granted. [The police] are to work closely with the SS."[51] Furthermore, Göring directed the Landespolizei in Prussia to maintain a "close relationship" with the army.[52]

The role played by the police in actions against the SA varied widely. For example, Landespolizei forces participated in the seizure of SA headquarters in Berlin, guarded SA prisoners, and even carried out executions.[53] In one example, a Landespolizei unit engaged an SA garrison in a firefight during the storming of an SA watch station in the Upper Silesian town of Beuthen (present-day Polish Bytom), reportedly killing three men and wounding several others.[54] In this case, Silesia was the area, after Munich, in which opposition by the SA was most expected, which may in part explain the perceived need to employ police forces there.[55]

In the wake of the actions of June 30, Himmler praised the performance of the Landespolizei forces in a letter to Daluege on July 16, 1934. He wrote: "On the occasion of the cleansing action [*Säuberungsaktion*] the Landespolizei were employed in *many* areas of the Reich, [and] they, in perfect cooperation with the offices of the Gestapo and the Political Police, did their duty."[56] The fact that Göring's and Himmler's plans against the SA unfolded so smoothly removed the need for major police involvement; however, the readiness of the police to join in the suppression of the sons of the "second revolution" is more important than the scale of their participation. In this respect, the participation of the SS and the Security Police, especially the Gestapo and the Security Service (SD), in the purge of the SA marked their "esprit de corps and detachment from the traditional values of Western Christian education," a detachment that became a fundamental characteristic of the police under National Socialism.[57]

If the overall political inclination of the Landespolizei cannot be definitively established, such is clearly not the case with respect to their military orientation. After the initial transfer of the Landespolizei into the Wehrmacht in the spring of 1935, the Reichswehr minister General Werner von Blomberg sent a message to Daluege thanking him for his work with these policemen and expressing his confidence that these men had been "educated in the old soldierly tradition."[58] In an order promoting Daluege to the rank of general of the police, Hitler also thanked Daluege for shaping the police into "a powerful [*schlagkräftig*] instrument of the National Socialist state" and especially for his efforts in making the Landespolizei a valuable arm of the Wehrmacht.[59] The fact that almost 13 percent of all Landespolizei officers reached the rank of general in the German army prior to 1945 provides one indication of this success.[60] Daluege's success in shaping the Landespolizei into a militarized police formation would be repeated later with the formation of the police battalions, units that became political soldiers in support of the Nazi leadership.

The Incorporation of the Feldjägerkorps into the Police

The loss of the fifty-six-thousand-man Landespolizei to the Wehrmacht was, in one respect, a severe blow to Daluege's police empire as these men constituted 65 percent of the police officer corps and more than 30 percent of the Reich's Uniformed Police forces.[61] Himmler, in fact, later complained that the loss of the Landespolizei resulted in the Uniformed Police losing some of its best men.[62] The absorption of the Feldjägerkorps (Field Security Corps), or FJK, provided one measure for counteracting the loss of the garrisoned police forces. The chief of staff of the SA, Ernst Röhm, initially proposed the idea of creating an internal SA police force in August 1933.[63] This Feldpolizei consisted of an initial cadre of two hundred experienced SA and SS men in Berlin tasked with taking action against leftist groups. Subsequently, the members of the Feldpolizei provided valuable assistance to the Gestapo in the National Socialist campaign against the parties of the Left.[64]

On October 7, 1933, Röhm created the Feldjägerkorps in Prussia with the mission of "guaranteeing and monitoring public discipline and order." The ranks of the FJK were to be filled by SA and SS men who, with the dissolution of the Hilfspolizei, found themselves without a job, the men of the Feldpolizei forming the core of the leadership of the new FJK.[65] Furthermore, Röhm directed that the FJK would work closely with the Gestapo and the other Prussian state police agencies.[66] Four months later, Röhm established the FJK in Bavaria, once again primarily from former Hilfspolizei members.[67]

Röhm's motivation for spearheading the creation of the FJK was twofold. First, with the dissolution of the Hilfspolizei, many SA and SS men lost their jobs. Second, and most important, the end of the Hilfspolizei meant that Röhm had lost his own private police force. Although the FJK was authorized to assist regular police authorities, its jurisdiction extended only to policing the ranks of the SA or those wearing SA insignia. For example, the FJK in Hamburg received orders to enforce the pub-closing-time ordinance for SA members and to arrest any violators and deliver them to the local SA watch station.[68] In fact, the FJK was the only organization authorized to arrest SA members when so requested by police or judicial authorities. Regular police might arrest a member of the SA only if he was caught "in the act" of committing a crime.[69]

Röhm's hopes for the FJK included the expectation that they would enjoy the same level of respect within the SA as did the "military policemen" (*Feldgendarmen*) within the old army. In practice, some within the FJK saw themselves more as "policemen" than simply "the internal police of the SA," leading them to describe themselves as *Feldjägerpolizei* and to request to wear the distinctive police star on their uniforms.[70]

During the events of June 30, 1934, Hitler transferred authority over the Prussian FJK to Göring, who in April 1935 ordered the incorporation of the SA's thirty-one-hundred-man Feldjägerkorps into the ranks of the Prussian Uniformed Police.[71] This transfer occurred at a time when the Uniformed Police had lost most of its Landespolizei forces, and, in this respect, the FJK provided a welcome addition to the dwindling ranks of the police. In order to ensure the quality and eventual fitness for duty of the FJK recruits, the police devised a training program to allow for the incorporation of only those men competent to conduct police duties.[72] Although Daluege gave lip service to the need for technically qualified policemen, in practice he valued ideological commitment above competence and envisioned the addition of the FJK as a means by which to continue the ideological coordination of the police. In an address to his police commanders, he exclaimed: "In order to create a more uniform and high-quality police many paths have been trodden. The latest is the transfer of the Feldjägerkorps to the Uniformed Police. Old fighters, who in the beginning took up the job as Hilfspolizei with heart and soul, shall now become comrades of the old corps [of the police]."[73] Later that year, Daluege admitted that the men of the FJK required some training in preparation for their police duties and a probationary duty period; however, he described them as a "valuable addition" to the police as they constituted the "superior selection and the best forces of the SA and the SS."[74]

With regard to their duties, Daluege intended for these men to constitute a motorized highway patrol and only in "exceptional cases" to perform the duties of a beat cop. Still, in his speech to his police commanders, he once again emphasized that the incorporation of the FJK into the police offered the opportunity to "build up the relationship between the [National Socialist] movement and the police and to bind the two more closely together." He also prophesied that the tasks facing the police in the future demanded a "militarily first-rate" officer corps, and he emphasized that no policeman could afford to forget or lose his ability to "feel and think like a soldier."[75] Daluege's glorification of a military identity among these Party soldiers once again demonstrated the close linkage of martial values with the objectives of the National Socialist movement among the senior police leadership.

With the inclusion of the Feldjägerkorps into its ranks, the Uniformed Police gained many men who had used the Reichstag fire decree and the tumultuous events of early 1933 "as a warrant for every form of political 'counterattack' and terrorism," including the persecution of Jews and members of the political parties of the Left.[76] These men certainly married martial attributes with National Socialist ideals, a mix that had proved deadly to many already in the early years of Hitler's revolution but would prove deadlier still during operations on the Eastern Front.

Promoting the Martial Ideal

During the initial years of the consolidation of National Socialist power, Daluege continued to propound his vision of a Uniformed Police built on martial values and a commitment to the Party. In a scripted answer to a question concerning the "new inner and outer attitude" of the police, he once again emphasized the martial character of the National Socialist police. He responded: "To be sure, the soldierly thought and feeling within the new police of the National Socialist state can no longer be denied. Although the member of the German police corps is also a civil servant, so will and must he feel himself to be a soldier; his duty demands this from him."[77] The emphasis on the martial character within the Uniformed Police remained a central element in Daluege's public statements throughout 1935. In a speech to police administrative trainees in October, he reminded his audience that, despite the presence of Social Democratic appointees at the highest levels of police administration under Weimar, police civil servants composed mostly of "old soldiers" had successfully resisted "the poison of Marxist propaganda." He also remarked on the necessity of conducting a "cleansing" of police personnel who "had forgotten their old soldierly traditions under the Marxist system [Weimar] and had allowed themselves to become tools of the black-red despot." Finally, he returned to his vision by declaring that the police must be inculcated with fundamental values, including complete subservience to higher authority, soldierly discipline, absolute obedience, and the "spirit of National Socialism."[78] Daluege's speech once again highlighted his advocacy of a police force based on martial values, values that he felt were by their very nature antithetical to "Marxist ideology" but clearly amenable to National Socialism.

These early efforts to inculcate martial values in the police were aimed at every member of the police establishment from the city beat cop to the rural policeman and even the police administrative official. They also extended to men within the Security Police and the SD.[79] In the case of police administrators, these men found themselves mobilized for combat operations at the front by the end of the war. Not surprisingly, the police officer corps remained a key audience for the martial message as they set the everyday tone for duty within their units and exercised a critical role in shaping the organizational culture of the police. In an entry in the 1936 police yearbook, Lieutenant Colonel of the Police Rudolf Querner, later a higher SS and police leader (HSSPF), described the new attitude. He emphasized the need for police formations built on a "martial point of view" as well as that for an "elite" police officer corps displaying a high level of "National Socialist, military, and police" expertise.[80] Querner's conflation of ideological predisposition with martial and police capabilities expressed the model for the police, but translating the ideal into reality at times proved difficult.

In an address to a gathering of small-town civil authorities, Himmler reflected on the progress made by the Community Police (Gemeindepolizei) since 1933. Although he criticized them for their motley collection of uniforms, their nonstandard rank insignias, and their reputation as "jacks-of-all-trades" in the pre-1933 period, Himmler noted that the "spirit of the political soldier" most prevalent in the Party and its organizations needed to take root in these policemen as in their big-city counterparts.[81] According to Himmler, the Nazi leadership recognized from the beginning the necessity of bringing forth the principles of authority, leadership, soldierly discipline, and absolute loyalty in the Community Police, just as in their city and rural counterparts. He later reinforced this idea by emphasizing the education of the police in a "soldierly spirit" as a central objective of the National Socialist leadership and reminding his audience that only a "soldierly police" could accomplish the tasks facing the Reich in the future.[82]

The Prussian Model

In addition to the promotion of the military ideal, Nazi leaders and police literature also reflected on the importance of the Prussian model for the men of the police. In his speech to the police in February 1933, Göring demanded that his police officers display the "old virtues of a Prussian officer." Delivered to a gathering of Prussian policemen, this message certainly found a receptive audience; however, its appeal extended beyond the geographic confines of Prussia. In the 1936 edition of the *Police Yearbook*, Helmuth Koschorke, a public spokesman for the police in the Reich and Prussian Interior Ministries, extolled the reemergence of "soldierdom" (*Soldatentum*) in the "new police" and noted that the source of the National Socialist policeman's authority was his "soldierly honor" (*Soldatenehre*). Koschorke also praised the National Socialist renaming of the rural police from Landjägerei to Gendarmerie, a measure that he described as "a symbol that signified the return to the old military virtues of the glorious Prussian Gendarmerie Corps."[83]

Clearly, the exaltation of "Prussian virtues" in the Third Reich was inextricably tied to the concept of a military ideal. For example, Hitler and Reich Propaganda Minister Josef Goebbels both cultivated a cult of Frederick the Great and Bismarck and repeatedly used both as exemplars of the Prussian forebears of the National Socialist movement.[84] The portraits of Frederick the Great adorning the "Brown House" in Munich and Hitler's headquarters and the launching of the battleship *Bismarck* provide but two examples of the symbolic unity and continuity of an idealized Prussian state for the National Socialist leadership. In the case of the latter, Hitler delivered a speech during the launching of the *Bismarck* on February 14, 1939, in which he explained that it was not coincidental that the three greatest warships of the Reich bore the names of Scharnhorst, Gneisenau, and now Bismarck. He then noted his own resolve "to honor the memory of those whose undertakings in their day and age created the preconditions for this Greater Germany of today."[85]

The appeal to Prussian virtues did not fall on deaf ears. The police president of Flensburg, Dr. Konrad Fulda, exalted Prussian militarism and attempted to inculcate this tradition in the city's Uniformed Police force. In a speech on March 21, 1933, Fulda equated the "good soldier" with the "good policeman in Adolf Hitler's Reich." He praised the elements of the "martial spirit," including discipline, order, loyalty, honor, camaraderie, courage, and duty and exclaimed: "This martial spirit is a National Socialist spirit."[86] In another example, a Gendarmerie officer stationed in the Ukraine in 1942 exhorted his troops to action with the following words: "We are not commissars with all their evil vices. We are soldiers of Prussian rearing and stand before a task, [one] that demands from us our greatest efforts." He continued: "We must only learn in this task which the Führer charged us with here in the Ukraine to see something very important and very beautiful; something upon which depends the fate of Germany for the coming centuries."[87]

Putting Words into Practice

Talk of the education of the police in a "soldierly spirit" was not mere rhetoric. In fact, police candidates were expected to pursue, not just training in police techniques, but a "complete military" training regime as well.[88] In truth, the military training of the police began prior to the Nazi seizure of power. Already in early 1931, there were press reports that uniformed policemen (*Schutzpolizisten*) were participating in training with the Reichswehr. One such article reported that the military officers supervising the training told the policemen to think of themselves, not as civil servants, but as "a company of soldiers."[89] In addition, reports smuggled out of Germany by members of the Social Democratic Party disclosed the military training of groups of up to two hundred policemen by the Reichswehr in the state of Saxony. By December 1934, numerous allegations of Reichswehr training of the police flooded in from across the Reich, including reports of the training of the police in the use of antitank and antiaircraft weapons, machine guns, and even artillery.[90] By the end of the year, the participation of the Uniformed Police in Reichswehr exercises and training courses became a routine occurrence and a poorly kept secret, despite the military leadership's attempts to conceal it.[91]

In another effort to improve the appearance of and military proficiency within the Uniformed Police, Frick recommended the institution of an annual physical fitness test in 1936.[92] The test was intended to prepare the policemen for the annual police sport championship. The participation of eighty thousand policemen in a modern pentathlon competition involving events designed to test running, swimming, broad-jumping, shooting, and hand-grenade-throwing skills provided another showcase for demonstrating the physical aptitude of the "new" police, with the top seventy performers from across the Reich meeting in the city of Halle to compete for the championship.[93]

The institution of the annual physical fitness test and the sport competitions served several purposes. First, these activities provided a demanding trial for evaluating the physical fitness of the police. Second, they represented a perfect test of the complete range of military skills envisioned by Himmler and Daluege for their soldierly corps, a point made explicitly in Daluege's comparison of participants in the march competition with the "storm troops" (*Stoßtrupps*) of the Great War. Finally, the emphasis on the "cult of the body" provided an image to the public of a strong, sleek, and well-trained police corps as the "forerunners" (*Wegbereiter*) of a "new sex" embodying the ideal of the physically fit and tough National Socialist man.[94]

Recruiting Those with Soldierly Virtues

The Landespolizei clearly had during the early years of the Nazi regime, until their transfer to the Wehrmacht, been a focus of military training within the police, and the admission into the police of SA, SS, and Stahlhelm members and the FJK demonstrated the continuing emphasis on inculcating a martial character in the entire police corps. In fact, Himmler and Daluege pursued a dual strategy for targeting applicants to the police. On the one hand, Himmler instituted measures aimed at enticing men who had finished their military enlistments to join the ranks of the Uniformed Police. The fall 1936 decision to allow Wehrmacht personnel, released after two to five years of military service, direct entry into the police enlisted ranks constituted another step down the road to militarization. The entry of these former soldiers carried the stipulation that they had previously belonged to the Party or one of its associated organizations, a restriction aimed at reinforcing, not only the military foundation of the organization, but the political reliability of these men as well.[95] Similarly, Himmler agreed to allow former members of the

Landespolizei who had finished their enlistment with the army reentry into the police as noncommissioned officers (*Hauptwachtmeister*) and official civil service status.[96] The acceptance of former soldiers into the ranks of the police injected an immediate military character into the police and provided a potential training cadre for the further militarization of other Ordnungspolizei members. In a related measure, Himmler issued an order on September 4, 1936, for "the official basic and continued professional training" of the entire German police to be based on a "military foundation."[97]

On the other hand, recruiting efforts highlighted the military nature of police duty. *Do You Want to Join the Police?*—a pamphlet specifically issued to support efforts to recruit young men finishing their secondary education—covered topics ranging from organization, to racial and health standards, to sport and physical fitness requirements. In the section "Police Service Is Honorable Service," the applicant read: "The young man who today has generally acquired a soldierly attitude through training in the Hitler Youth, the SA, and the SS as well as in his private life wants now to take on the outward appearance of the soldier as well." He also read that the German policeman in his role as protector of the inner security of the nation stood on the same level as the soldier of the Wehrmacht and that those entering the police "remained soldiers, wearers of a uniform," respected by the *Volk,* and charged with the preservation of the nation.[98]

Creating a Military Appearance

The fact that the policeman was "a man in uniform" was an important distinction to Hitler and the senior leadership of the police. In a state built on the conception of apocalyptic struggle, a uniform epitomized, by itself and for its wearer, the martial ideal. In turn, the introduction of the standardized green uniform for all policemen on June 25, 1936, symbolized the new military character of the police and constituted a measure to remove the visible vestiges of Weimar with its diverse collection of uniforms.[99] For Daluege, the new uniforms represented the unity of the entire Reich police as well as the close relationship between the police and the people.[100] Additionally, Hitler personally approved the new duty uniform, and the uniform jacket was consciously designed to resemble the military style of the former Landespolizei uniform, another symbol of the policeman's martial identity.[101] Another visible symbol of the changed status of the police involved the reintroduction of the sword for police officers and the bayonet for enlisted police ranks. A further expression involved the authorization of the police to wear military badges and decorations won during the Great War, a practice that continued into World War II with the authorization of policemen wounded in combat to wear the "war wound" badge and other military decorations.[102] It would be a mistake to underestimate the significance of seemingly minor uniform changes; indeed, for the professional soldier or policeman, awards and decorations constitute badges of honor and play an important role in establishing an individual's identity and status within a hierarchical organization.[103]

Views from the Party

In the initial phase of National Socialist rule, Daluege was not the only member of the political leadership emphasizing the soldierly character of the new police. For example, the newspaper *Der märkische Adler* devoted an entire front page to an article entitled "Police and National Socialism" by Wilhelm Kube, the district leader of the Kurmark and future Reich commissar for Belorussia. Kube began his article by noting that the love of bearing arms had been in the blood of a northern people like the Germans for thousands of years. He then praised the racial composition of the police as well as the "noble soldierly" leadership of the Prussian police and concluded with an appeal for an internal and external "comradely relationship" binding the police to the army, the SA, and the SS as well as all the organizations of the Party.[104]

In a December 1935 letter to Daluege, Martin Bormann also agreed on the "great importance of military qualifications" in the selection of police leaders.[105] Likewise, a confidential memorandum of November 2, 1936, to Hans Pfundtner, a state secretary in the Ministry of the Interior, called for the "strict military organization of the police" and the "standardized military training of police forces."[106] Later, Rudolf Hess, the deputy leader of the NSDAP (National Socialist German Workers' Party), indirectly highlighted the soldierly character of the police in a letter of July 29, 1938, to Viktor Lutze, SA chief of staff. In response to a query from Lutze concerning the possibility of uniformed policemen joining the SA, Hess responded that he did not find it appropriate for members of the police, "as [members] of a soldierly, armed formation approaching that of the Wehrmacht," to be "active at the same time in two organizations built on martial principles."[107]

Hess's reply is interesting in two respects. First, his rejection of Lutze's request provided a clear testament to the existing "soldierly character" of the police. Second, by 1938, Himmler had made significant progress in his merging of the Party soldiers of the SS with the police, a fact ignored by Hess in his response. As will be seen in the next chapter, this was, not an oversight on Hess's part, but rather recognition of the special relationship between the soldiers of the Party, the SS, and the political soldiers of the police.

Training the Police

Desire to serve the regime and political reliability, although important, were not the only determinants in deciding who could become a member of the police. In the case of the FJK, Daluege had given lip service to the requirement for training in police duties, but he was willing to overlook certain deficiencies in the case of the "old fighters" of the NSDAP. For new recruits, however, this was not the case. Although each applicant was expected to display the "true spirit of National Socialism" and ideology was one of two major areas of instruction during initial training efforts, recruits also needed to attain a level of technical expertise in order to enter the ranks. In addition to ideological instruction (*weltanschauliche Schulung*), training for candidates included physical fitness, weapons handling, and technical knowledge.[108]

Physical fitness emerged as a major area of emphasis for both candidates and active policemen. In contrast to the Weimar period, under the Reich physical fitness training involved all ranks and ages and included calisthenics, boxing, and judo. As in all areas, training was married to practical exercises, including the running of obstacle courses in uniform while carrying a rifle and lifesaving exercises where the candidate in full uniform was expected to rescue a simulated drowning victim.[109] Himmler took an almost obsessive interest in promoting physical fitness within the SS and the police. In a speech before a gathering of Hitler Youth in 1936, he explained the importance that he placed on sports badges by declaring: "Sport and the performance badges again select and kick out the man who does not achieve. . . . Further, I avoid in this way having a leadership corps which at the age of forty or forty-five puts on paunches."[110] In 1937, over two thousand policemen earned the SA sport badge and received authorization to wear it on their uniforms. The chief of staff of the SA, Viktor Lutze, warned, however, that persons should not seek the badge only in the hopes of adding an ornament to their uniform. Instead, he argued, the badge represented a visible symbol of "the will to assist in the great tasks involving the spread of the worldview and the ideas of the Führer."[111] Lutze's words perfectly framed the conflation of physical fitness with ideological duty espoused by senior SS and police leaders, a world in which athletic prowess became a symbol of racial superiority.

For the police candidates, weapons training involved initial familiarization with the weapon as well as practice at the firing range; however, it also included practice in riot-control measures involving large formations. Other training areas included command techniques, orientation and map reading, tactical reconnaissance, and communication. Finally, there were theoretical and academic exercises involving the study of technical subjects, decrees, ordinances, laws, and regulations as well as general legal principles. In the case of theory, however, the police candidate was admonished "never to let an examination of legality [*Rechtsmässigkeit*] prevent [taking] action."[112] This last statement was reminiscent of Göring's promise to the Prussian police that "police officials who in the execution of their duties make use of their firearms . . . [should do so] without consideration for the consequences of the use of their weapon."[113] It also demonstrates once again the effort of the police leadership to develop "men of action," unafraid and unhesitating in their use of force should circumstances so demand.

Selection for and attendance at a candidate-training course were not automatic guarantees of graduation. In the period between May 1934 and September 1935, there were thirty police-candidate-training courses throughout the Reich. Of the 2,087 candidates, 128, or a little over 6 percent of the applicants, failed the training. Graduation rates varied widely throughout the Reich, from a high of 204 of 207 candidates graduating from a total of three courses in Dortmund to a low of 646 of 730 candidates graduating from a total of four training courses in Berlin.[114]

It might be tempting to dismiss the expectations for police training as limited to the young men entering the profession, who, like their predecessors, were expected to endure a rite of passage prior to acceptance in the ranks. In fact, Himmler recognized this danger and issued an addendum to the regulations governing the training of the Uniformed Police in August 1936. In it he underlined his demand that all branches of the Uniformed Police exhibit the "soldierly virtues" (*soldatische Tugenden*) that characterized the German *Volk*. In addition to a "strict soldierly bearing in public," police officers and enlisted men were expected to maintain their level of physical fitness and their proficiency in the use of their weapons, with both identified as special areas of emphasis for the entire police. In the case of the rural Gendarmerie, the regulation raised the physical fitness standard to that of the Wehrmacht and the former Landespolizei.[115]

Preparing the Police for War

Himmler's goal of creating a physically fit and well-trained police force, displaying "soldierly virtues," extended to all branches of the police, and training guidance established for the police in October 1937 provided the unambiguous rationale for these efforts. Prepared for Daluege's signature, the guidance begins with the statement: "The training shall put the policeman of the Uniformed Police in the position to be able to handle the tasks that he will confront in peace and war." It also highlights the need "to maintain and if possible to increase" the physical fitness standards for the police

formations.[116] In other words, the continuing efforts by Himmler and Daluege
had behind them a specific objective beyond the everyday requirements of
police duty. That specific objective was the use of the police forces in the
coming war, a plan that Hitler shared with the senior members of the
Wehrmacht less than one month later, on November 5, 1937, during the so-
called Hossbach Conference, in which he outlined his vision of a war of conquest in the East to gain living space (*Lebensraum*).[117]

The training guidance prepared for Daluege's approval divided the police
into several categories, including police recruit companies and schools, police
companies, motorized Gendarmerie alert groups, individual duty posts, and
mounted and special detachments. These categorizations proved significant,
especially with respect to the differences in training received by the "police
companies" (*Polizeihundertschaften*) and the "police recruit companies" (*Aus-
bildungshundertschaften*) when compared to that received by "individual duty
posts." In the case of the former, weapons instruction included pistol, rifle,
machine pistol as well as light- and heavy-machine-gun training. Furthermore,
the guidance ordered the "main effort" (*Schwerpunkt*) to focus on tactical
combat training in both field and urban environments for the police companies, with training conducted in groups up to battalion strength.[118]

The military training of the Uniformed Police encompassed, not only the
lower ranks, but the senior leaders as well. During meetings with the regional
inspectors of the Uniformed Police in 1937 and 1938, Daluege repeatedly
stressed their military duties. For example, at a meeting in December 1937,
he emphasized the role of the inspectors in coordinating with Wehrmacht
authorities concerning the inclusion of police forces in army maneuvers.
Additionally, he recommended that the inspectors read the recently published
Paratroopers and Airborne Infantry, studying especially the presentation of
interesting tactical problems in the work.[119] During a subsequent meeting in
May 1938, agenda items included a report on the experience gained during
the march into Austria as well as a discussion of the topic "the military conception of the police civil service, not bureaucratization."[120] The latter subject was clearly in line with Daluege's intention to ensure that his policemen
become, not civil service bureaucrats, but rather soldiers wearing the uniform of a civil servant.

By 1938, Hitler and the National Socialist regime enjoyed widespread
approval and acclamation within German society as a whole. There were
clearly no internal threats facing the regime and no reason related to domestic policy for training the police formations in the use of light and heavy
machine guns or preparing them for combat-related duties. In fact, the formation and the military training of the police companies reflected Himmler's

and Daluege's plans for the creation of a combat-capable force in a coming war, plans that Himmler clearly was familiar with.

In a 1938 article in the police journal *The German Police* (*Die Deutsche Polizei*), the journal's chief editor described the new political and military character of the police. Contrasting the past with the present, he observed that the policemen of the Third Reich "no longer follow the instructions of today this, and tomorrow that, political authority [*Machthaber*] with police baton in hand, but rather [they are] soldierly in character and attitude, trained as weapons bearer for the usefulness and benefit of domestic peace."[121] With respect to the military character of the police, this comment was clearly correct; however, the maintenance of "domestic peace" was not the only rationale for the creation of a militarized police in company-sized formations, as events soon demonstrated.

Police Formations outside the Reich

Himmler did not wait long to take advantage of the capabilities of these police formations in support of the National Socialist plans for expansion. Already in 1938, nearly 9,000 men conducting duties with the police companies were concentrated in major industrial areas, including the Ruhr, as well as in cities such as Stettin, Königsberg, and Berlin, with an additional 3,400 men serving in the police recruit companies.[122] The annexation of Austria in March 1938 witnessed the employment of 18,000 policemen, including almost all the police companies.[123] Almost 1,000 policemen from Hamburg alone divided into three battalion-sized formations participated in the Nazi "march on Vienna." It is clear that the use of Uniformed Police forces in this operation was the result of neither last-minute nor ad hoc decisionmaking. In fact, for the move against Austria, police formations received coded instructions to begin preparations for a "parade" in January.[124] Later that year, 412 police officers and 9,350 police troops participated in the occupation of the Sudetenland. In this case, not only did the Uniformed Police troops perform well in the initial occupation, but they also received high marks for their propaganda work with Party officials among the local population in preparation for elections on December 4, 1938.[125] Finally, 6,500 policemen, now organized into two police regiments with a total of ten police battalions, assisted in the German takeover of the Czech provinces of Bohemia and Moravia in March 1939 with orders from Hitler "to remain continually in the Protectorate."[126]

The use of police companies in these extraterritorial operations established

a fateful precedent that would find its ultimate fulfillment in the use of Ordnungspolizei formations in the conduct of the campaigns in the East against
Poland and the Soviet Union. Additionally, the successful employment of the
police in these early "bloodless" campaigns constituted the first steps in the
realization of Himmler's plans for a soldierly police corps. Himmler
addressed this issue and the success of the police companies in a speech in
May 1939 in which he declared: "On account of the National Socialist outlook, it was for us a foregone conclusion to train the German police in a military spirit, and we have been proved correct by the newly acquired duties
of the police, in particular, the demands placed on the German police of the
last year."[127]

Despite the success achieved by early 1939, the realization of the ideal of
a soldierly police corps imbued with the National Socialist ethic required further efforts. In a speech on January 23, 1939, to the HSSPFs, Daluege admitted that, despite the progress made, there was still work left to be done. Still,
he stressed that the Uniformed Police with its "soldierly–National Socialist
attitude" had advanced far along the path toward the attainment of this
goal.[128] The request by the chief inspector of the Spanish police for Daluege's
help in creating a "powerful, military disciplined" Spanish police "filled with
a soldierly ethos" according to the German model offered one indication of
the progress made by the police along the road prescribed for it by the senior
SS and police leadership.[129]

Police for a Colonial Empire

The preparation of uniformed policemen for future colonial duties provides
another indication of the breadth of Himmler's and Daluege's ambitions for
the police in the prewar period. Certainly, a Nazi colonial empire could not
be attained without war. Already in 1936, Himmler had designated Uniformed Police units in Bremen, Kiel, and Hamburg as the heirs of units that
had served in German South West Africa, Cameroon, and the Chinese
enclave of Kiautschau, respectively. Furthermore, these units received the
right to wear the emblem of the Southern Cross on the left sleeves of their
uniform jackets.[130] In May 1937, Daluege's interest in the creation of a colonial police force led to his assigning a personal representative to attend the
meeting of the Reich Colonial League (Reichskolonialbund) in Düsseldorf.
Major of the Police Kummetz provided Daluege with a comprehensive report
on the events of the meeting and the colonial exhibition, including details of
a combined ceremony involving the Wehrmacht, the police, colonial war veterans, and Party formations at the Colonial War Memorial. With respect to

concrete initiatives, Kummetz suggested that, in the future, the police fellowship evenings provided an excellent forum for presentations and films dealing with colonial questions, evidence of the use of these informal gatherings as mechanisms for shaping the thinking of the police.[131]

The police involvement with the colonial question was not limited to the rhetorical realm. In a letter to Himmler on March 9, 1938, Daluege demonstrated his continued interest in the colonial question by proudly informing the *Reichsführer* of the success of his program involving the teaching of African-language courses within the police. He noted that a partial explanation for the success of the program involved the presence of a "large number of former colonial police troops within the police."[132] For his part, Himmler made his views on the subject of German colonies absolutely clear in a letter to Martin Bormann in January 1939. Himmler informed Bormann that any African possessions acquired by Germany existed simply to provide the Reich with products and produce otherwise unavailable. He envisioned sending civil servants and soldiers to run the farms and firms in these colonies "only for a limited number of years" before their return to Germany. He emphasized that he had no intention of creating a romanticized ideal of a generation of German expatriates living in Africa. In pursuit of this objective, Himmler personally had chosen and prepared the police officers for attendance at the Italian Colonial Police School.[133] Likewise, Daluege referred to successful completion of the initial efforts within the police in preparation for a future colonial police force in a speech in June 1939.[134]

In January 1941, Himmler created a Colonial Police Office under the Uniformed Police Main Office. The charter of the Colonial Police Office encompassed the "uniform preparation and later conduct of the employment of the Uniformed Police in the future German colonies and protectorates."[135] Subsequently, a Colonial Police School was established in Oranienburg near Berlin, with courses taught by members of the police as well as by members of the SS Colonial Political Institute and the Security Police Leadership School. Additionally, "specially selected SS and police officers" attended the Italian Colonial Police College near Rome in order to gain insights from the Italian experience in the colonization of Africa, and graduates of this program were serving in Libya by the end of 1941.[136]

In addition to the special selection of SS and police officers for colonial duty, Himmler's plans for future African colonies included the creation of an HSSPF subordinate to a colonial governor. Himmler also envisioned the cooperation of Security Police and Uniformed Police forces in the administration of these areas. Additionally, Hitler had approved the use of "active SS formations" for colonial duty.[137] The discussion of these issues at a time during which plans for the creation of an SS-monitored "Jewish reservation" on the island of Madagascar were being hurriedly made hardly seems coincidental.[138] It appears that the euphoria following the German victory over France, the possibility of taking over French colonial possessions, and the opportunity of ridding Europe of the Jews had generated renewed enthusiasm for colonial ventures among the senior SS and police leadership. It was not until March 1943, after the collapse of the German offensives in the East and in North Africa, that Himmler disbanded the Colonial Police Office; however, the very fact of its existence and of the effort taken in the special selection of SS and police personnel for this training provides another indication concerning Himmler's ambitions for his policemen in a coming new world order.[139]

The Creation of the Police Reserve

The actual demands placed on the police by their employment outside the borders of the Reich, not future visions of colonial empire, began to take their toll. The Uniformed Police had yet to fully recover from the loss of the Landespolizei, and extraterritorial missions stretched the organization to the breaking point. In fact, Daluege voiced this complaint to the regional and local leaders of the Party in a speech of June 26, 1939. The initial planning for the creation of a 100,000-man Police Reserve (Verstärkter Polizeischutz) began in 1937 with the intent of creating an Auxiliary Police that would be mobilized for internal security duties in the event of war but trained and led by regular police officers and noncommissioned officers.[140] Daluege envisioned a Police Reserve composed of men who had completed military training either as members of the former Reichswehr or, for nonveterans, through a comprehensive military training program conducted by the police.[141] Primarily, the Police Reserve was designed to counteract Wehrmacht plans for the mobilization of several thousand policemen into its ranks in the event of war. In turn, these reservists would assume police-type duties within the Reich, thereby helping alleviate the most pressing manning shortfalls.[142] To a large extent, the members of the Police Reserve came from the ranks of the SA reserve, continuing the tradition within the Uniformed Police of drawing on Party organizations for its personnel needs.[143]

With the outbreak of war in September 1939, the necessity of the Police Reserve became more urgent with the transfer of 13,604 police personnel into the Wehrmacht. The Gendarmerie was hardest hit, losing 8,451, over one-third of its members, to the German Military Police (Feldgendarmerie).[144] The remainder of these mobilized policemen entered the other services, resulting in the loss of 13 percent of the entire strength of the Uniformed Police.[145]

In one respect, the fact that one of every eight uniformed policemen entered service with the Wehrmacht provided an outward sign of Himmler's success in molding a police with martial capabilities, while the success of these men with the German armed forces during the war offered a testament to their martial skills. Himmler and Daluege ensured that the achievements of these former policemen with the Wehrmacht were well-known within the green corps by including pictures and stories on former policemen who won the Knight's Cross in issues of *The German Police*.[146]

The Search for Recruits

Already in the summer of 1939, the police and the army High Command had reached agreement concerning the recruitment by the police of twenty-six thousand men from several year groups. In a subsequent ministerial meeting on September 18, Göring notified those in attendance that Hitler specifically prohibited the enlistment of men between the ages of seventeen and nineteen into the police, year groups reserved for the Wehrmacht. Daluege, however, did not give up without a fight. In a memorandum of September 19, he fumed: "This order could only have been given without an understanding of the entire police organization." He continued: "Without the enlistment of younger recruits it is not at all possible to bring the police numerically up to the target manning strength."[147]

In the wake of the successful campaign in Poland, Daluege's argument carried the day, and, on October 31, 1939, acting on Himmler's authority, Daluege referenced a Führer Order calling for the immediate enlistment of 26,000 recruits for the Uniformed Police into "training battalions." The order designated 6,000 recruits between the ages of eighteen and twenty to form police "candidate [*Anwärter*] companies" and to undergo a twenty-eight-week training program. The stated goal for the training of the candidate companies included "full employment capability as marksmen in police and military engagements" and basic instruction in police-type duties, including search and arrest procedures, traffic regulations, and patrol duties. In addition, Hitler approved the enlistment of 20,000 men between the ages of twenty-seven and thirty as "*Wachtmeister* companies." The stated goal for the training of these men involved a one-year paramilitary and police training program to prepare them for individual and precinct duties. This 26,000-man police draft subsequently established the backbone of the police battalions. In addition, 327 officers and 9,599 troops from the earlier year groups entered the ranks of the SS Police Division, replacing "older officers and men."[148]

Significantly, prospective volunteers had to meet the criteria for entry into the SS, including a vetting of political reliability by the responsible Party office.[149] The requirement for police candidates to meet SS entry requisites proved a double-edged sword as the SS dipped into the pool of police recruits to fill its own formations. The joint SS and police recruiting office further complicated the situation as the Uniformed Police could not shield applications from their SS counterparts, an unintended disadvantage of the close relationship between the two organizations.[150] By the beginning of 1940, the total number of applicants for the 26,000 positions reached approximately 160,000; however, only one in four met the strict entry requirements.[151]

The reliance on SS enlistment standards and the emphasis on military training provided one indication of the special status enjoyed by the police battalions, and this special status found repeated expression in the words and orders of the police leadership during the war. In a letter of April 27, 1940, to the head of the Uniformed Police Operations Office (Kommandoamt), Lieutenant General of the Police Adolf von Bomhard, Daluege expressed his displeasure with the progress in the selection of officers and noncommissioned officers for the police training battalions. In fact, Daluege noted, he had taken personal action in two separate cases the day before. He then reminded von Bomhard: "At present the identification of officers and noncommissioned officers for the training battalions is the priority task." One of the cases that aroused Daluege's ire involved the assignment of a police sergeant from Hamburg who had received administrative punishment on four occasions and whose personnel file called for his investigation by the Gestapo. Daluege remarked that he had contacted the commander of the Uniformed Police in Hamburg and that the officer who had recommended this sergeant for duty with the training battalions would be "strictly called to account." In the second case, it was, not the quality of the men recommended by the Munich office, but the delays in getting the four officers and twelve noncommissioned officers to the police battalions that concerned Daluege.[152]

In order to underline the importance of finding the right men for the police training battalions, Daluege stated his intent to issue "another" detailed directive concerning this subject.[153] The personal interest displayed by the head of the Uniformed Police concerning the leadership of these battalions provided an unequivocal indication of the importance that he attributed to these formations. Likewise, in a speech to visiting Spanish dignitaries in the fall of 1940, the commander of the Uniformed Police in Hamburg, Major General of the Police Rudolf Querner, highlighted the "special training and schooling" of these formations for "future police duties."[154]

Shaping the Police Battalions

By the time of Querner's speech, the police battalions had firmly established their value as instruments of National Socialist racial policy in the invasion and occupation of Poland and in the campaigns in the West. Hitler provided an indication of his satisfaction with the performance of the police and his future vision for the police formations by ordering the preparation of "motorized police formations of considerable scale for occupation duties."[155] Likewise, Himmler and Daluege recognized the performance of the police battalions in the campaign against Poland and clearly saw the possibilities for the expanded use of the police in the future. In a memorandum to Himmler on March 7, 1940, Daluege requested an urgent meeting with the Reich leader of the SS on that same day in order to discuss "fundamental questions concerning the further missions of the Uniformed Police in many new tasks."[156] In truth, the war had brought many new tasks for the police, both malevolent and more benign, including the responsibility for air-raid protection; however, the performance of the police during the campaigns in Poland offered a clear portent of things to come.

Already in November 1939, Daluege had made a clear distinction between the activities of the individual policemen serving in Poland and the police battalions. The latter, he noted, had a "purely military" nature and organization. He then listed the duties of the battalions, including training activities, patrol duty, combat of public disorder, supervision of the Polish police, and the "maintenance of peace and order as far as is demanded in the interests of the Reich." The final task listed by Daluege involved "special tasks, for example, in the resettlement of Volhynian and Galician Germans."[157]

Daluege's conflation of the martial character of the police battalions with duties that went beyond traditional police activities and his distinction between individual police duty and the activities of the police formations once again highlighted the special status of the battalions. He also made his intentions with respect to the police battalions clear in a later memorandum concerning officer candidates for the Uniformed Police. In this document, he stressed the importance of drawing officer candidates from the ranks of the police battalions, especially those who had served in Poland and the Czech Protectorate. He ordered that first consideration be given to "militarily exceptional and gifted men," whose fitness for police duties would be a concern only after the war.[158] In other words, martial character and ability, not investigative expertise, became the desired standard for these future leaders of the platoons and companies of the police battalions.

The SS office of ideological indoctrination provided its guidance for the training of the entire Uniformed Police during the war in a letter of June 2, 1940. Again, a clear distinction was made between the ideological training of the police battalions and that of the individual duty policeman. In the case of the former, the goal of the schooling focused on "the training of the *martial combatant.*"[159] In order to accomplish this objective, the ideological training office suggested that weekly training sessions draw from World War I literature, including Rudolf Bathe's discussion of the "duties of the soldier." In an addendum to this guidance, the commander of the Uniformed Police forces in the General Government in occupied Poland expressed his own expectation that the objectives outlined in the guidance become "the spiritual property of *all* police soldiers [*Polizeisoldaten*] in the General Government."[160] Once again, a senior police leader equated the martial identity of the police soldier with the "spiritual" offerings of National Socialist ideology, a deadly admixture, as the events of the previous months and coming years demonstrated.

Facing a Manpower Crisis

In a report of August 20, 1940, Daluege detailed the training progress of the entire Uniformed Police. The progress of the police battalions assumed first place in his review of the state of training. He reported that sixty police battalions composed of police reservists had finished combat training up to the platoon level, with company and battalion combat training in progress. Likewise, thirty-eight police battalions composed of those from the 26,000-man recruit pool had finished parts of their training, while three police battalions within the occupied Eastern territories composed of 6,000 ethnic Germans had completed their combat training up to the company level, with battalion-level training in progress. Furthermore, Daluege noted the completion of basic military training for the 134,000 men tasked with individual duties or precinct duties.[161]

The fact that the 101 police battalions mentioned by Daluege with slightly over 59,000 men constituted forty-seven percent of the entire police force, excluding the Police Reserve, demonstrates the dominant role played by these formations within the Uniformed Police by the summer of 1940. Likewise, their distribution outside the borders of the Reich highlighted their role and importance in the prosecution of German occupation policies. At this time, the distribution of the police battalions outside the Reich included ten in the Czech Protectorate, thirteen in the General Government, seven in the annexed Polish provinces, six in Norway, and four battalions in Holland, for a total of forty. In addition, the number of individual duty policemen and men from the battalions operating outside the boundaries of the "old Reich" was 33,750, or 27 percent of all police forces.[162]

The Uniformed Police faced a personnel crisis by the summer of 1940, with the number of policemen, not including the Police Reserve, standing at 125,108, an increase of fewer than 4,000 men since the start of the war.[163] In a report concerning the personnel strength of the police, Daluege noted that the demands of war and extraterritorial duties had created a 69,000-man shortage within the police by August 1940. In fact, the ratio of policemen to inhabitants ranged from 1:400 in the annexed Polish territories and 1:860 in the General Government to 1:3,323 in the Netherlands.[164]

If expansion had not kept pace with the new demands placed on the Uniformed Police by the outbreak of war, such was not the case with respect to outfitting. Table 1 provides a comparison of equipment inventories on September 1, 1939, and August 1, 1940. On the one hand, this comparison highlights the dramatic increase in weapons stocks within the police and, in particular, in machine guns. On the other hand, it also indicates a significant increase in motorized and mounted transport as well as a more than twofold increase in the number of field kitchens. The upsurge in the equipping of the police for combat provides further evidence of the changed nature and missions of the Uniformed Police and its continued fashioning as a militarized instrument meant to support the expansionist policies of the Nazi regime.

The Martial Ideal in Wartime

During the war, the leadership of the Uniformed Police continued to maintain a focus on the martial character of the National Socialist police corps. This emphasis found expression in the words and actions of the policemen themselves, in the police literature of the period, and in the image of the police as presented to the public.

In the case of the reaction of the policemen themselves, Rudolf Querner, the commander of Uniformed Police forces in Hamburg, provided his response to the outbreak of war in a letter to Daluege dated September 14, 1939. Querner notified Daluege that he and his men stood ready to defend the Reich and the *Volk* at home or on the battlefront. "Although the primary task of the Uniformed Police is the protection of the domestic front in the homeland," Querner continued, "still we request that we be given the opportunity to demonstrate that we also know how to combat external enemies, whether in conjunction with the SS-VT [SS-Verfügungstruppe] or as a part of the Wehrmacht."[165] In September 1939, Daluege responded to a flood of such requests by issuing a letter prohibiting further requests for transfers to

Table 1. Comparison of Equipment Inventories

Item	September 1, 1939	August 1, 1940	Percentage Change
Heavy machine guns	290	1,100	+279
Light machine guns	190	1,736	+814
Machine pistols	7,400	10,400	+41
Rifles	78,841	143,138	+82
Pistols	90,000	178,820	+97
Armored cars	37	39	+5
Trucks	2,480	3,740	+50
Motorcycles	3,209	3,684	+15
Horses	1,690	2,105	+25
Field kitchens	104	225	+116

Source: "Der Chef der Ordnungspolizei, Der Aufbau der Ordnungspolizei für den Kriegseinsatz (August 20, 1940)," T480, reel 96, National Archives and Records Administration.

the front and emphasizing the importance of manning police posts inside the homeland (*Heimat*) now that the war had begun.[166]

Senior police leaders were not the only ones who embraced the identity of the martial combatant. Police Sergeant Gustav Berger penned a letter to his hometown newspaper in November 1939 in which he mocked the overzealous deference shown by Polish Jews to their German occupiers and reiterated the stereotype of Polish ineptitude and bureaucratic mismanagement. He also framed his service in Poland as that of a "soldier."[167] In the case of Police Battalion 310, the battalion commander reminded his men before their departure for Poland in October 1940 of his expectations that each one conduct himself as a "National Socialist and martial combatant of Adolf Hitler" and dedicate his entire strength to enforcing Germany's right to rule in the East.[168]

One way of enforcing German rule involved the conduct of antipartisan operations. In this regard, a police reservist serving in Poland described his company's participation with SS forces in an action aimed at Polish "bandits." During a daylong operation, the company marched for miles through swampy terrain and in the winter cold in full combat gear. In spite of the conditions, this police reservist remarked: "One grits one's teeth. When one is a soldier, there are no obstacles and no getting tired."[169] In a similar account, a member of a police battalion from Flensburg reflected on his unit's actions in Russia after his transfer to the Netherlands: "The achievements that we demonstrated in battle against the bandits in the East are and remain for us good memories. Life is good here in the West, but we old soldiers of the East don't know anymore how one sleeps in a clean bed."[170] These policemen clearly identified themselves as martial combatants who took pride in their former service in the East.

Portraying the Political Soldier

Practical as well as propagandistic police literature of the wartime period highlighted the martial nature of police duty. For example, two Uniformed Police officers authored a book entitled *Uniformed Police in Combat: Tactical Handbook of the Police Battalions,* dealing with the tactical combat skills required by the police formations in a range of military activities, including pacification and antipartisan operations. In their discussion of pacification operations, the authors commented that no other police duty demonstrated more clearly Himmler's demand for the combination of a "soldier and civil servant in the same person."[171] Likewise, Hans Richter, a captain in the police reserves, authored a popular account of Uniformed Police actions in the campaigns in Poland, Scandinavia, and the Low Countries. A veteran of the Great War, Richter expressed his excitement as he traveled to Poland on a trip that brought back the feelings of the "old soldier." He also discussed the role of the police in the "resettlement" of the Polish population, the necessity for summary executions, and police activities to break the "supremacy" of the Jews. Finally, Richter ended his work by noting that the men of the police were no less important than their counterparts in the Wehrmacht and described the latter as "conquerors" and the former as "guarantors" of German victory.[172]

Popular images in postcards, placards, and the public media during the war also reinforced the image of the policeman as a soldier. The cover of Helmuth Koschorke's *The Police Intervenes!* showed a squad of seven policemen patrolling a railroad track as they marched over a frozen, desolate landscape. The security of lines of communication and the need to protect them from partisan attack emerged as a critical military task in the East, and the picture of these policemen in their winter greatcoats, wearing steel helmets, and carrying rifles provides the impression of soldiers engaged in a thankless task under harsh conditions.[173] By mid-1941, issues of *The German Police* repeatedly carried stories concerning the combat actions of the police battalions, including those of the formations in the occupation of the Balkans, the "cleansing" of the Ukraine, and the battle against the "Bolshevist world enemy" in the Soviet Union.[174] These stories highlighted the operations of the police working "hand in hand" with the Wehrmacht.[175] A

February 1944 issue of the magazine highlighted the martial character of the police with a pen-and-ink drawing of a uniformed policeman standing in front of a ruined building with a machine gun in his hands and two hand grenades stuck into the front of his belt.[176] By 1944, many within the Uniformed Police would have identified closely with the sight of a colleague armed for close-in combat as experience in the East had taught.

Other popular images combined the martial character of the police with that of the SS. For example, a wartime postcard from a series of SS-related art displayed a police mountain trooper (*Polizei-Gebirgsjäger*) dressed in winter camouflage and cradling his machine gun.[177] Similarly, a police recruiting poster for 1942 showed two policemen in greatcoats staring out across the Russian steppes and standing above the caption "The Police at the Front." In the background, destroyed Soviet tanks litter the landscape, while, in the foreground, a policeman and a member of the SD, flanked by the police crest and the runes of the SS, hold their weapons at the ready.[178] The poster presented the twofold message of a soldierly police locked in combat against an enemy army while standing shoulder to shoulder with their counterparts in the SS.

In the period between 1933 and 1945, the Uniformed Police experienced a sustained and consistent campaign emphasizing soldierly virtues and glorifying the martial combatant. The "police soldiers" that Himmler and Daluege sought to mold from the ranks of the Ordnungspolizei were, however, intended to be, not apolitical servants of the state, but rather "political soldiers" of the National Socialist regime and executors of racial policy. In this respect, the "police companies" and "police recruit companies" acted as the bridge between the earlier Landespolizei formations and the later police battalions. In reality, Himmler's objective of instilling a military character into the German police extended to the ranks of both the Uniformed Police and the Security Police. In the case of the Security Police, the Einsatzgruppen (Special Mission Groups) acted as a deadly instrument for the prosecution of racial war. Likewise, within the ranks of the Uniformed Police, the police battalions emerged as a ready and capable tool of annihilation that would cut a bloody path across the East.

The symbolic unity of the police soldier with the SS was not simply the product of propaganda and artistic representation. In the wake of the Soviet winter offensive of 1941–1942, the men of the Uniformed Police had been thrown into the front lines in order to stem the assault. Himmler recognized this performance in a message to his policemen in which he paid tribute to the police with the words: "In the front ranks of the battle with units of the Wehrmacht and the Waffen-SS, you proved [your] soldierly courage, loyalty, and devotion to duty as model National Socialists and SS men."[179] As chapters 4 and 5 will show, the men of the police had ample opportunity to demonstrate their soldierly courage, loyalty, and devotion to duty in the years ahead. However, Himmler's praise of the police as model National Socialists and SS men was not intended as empty rhetoric as the Reich leader of the SS had gone to great lengths in his quest to merge the soldierly corps of the police with the black corps of the SS.

THREE

INSTILLING THE SS ETHIC

It can only be a question of time before the entire police coalesces with the SS corps into a permanent unit and the SS and police form a protective corps that in every respect guarantees the internal strength and the steel-like toughness of the greater German Reich.
—Kurt Daluege (January 1939)

In conjunction with the effort to build a martial character within the police, Himmler and Daluege pursued a parallel effort designed to achieve the unification of the police with the SS. Himmler's vision for the Uniformed Police involved the creation of an SS ethic within the police that fused the aspirations of the NSDAP (National Socialist German Workers' Party) with the identity of the police soldier. Hitler's appointment of Himmler as Reich leader of the SS and chief of the German police on June 17, 1936, offered Himmler the opportunity to turn his plans for the fusion of the SS and the police into reality.

The goal of uniting the police with the SS was not the result of a spur-of-the-moment decision but, in fact, the product of a long-term vision. Rudolf Querner, a police general, informed a visiting group of Spanish police officials in September 1940: "Already long before the [National Socialist] takeover of power, the Reich leader of the SS and his colleagues intended to create a future German police organization in such a way that its officers and men should comply with all the stringent requirements of the Schutzstaffel." Querner continued: "The more the state and the Party became one, the police of the movement [the SS] and the police of the state were supposed to be united in a great protection corps [*Schutzkorps*] of the Third Reich."[1] In a similar vein, prior to the war, Hitler intended "the police to become a part of the [National Socialist] movement."[2] Himmler's appointment provided him with the necessary authority to realize his dream for merging the green-clad corps of the police with the black corps of the SS.

Describing the SS Ethic

The often-cited motto of the SS inscribed on the blades of their daggers— "My honor is loyalty"—offers one perspective on the central importance to the men of the black corps of the concept of absolute commitment. From a sense of obligation to the order and, by extension, to National Socialism, the SS man accepted the responsibility to "protect" the movement and guard its message from internal and external foes alike. The designation of the SS as Schutzstaffeln, literally "Protection Squadrons," itself indicates an important distinction between the SS and its erstwhile parent organization, the SA, or "Storm Troops." Indeed, it is not coincidental that the protection of the movement's own "messiah," the Führer, fell to the SS, and this fact itself offers the ultimate expression of this role. In addition, the SS "came to see itself not only as the loyal elite of the movement but also the future Nazi police."[3]

In a speech of October 1943 to SS and Party leaders, Himmler laid out his expectations for the men of the black corps to remain "honest, decent, loyal, and comradely," but he warned that these traits applied only to "members of our own blood" and "otherwise to none other." After establishing this "fundamental principle" (*Grundsatz*), he went on to outline the "most important virtues" of the SS man, including loyalty, obedience, bravery, truthfulness, honesty, fellowship, acceptance of responsibility, industry, and abstinence.[4]

In Himmler's mind, these nine virtues provided the foundation for the SS ethic, and their ordering was not coincidental. Not only did Himmler cite loyalty as the central virtue of the order, but he also described the kind of loyalty he had in mind as inextricably binding the men of the SS with the person and ambitions of Adolf Hitler. Likewise, his placement of obedience second and his praise of the "sanctity" of orders given by superiors to subordinates held specific meaning in late 1943. In a speech in which the physical and psychic burdens placed on the men of the SS and the police in the "extermination of the Jewish people" had already been noted, a reference to obedience and the sanctity of orders could not have been more clear.[5] Loyalty and obedience in fact constituted the bedrock on which the entire SS edifice rested, but it was the marriage of these "virtues" to a martial mentality that laid the foundation for annihilation and genocide.

The military identity of the SS was, in fact, no less important than a listing of the desired character traits of an SS man, as that military identity provided the context in which those character traits would find their ultimate expression. In discussing the SS, the German historian Hans Buchheim reflected: "The word 'soldierly' played a major role in the SS. The term had of course been stripped of its normal military connotations and turned into an expression signifying a general belligerent attitude in accordance with the National Socialist 'political soldier' concept."[6] In the case of the SS-Totenkopfverbände (or Death's Head) units, it was not a large step for men who had brutalized concentration camp inmates and "learned to hate absolutely the 'enemies

behind the wire' as subhumans who were a political and racial threat to the
security of the Reich" to transfer their hatred and their sense of mission as
"soldiers of destruction" in an apocalyptic battle against Jewish-Bolshevism.[7]
However, the scope of Himmler's ambitions in this respect was not limited
simply to the men of the Death's Head formations under Theodor Eicke's
command; rather, it extended to the entire SS empire.[8] In this respect, the Uniformed Police became under Himmler's guidance part and parcel of this larger
effort to merge, not only the organizational direction of the police with that
of the SS, but also the values and beliefs of the green-clad men of the police
with the political and racial "elite" of the SS.

Cooperating in the Conduct of Genocide

Despite the personal differences between Heydrich (chief of the Security Police
and Security Service [SD]) and Daluege, the initial investment in creating a cooperative relationship between the Security Police and its uniformed counterpart
paid significant dividends after the outbreak of war and during the German
occupation in the East. The integration of regular policemen into the activities
of the Einsatzgruppen (Special Mission Groups) in Poland and the Soviet Union
provides one of the most visible expressions of the symbiotic relationship
between the Security Police and the Uniformed Police; however, throughout the
period of the German occupation in the East, the men of the police worked
closely with their counterparts in the Security Police and the SD in the prosecution of racial war.

The division of Poland and the creation of the General Government in
October 1939 provided the perfect setting for cooperation. A situation report
of January 1940 provides details of a joint action involving the Police Regiment Lublin with the SD during the conduct of "a large-scale action against
professional criminals [*Berufsverbrecher*]."[9] Later that same year, Uniformed
Police forces supported an operation led by the commander of the Security
Police and the SD the aim of which was the rounding up of able-bodied Polish men, presumably for forced labor.[10] The higher SS and police leader
(HSSPF) East, Friedrich-Wilhelm Krüger, provided further evidence of the
full extent of this relationship in an order directing the execution of "political commissars and Communists"—"without exception"—by specific units
of the Uniformed Police, Security Police, and Waffen-SS under his command.[11] Similarly, a situation report by the Criminal Police office in Bilgoraj
in December 1942 noted that the "cooperation with the stationary [Uni-
formed Police] units can be described as satisfactory." The report continued:
"The named police units are of their own accord endeavoring to clear up

crimes [*Straftaten*]."[12] By 1943, the close coordination of the two organizations found expression in a police report arguing that greater success in anti-partisan operations was directly related to the degree of cooperation between the Uniformed Police and the Security Police.[13]

Himmler ante Portas

The early record of the various branches of the Uniformed Police in support of the Gestapo, the Criminal Police, and the SD certainly indicated the willingness and the ability of the Ordnungspolizei to carry their share of the load in the battle against the political and racial enemies of the Reich. The participation of the Uniformed Police in actions aimed at the parties of the Left, the use of police to enforce racial statutes and to provide political evaluations of their fellow citizens, as well as the infusion of men from the Party and its paramilitary organizations provide strong evidence concerning the regime's initial success in transforming the police into an instrument for the prosecution of National Socialist policy.

The involvement of the Uniformed Police in the political activities of the state was, in fact, part and parcel of the regime's plans for the police. Indeed, party ideologists identified the primary tasks of the police as the ability to "execute the ideology of the state leadership and help create and maintain the order willed by it" as well as the safeguarding of "the German people, as an 'organic, corporate entity,' its vitality and institutions, against destruction and disintegration."[14] In an October 1935 speech to a group of police instructors, Daluege addressed the progress made by the Uniformed Police under National Socialism. He remarked that the police had undergone a "far-reaching and comprehensive transformation" in the prior two years, including the removal of those who had forgotten their "soldierly traditions" under the "Marxist system" (Weimar). He discussed the elements of the transformation of the police, including their acceptance of the leadership principle, soldierly discipline, and absolute obedience. He then called on the assembled police instructors to educate the police in the "spirit of National Socialism."[15]

The effort to bind the police to the SS and the Party remained an important objective for the National Socialist leadership during the interwar period. In a series of guidelines prepared for Prussian police officials in September 1935, Daluege focused on several issues concerning new accessions to the police. First, he emphasized the importance of recruiting from "regions with racially and mentally better human material." Second, he directed that preference in recruiting police officers be given to those men who were members of the Hitler Youth, the SA, or the SS. Finally, he discussed the possibility of seeking out men from the SS-Leibstandarte and the SS-Verfügungstruppe (SS-VT) for duty with the police. In this last case, he warned of the sensitivity of this effort given its potential of encroaching on Himmler's personnel base. But the lure of the SS racial reservoir proved too strong a temptation, as exemplified by Daluege's remark: "Doubtless this concerns a physically, racially, and mentally good human material that has already passed through physical and ideological training in line with our interests."[16]

With the naming of Himmler as chief of the German police in June 1936, such concerns became moot. Himmler made this point explicit in a speech on May 5, 1937, to the Uniformed Police officer corps in which he explained his plans for recruiting from the SS for the police. He then emphasized the need for a close relationship to the Party. He exclaimed: "The police will fulfill its present and future tasks only if it is the most dependable and most National Socialist penetrated part of the German civil service and remains hard and uncompromising even in the times of greatest burden."[17] This speech provides a further example of the importance that Himmler attached to the transformation of the police and his continuing efforts to make sure that this message reached its intended audience, an audience that would set the expectations and the day-to-day standards of the police force. In one respect, Himmler was preaching to the choir as, by December 1937, over half the police officer corps, 1,083 of 2,035, belonged to the Party and, by mid-1938, this number was expected to reach an astounding *70 percent*.[18]

The Use of Ritual and Ceremony

The Nazi government had already succeeded in bringing its message to the police at least at the symbolic level. The newly instituted Day of the German Police provided the platform for the introduction in December 1934 of the "Hitler salute" or "German salute" for the police. Unlike the members of the Wehrmacht, the police received the "distinction" of using the Nazi Party salute instead of the traditional military salute.[19] In comparison, the law of August 20, 1934, mandating an oath of allegiance to Hitler applied, not only to the Wehrmacht, but to the entire civil service as well, including the police.[20] In terms of organizational culture, the significance of these measures extended beyond mere formalism. Using the Hitler salute and taking an oath of loyalty to the person of the Führer by themselves did not make true believers out of the police, but they represented two powerful symbols of the organization's allegiance to the National Socialist state and its Führer.

Likewise, the use of ceremony and ritual to commemorate fallen policemen offers some examples of the effort to tie the participation of the police in the suppression of leftist "uprisings" under Weimar to the objectives and historical traditions of the Party. Speaking at the dedication of the monument to the Ruhr fighters (*Ruhrkämpfer-Ehrenmal*) in April 1937, Daluege railed against the Marxists and the "Jewish traitors," whom he described as a "world pestilence" that threatened the German state in the 1920s. He remarked that it was the "men in police uniforms" who fought an "almost hopeless war between two fronts," the "Spartacist horde" on the one side and the "Marxist government in Berlin" on the other. "Through the incorporation of the police into the protective corps [the SS] of the movement," Daluege observed, "our fallen comrades [in this 'battle of annihilation'] have become on the outside what they were in their hearts, even if unconsciously: the forerunners and pioneers of National Socialist philosophy."[21] Daluege's appropriation of police sacrifice for National Socialism, combined with his anti-Marxist and anti-Semitic rhetoric, including his use of the term *Vernichtungskampf* (battle of annihilation), demonstrated one method by which ceremony was used to reshape historical experience and at the same time to condition contemporary members of the organization for an apocalyptic struggle already in 1937.

In another example, Hitler awarded unit flags to the police in the "Blood Banner" ceremony during the Nuremberg Party rally in September 1937. During this ceremony, Hitler grasped the unit colors of the police with one hand while holding the "Blood Banner" carried by the Nazis in the abortive beer-hall putsch in the other hand. And at one point he exclaimed: "The German police shall be brought together more and more in a living connection with the [National Socialist] movement, which not only politically represents Germany today but symbolizes and leads [it]."[22] With the award of SA- and SS-style flags and standards to the police, Hitler intended to demonstrate the blood bond between the Party, the SS, and the police.[23]

Merging the Police with the SS

The ascendance of Heinrich Himmler to a position of control over the entire police apparatus of the Third Reich initiated a further radicalization of the police in the remaining years before the war and, especially, during the war. In one respect, Himmler's appointment "embodied at the highest position the constant connection between the SS and the police."[24] His successful unification of the various state Political Police organizations under his control proved to be the first step in a larger plan for the unification of all the various state police organizations under National Socialist control. Already in October 1935, Hitler had agreed in principle to the appointment of Himmler as the head of the entire Reich police apparatus as a key step to ensure the "maintenance of the health of the German national body [*Volkskörper*]."[25]

After his selection as chief of the German police in June 1936, Himmler initiated a series of systematic measures aimed at the "merging" (*Verschmelzung*) of the SS and the Uniformed Police. In a January 1937 radio address, he outlined his strategy: "The German National Socialist police . . . will continually and ever more firmly coalesce with the SS, supplemented increasingly by leaders and men of the SS, and above all will be an example of the growing together of Party and state."[26] He continued by noting that the "anchoring" of the German police within the order of the SS and the adoption of the "strict laws of the SS" would provide the police with the "strength" to be "hard and unyielding" when required and "understanding and generous" when possible.[27]

Hitler's selection of Himmler to lead the police provided unambiguous proof of his desire to see the police merged with the "soldiers of the Party," the SS, in both an organizational and a spiritual sense. Later, Daluege explicitly highlighted the long-term goal of a Uniformed Police force composed of officers and men solely from the SS.[28] Hitler later made this ambition explicit in a directive dealing with the SS on August 17, 1938.[29] At the official ceremony marking Himmler's appointment, Daluege exclaimed: "We can be proud that at this moment a dream is coming true, something I dreamed of as an SS leader before the [National Socialist] revolution, that is, the unification of the police of the movement [the SS] with the police of the state in the person of Reich Leader of the SS Himmler."[30] When it was Himmler's turn to speak, he identified one of his key tasks as "welding the police together with the order of the SS" in order to strengthen the Third Reich.[31] In his quest to weld the SS and the police together, Himmler pursued several tracks, involving symbolic, instructional, and organizational initiatives.

Symbols of Unity between the Police and the SS

Not only did Himmler's and Daluege's words present their expectations of the police, but they also created an organizational culture within the police in which anti-Semitism and anti-Bolshevism emerged as institutional norms. It is clear that not every policeman may have embraced the extreme implications of Himmler's rhetoric, but it is equally clear that the *Reichsführer*'s vision established an atmosphere favoring the development of a police mentality that promoted the ideal of a soldierly corps locked in an apocalyptic battle with "Jewish-Bolshevism." In addition, Himmler's remarks made it apparent that one of his objectives included the "merging" of the SS with the police, a goal that he pursued through several initiatives in the following years. These measures included the authorization in 1937 for SS personnel serving in the Uniformed Police to wear the SS runes as well as introduction in 1938 of the SS sword for police officers.[32]

The display of the SS runes on a policeman's tunic or the wearing of the SS sword provided inferential evidence of the racial and political sympathies of the specific individual and offered visible symbols of the special status enjoyed by the SS within the police. In another measure, policemen who qualified as Party "old fighters" received authorization to wear the honor chevron (*Ehrenwinkel*) of the NSDAP on the sleeve of their uniform jacket.[33] In addition, policemen *accepted* into the SS received an SS rank corresponding to their police grade.[34] Admittedly, the reaction of the individual policeman to SS titles, the SS runes, the honor chevron, and the sword might vary from envy to disinterest; however, the presence of these symbols and the distinction implicit in their wear sent an unambiguous message to the rank and file concerning the larger organization's values, objectives, and ideals.

Grooming a Police Elite

A more concrete example of the "merging" of the soldiers of the Party (the SS) and the police occurred with the acceptance of both officers and enlisted men from the ranks of the SS-Verfügungstruppe and the SS Death's Head units into the Uniformed Police. In a lecture to Wehrmacht officers in January 1937, Himmler informed his audience of the importance that he placed on these initiatives, especially with respect to the police officer corps, and he highlighted his efforts to incorporate commissioned graduates of SS officer candidate schools (*Junkerschulen*) into the Uniformed Police. In fact, he discussed his idea of requiring every SS candidate from these schools to spend six months in the Uniformed Police.[35] It is important to note that Himmler viewed the SS *Junkerschulen* as the crucible from which the elite of the SS was to emerge.[36] His emphasis on the introduction of these demonstrated "true believers" into the police officers corps was not empty rhetoric as, in 1937 and 1938, 40 and 32 percent, respectively, of all *Junkerschulen* graduates entered the ranks of the Uniformed Police.[37]

In his lecture to the participants in the Wehrmacht training course, Himmler made it absolutely clear that the SS and the Uniformed Police had an important role to play in the coming war against the "Jewish-Freemason-Bolshevist" enemy. He then unveiled his plan for the employment of his SS Death's Head units inside and outside Germany as well as the rotation of officers and enlisted men from the Uniformed Police between the field and the homeland in order to ensure the preservation of "decent men" within the police. This speech offers an early glimpse into the crucial role of the SS and the police in Himmler's plans for the future security of the Reich and in the expansion of the Nazi empire. In closing, he reminded his audience that a future war would be a "battle of annihilation" (*Vernichtungskampf*) between the "bearers of culture" of the Nordic German race and a "subhuman" array of enemies. Finally, in a comparison to the birth of Christ, he remarked that Germans had the good fortune of living in a time when an Adolf Hitler had been born, something that happens only once every two thousand years.[38]

Himmler's and Daluege's repeated use of the term *battle of annihilation* when discussing the racial and political enemies of the Third Reich is striking for two reasons. First, these prewar utterances offer strong inferential evidence of their plans for the police in a coming conflict. Second, their use of apocalyptic and religious imagery framed this contest in absolute terms for the men of the police, with direct implications for the measures and methods to be used in this looming confrontation.

Recruiting efforts deliberately sought to portray the SS and the Uniformed Police as an organic whole, thus conjoining the organizations in the minds of potential applicants.[39] In fact, local police authorities received instructions to "take up their advertising duties and endeavor to promote a constant and effective recruitment campaign for the police, as well as for the SS."[40] Himmler's expectations for local police officials included the identification of suitable Hitler Youth members as well as those young men who had completed their preparation exams (*Abitur*) for entrance into university. This latter group had the opportunity to submit a joint application for entry into police officer candidate school and the SS with the added privilege of applying for acceptance into the SS *Junkerschulen*.[41]

By September 1938, Himmler appeared to be satisfied with his initial efforts, and he remarked on the "favorable progress" made in the recruitment of uniformed policemen and the incorporation of "numerous" members of the police into the SS.[42] In fact, Daluege provided a statistical overview of SS and Party membership in a speech to HSSPFs on January 23, 1939. He remarked that 70 percent of the 1,400 officers and 30 percent of the 30,000 senior enlisted force belonged to the Party, with 26 percent of the officers and 14 percent of the senior enlisted force qualifying as "old fighters." Additionally, 16,200 police civil servants belonged to the SS, including 362 (26 percent) from the police officer corps. Furthermore, from a total of 91 police presidents and police directors, 48 (53 percent) belonged to the SS, 23 (25 percent) to the SA, and 3 (3 percent) to the National Socialist Driving Corps (NSKK).[43]

It should also be noted that Himmler's efforts to increase the numbers of SS men within the ranks of the police came on the heels of a period (1933–

1935) in which approximately 60,000 men had been released from the ranks of the SS as unsuitable for duty in the black corps.[44] In other words, the police were intended, not to pad the ranks of a swollen organization, but to augment the political and racial elite of the Third Reich. In fact, the entry requirements for police members into the SS were exactly the same as those for any other applicant, including the same physical and medical requirements as well as the validation of "Aryan ancestry" from 1800 for enlisted men and from 1750 for officer candidates. Additionally, acceptance into the SS meant that these policemen needed to receive prior approval before becoming engaged, including providing the necessary proof of the Aryan ancestry of the woman they wished to marry. Likewise, the requirements for earning the SS sport badge as well as the payment of organizational dues applied to these policemen.[45] Furthermore, Himmler directed that policemen who were SS members were to "participate regularly" in SS duties, and he ordered the formation of unique SS formations (SS-Polizei-Stürme) composed entirely of policemen.[46]

The movement of policemen into the SS was complemented by plans for the accession of SS members into the police corps. Already in early 1938, Himmler had crafted a plan for the transfer of men finishing their enlistments with the SS-Verfügungstruppe on October 1, 1938, to the ranks of the Uniformed Police.[47] In the summer of 1939, the personnel office of the Ordnungspolizei released expanded guidelines for the incorporation of former SS-VT enlisted men at the conclusion of their enlistments in October. This initiative included an abbreviated training course for the SS-VT men, with the possibility of accelerated promotion to the rank of *Polizeioberwachtmeister* (staff sergeant).[48] The outbreak of war in September made the 1939 initiative moot as these men would be mobilized back into the ranks of SS formations.

Even if the war prevented the full implementation of the effort, one contemporary writer still observed: "With the entrance of the young SS-men into the police, the ties between the two organizations become stronger."[49] The simple fact that the Uniformed Police and the SS had reached an agreement is significant and provides further evidence of the activities pursued in order to fuse the two organizations. In another example, Himmler broadened the pool of applicants for admission into the SS from the Uniformed Police, including the Fire Service, in November 1940 by favoring applications from those who had served with the SS Police Division, policemen who had received a wartime decoration, and those who had received field promotions to officer rank.[50] In addition, it would be a mistake to overlook the transfer of policemen into active SS field units. For example, almost 15 percent of Waffen-SS generals and colonels and over 11 percent of Waffen-SS lieutenant colonels and majors had started their careers as policemen.[51]

By 1941, Himmler's dual-track strategy of, on the one hand, introducing SS personnel into the police and, on the other hand, focusing on ideological indoctrination appeared to be working as 30 percent of all regular Uniformed Police officers belonged to the SS, compared to 7 percent of all reserve Uniformed Police officers, while over 65 percent of both groups belonged to the NSDAP.[52] However, still not satisfied, Himmler sought to increase the number of *regular* policemen from the enlisted ranks within the SS by expanding eligibility preferences for this group in June 1942. For example, policemen serving with the SS Police Division and members of the police battalions who had "proved themselves in duties outside the Reich" were to receive preferential treatment in their applications for admission to the black corps.[53] In this respect, Himmler's directive provided direct recognition of the important role played by the police battalions in the subjugation of the occupied territories and mass murder.

Creating a Reichstruppe

During the course of the war, Himmler and Daluege pursued measures to make the bond between the SS and the police even more explicit by anchoring it in a directive to be signed by Hitler entitled "Decree of the Führer concerning the SS and the Police" and an associated law entitled "Law concerning the Reichstruppe." In the case of the former, Himmler provided the head of the Reich chancellery, Hans Heinrich Lammers, with a copy of the draft decree in early 1942. Through the decree, Himmler sought to achieve a further merging of the two organizations with respect to entry standards, privileges, and duties.[54] In the case of the latter, Daluege received a draft copy of the law in October 1942 from the head of the police Office for Administration and Legal Affairs, Dr. Werner Bracht. In his cover note, Bracht noted that the document itself had not been coordinated outside the Uniformed Police organization and had not even been shared with offices within the Ordnungspolizei.

The primary missions of the Reichstruppe involved the protection of the "blood and unity" of the German *Volk* as well as the guarding of the Party and its "National Socialist ideas." Members of either the SS or the police could apply for admission to the Reichstruppe with the following understanding: "The member of the Reichstruppe is allowed to be neither only a civil servant nor only a soldier, but he must be above all else a political fighter. Only the political soldier . . . will be in the position to fulfill the tasks placed on the Reichstruppe." With the creation of the Reichstruppe, Himmler sought to achieve his quest for a "National Socialist soldierly order of ideal Nordic men."[55] In the end, opposition to the proposal in the Reich chancellery and the Party chancellery doomed it to a slow, bureaucratic death; however, the effort once again highlighted Himmler's vision of a conjoined SS and police racial elite.[56]

By the last years of the war, Himmler's dreams for the SS and the police faded further into the past as the elite nature of the SS and its armed formations experienced a gradual decline with the introduction of foreign volunteers and as the award of the SS imprimatur became an increasingly ordinary occurrence.[57] In February 1943, Himmler changed the designation of the Uniformed Police Regiments to the SS Police Regiments in recognition of "their particularly courageous and successful operations" in the East.[58] Although this designation did not automatically qualify the men of the police battalions for membership in the SS, it served as Himmler's recognition of the "special services" rendered by the police in the prosecution of the Third Reich's racial policies.

Already in 1940, Himmler had made exactly this point during a speech to SS officers in which he exclaimed: "I will tell you something. Throughout the entire Waffen-SS, we must begin to perceive and see the other great activities of the entire SS and police. You must also look at the activity done by the man in the green uniform as equally valuable as the activity you yourselves do." It was not coincidental that Himmler chose to make this statement immediately on the heels of his discussion of the difficulties of "suppressing a hostile population . . . to carry out executions, to transport people away, to take away howling and crying women and to bring over and care for ethnic German comrades from across the border with Russia."[59] In this way, Himmler paid tribute to the work of the Uniformed Police in occupied Poland and ranked their work as no less important than that of the rest of the SS.

The Ideological Instruction of the Police

Himmler's ambitious plans for the police corps required, not just the introduction of visible symbols of unity with the Party and the SS, but, more important, an education program aimed at shaping the worldview of the police leading to the internalization of belief along National Socialist lines. In April 1937, Himmler released guidelines concerning the ideological indoctrination of the police and assigned the responsibility for these efforts to the Race and Settlement Main Office (RuSHA).[60] In addition to giving responsibility to the RuSHA for ideological instruction, Himmler's decree also included several further requirements, including the ideological education of the entire Ordnungspolizei, the use of training directors (*Schulungsleiter*) from the SS to coordinate with the RuSHA on training curricula and to carry out the indoctrination of the police, and the assignment of special lecturers (*Schulungsredner*) to be drawn primarily from the SS. The decree also underlined the necessity for the training directors to work closely with the RuSHA.[61]

The RuSHA created the training syllabi, and the regional inspectors of the Uniformed Police identified training directors to represent their jurisdictions. One indication of the importance attached to the ideological instruction involved Daluege's decision to personally address the first training course for the *Schulungsleiter*. Daluege reminded the training directors of their crucial role "to fill up and penetrate the great corps of the German police with the spirit of the National Socialist Schutzstaffeln [SS]."[62] As the first group of *Schulungsleiter*, composed of 450 police officers, met in Berlin in May 1937 to begin training, both Himmler and Daluege had provided the clearest of marching orders concerning their plans for the fusion of the SS and the police. Subsequently, the drain on RuSHA resources caused by the large-scale training program led Himmler to transfer responsibility for the ideological training of the police to the SS Training Office in 1938,[63] a measure that Daluege described as "of fundamental significance for the ideological adjustment of the Uniformed Police corps."[64]

Ideology in the Classroom

Recommended attributes for the training directors included that they "should have special training as teachers or lecturers, hold SS-leadership ranks, and should be capable of lecturing . . . [and] especially competent in the areas of history and national politics."[65] In support of the lecturers, the SS Main Office published a monthly pamphlet designed to introduce a general theme to guide and to focus classroom discussion as well as numerous recommendations for establishing the most favorable conditions for student learning. For example, the designated theme for November 1940 was "Germany's right to colonies" a topic that was intended to serve as a justification of German conquests in Europe and beyond. In order to allow sufficient time for lesson preparation, the Office of Ideological Instruction issued the topic by telegram on September 20, 1940.[66] In addition to ensuring adequate time for preparing lesson plans, lecturers received instructions to make liberal use of visual aids and were strictly admonished not to simply read their presentation. In addition, lectures were not to be scheduled immediately after "strenuous police duty" or to last more than an hour.[67]

The number of students was limited to no more than ninety, and the guidelines encouraged the selection of a speaker with a previously established personal relationship with his listeners. The latter measure was intended to encourage questions and the free exchange of ideas between comrades united in a shared mission. The ability of the lecturer to relate the material to the everyday life and experience of his listeners was also viewed as critical to successful instruction. Guidelines for these presentations, however, reminded the lecturer of his responsibility to "reflect on the fact that he is neither political prophet nor priest but rather stands as a political soldier in front of political soldiers."[68] The conjoining of religious imagery with one "political soldier" instructing a group of his fellows once again highlights the marriage of martial identity with an idealized SS ethic, a union that created both an ideal type and an expectation for the men of the police.

The level of effort that went into laying the foundation and building the structure of ideological indoctrination within the police corps was not intended to conceal a theoretical "Potemkin village." Overwhelming evidence demonstrates that Himmler placed great emphasis on the inculcation of National Socialist ideals in the police. One indication that ideological instruction was not simply a pro forma right of passage or intended to serve as rhetorical window dressing can be seen in a report detailing the results of the tenth officer candidate training course conducted at the police school in Fürstenfeldbruck between November 1938 and April 1939. Despite the devotion of two hours per week to ideological instruction, some three-quarters of the 110 participants failed to meet the course objectives in the combined area of national politics and ideological instruction (*Nationalpolitik und weltanschauliche Schulung*). In this case, the graders showed a great degree of leniency, as evinced in their evaluation of the majority of these men as "truly idealistic fighters of the movement of first-rate character."[69]

The apparent failure of this officer candidate group to meet the standards of ideological instruction can be read in two ways. First, it might be argued that the failure of these men demonstrated their lack of interest in the subject. Second, it might have arisen as the result of very high standards associated with the subject itself. Absent further evidence, the latter explanation seems more plausible given the evaluation of the instructors with respect to the National Socialist attitudes of the candidates. Still, whatever the case, it is absolutely clear that ideological instruction cannot be dismissed as simply "empty hours" in a busy curriculum—the subject of ideology mattered to those who taught it. Similarly, the officer evaluation form introduced in 1937 provided a single line each for discussions of character, knowledge, training, and ability to learn but *eleven* lines on which to detail the officer's National Socialist worldview.[70]

War and Ideology

Significantly, the outbreak of war resulted in the acceleration of ideological training activities in spite of the increased demands placed on the personnel and resources of both the SS and the police. In October 1939, Himmler named Dr. Joachim Caesar to the newly created position of chief of the Office of Ideological Instruction. With his appointment, Caesar assumed responsibility for the formulation, standardization, and evaluation of the entire ideological training curriculum. Additionally, a key part of his duties included monthly visits to monitor and evaluate training sessions and to provide Daluege with a report detailing his observations and recommendations.[71] In June 1940, Himmler ordered the commencement of daily indoctrination sessions (*Tagesschulung*) consisting of fifteen- to twenty-minute periods three times per week. The purpose of these abbreviated lessons was, not to review and discuss current events, but, more important, to focus on the "inculcation of National Socialist ideas" and the Führer's work in the creation of a German empire.[72]

The "Guidelines for the Conduct of Ideological Instruction of the Uniformed Police during the War" provides further strong evidence of the importance placed on ideological instruction with the outbreak of war. The guidelines began with the demand: "All the men of the Uniformed Police must not only know the events but must also be able to see and understand the larger connections. They must be able to correctly evaluate the measures taken and correctly carry them out. They must prove themselves as politically schooled organs of the National Socialist state leadership in their relations with the people." In one respect, the guidelines did distinguish between the ideological instruction of the men of the police battalions and that of other policemen by establishing the goal for the training of the former as the "formation of the political will of the martial combatant." In comparison, the goal for the individual duty policemen involved training these men as "bearers of political will" (*politische Willensträger*).[73] In both cases, the directive stressed the importance of the political nature of police duties. It once again highlighted the role of the police battalions, not only as police soldiers, but also as "political soldiers" whose police identities were inextricably tied to a martial character and the political aims of the National Socialist regime. It thus created a special status for these men, which, in turn, implied a special role for these units.

Ideology and the National Socialist Message for the Police

The print media provided an important mechanism through which Himmler's message to the men of the police was both reinforced and supplemented. Such printed matter can be separated into three general categories: that meant specifically for the police and used for guiding indoctrination sessions; that meant for the SS and the police generally and intended to supplement police-specific material; and, finally, that aimed primarily at the general reading public and meant both to mold the public image of the police and define the self-image of the individual policeman with respect to his place in the *Volksgemeinschaft* and his contribution to the political objectives of the National Socialist government.

A series of SS study guides (*Leithefte*) provided the initial basis for the ideological education of the SS and the police and served a central function in this process.[74] The study guides attempted to frame an overarching National Socialist worldview. On the one hand, they provided a "positivist" ethnocentric image encompassing an idealized depiction of German history and the glorification of a "Teutonic" identity based on shared blood and a mystical relation to the soil. On the other hand, they exalted National Socialist political and racial ideals and highlighted the mortal danger that the elements of a symbiotic Jewish-Bolshevist-Freemason threat posed to the *Volk*.[75]

The SS study guides provided a ready resource for initiating and standardizing an ideological indoctrination program within the police; however, Himmler went one step further and, in late 1940, introduced the biweekly publication, aimed specifically at the Uniformed Police, the *Political Information Service* (*Politischer Informationsdienst* or *PID*). The *PID* was a two- to four-page pamphlet divided into two sections: section A examined "fundamental questions of ideological, political, cultural, and economic content" intended to provide the foundation for weekly indoctrination sessions; section B provided supplementary information focused on the local level and intended to clarify specific issues, questions, or rumors faced by individual units. The distribution of the *PID* ranged from nine copies per each police company down to two copies for each small Gendarmerie station, with the requirement for each unit to maintain a central file of at least one copy of every pamphlet.[76]

The decree announcing the *PID* established specific requirements for the dissemination of the document to the police battalions, the Gendarmerie, the individual duty policemen, the police schools, and even police hospitals and health resorts, including the stipulation that discussion of the subject covered by a particular issue of the *PID* occur within one week of receipt of that issue. However, the instructional guidelines noted that not every topic needed to be discussed at one session, that discussion might instead be spread out over the week. Significantly, the decree placed the responsibility for the conduct and documentation of training squarely on the shoulders of the senior police commanders, once again highlighting the importance of this effort to the senior SS and police leadership. Making the senior police commanders directly responsible for this training dramatically lessened the chance that it would be neglected, whether deliberately or unintentionally.[77]

In practice, the publication and distribution of the initial editions of the *PID* experienced some difficulties at the local level. For example, the office of the senior commander of Uniformed Police forces in the General Government noted in a letter of December 6, 1940, that the *"Political Information Service* is to be distributed *immediately* on delivery to your subordinate commands and attention is to be paid to the detailed study of them."[78] The letter also noted that distribution delays owing to insufficient numbers of copies of the first two issues should not prevent the discussion of the third and fourth issues on their arrival. One indication of the importance attached to the discussion of the pamphlets can be found in an order from the office of the senior police commander in Lublin requesting the names of those policemen entrusted with the indoctrination sessions within the police battalions and Gendarmerie in order that they might receive copies of the book *Under SS Runes and the Eagle* (*Unter Sigrune und Adler*) personally inscribed by the regimental commander on the occasion of the SS Julfest, Himmler's secularized SS version of the Christmas celebration.[79]

The *PID* pamphlets approached ideological instruction in a more sophisticated manner than did some other publications, including the rabidly anti-Semitic *Der Stürmer* and the SS study guides. For example, the first issue (published in October 1940) began with an essay by Alfred Rosenberg, the Party's designated ideologue, offering a justification for the present war by trooping out the standard complaints of "the shame of Versailles" and the exploitation of Germany by "international high finance." Rosenberg exalted the role of the NSDAP in bringing the new Germany forth from this position of destitution into a new era of "national honor, social justice, and comradeship among the *Volk*." The essay makes no mention of a "Jewish-Bolshevist" threat, and, in fact, apart from the coded phrase "international high finance," neither the term *Jewish* nor the term *Bolshevist* appears in it. Rosenberg concluded with a description of the nature of ideology: "For us a worldview [*Weltanschauung*] is, not the sum of abstract doctrines, but instead the living, standing representation of a great ideal. Not the defense of dogmas, but instead [the defense] of spiritual and character values."[80]

The choice of Rosenberg's essay to lead off the political indoctrination of the police demonstrated a strategy that combined existing "hard-core" ideological initiatives with a "soft-core" approach that appealed to the reader at the more abstract level of national mission and duty to the *Volk*. Similarly, the eighth issue (February 1941) of the *PID* began with an article entitled "The Effort for the Biological Victory." Quoting liberally from the Reich health minister, Dr. Leonardo Conti, the article contrasted the present state of Germany with that prevailing during the blockade during World War I and discussed the health of the German people with respect to the prevention of disease, including the distribution of vitamin C doses to schoolchildren.[81] The utility of this type of article for an indoctrination session was twofold. On the one hand, it presented an issue, the health of one's family, of very real concern to the policemen. Raising the specter of the Allied blockade also framed the present war in terms that could be used to justify severe measures such as those visited on the German people during World War I.

During the course of the war, the *PID* adopted an increasingly stronger line with respect to the ideological and racial views of the Third Reich, a fact in part highlighted by the renaming of the *PID* as the *Newsletter for Ideological Instruction of the Uniformed Police* in mid-1941. In fact, the explicit nature of the anti-Semitic indoctrination of the police increased considerably in the months following the invasion of the Soviet Union.[82] The historian Karl Heller noted evidence that the editors and writers of the *Newsletter* became "increasingly concerned with the German conquest and settlement of the *Ostraum* [Eastern areas]." By 1942, little imagination was required on the part of the police reader to understand the implications of describing Jews as "enemy number one" or articles with titles such as "One War Aim: A Europe Free of Jews" or "The Devil in Paradise." The framing of the National Socialist ideal for the police also found increased emphasis, as an article in the March 10, 1943, issue noted: "The policeman of today has become a political soldier and a bearer of the Nazi idea." The passage continues: "To be a policeman today means to do one's duty in tireless dedication to the state, and beyond that duty to be a standard bearer of National Socialism and a fanatical propagandist of our ideology." Another article warned that "the Satanic grinning of international Jewry is already visible behind the mask of Bolshevism" and exhorted the police to a "total effort" to oppose this danger.[83]

Getting the Message?

For the men of the police battalions, the practical implications of the exhortations against Jewish-Bolshevism were very clear by 1942. These men had been putting ideological precepts into almost daily practice on the Eastern

Front. Still, the answers to questions of reception and the importance of indoctrination sessions aimed at the police remain crucial to determining the effectiveness of these efforts. Records from the Gendarmerie station at Zamosc in the district of Lublin provide some insights into the progress and effectiveness of ideological education, at least as far as a specific unit is concerned.

In March 1942, a captain of the Gendarmerie filed a required report detailing the conduct of ideological training between January 21 and March 20, 1942. He noted: "In the Uniformed Police, the ideological education is strong and has become a general possession of officer and enlisted man." Still, he cautioned on the need to bring the "National Socialist philosophy" (*Gedankengut*) more closely to the men in order to "harden them for the conduct of their difficult duty." The report remarked that the men showed great interest in the subject and that the supplied materials allowed for successful completion of the objectives. It also commented that daily indoctrination sessions included the use of radio news reports followed by a discussion; that weekly indoctrination employed the SS study guides, the *PID*, and newspaper and radio accounts; and, finally, that the senior Gendarmerie commander personally conducted monthly indoctrination sessions using the issued instructional materials.[84]

The March report is interesting in several respects. First, it provides a picture of an organized and established indoctrination program but admits the need for continued work to "harden" the men for their "difficult tasks." Second, it notes that, because no SS personnel were available, twelve Uniformed Police officers have conducted the training. The assignment of twelve officers to this task within a two-month period tends to demonstrate a broad range of responsibility for instruction and refutes the stereotype of the "one" true Nazi tasked with ideological instruction and ignored by all. Finally, the fact that the senior commander led the monthly sessions and was required to note his success in a written report to his superiors again denotes the importance attached to the activities even if their impact cannot be fully discerned in the minds of the men receiving the instruction.

By the fall of 1942, the Gendarmerie units in the district of Lublin experienced significant problems in meeting the schedule for indoctrination sessions. A report of September 28, 1942, from the commander of Gendarmerie forces to the commander of the Uniformed Police observed that the "continuous operations of the Gendarmerie in combat against bandits and the bringing in of the harvest" prevented the conduct of all planned ideological instruction. Still, the report noted that every available opportunity to conduct indoctrination training was used, with special emphasis being placed on the training of the "younger gendarmes," and with sessions led by the post commander or his deputy.[85]

Despite the press of daily duties, including combat against "bandits," the scope of ideological instruction actually increased in September 1942 with the requirement for police administrative officials to document their attendance at the sessions.[86] However, complaints continued to come in from the field that operational duties were impinging on ideological training. For example, the March 1943 monthly report from the commander of the Gendarmerie to the commander of the Uniformed Police in Lublin again noted difficulties in achieving training objectives owing to ongoing antipartisan operations (*Banditenbekämpfung*). The report admitted that weekly and monthly indoctrination sessions were not completed and that only daily sessions involving the discussion of current events had been conducted. In an effort to defend the cancellation of ideological training, the report remarked that National Socialist philosophy was "firmly rooted" in both officers and men and noted the wide availability of the SS study guides and the *Newsletter*.[87]

In one respect, the assertions of the Gendarmerie commanders that their men were "firmly rooted" in National Socialist philosophy seem formulaic and unconvincing; however, one must keep in mind that these men were on the front lines of a racial war in the East that encompassed the murder of Jews, the Polish intelligentsia, the clergy, and partisans. One might then expect a certain degree of exasperation on the part of a unit with the "paperwork" of ideology when demonstrated actions had repeatedly spoken louder than words.

Professional Literature and the Shaping of Police Attitudes

The professional publications of the SS and the police provided another medium through which to shape the attitudes of the Uniformed Police. As is true today, professional journals served an important function in the dissemination of the most current ideas, findings, beliefs, or debates within a specialized community. The primary professional police publication was *The German Policeman* (later *The German Police*), published twice a month by the Fraternal Association of German Policemen and provided to all members.

Like similar organizations for lawyers and doctors, the Fraternal Association of German Policemen served as a body designed to look out for the welfare of its members, to centralize the various interest groups representing them, and to provide a structure for Party influence and control, a move made explicit in a circular decree of January 29, 1935.[88] The association's statutes noted that its primary purpose was "to cultivate true German camaraderie among its members who are bonded by German blood and German soil to the National Socialist worldview."[89] Membership—initially optional—was, by early 1939, mandatory for all policemen.[90] The association served the function of a professional organization designed to promote expertise as well as to acculturate its members with National Socialist values, as the organization's charter clearly stated. One proposal aimed at accomplishing the latter goal called for using the organization's meeting facilities for the ideological indoctrination sessions conducted by the *Schulungsleiter.*[91]

A report issued under Daluege's signature in October 1937 concerning the professional training of police enlisted personnel emphasized the use of police specialist literature for this purpose, with priority given to *The German Police.*[92] This magazine, however, was not a simple technical or professional periodical devoid of political content; instead, it was heavily overlaid with the racial and ideological beliefs of National Socialism. For example, the May 1, 1937, issue contained an article entitled "The German Woman," which offered the idealized vision of the German woman as the "bearer of German civilized behavior [*Gesittung*]."[93] An issue published in November 1937 carried a more ominous message with respect to the Party's views on Bolshevism. An article entitled "Twilight of the Bolshevists?" noted the opening of an anti-Bolshevist exhibition in the Reichstag, "the historical site of the last great Communist attempted assassination in Germany." Furthermore, the article contrasted the celebration of the signing of the anti-Comintern Pact with the festivities in Moscow marking the twentieth anniversary of "terror and bloody rule in Soviet Russia."[94]

The war brought about a further radicalization of the topics and themes carried in the pages of *The German Police.* In 1940, issues of the magazine reinforced the racial prejudice against the "Jews of the East" (*Ostjuden*) by associating them with "dirt, stench, epidemics, and lice," among other things.[95] The front cover of a July 1941 issue trumpeted "Police Battalions in Operation against the Bolshevist World Enemy," the title of an article that referred to "drastic measures" taken against "plunderers" and the cooperation of the Uniformed and Security Police against the "Bolshevist underworld."[96] Finally, the October 1, 1941, issue contained an article entitled "Gypsy Transport" written by a police sergeant, Wilhelm Drechsler. Drechsler described his participation in the transport of a group of fifty-two Sinti and Roma to a holding camp. He recounted the dirty "black fingers" of the children and a woman who cleaned herself with a spit-moistened rag. Drechsler concluded: "The truth is: [the case of] the Gypsies concerns an asocial race or better yet a mix of races. Unable to remain in one place . . . [they] lead a parasitical existence, spreading the worst superstitions."[97] These are but three examples of the role played by the journal in disseminating and reinforcing racial stereotypes among the police.

The practice of linguistic dehumanization found its ultimate expression in numerous official police reports, where terms used to euphemize murder ranged from relatively benign expressions (e.g., *to turn off, to render harmless,* and *to cleanse*), to more obtuse or opaque terms (e.g., *special treatment* and *executive measures*), and to lethal words (e.g., *exterminate, annihilate,* and *liquidate*). In the case of the latter, the police reports often married them to a specter of imminent biological danger. The use of the terms *plague* and *epidemic* to describe both Jews and Bolshevists offers but two examples. And, when used in conjunction with *combat (Kampf)* (i.e., that against a Jewish or Bolshevist *pestilence*), such terms as *extermination* and *annihilation* provided the perfect linguistic complement to this biologically prescribed threat.[98] Similarly, an article from the January 1, 1940, issue of *The German Police* remarked on the "cleaning up" taking place in Poland, a process aimed at "bacillus" and "caftan wearers" (i.e., Jews).[99]

The SS weekly newspaper *The Black Corps* constituted another important venue for propagating the SS ethic and the Nazi worldview. Published between 1935 and 1945, with a maximum circulation of 750,000 copies, the newspaper "had a strong impact on the public" and was described as the "most extraordinary and most widely feared organ of the National Socialist press."[100] Within the ranks of the police, the newspaper received special attention as many police units subscribed to it for the purpose of incorporating it into their ideological training program.[101] An order of October 1939 prepared for Daluege's signature outlined the distribution of free copies among the police corps and detailed plans for finishing the construction of public display cases specifically for *The Black Corps* within the police stations. Daluege's order also included the requirement that copies be posted soon after being received and that only "undamaged" copies be displayed, a further indication of the importance attributed to this effort.[102] The use of display cases was particularly significant for all Germans in this period as many readers unable or unwilling to spend their money on newspapers regularly stopped at public display cases to read them.

Throughout the newspaper's history, Himmler maintained a deep personal interest in it, and the major themes presented in *The Black Corps* mirrored those of the SS ideal: anti-Bolshevism and racism. When it came to racism, the message varied. Sometime the Jews were targeted: for example, a two-part series entitled "The Plague of Vienna," a pictorial depiction of the "Jewish ghetto" in Vienna, was, according to William Combs, designed to "evoke revulsion and disgust from the readers." Sometimes the physically and mentally handicapped were targeted: for example, an article entitled "Money out the Window" compared the costs of a program to build low-cost housing for newlyweds with the "waste" of almost a million reichsmarks on housing the mentally and physically handicapped in the city of Breslau. As Combs reports: "Nearly every issue and, so it seemed, every article had some reference to race."[103]

After the invasion of Poland, and especially after the attack on the Soviet Union, the image of the "dirty" Jew became a standard trope in the pages of *The Black Corps,* and the themes of anti-Semitism and anti-Bolshevism became inseparably merged. Although the newspaper's editors made no direct mention of the Final Solution, the association of terms such as *annihilation* and *extermination* with references to the Jews established an explicit image for the reader. Stories concerning cooperation between the SS and the police in bringing "order" to Poland, as well as articles on the actions of SS and police units in antipartisan operations aimed at "bandits" and "Bolsheviks," intimated the prosecution of the racial war in the East.[104] For most readers— policemen who had served in the East or who had colleagues and friends there—the real meaning could hardly be missed.

Depictions of the Police in Popular Literature

In addition to literature aimed specifically at the police, Himmler and the senior police leadership supported efforts by members of the police as well as other writers to provide the general reading public with a positive image of the police. For example, Roland Schoenfelder wrote a popular history of the German police in a folio edition published in 1937 under the title *The Origins of the German Police.* Schoenfelder was, in fact, a member of the writing staff of the police periodical *The German Policeman,* and his work provided a general account of the various German police forces, including those of the Gendarmerie, a force based on the French model; the police forces of occupied Alsace and Lorraine prior to World War I; and German colonial police forces in the same period. With respect to the last, Schoenfelder noted the importance of military and police cooperation in the institution of "order and security" within German colonial possessions, a theme that would later prove relevant to the occupation of the East during World War II. *The Origins of the German Police* also highlighted the importance during the Great War of German police forces in the maintenance of the internal security of the home front. And it ended with a mere three pages dedicated to the National Socialist police, a curiosity explained by the author's note that a second volume devoted entirely to that topic was currently being prepared.[105]

Despite its brief length, the last chapter provided several powerful images of the National Socialist ideal for the police. A pen-and-ink drawing of a policeman carrying the newly acquired police flag with eagle and swastika, appearing above the caption "Finally a Peoples' Police," covers the top half of its first page. The following page also used a large pen-and-ink drawing depicting the murder of Police Sergeant Zauritz and the SA leader Maikowski on the evening of January 30, 1933, by "murderous Communist gunmen." Both men are shown being shot in the back, with Zauritz bent over backward, hands in the air, and Maikowski falling forward toward the pavement. The accompanying narrative details the triumphant celebration of Hitler's appointment as chancellor and the torchlit parade of SA, SS, and police units in front of the chancellery. The assassination of the two men occurred after the parade, as Maikowski's SA unit, escorted by Zauritz, marched through Charlottenburg.[106] The use of this story as the centerpiece of the chapter was intended to demonstrate the bond between the Party and its fighting organizations and the police, as from the first hours of National Socialist rule the SA and the police had been joined by shared blood in martyrdom for the movement.

The outbreak of war in 1939 engendered a veritable flood of popular literature describing the role of the Uniformed Police forces in the various theaters of war. A popularized account of police activities published shortly after the conclusion of the campaign in Poland entitled *Mounted Police in Poland* exemplifies the technique of conjoining racial stereotypes with criminal activity. In this work, Helmuth Koschorke, an Ordnungspolizei officer, described the activities of the mounted police forces during the invasion. Koschorke overlays the imagery of the "Asian" other on the Poles. He also emphasized the "criminal" nature of Polish opposition to the German occupation and generally portrays Poles as indolent, shifty, dishonest, malicious, and drunken. Koschorke began his introduction with a description of police responsibilities to hunt down "snipers" and "marauders" in order to reestablish "order." He then described the responsibility of the police units for "suppressing . . . flare-ups of guerrilla warfare [*Bandenkrieg*] with an iron fist." Later in his narrative, he quotes a police officer instructing his men on their unit's mission, which involves the "cleansing" of "murderous arsonists" and "the rendering harmless" of "murderous scoundrels."[107] The officer's choice of expressions provides a perfect example of the way in which the object of the action was delegitimized while the phrasing concerning the methods used employed relatively benign euphemisms, an attempt to play down the significance of the act itself. Indeed, one might expect the use of both devices in a popularized account aimed at the general public.

Koschorke's account focuses specifically on reinforcing racial prejudices with respect to the Slavic stereotype of the Catholic Pole. Likewise, Catholic clerics are depicted as hypocritical prevaricators who use their positions and their churches as cover for murderous acts aimed at the ethnic German population or the occupying German forces.[108] Noticeably absent from this account is a discussion of Poland's large Jewish population, a fact in part explained by Koschorke's publication in 1941 of *The Police Intervenes!* In this work, which adopts the narrative style of diary entries to track the progress of the German campaigns in 1939 and 1940, besides emphasizing the military tasks of the police in the Polish campaign, Koschorke gives full vent to the crudest expressions of anti-Semitism.[109]

In a manner similar to *Mounted Police in Poland*, *The Police Intervenes!* employs the strongest form of racial caricature in its depiction of Polish Jewry. In one entry, Koschorke deftly indicts both the Jews and the Polish aristocracy in the words of a simple Polish peasant who is ostensibly quoted as saying that he does not care who rules the country, as long it is neither of these two groups. In a subsequent entry, Koschorke describes a small town near Radom as a "nest of Jews" (*Judennest*) and later details his own response to his early encounters with Polish Jews: "When I think back on the last two days, I become nauseous. Jews, Jews, and again more Jews. We rounded up hundreds and hundreds of the most abominable examples."[110]

If Koschorke's use of extreme racial stereotypes in some cases overshadows his discussion of the activities of the police units themselves, such was not the case with the works of the police reservist Captain Hans Richter. In a foreword to the 1942 edition of Richter's *Police Operations*, Daluege remarked on the presence of the men of the police and the police battalions "standing by the side of the units of the Wehrmacht and the Waffen-SS," once again reinforcing the relationship between and shared mission of the three.[111] In contrast to Koschorke's, Richter's narrative primarily focuses on the activities of the police in Poland, Belgium, Holland, and France.

The chapter on Poland accounts for a little over one-third of the narrative and includes a description of the role of the police in the "resettlement" of ethnic Germans in areas confiscated from Polish owners. Police actions against the Polish population are downplayed, with only short descriptions of Poles shot while trying to steal or executed by summary courts and a brief discussion of a "pacification operation" that was broken off owing to poor weather. And Richter's racial prejudice with respect to Poland's Jewish and non-Jewish population was clearly evident, but much less directly expressed than Koschorke's. For example, Richter described the town of Rzeszow, the battalion headquarters, as a "dirty, poorly built nest inhabited by Jews." And of the difficulties experienced by the police in forcing the Jews of Łódź into a closed ghetto he remarked: "For the Jews did not want to understand that their supremacy also here in the East was ended for all time." The words *also here* referred to the continuation of a process that had begun in the Reich and was now being realized in the East. Finally, Richter noted that the creation of a "sterile living space" could not be achieved without taking the necessary action against this "nucleus of destruction," meaning the Jews.[112]

Richter's discussion of the people and places of Norway offers a dramatic contrast, Norway being a land in which the German policeman had been instructed to conduct himself, not as an occupier, but as a "friend and a guest."[113] (This same point was made by Daluege in a February 1941 speech to members of the National Socialist Driving Corps: "Operations in Norway and Holland yielded different tasks than in Poland because here [in Norway and Holland] other peoples stood before us.")[114] Whereas Richter depicted Norway as modern and developed and as inhabited by a civilized, Nordic people, like Koschorke he created the image of a backward and underdeveloped East inhabited by simpleminded Slavs and nefarious Jews, a message that any reader familiar with the propaganda of the Third Reich would be sure to recognize.

A final example of the police literature is a posthumous account of Uniformed Police actions during the initial invasion of Russia that appeared under Hans Richter's name in 1943. The volume—an oversized pictorial edition supplemented by short combat anecdotes—begins with a description of Richter's trip through swamps with his weapon at hand and a round in the chamber on his way to the headquarters of a police regiment to receive a briefing on the partisan war (*Bandenkampf*). This posture of readiness was made necessary by the presence of an enemy "lurking," like the omnipresent swarms of mosquitoes, in the inhospitable terrain, the "Bolshevist." According to Richter, this was a war that presented the men of the police with "completely new tasks." The pictorial format and the brief narrative offer little room for in-depth discussion; however, the description of "treacherous" inhabitants and the discussion of the "cleansing" of forests and towns as well as the "annihilation of numerous Bolshevists" offers a glimpse into the mentality of the German war in Russia.[115] It also served as a "short, precise spiritual preparation for policemen for a possible future employment in the war against the Soviet Union."[116]

Evaluating the Printed Message

Strikingly revealed in the examination of the various types of ideological literature related to the police are the sheer amount of material available as well as the various levels at which that material was targeted. The *PID* and the *Newsletter* offer examples of literature aimed at the political, ideological, and cultural indoctrination of the policemen, and the practice of using them as a basis for weekly indoctrination sessions reinforced their effect. Likewise, publications such as *The German Police* and *The Black Corps* offered an ancillary approach to the mind of the policemen under the guise of professional literature. Just as today's professionals in the areas of law, medicine, and academe look to their professional journals for information on the latest developments, information, techniques, or themes, so too did the German police, these types of magazines playing an important role in shaping their mind-set and establishing their internal culture. Finally, the popular accounts of police activities, especially after the outbreak of war, played a crucial role in creating a self-image of the police soldier standing side by side with the Waffen-SS and the Wehrmacht at the front, engaged in a difficult, dangerous, but necessary task. Policemen reading accounts of their green-clad colleagues receiving combat decorations would certainly feel a sense of pride and, perhaps, envy. Still, even those policemen sitting in a precinct building far from the fighting benefited from this image, especially those who fought a different war, one against Allied bombers in the cities of the Reich. These accounts, heavily laden with ideology, demonstrated that the police were, not second-class soldiers, but an important instrument in the expansion and consolidation of the Nazi empire.

Informal Mechanisms for Ideological Instruction

In addition to formalized indoctrination sessions and printed materials, a number of informal activities also supported the inculcation of ideology and group identity in the police corps. These activities ranged from the benign, such as visits by theater groups performing Bavarian folk comedies, to the malign, such as the showing of ideologically laden films.[117] Guidelines for the ideological training of the police included visits to movie theaters and the use of films to supplement classroom instruction.[118] In June 1940, Himmler reached an agreement with the Propaganda Ministry concerning the screening of popular films for the men of the Waffen-SS and the Uniformed Police serving in the occupied Eastern territories. In fact, Himmler ordered the viewing of the virulently anti-Semitic film *Jud Süß* by the "entire SS and police" during the course of the winter of 1940–1941. After viewing the film, one SS leader in the concentration camp at Sachsenhausen took out his rage on eight of the camp's inmates by beating each repeatedly with a wooden rod.[119] The practical effect of such films in forming group attitudes and dictating actions is, of course, more difficult to measure, but they certainly contributed to the reinforcement of existing racial prejudices within the organizational culture of the police.

In his work on the SS and the police, the German historian Jürgen Matthäus identified "fellowship evenings" (*Kameradschaftsabende*) as a powerful informal mechanism for increasing group cohesion among the police units.[120] An examination of the unit diary of Police Battalion (PB) 322 from July to December 1941 provides ample evidence to support this view. The scene of Gerhard Riebel's police company gathered around a candlelit tree on Christmas Eve to hear an ideological homily aimed at Jews and Bolshevists offers but one example. The men of PB 322 regularly attended "cozy fireside gatherings" in the wake of killing actions. On special occasions, beer might be dispensed, not as a prelude to drunken debauchery, but as a special ration designed to increase the festive feeling of the gathering. Likewise, after the conclusion of a major action to clear a forested area as a personal hunting preserve for Hermann Göring, one involving the "evacuation" of the area's inhabitants and the outright execution of many, members of the unit took a guided tour of the area on a small local railroad.

In another example, the unit celebrated its first-year anniversary in a "cozy get-together" on the evening of October 1. The following day, these same men rounded up 2,208 Jews and executed an additional 65 caught in the process of "escape attempts." On October 3, they executed 555 of the incarcerated Jews in a nearby forest camp.[121] Similarly, a visit by the head of the antipartisan effort in early December 1941 provided another opportunity for celebration and reflection as the men listened to a music recital commemorating their fallen comrades. Afterward, SS Obergruppenführer Bach spent an hour providing guidelines to the policemen concerning winter training objectives. Bach praised the policemen for their past performance and identified "new tasks" for the coming spring, tasks associated with the "contest between two worldviews that would not always be easy." Finally, the evening ended with a "Sieg Heil" to the Führer and the singing of national hymns.[122]

The camaraderie shared by the men of PB 322 was not unique. For example, Himmler emphasized the importance of such comradely get-togethers on the evening of execution actions to help prevent these "difficult duties" from "harming the minds and character" of participants.[123] Likewise, Bach advocated the use of "fellowship evenings" as a means to increase camaraderie and promote relaxation among antipartisan "hunting platoons" (*Jagdkommandos*) in the wake of their operations, operations that often involved the summary execution of partisans and Jews as well as the "elimination of bothersome witnesses" (*lästige Zeugen*).[124] Hans Richter also discussed the "good comradely relations" enjoyed by the policemen in their quarters in Poland as they sat by candlelight or around a fire enjoying a music recital by their colleagues and a group of Ukrainian folk dancers.[125] In another example, a theater group dedicated specifically to the entertainment of the police provided a show for the men of the Gendarmerie in Lublin in the middle of their "difficult duty" (antipartisan operations) in March 1943.[126]

Such fellowship evenings served an important purpose, instilling in the police a shared sense of comradeship and duty. The significance of these get-togethers is even more apparent when viewed as but one piece of a much larger effort including indoctrination sessions, literature, films, and visits by senior leaders to units at the front. Of course, these initiatives may not have been uniformly successful; still, it is impossible to ignore their breadth and the clear influence that they had in establishing an individual mentality and an overall organizational climate in which the fundamental precepts of National Socialist racial and ideological philosophy became the institutional norm.

Visiting the Troops

One striking aspect of the operations of the police units on the Eastern Front is the number of visits made to them by senior SS and police leaders—especially Himmler and Daluege—during the early stages of the invasion of the Soviet Union (July 1941 and after). These visits served two functions. First, Himmler and Daluege used them to check on the progress of their units in the apocalyptic battle with the forces of Jewish-Bolshevism that Himmler had prophesied in June 1936. Second, they used them to bring their ideological message directly to the troops, their trips coinciding on numerous occasions with killing operations.[127]

Despite the ideological indoctrination and the hammering home to the troops of the idea of their special mission in the East, Himmler clearly recognized that some policemen would not be able to kill in cold blood or would eventually reach the limits of their physical and psychological endurance. Therefore, he provided a way out by ordering that no one should be forced to participate in the killing operations,[128] informing his senior SS and police leaders, for example, that, despite the "sanctity" of orders, men who were at the "end of their rope" (*mit den Nerven fertig*) should be sent into retirement.[129] On the one hand, Himmler sought to encourage his subordinates by demonstrating that he did not merely give orders from behind a desk several thousand kilometers away from the fighting. On the other hand, he attempted to make the job easier for his policemen by placing responsibility for it in his and the Führer's hands.[130]

Creating SS and Police Leaders

Efforts to transform individuals into true believers represented only one part of a larger, overall plan. For example, the creation of the Main Office of the

Uniformed Police—a novel government institution—undoubtedly represented an effort on Himmler's part to shift the identification of the police from the Ministry of the Interior to the SS.[131] In this respect, the use of the term *main office* provided a semantic link and implicit association with the existing SS Main Office.[132]

One man sitting in Berlin, regardless of the extent of his power, could not by himself accomplish the goal of binding the police to the SS. Therefore, Himmler moved forward quickly to improve the cooperation between various branches of the police and increase his control at the regional level. One initiative was the creation on September 1, 1936, of the inspectors of the Uniformed Police to serve as the police representatives to the Reich governors. (Initially, the inspectors' authority was largely administrative—for example, they were responsible for ensuring the "smooth cooperation" of all police authorities during "large operations"—and their direct command authority was extremely limited.)[133] Another initiative, the appointment in February 1937 of an inspector general within the Schutzpolizei, the Gendarmerie, and the Community Police, was part of an effort to "tie theory to practice" by establishing a single position for evaluating the "organization, training, and continuous further development of the police."[134] While the effect of the latter initiative remained confined to the Uniformed Police, that of the former was felt immediately by all SS and police forces with Himmler's move to create a new position that conjoined the powers of the SS and the police at the regional level just as his appointment had accomplished at the national level.

On November 13, 1937, the Reich and Prussian Ministry of the Interior created the position of HSSPF. The original decree noted that, in the event of wartime mobilization, Himmler would appoint HSSPFs to control and coordinate the activities of all police forces within a given military district (*Wehrkreis*) in order to assist the civil administration.[135] The creation of the HSSPFs represented the ultimate merging of the SS and the police at the regional level, at which a single individual could act as a "guardian of unity," thus ensuring the implementation of political and racial policies coming from SS headquarters.[136] Himmler did not, however, wait for the outbreak of war and on September 15, 1938, ordered the establishment of HSSPF positions throughout the Reich "in order to finally ensure the union of the SS and the police in the highest positions of command authority."[137]

As later events clearly demonstrated, Himmler's ultimate plans for the HSSPFs were decidedly more ambitious and included the expansion of the SS and police power base throughout the Reich and especially in the occupied territories. The significance of the HSSPFs centered, not just on the title itself, but, more important, on the men chosen to fill these positions. In her

seminal study of the HSSPFs, Ruth Bettina Birn provided a demographic profile of these men and identified a number of similarities in their professional
backgrounds. First, the majority of the HSSPFs belonged to the "front generation," or men who had served in the German military in World War I.
Second, 40 percent received the Iron Cross, first-class, while almost 30 percent had been wounded in combat. Birn contends: "For most [of the HSSPFs]
the war [World War I] represented the fulfillment of their professional ambitions." In fact, the personal identity of these men was inextricably linked to
their military experience and their own self-image as soldiers, and many continued to describe themselves as soldiers even after their demobilization at
the end of the war.[138]

The HSSPFs were not merely "soldiers" shaped by their military experience; they were the elite of the SS, "Party soldiers" who were tasked with
shaping the police forces under their control in their own images and defining the organizational culture within their commands. Not only did they
establish for the policemen under their command parameters for expected
behavior, but they also created an environment that linked martial values
with National Socialist racial ideology.

The position of HSSPF was perfectly suited to the coordination of wartime
police and military duties, a not coincidental aim of the *Reichsführer*. Indeed,
after the outbreak of war, the HSSPFs played a central role in the initiation
and coordination of National Socialist racial policies in the East. In the occupied Eastern territories, Himmler's authority as Reich leader of the SS led to a
situation in which "the HSSPF[s] were in practice independent even of those
civil administration authorities to whom they were in theory 'subordinate.' "[139]
Guidelines issued in December 1939 noted the authority of the HSSPF to lead
"all joint preparations of the SS, the Uniformed Police, the Security Police,
and the SD that serve the fulfillment of Reich defensive measures of these institutions." The guidelines further directed that the HSSPF "assumes command"
of all SS and police forces in "all cases" involving joint operations for "specific tasks."[140]

As the war progressed, Himmler focused on increasing the influence of
the HSSPFs both in the Reich and abroad by expanding their charter beyond
an "equal responsibility for police and political matters" to "giving priority
to the *political side* and making the HSSPF[s] responsible within their area
for representing the political interests of the RFSS [Reich leader of the SS] or
the SS overall in negotiations with the Wehrmacht, Party, or State authorities."[141] For example, in a letter of June 15, 1943, Himmler informed Gottlob
Berger, the head of SS Main Office, of the necessity to "build up and
strengthen" the position of the HSSPF in order to prevent loss of HSSPFs'
areas of responsibility and span of control. Himmler warned: "In one hand

we are strong, but in many hands we are weak."[142] Not coincidentally, the letter to Berger came at a time when Himmler was in a struggle with Alfred Rosenberg, the minister for the occupied Eastern territories, over the authority of the HSSPFs in the East.[143] In the end, Himmler's ability to strengthen the position of the HSSPFs allowed him to impose himself directly into the chain of command in the occupied Eastern territories, and this proved decisive in the conduct of genocide. The HSSPFs emerged as the Reich leader's trusted agents in the conduct of racial war, and their ability to martial the entire force of the SS and the police proved critical to the success achieved in this endeavor.

During the prewar period, Himmler and Daluege pursued a series of administrative, organizational, training, and operational initiatives designed to bind the green corps of the police with its SS counterparts. The incorporation of SS and SA men into the police ranks, ideological initiatives, focused recruitment efforts, and the creation of the HSSPFs all combined to move the police toward Himmler's ultimate goal of fusing the two organizations into an organic whole. Without a doubt, the outbreak of the war in 1939 affected these plans and forced numerous changes as the size of both the SS and the Uniformed Police grew. Still, the war also provided an opportunity to test the effectiveness of Himmler's and Daluege's prewar efforts to shape the police into both a military and an ideological instrument, and it was in Poland that these "political soldiers" faced their first test.

FOUR

BAPTISM OF FIRE

We police went by the phrase, "Whatever serves the state is right, whatever harms the state is wrong. . . . [I]t never even entered my head that these orders could be wrong. Although I am aware that it is the duty of the police to protect the innocent, I was however at the time convinced that the Jewish people were not innocent but guilty. I believed all the propaganda that Jews were criminals and subhuman. . . . The thought that one should oppose or evade the order to take part in the extermination of the Jews never entered my head either."
—Policeman Kurt Möbius (November 1961)

The invasion of Poland on September 1, 1939, opened the first act of Hitler's racial war in the East. In comparison to the activities of the Uniformed Police in Poland, those in the earlier occupations of Austria and Czechoslovakia constituted mere dress rehearsals for the start of a series of military campaigns that would put the entire SS and police complex to the test. In the execution of National Socialist racial policy, the men of the Uniformed Police would not be found wanting. As the early activities in the conquest and occupation of Poland demonstrated, the Uniformed Police played a key role in the subjugation of the Polish nation. Himmler and Daluege received handsome dividends for their efforts to inculcate in the police leadership a martial spirit bound with an SS ethic. In truth, the prewar cooperation of the Uniformed Police with the Security Police and the use of the former against the domestic enemies of the Third Reich, including Communists, Jews, and members of the clergy, laid a foundation on which increasingly more radical measures could be built. The ease by which the men of the police transitioned into the role of occupiers and their conduct in the prosecution of both war and atrocity provided clear indications of the poisonous effects of National Socialist indoctrination when coupled with the ideal of the political soldier.

Preparing for War

According to one historian, the decision to employ police battalions in the campaign against Poland was made several months prior to the actual attack.[1] Without doubt, the performance of the police formations in the occupations of Austria and Czechoslovakia provided ample evidence of their utility and justified their continued use. However, the invasion of Poland proved different from these earlier campaigns in two key respects. First, this would be a "hot war," involving significant combat between the armies of both countries. Second, unlike in the cases of Austria and the Sudetenland, in which the Third Reich was reclaiming and embracing lost Aryan brethren, Nazi racial policy cast Poland as backward and illegitimate and its inhabitants as degenerate and racially inferior.[2] In a meeting with his senior military leaders on August 22, 1939, Hitler provided clear marching orders calling for the "annihilation of Poland": "We seek the annihilation of the enemy, which we must pursue in ever new ways."[3] After the outbreak of hostilities, Hitler again emphasized the need to "annihilate the Polish people," setting a tone that boded ominously for the course of the war and the fate of the Polish nation.[4]

In some respects, the invasion of Poland found the Uniformed Police ill prepared for the task of conducting sustained military operations. For example, the police formations suffered from a lack of heavy and light machine guns.[5] Additionally, the lack of adequate motorized transportation plagued the police battalions and remained a significant problem as late as February 1940, with the Wehrmacht forced to assist in the transport of supplies to the police units stationed in Poland. The shortage of sufficient transportation resulted in large part from the earlier transfer of some 60 percent of police vehicles to the armed forces during the mobilization of the Landespolizei into the Wehrmacht in 1935 and 1936.[6] In one respect, it appeared that the planned scale of police operations caught Daluege and his staff unprepared. In a letter of September 5, 1939, Daluege noted: "The assembly of new police battalions is greatly hampered owing to the question of equipment. . . . [W]ithout knapsacks and tents, mess kits and canteens, it is impossible to employ these troops." He then emphasized the importance of the request given the "urgency of [the] employment of the police battalions in Poland" and concluded: "At the present time, police battalions are being considered in a strength of 20,000 men."[7] In fact, the general quartermaster of the German army, General Eduard Wagner, urgently requested the assignment of additional police battalions during a meeting with Daluege on the same day.[8]

Daluege's appeal produced the desired results, as revealed in a letter from Himmler to the treasurer of the NSDAP (National Socialist German Workers' Party), Francis X. Schwarz, thanking him for the delivery of twenty thousand sets of equipment for the police battalions. In a letter of September 13,

Himmler remarked: "These police battalions . . . are already situated here in Poland and have their hands full, in order to overcome and take prisoner the roaming 'franc-tireur' and scattered elements of the Polish army."[9] The use of the imagery of the *franc-tireur* (guerrilla) was not coincidental. In one respect, Himmler was consciously pursuing a policy of criminalizing popular resistance, a policy reminiscent of the reaction to the resistance offered by guerrillas during the Franco-Prussian War of 1870–1871. In this case, German forces conducted acts of retaliation against French men and women accused of sniping or other acts of aggression. In fact, Bismarck remarked: "We are hunting them down pitilessly." And he continued: "They are not soldiers: we are treating them as murderers."[10] In 1914, the ghosts of the *francs-tireurs* arose once again as an apparition that haunted the imperial forces contributing to German atrocities in the early stages of the Great War.[11] Likewise, Wehrmacht, SS, and police forces labeled members of the resistance *francs-tireurs* and *Freischärler* (guerrillas) in order to justify executions during the Eastern campaigns of World War II.[12]

Going to War

The role played by the Uniformed Police during the opening weeks of the war ran the spectrum from traditional police and security duties to those associated with the implementation of National Socialist racial policy in its most destructive form. In the initial days of the war, Daluege assembled twelve police battalions, a number subsequently increased to twenty-one battalions and two mounted police units, by the end of September.[13] These police battalions were assigned to each of the Wehrmacht's numbered armies and subordinated to the military commander of their respective army with orders to "sweep behind the advancing Armies."[14] The rapid advance of the Wehrmacht proved a mixed blessing for these units as numerous police battalions became engaged in combat with portions of the Polish army bypassed by the army. For example, Police Battalion (PB) 41 received a commendation from the army for its actions on September 9 in the occupation of Łódź and the protection of the Eighth Army's flank. Several days later, PB 41 once again played an important role in the "decisive" battle for Kutno by "cleansing" the battlefield of "fleeing and scattered remnants of the Polish armed forces."[15] In October, the battalion received orders to "subdue Polish bands and guerrillas [*Freischärler*]" in the rear of the German army.[16] A senior police leader also referred to the use of the police battalions in "action[s] during pacification operations to battle Polish gangs that had been formed from freed prisoners."[17]

Words and Meanings

As with the use of the term *franc-tireur,* the description of Polish armed resistance as *bands* or *guerrillas* was not coincidental. During the course of the war, the police reports became an important forum for highlighting efforts to delegitimize any form of Polish resistance, whether verbal or physical. For example, the reports consistently employed the terms *bandits* (*Banditen*) and *gangs* (*Banden*)—instead of, for example, *resistance fighters* and *partisans*—to describe armed opposition to German authority. On the one hand, the terms themselves highlight a mentality that heightened German racial prejudices with respect to Poles. On the other hand, the linguistic criminalization of these groups provided the ostensible pretext for the actions taken to reestablish law and order.

During a speech in 1940, Major General of the Police Rudolf Querner remarked that the experience of PB 41 in direct combat was not atypical, as "every other battalion had battles with scattered elements of the Polish army during the months of September and October 1939."[18] In addition to frontline fighting, the police units also conducted more traditional police tasks, including the guarding of prisoner and weapons transports and the protection of power plants and important industrial sites. Even these traditional security tasks were not free of racial implications. For example, the use of the police battalions in guarding large groups of Polish prisoners of war had racial implications as the police separated these men into groups of Jews, Poles, and ethnic Germans.[19] Similarly, the use of the police to provide "immediate protection for important armament and economic firms" represented one of the first steps in the economic exploitation of the country, a practice that became part and parcel of National Socialist occupation policy throughout Europe.[20]

Operation Tannenberg

In addition to the units of the Wehrmacht and the Uniformed Police battalions that entered Poland, Himmler had established five Einsatzgruppen (Special Mission Groups) to accompany each of the numbered German armies at the start of the campaign. Shortly after the invasion, Himmler ordered the creation of two additional Einsatzgruppen, including one under the command of SS-Obergruppenführer Udo von Woyrsch, a man who had "earned his bones" for his demonstrated brutality during the suppression of the Röhm putsch in 1934.[21] The Einsatzgruppen provided a ready-made and deadly instrument for the implementation of racial policy against the Polish people.

Under the code name Operation Tannenberg, the leaders of the Einsatzgruppen were carefully selected from among SS officers for their ability
"ruthlessly and harshly to achieve National Socialist aims."[22] The stated mission for these units involved the "combat of all enemies of the Reich and the
German people in the rear area of the fighting troops."[23] However, early in
September, Heydrich (chief of the Security Police and Security Service [SD])
revealed that their real mission was the liquidation of Poland's nobility,
clergy, and Jews.[24] In 1940, Heydrich repeated this assertion and informed
Daluege that Hitler directed the "extraordinarily radical . . . order for the
liquidation of various circles of the Polish leadership, [killings] that ran into
the thousands."[25] In human terms, Poles caught within the destructive mael-
strom of the German assault included Polish nationalists, Jews, Communists,
and members of the Catholic clergy, the intelligentsia, and the Polish nobility.[26] Operating from copies of lists of suspected "anti-German" elements
compiled by the SD in Berlin, the Wehrmacht, the Einsatzgruppen, and members of the Uniformed Police were well prepared to deal with these putative
enemies of the Third Reich during the German occupation.[27]

If Hitler selected the Einsatzgruppen as the cutting edge for the enforcement of racial policy, this task was not entrusted only to the men of the Security Police, the SD, and the SS. In the case of Einsatzgruppe von Woyrsch,
over half the unit's members, 2,250 men in five battalions, came from the
ranks of the Uniformed Police.[28] Einsatzgruppe von Woyrsch supported the
Fourteenth Army on its march into Galicia and received orders for the "radical suppression of the flickering Polish uprising in the newly occupied portions of Upper Silesia."[29] Himmler's order to von Woyrsch to provide him
with situation reports every three hours also indicates the high level of interest in the activities of the unit, a level of interest repeated in the reporting
procedures of both the Einsatzgruppen and the Command Staff RFSS (Kommandostab Reichsführer SS) during the campaign in Russia.[30] Finding no
uprising on their arrival into the area, von Woyrsch's men, including his uniformed policemen, burned down synagogues in the cities of Kattowitz
(Katowice) and Bendsburg (Będzin) and massacred Jews and Christian Poles
in the vicinity of Przemyœl and Tarnów.[31] In the case of the massacres, uniformed policemen killed almost 100 Polish civilians, including Jewish children, and set fire to the synagogue in Będzin on September 8.[32]

The Uniformed Police and the Conduct of Racial Policy

That the police formations were used as security forces should not be surprising, just as the employment of police forces in direct combat, although

perhaps unexpected, should be seen as a natural extension of prewar efforts to shape them into a capable military instrument. The incorporation of the police into the Einsatzgruppen, however, reflected the equally important prewar effort to create political soldiers to enforce the racial policy of the Third Reich. In this respect, it was not just the battalions assigned to von Woyrsch that demonstrated their capability and willingness to pursue the regime's ideological objectives.

In their first battle campaign, the police formations attached to the German army demonstrated their adaptability and utility in the conduct of reprisal and the prosecution of the Third Reich's racial policies. These actions ranged from the threatening to the horrific. For example, at Himmler's orders, the police established "sentry posts" at synagogues.[33] The mistreatment of Jews by the police ranged from their use in forced labor (e.g., the cleaning of streets and sidewalks) to the widespread cutting of their hair and shaving of their beards.[34] Policemen also routinely participated in the public abuse or beating of Jews.[35] That policemen publicly humiliated Jews and took satisfaction in doing so provides additional evidence of Himmler's and Daluege's success in instilling a profound antipathy toward the Jews in the entire police organization. Clearly, men who shaved the beards of Jews, gloated at the sight of them cleaning streets with toothbrushes, or even physically abused them were not necessarily prepared to murder Jews; however, the overall effect of these actions, combined with the senior leadership's acceptance and promotion of them, further extended the boundaries of what was considered permissible and desirable police behavior and affected the organizational culture of the institution. Such acts of cruelty, brutality, and atrocity proved a natural extension of prewar rhetoric and actions and provided the springboard for further radicalization in the following years.

The tendency toward radicalization and the move to expand the boundaries of the permissible proved to be a surprisingly rapid process, as demonstrated in a directive from the Uniformed Police Main Office on September 5. The directive outlined the methods for the conduct of pacification operations in the most explicit terms. It discussed the use of a police battalion in planned reprisal actions in the vicinity of Częstochowa (Tschenstochau) and directed the battalion commander "to take the most drastic actions and measures such as those in the upper Silesian industrial area, [including] the hanging of Polish franc-tireurs from light poles as a visible symbol for the entire population."[36] In this case, the Wehrmacht beat the police to the punch by executing ninety-nine Polish civilians, but the police formations had numerous opportunities to create "visible symbols" of their own.[37]

The willingness of the police to participate in the pacification of the Polish resistance found its testimony in a letter of September 15, 1939, from Walter von Keudell, a committed German nationalist and former district president (*Landrat*) in Königsberg, praising the performance of police forces in the occupation of Poland. Keudell commended the police for "courageous activities" and remarked: "I can give the police formations and their leaders only the absolute best marks for their activities during the first thirteen days of the war." He continued: "Especially since the police possessed absolutely no case files [*Aktenvorgänge*] or other guidelines for these activities but instead had to rely on their own courage and common sense." Keudell then intimated the reason for his glowing evaluation: "For obvious reasons, I do not want to provide a written report of the specific activities of the police, quite extensive [activities] that were bound up with the energetic use of their weapons."[38]

Keudell's letter provides two insights into the actions of the police forces in the first weeks of the campaign. First, even in the absence of specific guidance, the police knew what actions to take in order to master the situation and to secure the German occupation. Second, they proved ready and willing to use their weapons to do so. In fact, Keudell's letter offered direct evidence of Himmler's success in shaping the police into model political soldiers, and the actions of these men spoke louder than words.

The activities of PB 61 in the opening two months of the campaign offer several examples of a unit that did not hesitate to energetically use its weapons. The battalion departed Dortmund on September 6, reaching the Polish city of Poznań (Posen) six days later. Soon after its arrival, it conducted "cleansing" operations aimed at Polish "bandits" and "snipers." It also captured hundreds of former Polish soldiers and turned them over to the Wehrmacht. In addition, individual companies and platoons routinely participated in the execution of small groups of twenty to thirty Poles sentenced to death by Wehrmacht court or by a summary court composed of officers within the battalion for opposition activities or weapons possession. These "court proceedings" normally lasted ten minutes and seldom more than twenty minutes, offering one indication of their perfunctory nature.[39] PB 103 offers another example. Operating in Poznań in early October, it concentrated on house searches, looking for weapons. This unit, composed mostly of police reservists, relied largely on information from ethnic Germans and "rapidly delivered the just judgment [execution]" for weapons owners.[40] Speed in conducting the executions clearly outweighed judicial process.

Polish Jews were not, however, the only objects of police brutality. The commander of PB 61, Major Friedrich Dederky, sentenced Roman Pawlowski, a Catholic priest in the town of Kalisch, to death for possession of ammunition on October 18, 1939. According to a German report, the execution of Pawlowski led to several attempted acts of resistance, which in turn provided the necessary pretext for the arrest by the Security Police of "dangerous Poles" among the senior ranks of the clergy. The report also remarked that the Security Police, "in cooperation" with the Uniformed Police, ensured that these Catholic priests received their "just punishment."[41] The cooperation of the Security and Uniformed Police in these executions is reminiscent of their prewar collaboration in the investigation and surveillance of German clergy and once again highlights the close relationship between both branches of the police, a relationship that remained strong throughout the war.

The execution of Father Pawlowski proved to be the first in a series of violent acts that claimed the lives of over thirty Poles (most executed on charges of weapons possession) and included a pogrom aimed at Kalisch's Jewish population and involving widespread mistreatment, including beating and incarceration in forced labor camps.[42] During this period, the battalion's Second Company and Gendarmerie personnel arrested forty-six Poles on charges of mistreatment of or incitement against ethnic Germans. The report does not detail the fate of these persons, but it does note that, in another area, seven Poles accused of being "German haters" and "gang leaders" were shot by members of the Gendarmerie while trying to escape.[43] During the course of the war, the phrase *shot while trying to escape* became a routine part of the police lexicon and provided an expedient means of bypassing administrative or legal requirements and implementing summary execution.

Wehrmacht and Police Cooperation

The participation of Wehrmacht and police forces in the prosecution of pacification and reprisal actions indicates an important point. The German army's almost pathological fear of the actions of civilians and irregulars, which traced back to the experience of Prussian forces in France in 1870–1871, coupled with real and imagined Polish atrocities, helped create a situation in which preexisting racial prejudice facilitated atrocity. As in the case of Belgian Louvain in 1914, the Polish city of Bydgoszcz (Bromberg) provided German propaganda with a ready-made cause célèbre.[44] In this case, however, pro-Nazi sympathizers among the city's ethnic German population engaged retreating Polish troops. The resultant retaliatory actions by the Polish army claimed the lives of over a thousand ethnic Germans, including insurrectionists as well as innocent bystanders.[45]

By the time German forces reached Bydgoszcz on September 5, "Bromberg's Bloody Sunday" became a symbol of Polish perfidy and provided the pretext for bloody retribution against the city's Polish inhabitants. Continued sporadic resistance throughout the city and several instances of sniping led the military administration to institute a large-scale pacification operation, resulting in the arrest of several thousand Poles as well as the summary execution of those found with any weapons, including flintlock rifles and bayonets.[46] During this operation, the military authorities relied heavily on the Security Police and the Uniformed Police forces assigned to Einsatzgruppe IV, a precedent that would find repeated expression in the coming years. Furthermore, the men of the Uniformed Police proved up to the task. Lieutenant General of Police Arthur Mülverstedt supervised the actions of PB 6 as the battalion conducted "cleansing actions" throughout the city, the policemen arbitrarily arresting and executing Poles within the community, including 370 persons in the period between September 9 and September 11 alone.[47] Mülverstedt, a former officer in World War I and "fanatical National Socialist," proved to be a perfect choice for this duty. In fact, Daluege recognized his leading role in the "annihilation of the Polish enemy state" by naming him as the commander of the effort to create the training battalions and, later, commander of the SS Police Division.[48]

This radicalization of the police—their use in enforcing draconian Wehrmacht antiresistance and antipartisan objectives—stemmed, not just from the September 5 Uniformed Police Main Office directive, but also from several directives issued by senior Wehrmacht officers during the first week of the invasion under the pretext of military necessity. These directives—mandating the summary execution of those found with weapons and legitimizing reprisal in the event of resistance—proved important in two respects. First, they began a process that undercut traditional protections for Polish civilians—specifically those accused of resistance activities—broadening the charter of the police units operating under army control beyond simple security duties to include the commission of atrocities. Second, they demonstrated the emerging bond between the Security and the Uniformed Police and they highlighted the German army's reliance on these forces to execute pacification operations.

This reliance on the police also places Wehrmacht commanders' subsequent complaints of SS and police excesses during the campaign in another light. When one makes a bargain with the devil, as the Wehrmacht had done with the SS and police forces, one must accept its full implications and natural consequences. And it must also be noted that some Wehrmacht commanders praised the activities of the police, indicating at least some measure of support for them within the armed forces. For example, General Conrad von Cochenhausen, the commander of the Tenth Infantry Division, praised the police battalions for their performance operating alongside his forces "since the march into [Poland]."[49] Cochenhausen's division was one of the primary units involved in the "murderous march of the XIII Corps" during the initial weeks of the invasion, the unit participated in numerous acts of reprisal and atrocity directed against Polish civilians, leaving a trail of dead bodies and destroyed communities in its wake.[50] In short, Cochenhausen's recognition of the actions of the police battalions provides another piece of indirect evidence concerning the complicity of the formations in the conduct of atrocity.

By the second week of the war, the guidelines for Wehrmacht and police cooperation were no longer being made in the field but in the offices of the Bendlerstrasse. On September 12, 1939, the headquarters of the commander in chief of the army issued a directive mandating the voluntary turn-in by Polish civilians of "all firearms and ammunition, hand grenades, explosives, and other war equipment" within twenty-four hours to the nearest military post or police station at the penalty of summary execution. In addition, the directive warned: "Violent acts of any kind against the Wehrmacht or its members will be punished by death."[51] Similarly, the commanders (*Kommandeure*) of the Uniformed Police directed their men to closely study the Wehrmacht-issued *Instructions for the Conduct of German Soldiers in Occupied Poland*. These instructions admonished German soldiers to behave as representatives of the Reich and warned: "Behavior toward the Jews requires no special discussion for soldiers of the National Socialist Reich." Klaus-Michael Mallmann correctly contends that these instructions sent the unambiguous message that Poles were "subhuman" and the Jews "free game."[52]

Even after the end of the campaign, some Wehrmacht commanders continued to rely on the police to control the behavior of their men. In a letter of November 13, 1939, the military commander of Warsaw, Lieutenant General Neumann Neurode, informed the commander of the city's police regiment that, despite several warnings and numerous punishments, some soldiers continued to act with complete disregard for the "honorable conduct of a soldier." He cited several examples of "dishonorable" conduct, including German soldiers visiting Polish prostitutes, walking arm in arm with Jewish women, and bartering with Jewish merchants. Neumann Neurode's worries about the effect of such activities on "discipline and order" and his request that police patrols be on the lookout for them highlight both the acceptance of the racial precepts of German occupation and the expectation of their enforcement by the police.[53]

When coupled with orders from Berlin, including Himmler's directive of early September calling for the summary execution of all "insurgents," these directives created an environment that was not only conducive to but in point of fact promoted the use of the most severe measures in dealing with the Polish population.[54] Interestingly, this pattern of transmitting selected army orders to police formations occurred again in April 1940 after the Wehrmacht High Command notified military units in Poland of the forthcoming Foreign Ministry pamphlet entitled *The Polish Atrocities against the Ethnic Germans in Poland.* The High Command was sending copies of the pamphlet to selected commands, but especially to Wehrmacht personnel serving at prisoner-of-war camps to ensure that "every German soldier guarding Polish prisoners of war must know [*sic*] of the shameful acts in Bromberg and Uniejow." In turn, the head of the Uniformed Police Operations Office, Adolf von Bomhard, forwarded the Wehrmacht letter to *all* police offices with the remark to pay especially close attention to the admonition that "one does not give one's hand" or "provide special favors" to such persons.[55] Similarly, after the invasion of the Soviet Union, the senior leadership of the SS and police forwarded a copy of the virulently anti-Bolshevist and anti-Semitic "Reichenau Order" of October 1941 to police units serving in the East.[56] These examples all demonstrate that the senior leadership recognized the value of using the Wehrmacht's messages for their own purposes.

In one respect, these "legal" directives normalized draconian measures and facilitated the transformation of the police by further underlining the military identity of units locked in combat with racial inferiors, and, in the case of the Jews, racial enemies. But not just police battalions became involved in actions directed at the Polish population. Members of the Gendarmerie did as well. Already on September 10, the operations officer of the First Army Corps noted the execution of "eighty Jewish civilian prisoners" by members of the Gendarmerie.[57] In addition, Gendarmerie personnel reportedly conducted public executions in Bydgoszcz of forty and fifty-one persons on September 5 and 10, respectively, and of twenty-eight persons in Kostrzyn on October 20.[58]

Controlling the Countryside

These Gendarmerie personnel were part of a force of 103 officers and 5,805 men from the Schutzpolizei and the Gendarmerie mobilized, in addition to the police battalions, for individual duties (*Einzeldienst*) during the initial military occupation. According to Querner: "These forces took over the police duties of providing order in the cities and the countryside." Querner continued by describing their main duties as, "first and foremost, the prevention of food profiteering, destruction of vital goods, looting, raids, attacks, etc."[59] Gendarmerie personnel played a key role in ensuring public compliance with published administrative regulations, especially those concerned with food hoarding and price speculation. Primarily organized into small units in the countryside, they also assisted in the search for weapons caches as well as in the conduct of operations against "bandits" and partisan bands.[60]

On the basis of the continuing need for more forces in the East, on September 20 the Uniformed Police Operations Office issued mobilization orders for 1,279 members of the Gendarmerie to report within twenty-four hours for individual duty in the East.[61] The shortage of personnel emerged as a chronic problem for German military and police forces throughout occupied Europe during the course of the war and led to repeated complaints within Germany and in the occupied territories.[62]

Explaining Motivation

During Hitler's blitzkrieg against Poland, the men of the SS, the SD, and the Security and Uniformed Police demonstrated their abilities in the conduct of military duties as well as in the prosecution of reprisal actions and racial policy. In the case of the Uniformed Police, many among the men assigned to the police battalions as well as those mobilized for individual duty proved themselves to be first-class soldiers and executioners. In Poland, Himmler and Daluege had their first opportunity to test the effectiveness of their prewar efforts to shape the police into political soldiers, and the results justified their efforts. Clearly, Himmler had realized his January 1937 vow that his police officer corps would not become a second-class officer corps. However, if we are to explain his success, we must examine the motivations of the policemen involved in this first campaign, their actions being what set the precedent for later events.

The words of individual policemen provide some of the clearest indications of motivation. On September 14, 1939, like other police leaders, Rudolf Querner, a senior police commander in northwest Germany and a future higher SS and police leader (HSSPF), eagerly volunteered for action, notifying Daluege that the policemen under his command stood ready to defend the German Reich and the *Volk* wherever they were sent. As noted earlier, Querner remarked: "Although the primary task of the Uniformed Police is the protection of the domestic front in the homeland, still we request that we be given the opportunity to demonstrate that we also know how to combat external enemies, whether in conjunction with the SS-VT [SS-Verfügungstruppe] or as a part of the Wehrmacht."[63] Querner's zeal and willingness to assist either the SS or the Wehrmacht provided evidence of his knowledge of the activities of the Einsatzgruppen and the cooperation provided by the Uniformed Police in the prosecution of their gruesome tasks.

His offer thus demonstrated his commitment to support both the regime's military and its racial initiatives in Poland.[64]

The identification with martial values and the belief in the ideological underpinnings of the campaign against Poland were not limited to the senior members of the police leadership. One example of the martial attitude in the police can be seen in a letter from Gustav Berger, a policeman from Offenbach, to his hometown newspaper in November 1939. Berger reported: "Our friends in Offenbach have probably often asked themselves the question, 'Where are our old Offenbach policemen, one doesn't see them around anymore?' Well, they, like so many other German men, are deep in enemy territory in order to fulfill their duty, just like all other German soldiers."[65]

Descriptions of Polish Jews by members of the police in the first month of the campaign also demonstrate the effectiveness of prewar efforts at shaping an anti-Semitic mind-set. A situation report prepared by PB 102 provided the following evaluation of the Polish Jew: "He is doglike servile, faking submissiveness, [he] is and remains a dangerous element within the body of the Polish people [*Volkskörper*]." The report then suggests a method for dealing with the "perfidious Jew": "He must be . . . strictly supervised and relentlessly covered by the most severe punishments on the slightest pretext."[66] In another example, a police company diary discussed the unit's actions in conducting house-to-house searches in Poznań. The diarist noted: "The worst part of all is the appearance of the unsightly [*unappetitlich*] Jewish women, scantily clad or not dressed at all, but with made-up red lips, who run around the apartments like startled hens." He continued: "For us, this is a typical sign of the moral depravity of the Jews in Poland." Apart from the barely suppressed eroticism, this unit diary is important in several respects. First, such war diaries served as open records for documenting the accomplishments of a particular unit as well as the major events experienced. Second, the writer's use of the phrase *for us* provides a clear indication that this reflected, not a single impression of one specific person, but a feeling universal among the company's members. Similarly, an entry recording the capture of sixty-one prisoners in the search of a village and farmhouses and another noting that "one of the most important duties of this watch period involved the guarding of hostages" illustrate the familiarity of these men with the conduct of actions supporting the Third Reich's political and ideological efforts.[67]

Evaluating the Performance of the Police

In their baptism of fire, Himmler's police formations had shown themselves as versatile and capable military units, a fact recognized, not only by the leadership of the SS and the police, but by senior commanders within the German armed forces as well. On September 21, General of the Infantry Hans Beyer, commander of the Eighteenth Army, personally commended the men of PB 63 for their actions during the campaign. Beyer described the complete range of the battalion's duties, including providing security for captured material, the guarding of prisoners of war, enforcing traffic regulations, and creating and arming Ukrainian auxiliary formations; however, he began his commendation by highlighting the role of the police in "mopping-up and pacification actions," a clear indication of the important role played by this unit and other police formations in direct combat.[68]

One of the most evident indications of the satisfaction with the performance of his policemen in Poland involved Hitler's September 18, 1939, decision to create an independent SS Police Division, composed entirely of officers and enlisted men drawn from the Uniformed Police.[69] Not only did the creation of an SS division composed of policemen offer direct recognition of the role of the police in the attack on and subjugation of Poland, but it also served as another step in the achievement of Himmler's vision for the institutional and ideological merging of the police and the SS. Likewise, the later selection of Mülverstedt as the commander of the division provided unambiguous evidence of the organization's ideal leadership type as well as the rewards to be gained by faithful prosecution of the regime's racial policies.[70] The SS Police Division fought in the campaign against France, but it was the unit's performance in Russia that resulted in Himmler's decision in February 1942 to accept all policemen in the division not currently in the SS directly into the organization.[71]

On the one hand, the establishment of the SS Police Division provided a cadre of men who would later receive special consideration for entry into the ranks of the police.[72] On the other hand, it directly supported Himmler's plans for the creation of militarized SS formations on an equal footing with their army counterparts in capability and firepower. In turn, the Polish campaign provided the catalyst for "the explosive growth of militarized SS formations," and it was not coincidental that this expansion included the police.[73] Likewise, after the campaign, Himmler took advantage of the opportunity provided by the war to place the police battalions serving in Poland under the special jurisdiction of the SS and police courts and, thus, effectively of the SS, an organization openly committed to the regime's ideological precepts and demonstrably complicit in the prosecution of its racial policies.[74] This initial move to place police forces under SS jurisdiction provided another important step in further loosening the restrictions on police behavior and further shaping the organizational culture of the police by expanding the bounds of acceptable behavior among its members.

In the aftermath of the campaign, Daluege also recognized the important role played by the police battalions and their potential utility for future campaigns. In a letter of March 7, 1940, Daluege wrote to Himmler requesting an immediate meeting to discuss "fundamental questions of the further employment of the Uniformed Police in many new tasks."[75] Two weeks later, in a letter concerning replacements for the officer corps of the police battalions, Daluege ordered that priority be given to graduates of SS leadership schools, qualified policemen from the ranks, and, finally, officers from the Wehrmacht who had been demobilized owing to war injuries, in that order. Furthermore, he directed that police training battalion officers should be selected solely on the basis of their military talents and that only *after* the war would they be evaluated on their potential for police duties.[76] This comment aptly demonstrated the ascendancy of the martial identity within the police being prepared for imminent campaigns in Scandinavia and the West.

A Younger Man's War?

Himmler's and Daluege's initiatives both provide further evidence of the special status enjoyed by the police battalions in the wake of the Polish campaign. They also highlight the police leadership's continued efforts both to militarize these forces and to merge their identities with that of the SS. Still, not all had proceeded as smoothly as Himmler and Daluege had wished. For example, the mass mobilization of older police reservists concerned both and had resulted in cases in which men over the age of sixty received orders for duty in the campaign.[77] In a visit to Poland during the campaign, Daluege recalled meeting a group of five police reservists between the ages of fifty-five and sixty-five. The men were all volunteers, and each wore an Iron Cross first-class awarded for combat in World War I. According to Daluege, these men stated that they had joined the battalion because it was their duty as "participants in the World War and as National Socialists."[78] For Daluege, these men represented the true spirit of the police reservists, men of martial bearing committed to Hitler and his movement. Still, the use of overaged reservists was not the standard sought by the chief of the Uniformed Police, and, in early 1940, police reservists over the age of forty-five conducting individual duty received transfers from Poland for duty in the Reich.[79]

In January 1940, Daluege also signed an order prohibiting the assignment of "police reservists" over the age of thirty-nine to duty with the police battalions in the occupied Eastern territories.[80] Significantly, this prohibition did not apply to "regular" or active-duty policemen, who had spent years in the organization, with immense efforts having been devoted to their socialization as political soldiers. Units composed of police reservists, however, were relatively recent creations, and their hurried mobilization allowed for far less certainty as to their political and military reliability, at least until they too could be fully trained and integrated into the ideological and martial ranks of their regular counterparts.

Daluege's prohibition on the employment of men over the age of thirty-nine (those born in 1900 or later) as reservists was not an arbitrary decision and reflected an important reality of the demographics of the Party itself. In fact, Daluege later directed the exchange of men *within the police battalions* from the year groups 1900 and earlier with those born in 1901 or later.[81] In short, it appears that the choice of 1900 marked less a chronological than an experiential divide. By January 1935, persons born between 1895 and 1904 represented twenty-eight percent of Party members, those born between 1905 and 1917 thirty-eight percent.[82] In particular, the age cohorts born between 1905 and 1912 were significantly overrepresented.[83] On the other hand, those born after 1913, and certainly those born after 1918, represented a promising pool of Party members, having reached maturity and embarked on their adult lives in a Germany under National Socialist rule. Still, Himmler and Daluege, born in 1900 and 1897, respectively, were themselves products of earlier cohorts, perhaps providing an additional explanation for the attempt to limit the use of policemen over thirty-nine.

In November 1940, Daluege once again addressed the issue of age among the police reservists by ordering that preference for discharging police reservists be given to those over the age of forty-five in order to release these older men from duty.[84] As late as 1944, Daluege remained reluctant to modify the guidelines for reservists serving with the police battalions, holding to the prohibition on those born in 1900 or later despite the increasing manning crisis caused by the regime's vast conquests in the East and the losses experienced in battle.[85] The distinction between the age restrictions on the men of the police battalions and those on the men of the Gendarmerie once again reinforced the special position enjoyed by the former in the eyes of the police leadership.

In May 1942, Daluege did, however, agree to allow gendarmes from the reserves up to the age of forty-five to assume individual duties in the East, but only if they "possessed the necessary toughness [*Härte*] and skill [*Gewandtheit*]." Still, priority in the training of these older police reservists was given to instruction in the use of machine pistols and light machine guns in order to perfect their shooting skills, an important indication of the types of duties expected in the East.[86] Despite Daluege's efforts to keep older reservists out of the East, 40 percent of the Gendarmerie personnel at the rank of sergeant largely performing duties with detachments and at small posts within the district of Lublin were older than forty-five by the end of 1942.[87]

Governing Poland

The defeat of the Polish armed forces and the conclusion of German military operations set the stage for the fourth partition of Poland. The end of military control with the annexation of previous Polish territories into the Reich proper and the creation of the General Government under German civilian administration on October 12, 1939, heralded the emergence of a regime in which the complete merging of SS and police functions found its first expression. The subjugation of Poland provided Himmler with a golden opportunity to create an SS empire and to translate the theory of racial policy into practice. And it was apparent that these objectives could not be attained without the cooperation of the police.

With respect to Himmler's goal of creating an SS empire in Poland, Hitler's appointment of Hans Frank as the governor general of the occupied Polish territories and his decree granting Frank complete administrative control seemed to provide an inauspicious beginning for these plans.[88] Ever the consummate political intriguer, Himmler did not, however, wait for the creation of a civil administration before appointing Friederich Wilhelm Krüger as the HSSPF for the area on October 4.[89] For his part, Frank allowed Himmler a small victory by accepting Krüger's appointment, but, in his first official decree, that of October 26, he expressly subordinated Krüger both to himself and to his deputy.[90] Through this decree, Frank sought immediately to delineate the chain of command within the General Government and prevent Himmler and his SS organization from undermining his position. In the end, the *Reichsführer* proved himself a more than worthy opponent for Frank, eventually emerging as the victor in this two-way battle for control of the police in 1942.

The Organization of the Police in the General Government

The structure of Security and Uniformed Police forces in the General Government largely mirrored the regional structure of the Reich forces. They were headed by Krüger, an HSSPF, just as the regional Reich forces were headed by an HSSPF. A commander in chief of the Security Police and a commander in chief of the Uniformed Police worked directly for Krüger in a manner similar to that in which the inspector of the Security Police and the inspector of the Uniformed Police worked directly for HSSPFs in Germany. However, the use of the term *commander in chief* (*Befehlshaber*) instead of *inspector* provided a clear indication that these men exercised command authority over the occupation police forces, a precedent established during the invasion of Poland and the assignments of commanders in chief to each of the numbered armies. Similarly, the position of the HSSPFs in the occupied territories in general emerged as significantly more powerful than those of their counterparts in the Reich. This was based in large part on two factors. First, the political clout of Party leaders within Germany proper prevented Himmler's SS and police praetorians from accumulating excessive power, at least in the early years of the war. Second, the enforcement of occupation and racial policy and the prosecution of antipartisan operations largely fell into the hands of the HSSPFs in the occupied territories, providing these men with an ideal mechanism for increasing their power.

In addition to the senior SS and police leadership located in Krakau, the seat of the government, SS and police leaders (SSPFs) supervised the activities of police forces in each of the districts of the General Government—initially Lublin, Radom, Cracow, and Warsaw, with Galicia added in August 1941.[91] Although technically subordinate to district Party leaders appointed by Frank, the SSPFs' primary allegiance remained to Himmler and his representative in the General Government, Krüger.[92] Beneath the SSPFs, district

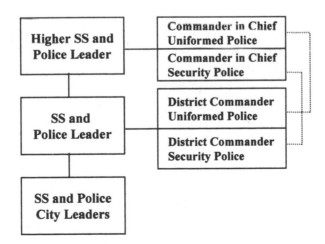

Figure 3. SS and Police Organization in the Occupied East

Source: Created by the author from Organizational depiction, T175, reel 229, frame 2768153, NARA.

police commanders (*Kommandeure*) of the Security Police and the Uniformed Police provided another level through which to exercise control over the specific branches of the police.

At the lowest levels, uniformed policemen operating in detachments and sections in cities and towns, combined with Gendarmerie personnel organized into posts, enforced a variety of laws and regulations, ranging from the prevention of food profiteering to the enforcement of traffic regulations.[93] In the initial months of the civil administration, many of these men not only acted as policemen but also assumed the governing responsibilities of local mayors and other civil officials.[94] The significant independence enjoyed by these men, as well as their subsequent actions, offers a telling insight into their commitment to and support for the regime's occupation policies. For example, Josef Kielar, a Pole, recalled the arrest of his brother and another man by Gendarmerie men from the post in Tomaszow Lubelski and the subsequent execution of both on January 11, 1940. He testified: "A short time after their arrest, they were taken by gendarmes into the forest . . . and shot and their bodies buried in a previously prepared grave." The ordeal of the Kielar family did not end there, however, as the parents, unaware of the executions, visited the Gendarmerie post to inquire about their son on the following day. A gendarme responded by striking and kicking the mother and shouting that there are no Poles here.[95]

In giving postwar testimony, Jan Krawczyk, a resident of Tomaszow Lubelski, remembered several members of the German Gendarmerie post and recalled one of these men "as a comparatively decent person": "One never heard that he had killed or tortured anyone." In contrast, Krawczyk remembered ten separate occasions of "groups of Poles or Jews" being led into the forest by policemen, followed by the sound of shooting. Krawczyk stated that he subsequently saw the bodies.[96] Krawczyk's testimony is revealing, not simply because only one of several gendarmes acted with comparative decency, but because it demonstrates that these policemen had a choice in the way they acted. Additionally, members of the Gendarmerie regularly participated in the conduct of operations against "bandit" and partisan groups.[97]

Despite the presence of over 10,000 policemen in August 1940, the General Government suffered from a chronic shortage of qualified personnel, especially gendarmes. The Gendarmerie as a whole had lost 280 officers and almost 8,000 men to the German army's Military Police, creating an especially difficult problem as most of these men came from the ranks of the motorized Gendarmerie. The result was shortages within and outside the Reich.[98] The number of Gendarmerie personnel requested for duty in the General Government totaled 2,226 in November 1940 alone. In an effort to induce more gendarmes to sign up for duty in the East, volunteers received

a promise of accelerated promotion and a choice of duty locations following the completion of a three-year tour. Furthermore, Himmler authorized
the assignment of qualified Hilfspolizei members for individual duty in the
General Government.[99]

In comparison to policemen conducting individual duties, the police battalions constituted by far the vast majority of Himmler's forces in the East.
For example, in August 1940, thirteen police battalions with 219 officers
and 8,245 men constituted almost 80 percent of the total of uniformed
policemen in the General Government.[100] By the end of 1941, this proportion changed slightly, with nine police battalions and five additional police
companies totaling 7,404 men compared to 811 individual duty policemen
and 2,199 gendarmes.[101] The large number of policemen assigned to these
formations provides direct evidence of the importance attached to them and
is crucial for understanding the role played by these battalions and companies in the prosecution of racial policy.

Massacre at Ostrów

More than any other example, the events in the Polish town of Ostrów
Mazowieck on November 11, 1939, offer a glimpse into the logical consequences of promoting an organizational environment built on racial hatred.
On November 9, a fire broke out in the town, and a rumor spread by a local
Nazi district leader (*Kreisleiter*) attributed it to Jewish arsonists. The official
then ordered a group of Jews to work the reciprocating arms of a water
pump in order to fight the fire. Then he and several other men, including a
soldier and a policeman, proceeded to beat the Jews, matching the rhythm
of the pumping action.[102] The next day, men from Reserve PB 11 gathered
the town's Jews together, men, women, and children, and sent word of the
arrests to the commander of Police Regiment Warsaw, Colonel Karl Brenner.
On November 10, Brenner ordered Captain of the Police Hans Hoffmann,
a company commander, to assemble a group of men and proceed with them
to Ostrów the next day to convene a police court and conduct any subsequent executions.[103]

In reality, the fate of the Jews was sealed before the men of PB 91 left for
Ostrów. The testimony of one of the policemen confirms that the decision to
execute them had already been made on November 10, prior to the unit's
departure.[104] According to a senior enlisted member of the unit, Hoffmann
approached him the night before the mission with orders to put together a
group of men who were "especially brave" and "in possession of the necessary toughness" for a "very important affair" the following day.[105] In selecting

Hoffmann to lead the action, Brenner had chosen well. The thirty-five-year-old Hoffmann had joined the police in 1924 at the age of twenty and became an officer five years later. He was also an "old fighter," having entered the Party in November 1932, and a member of the SS.[106]

Early in the morning of November 11, Hoffmann and a police contingent of some thirty-five men from PB 91 left Warsaw for Ostrów. When they arrived in the town, they were informed that a group of Jews had been condemned to death for arson. Shortly thereafter, members of PB 11 escorted the town's Jews to the execution site, placing them before freshly dug ditches prepared as mass graves. Armed with rifles, and led by First Lieutenant of the Police Otto Franz (a pseudonym), a platoon leader and member of the SS, the men of PB 91 proceeded to shoot men, women, and children as they approached the execution site in groups of ten. In his postwar testimony, Franz remembered that he had to give the command to fire on the first groups of victims but that this proved unnecessary as the executions proceeded, the men beginning to fire on their own. Franz also claimed that, when he saw children approaching the site, he requested to be replaced, a request refused by Hoffmann.[107] Interestingly, it was not until the appearance of the children that Franz appeared to have second thoughts about the executions, and it does appear that the appearance of children caused some concern among the men.

One participant remembered that, during a pause in the shootings, and perhaps in reaction to these concerns, Hoffmann, or a second officer, Captain of the Police Kurt Kirschner, justified the murders by alleging Jewish complicity in the assassination attempt against Hitler in Munich a few days earlier.[108] But, in the end, the men of PB 91 pulled their triggers and killed 156 Jewish men and 208 women and children in groups of ten, the whole process taking an hour and a half.[109]

The massacre was an important event because of its scale (an entire Jewish community) and the fact that the victims included women and children. Still, the murder of both Poles and Polish Jews having begun early in the campaign, the massacre proved less an anomaly than a natural extension of previous actions. During a campaign designed to enflame racial hatred and an occupation built on the principle of exploitation, it provided but one example of the boundaries of the possible for the men of the police. It also offered a clear example of "cold-blooded" atrocity. The victims had not fired on German forces, nor had the fire they allegedly set resulted in loss of life. Further, the fact that a policeman who joined the battalion after the Polish campaign remembered being shown pictures of the victims kneeling before the mass graves prior to their execution demonstrates that this was not seen as a dark chapter in the unit's history never to be opened again.[110] Indeed, showing pictures of executions to new members of the unit served two purposes. First, it demonstrated a sense of pride or accomplishment, and, second, it helped social-ize new members by establishing the limits (or lack thereof) of accepted behav-ior and creating expectations for the future. In the coming months and years, premeditated murder became a trademark of Himmler's green battalions.

Praising Atrocity

The massacre at Ostrów was not the only example of brutal police conduct in the final months of 1939. The precedent of reprisal actions and executions established during the campaign itself not surprisingly continued into the period of civil administration. The deaths of two Wehrmacht soldiers at the hands of two Polish "career criminals" on December 29, 1939, resulted in the dispatch of PB 6 to the pub where the shootings took place. The retri-bution taken included the hanging of the owner in front of his pub as well as the execution of an additional 114 Poles who had nothing to do with the officers' deaths. The scale and severity of the reprisal highlighted the brutal-ity of the battalion's actions, actions that received high praise in the daily orders of Police Regiment 31.[111] In this case, the recognition given to the men of PB 6 furthered the creation of an organizational atmosphere in which atrocity became, not just an acceptable, but a desirable attribute. However, it must also be emphasized that Himmler and Daluege wanted these actions to remain secret, or at least hidden from public view. For example, in a letter of December 13, 1939, concerning police formations coming home from Poland, Daluege ordered: "These men are to be sworn to secrecy concern-ing the conduct of *special tasks* that they were delegated during their duty [in Poland]."[112]

Opposing Atrocity?

If the German public remained largely unaware of the activities of Himm-ler's green battalions, such was not the case with the senior leadership of the Wehrmacht. For example, the description of the actions of PB 6 comes from, not a police report, but rather an army report prepared for General Wilhelm Ulex listing a series of atrocities committed by SS and police forces during the invasion. While the report represented a complaint, that complaint was not about the nature of the acts themselves but about how, in the general's opinion, they would not work and might prove counterproductive. Ulex wrote: "It is mistaken to slaughter several tens of thousands of Jews and

Poles, as is currently happening, because in the view of the majority of the [Polish] population neither is the idea of a Polish state laid to rest nor are the Jews gotten rid of [*beseitigt*]." He continued by describing both the Jews and the Poles as "our archenemies," but he argued that the public acts of violence were creating sympathy and support among Catholic Poles.[113]

Others opposed the atrocities being committed on similar grounds. General Eduard Wagner, the quartermaster general, noted that he had a "very important, necessary, and clear conversation" with Heydrich on September 19, 1939, presumably concerning the atrocities committed by the Einsatzgruppen. Still, Heydrich and Werner Best had briefed Wagner concerning the activities of these units on August 29. Wagner wrote about that meeting: "We quickly came to agreement."[114] Likewise, Franz Halder, the chief of the German army General Staff, euphemistically described the planned "housecleaning" of Polish Jews, intelligentsia, clergy, and nobility in a diary entry of September 19: "Army insists that 'housecleaning' be deferred until army has withdrawn and the country has been turned over to civil administration."[115] In this case, Halder and the army leadership may have found the actions distasteful, but only to the extent that they affected discipline or involved Wehrmacht forces.[116] In truth, recent scholarship demonstrates that numerous units within the army needed no assistance from the SS and the police to prosecute their own atrocities.[117]

Despite his own demonstrated racial convictions, Ulex did make several insightful points. First, he correctly observed: "If high officials in the SS and police demand acts of violence and brutality and praise these acts in public, then in a short time only the violent will reign." Ulex was certainly right, but he failed to understand that this was exactly the goal being pursued by Himmler in the creation of an empire in the East dominated by the SS and the police. Second, Ulex noted his opinion that the series of atrocities discovered by his command constituted "only a *small* portion" of those that had taken place. Finally, he suggested that the only solution to the current situation involved the complete replacement of "all police formations *including every one of their leaders*."[118] Ulex's solution is striking because it reflects his belief in the systemic nature of the problem within the SS and police leadership; however, he once again missed the point. The leaders of SS and police formations within Poland were neither unique in their outlook nor aberrant in their behavior. These men were part of an organization that had prepared them, especially the leadership within the officer and enlisted corps, for their duties by inculcating values and beliefs promoting a specific worldview in which actions taken against "enemies," whether Communists, Jews, or Polish priests, were acceptable and desirable.

Imposing Control

During the period of German civil administration, the police battalions became key instruments for realizing the Third Reich's objectives in the East. In the first months, police forces concentrated their efforts on the pacification of the Polish countryside. On November 29, 1939, Himmler sent a letter directly to Krüger inquiring about the status of a large-scale "cleansing action" that he had ordered during an earlier visit to the General Government. Himmler had suggested the action as a result of reports indicating the presence of Polish soldiers and large stores of supplies and munitions in the forests on both sides of the San River. In his letter, he also remarked that the action would require the employment of numerous police battalions and the support of mounted units.[119]

Himmler's letter is noteworthy in several respects. First, it was sent directly to Krüger, completely bypassing the Governor General, Frank, a clear indication of the relationship that Himmler sought to promote concerning the role of the HSSPFs in the occupied territories. Second, it provides an example of the *Reichsführer*'s early claim to SS and police priority over the German army in the conduct of pacification and antipartisan operations. As later events demonstrated, Himmler would eventually win the battle for primacy, but not without a fight from the Wehrmacht. Finally, the letter demonstrated Himmler's personal interest in these types of operations, an interest later exemplified in his meticulous and detailed following of events in the Soviet Union as the SS and police forces assigned to the Command Staff RFSS murdered their way through Russia.

On December 7, Krüger responded to Himmler's letter, reporting a delay in the planned action, and blaming it on a lack of sufficient SS and police forces, especially mounted units. In regard to the latter, he remarked that the Wehrmacht commander of military forces in the General Government (Oberbefehlshaber Ost), General Johannes Blaskowitz, had agreed to provide twenty-five hundred horses to the SS. As a result, Krüger was scouring the SS Death's Head formations within the General Government to find men who had riding experience. Furthermore, he informed Himmler that he was waiting for the availability of a third police battalion before commencing the operation.[120]

Krüger's response also bypassed Frank and indicated the desire of the senior SS and police leadership in taking the lead in the enforcement of occupation policy. It also demonstrated the now firmly established belief in the joint use of SS and police forces acting together. In a foreword to a history of SS and police actions in Poland, Krüger subsequently highlighted the key role played by the cooperation of the police and SS Death's Head formation in the Polish campaign.[121] The close cooperation of these SS and police formations offers additional evidence of the interconnections between and mutual dependence of the entire SS and police complex.

Competing Authorities

Without doubt, the Wehrmacht valued the efforts of the police in supporting military operations during the invasion; however, by the end of 1939, the expansion of SS and police authority into the realm of antipartisan operations soon proved a source of friction between the two organizations. The Wehrmacht's reservations concerning the Uniformed Police grew as the police formations increasingly became involved in military operations. Already in December 1939, General Blaskowitz had complained to Krüger about confrontations between police and Wehrmacht forces, incidents that damaged the political and military image of the Reich among the Polish population. As a result, Krüger informed the commanders in chief of the Uniformed and Security Police that he held them personally responsible for ensuring that the police forces under their command work harmoniously with the Wehrmacht, including the rendering of proper courtesies (e.g., saluting).[122]

Ironically, less than four months later, Krüger's conduct became the subject of a complaint lodged by the commander of Wehrmacht forces in the General Government with the commander of the German army, General Walther von Brauchitsch. The complaint concerned the employment of SS units and Uniformed Police battalions in the conduct of operations against Polish partisans. On March 29 and 30, two police battalions under the command of SS Brigadier General Friedrich Katzmann, the SSPF in Radom, initiated an antipartisan operation without informing the local military commander in spite of earlier promises to do so. In response to Wehrmacht requests to participate in the operation, Katzmann remarked that the "elimination of partisans is the business of the police."[123] The police operation proved a notable failure, leading to nine casualties among the police forces and the loss of significant numbers of weapons and equipment to the partisans. As a result of this debacle, Krüger, at Hitler's direction, took command of reinforced SS and police forces on March 31 in order to conduct a reprisal action (*Vergeltungsaktion*) aimed at "the entire male population in the battle area." On April 1 and 2, Krüger's SS and police forces succeeded in capturing or killing approximately fifty of the estimated one hundred members of the targeted partisan force. Again, Krüger refused the help of available German army units and went so far as to keep his plans hidden from the local military commander.[124]

Interestingly, the first reason cited in the Wehrmacht complaint centered on the efforts of the police to claim sole credit for these operations by excluding army units. Only in second place was the failure of police forces to notify the army of the impending operations. The final two grounds listed in the complaint included the alleged ineffectiveness of the police in antipartisan operations and the resulting disgrace for all German forces in the eyes of the Polish population. Additionally, the report facetiously commented that the police "shot at everything that moved, including women and crows," a remark reminiscent of Keudell's statement about the policemen's energetic use of their weapons, and a further indication of the willingness of these men to use deadly force.[125]

If, in the spring of 1940, Wehrmacht commanders saw the police as unwelcome competition and amateur soldiers, their counterparts would embrace SS and police formations for antipartisan operations by the fall of 1941. From the perspective of the police leadership, the use of the battalions in these operations reflected the unique status of the units. On June 2, 1940, Himmler made this unique status explicit in a directive entitled "Guidelines for the Conduct of the Ideological Education of the Uniformed Police during the War." The directive noted that a distinction needed to be made between the ideological instruction of the police battalions (*geschlossene Formationen*) and that of other branches of the police. In Himmler's view, the goal in training the men of the police battalions was their education as "martial combatants" (*soldatische Kämpfer*). Furthermore, Himmler directed that the weekly ideological instruction of the police battalions focus on the goal of "shaping the political consciousness of the martial combatant."[126]

Himmler's directive is important in two respects. First, it shows that he viewed the men of the battalions, not just as police soldiers, but as "political soldiers" whose police identities were inextricably tied to a martial character and the political aims of the National Socialist regime. Second, it created a special status for the men of the police battalions, which implied a special role for these units.

Coming Home to the Reich

The role of the police in the massive resettlement action aimed at bringing ethnic Germans from the territories outside of Germany "home to the Reich," and the resulting effort displacing hundreds of thousands of Poles from their homes in the process, offers another example of Himmler's reliance on his green battalions for the conduct of racial policy. Already at the end of October, Krüger had met with Frank in order to inform the governor general of Himmler's plans for the resettlement of all Jews from the newly

annexed Reich territories to the General Government, to be replaced by
"families of good blood."[127] The historian Christopher Browning described
this as a process by which "hundreds of thousands of people were shoved
around like so many pieces on a chessboard in pursuit of their [Hitler's and
Himmler's] vision of a racially reorganized eastern Europe."[128]

In the case of PB 91, the men received their orders to begin the resettlement
of both Polish Jews and Poles shortly before Christmas. One policeman, Wilhelm Hahn (a pseudonym), recalled the unit's participation in the action from
December 23 or 24, 1939 until its completion by mid-January 1940.[129] Hahn's
account, however, fails to address the brutality and hardship endured by those
selected for resettlement. For example, shortly before Christmas, police forces
herded sixteen hundred Jews from the town of Nasielek into a local synagogue, beating many with whips in the process, and even executing several.
The next morning, the policemen, again employing whips, forced the majority of the Jews to cross over a mud pit, dubbed the "Red Sea," en route to the
trains waiting to deport them to the General Government.

For those who reached the trains, journeys of hours, or even days, in freez-
ing temperatures in unheated railcars lay ahead.[130] One report compiled by the
Catholic primate of Poland, Cardinal Augustyn Hlond, for Pope Pius XII contained the following account of the typical course of the deportations: "It was
early in December 1939. The winter was extraordinarily severe, the tempera-
ture falling to thirty degrees (C.) of frost [−30 degrees Celsius]. At Mielec I saw
a train full of deportees from Bydgoszcz enter the station. The train was composed entirely of cattle-trucks [railcars], sealed without windows, without
water, lavatories, or any heat. The journey lasted three days and three nights.
The people confined in it [i.e., the trucks] were mainly women and children.
When the trucks were opened . . . I approached and saw that it [the 'cargo']
consisted of frozen, frost-bitten children. One, two, twenty, thirty or more."[131]
Many on this transport proved "luckier" than others as the bitter cold, combined with long periods of exposure, claimed the lives of the young, the old,
the sick, and the weak. One German general described the hatred and fear
being generated among the Polish population by the rail transports with their
"countless starving [and] dead children" and those "dead from exposure."[132]

In giving postwar testimony, one former policeman from PB 91 captured
the casual brutality associated with the guarding of Jewish and Polish
refugees during similar transports earlier in the war. Remarking on the practice of searching for valuables, he stated that, if a refugee was found to have
lied about having valuables, "then a thrashing was given [to him or her], but
it never came to the mishandling [of refugees]."[133] The reflection of a policeman some fifteen years after the end of the war that "a thrashing" (*eine Tracht
Prügel*) delivered to Jewish and Polish refugees did not constitute abuse pro-

vides evidence of the poisonous remains of a mind-set in which brutality was, not just commonplace, but natural.

This same former policeman, like so many of his colleagues after the war, could recall "hearing about" executions of Jews during transports, but he never witnessed them. After being shown a photograph of a Jewish transport departing Częstochowa (Tschenstochau), he did, however, admit that he had probably been the photographer.[134] That admission once again demonstrated the desire among some members of the police to document their participation in the enforcement of the Third Reich's racial policy. Taking pictures of Jewish transports does not equate to genocide, but it does suggest that the policemen performing acts of enforcement were not ashamed of or embarrassed by them. Indeed, the fact that Himmler repeatedly issued prohibitions concerning the photographing of such acts by his SS and police forces illustrates the widespread nature of the practice.[135]

The use of the police in resettlement actions had become standard practice by the summer of 1940. The men of PB 101 "evacuated" an average of 350 families per day, resettling a total of almost 37,000 people in the five months between May and September.[136] Gendarmerie forces also joined in the effort by evacuating 500 Poles who had displayed an "anti-German" attitude.[137] In many cases, German gendarmes from local posts "intervened" in the event that families refused to leave their homes voluntarily or attempted to take more personal articles than allowed.[138] During these actions, the police routinely cooperated with SS and SD men, establishing a pattern that would continue throughout the occupation of Poland and during the campaign in Russia. For those being resettled, these actions often meant short notice and permission to take only the items that could be fit into a single suitcase, along with enough food to last for fourteen days.[139] For some, the consequences of these actions proved fatal, as recounted by a policeman from PB 101: "They [the resettlement commission] objected that we struggled under the burden of the old and sick. To be precise, they did not initially give us the order to shoot them on the spot, rather they contented themselves with making it clear to us that nothing could be done with such people. In two cases I remember that such people were shot at the collection point."[140] Similarly, those attempting to return to their homes after being resettled risked their lives if they were recaptured by the German authorities.[141]

Forced Labor for the Reich

If the men of the Uniformed Police proved instrumental in supporting the racial policy of the Third Reich during the mass expulsions of Poles from their homes, they also played a key role in another aspect of the regime's exploitation of the occupied territories through their efforts in seizing Polish men and women for forced-labor duties in the Reich. One police report noted the continuing "unpopularity" of the drafting of Poles for forced labor in Germany. It also remarked Uniformed Police forces were often required to prevent those selected for work from fleeing the area.[142] On June 24, 1940, men from the Second Company of PB 104 cooperated with the SD and ethnic German auxiliaries and seized 814 Polish men between the ages of eighteen and sixty in the city of Lublin in order to determine their fitness for forced labor in Germany. One day later, men from the Second Company supported the First Company in the arrest of an additional 500 Poles, with 85 being taken to the prison in Lublin for subsequent transport to the Reich.[143]

The Uniformed Police became a key player in conducting raids to identify "work-shy" (*arbeitsscheu*) Poles for labor in the General Government and the annexed territories. In these cases, the police seized Poles and brought them to the German Labor Office (Arbeitsamt) in order to register them for prescribed mandatory work projects or for temporary heavy manual labor tasks, including the clearing of streets after snowfalls.[144] The conscription of Polish Jews by the police for forced-labor tasks within the General Government became a standard practice, including the roundup of 400 Jews by the Third Company of PB 104 and another 600 by PB 11 in June 1940.[145]

Not only was the policy of impressing workers unpopular among Poles, but it also became a major point of contention between various agencies within the German administration. The issue of forced-labor recruitment evoked controversy as the increasingly random conscription of armaments workers by the police threatened production goals and elicited complaints from the Armaments Inspection Office.

In a report issued in June 1940, the Armaments Inspection Office brought this issue to the attention of General Blaskowitz. The report described the raids to "recruit" forced laborers and contended that these actions evoked "great disquiet" among armaments workers as "the police have in numerous cases not accepted the identity cards of the armaments workers, and in some cases have destroyed them." Furthermore, armaments inspectors frequently had to take action to secure the release of these workers from police custody.[146] This complaint again demonstrated the zeal of Himmler's policemen in the prosecution of their duties even when their success was at the expense of the Wehrmacht's economic plans. The demand for workers both in the General Government and in the Reich continued to increase throughout the occupation. In an attempt to meet demand in the former, men from PB 314 conducted a sweep in Zamosc to net "work-shy Jews" in May 1941.[147] In an attempt to do the same in the latter, the police regiments in the

General Government were ordered on September 17, 1942, to create special detachments in order to collect 140,000 Poles for forced labor in the Reich by the end of the year. This was in addition to those already impressed during the first eight months of 1942.[148] The assistance of the police in the prosecution of the Third Reich's forced-labor policies provides another insight into the methods by which these policemen operated and their complicity in the exploitation of the occupied territories.

Cooperating with the Security Police and the SD

The examples of resettlement and impressment point to the continuing close relationship among the various branches of Himmler's SS and police empire. In fact, the practice of cooperation between the Security Police and their uniformed counterparts was well established by the summer of 1940 and became a prevalent feature of police operations throughout the occupied territories. For example, a police report in January 1940 mentioned that the Gestapo office in Thorn had requested the assistance of fifty-five men from PB 22 to guard a prisoner transport. It also remarked that the police had uncovered evidence of the support of Catholic clergy for "seditious elements" (*verhetzte Elemente*) in several communities of the former Polish province of Silesia and had passed this information to the Gestapo.[149] Likewise, a situation report of May 15, 1940, noted the employment of PB 82 in "numerous actions" supporting the Gestapo in Silesia, resulting in the arrest of 812 persons as well as the assignment of men from PB 11 to assist Gestapo actions in East Prussia. In this latter case, police forces arrested 308 members of the "Polish intelligentsia," turned them over to the Gestapo, and conducted a combined operation that led to the arrest of 107 persons in the town of Ostrolenka.[150] Policemen in the General Government also assisted the Security Police in a series of sweeps over five days that netted 59 Poles, "mostly academics," suspected of being members of the resistance.[151]

Concentrating Poland's Jews

The guarding of closed Jewish residential districts or ghettos constituted an additional contribution of the Uniformed Police to the prosecution of National Socialist racial policy in both the occupied Polish territories and the General Government. The creation of these ghettos reflected a highly decentralized process as local German authorities pursued independent initiatives, with ghettos first appearing in the occupied territories during the

winter of 1939–1940. The German administration of the Warthegau established the first large ghetto in Łódź (Litzmannstadt) in April 1940 with a
population numbering at least 162,000.[152] One indication of the scale of the
Łódź ghetto is the daily requirement for some 200 policemen to guard the
area in May 1940.[153] The enclosure of the ghetto on May 10 by the construction of a fence, not only resulted in the physical isolation of the incarcerated Jews, but also had a more ominous implication as the police forces
guarding the perimeter received orders to "shoot on sight" any persons
attempting to leave the ghetto without permission.[154] In addition to providing
the uniformed policemen guarding the ghetto with the authority to use their
weapons, police leaders "praised" those who actually made use of their
weapons in front of their fellow policemen.[155]

In the case of the Warsaw ghetto, PB 61 arrived in the city in January 1942
at the start of the battalion's second tour of duty in Poland. Its primary
responsibility involved guarding the enormous ghetto with its Jewish population of over 400,000.[156] The shooting of Jews became a routine part of
these men's daily duties. In fact, some policemen participated in a contest to
see who had killed the most Jews, keeping track of their totals by making
tally marks at the entrance to a local pub frequented by the battalion's men
after duty. The pub itself was "decorated" with paintings such as one showing a policeman shooting a Jew who was bent over in an attempt to pick up
some food or another showing a policeman beating an animal with a Jewish head. One member of the unit also recalled the singing of songs one of
which included the following verse: "When the blood of the Jews sprays
across the wall."[157] In postwar testimony, members of the battalion identified those who took pleasure in shooting Jews but also recalled that some
men never fired their weapons. The latter contention may or may not be true,
but it is also in one respect irrelevant as the standard of acceptable and
desired behavior was established by those who perpetrated atrocity on an
almost daily basis. Certainly, the norms and values expressed in the actions
of PB 61 demonstrated the nature of the unit's own organizational culture.

The public recognition of those men who shot "escaping" Jews offers
another example of the method by which senior leaders established organizational norms and standards for those within the ranks of the police. As in
the case of the open praise by the regimental commander for the reprisal
action conducted by PB 6 in the execution of the pub owner and 114 other
persons in December 1939, the commendation of policemen for the liberal
use of their weapons helped shape the values and views of the police and,
eventually, guided their actions. In truth, the promotion of this mentality
found its roots well before the campaign in Poland in Göring's infamous
"Shooting Directive" of early 1933. The encouragement of a policy of deadly

force with respect to the Łódź ghetto merely reflected a continuing glorification of violence against putative enemies.

Constructing the Enemy

The actions of the police units operating in Poland evolved from a number of sources, not least of which were historical stereotypes, personal biases, wartime propaganda, and, perhaps most important, the representations of their enemies imparted to them by police leaders, whether in ideological instruction and professional publications or in directives and orders. The postwar testimony of one former policeman demonstrates the deep-seated nature of these views. In discussing his participation in the Polish campaign, Philip Kutscher (a pseudonym) remarked: "During my entire duty in Poland, I personally was never actively or passively involved in any kinds of actions against Jews, prisoners of war, *or other potential enemies.*"[158] The wording of the police reports provides numerous examples of the effectiveness of the prewar efforts to create a view of the enemies (*Feindbild*) of the Third Reich. A report of May 26, 1940, by the commander of the police for the district of Lublin, Lieutenant Colonel of the Police Kintrup, to the commander in chief of the Uniformed Police commented: "The district of Lublin can be viewed as the storage place [*Abstellort*] for all dirty and unsafe elements of the great German Reich." It then identified these "dirty and unsafe elements" by noting: "1,100 Gypsies are already present in the district[, and] 100,000 Jews from Germany are expected soon." Three weeks later, a platoon of policemen from PB 104 transported a group of 125 Sinti and Roma (Gypsies), including men, women, and children, presumably to a detention camp in the district.[159]

With respect to Polish Jews, the reports indicate the level of paranoia within the ranks of the police concerning their alleged anti-German activities. A situation report of May 15, 1940, concerning activities in the General Government warned: "The Jews are without doubt also the carriers of anti-German propaganda." The report then accused traveling Jewish merchants of using their business dealings as cover in order to spread this "propaganda."[160] In the months prior to the invasion of the Soviet Union, another police situation report remarked on the growing anxiety among the Polish population over a coming war between Germany and Russia, fears allegedly fostered "by agents in England's pay, that is, by the Jews."[161] Such depictions of Jews once again illustrate a general organizational attitude. They did not necessarily make extermination an absolute necessity; however, combined with police acts of violence and brutality, they did facilitate the acceptance of and eventual movement toward annihilation.

Personnel Crisis in the East

Soon after the first outposts in the Eastern Empire of the Third Reich were established, it became clear that the number of SS and police forces available for duty in the occupied territories was insufficient to maintain the degree of control demanded by German administrative authorities, as evidenced by Krüger's complaint to Frank at the end of October 1939.[162] In one respect, draconian measures and the elimination of real and imaginary opposition provided one mechanism for sustaining an iron grip. Additionally, Himmler and Daluege pursued several other initiatives to address the shortage of available policemen for duty in the East. First, the German administration, using specially selected SS officers, recruited numbers of auxiliary policemen from the ethnic German population of Poland for duty in the Self-Defense Force (Selbstschutz), a practice that was in some respects analogous to the use of the Hilfspolizei within the Reich in 1933. These forces, subordinated to the Uniformed Police, provided a ready pool of recruits.[163] The use of ethnic Germans, many of whom were members of National Socialist–related organizations, in the role of auxiliary policemen provided these individuals with a ready-made opportunity to exact revenge for real and perceived injustices at the hands of their Polish neighbors, and many used the changed circumstances to settle old scores.[164] By the first week of October 1939, the West Prussian Self-Defense Forces, led by Himmler's personal adjutant SS-Oberführer Ludolph von Alvensleben, totaled over 17,000 men and had executed 4,247 Poles. In the case of the incorporated territories, the Self-Defense Forces emerged as an important additional instrument for the conduct of atrocity in support of National Socialist ethnic-cleansing efforts.[165] German administrative authorities within the General Government also recognized the value of these formations, and the number of ethnic Germans serving in the Self-Defense Forces reached 6,000 by August 1940, these forces receiving their training from senior enlisted members of the Uniformed Police.[166]

    Second, the recruitment of Ukrainians as auxiliaries provided another source of manpower, with the first group of Ukrainian auxiliaries being established in 1940 in the vicinity of Chełm in the General Government.[167] By 1942, over 1,500 Ukrainians served as auxiliaries (*Hilfswillige* or Hiwis) under German command.[168] Like their ethnic German counterparts, the majority of these men exhibited considerable enmity for their Polish neighbors, especially Jews, marking them as a willing instrument for the pursuit of National Socialist racial policy. Under the command of German police officers, these auxiliaries participated widely in the murder of Jews and other "enemies" of the Third Reich throughout the East.[169]

To supplement these forces, on May 6, 1940, Frank issued a directive establishing a Sonderdienst, or Special Service, consisting of men of German ancestry between the ages of eighteen and forty. The directive ostensibly limited the duties of the Sonderdienst to "tasks of administrative and technical nature" and prohibited the performance of police tasks unless "no police forces are available."[170] In truth, Frank's order constituted a thinly veiled attempt to bypass the established SS and police apparatus and regain control of a police apparatus loyal to Himmler. Despite its charter, the Sonderdienst emerged by 1942 as an important adjunct to the regular police forces by assisting in guard duties, patrols, and even antipartisan operations. However, by this time, Himmler had forced Frank to relinquish control of it to the HSSPF, using as leverage damaging information that he had collected concerning corruption in the General Government and the participation of Frank's wife in these affairs.[171] In addition, Himmler blackmailed Frank into naming Krüger as the "secretary for all police business and resettlement matters," subordinate to the *Reichsführer* alone in these affairs.[172] After March 1942, Frank was, in fact, compelled to govern without direct executive authority, and his directives relied largely on the consent and cooperation of the HSSPF and, ultimately, Himmler.

Cracking Down

When discussing the economic viability of the General Government in October 1939, Frank remarked that everything had to be done to maintain the ability of the Polish population to work. In contrast, he noted that he was "completely indifferent to the fate of the Jews."[173] At the end of February 1940, in a meeting with officials from the district of Radom, Frank stated that "the backbone of the Poles is broken for all time" but that he intended to "take all steps to shape the standard of life of the Polish people in such a way that it only just supports life." He also assumed responsibility for all the actions that had taken place within the General Government since October 11, 1939, by describing them as "regrettable from the point of view of humanity in general" but justified in the pursuit of Hitler's vision of a greater German world order. Finally, he also sought to inject himself into the administrative machinery of annihilation by ordering that he would act as the final authority, approving all death sentences passed by SS and police summary courts.[174]

Frank's effort to ensure that he had final authority on the implementation of capital punishment within the General Government might be interpreted in two ways. It might have been an attempt to gain a tighter hold on such activities and to put an end to mass executions.[175] And it might also have been an attempt to reexert authority over Krüger's SS and police forces. Although neither interpretation can be ruled out, the second is most probably correct, given the nature of the Government General and its charter. In any event, Frank's efforts proved largely futile, as evidenced by the continued widespread use of summary execution by SS and police forces.

Despite the incomplete coverage offered by surviving police reports from the first half of 1940, these documents demonstrate the consistent use of capital punishment by the police for a wide variety of reasons throughout the annexed Polish territories and in the General Government. The number of those executed ranged from single individuals to large groups. In the town of Konski alone, the Uniformed Police executed 257 Poles between March 31 and April 8. Targets varied. "Communist agitators" paid for their activities with their lives, as did one Russian prisoner of war and five Jews accused of "spreading disturbing rumors."[176] In the General Government, a Jew accused of calling a soldier "a German pig," a Pole accused of spitting on a German official, and a Pole who allegedly "jostled" a gendarme were all put to death, evidence of the low toleration of any signs of opposition as well as of the low threshold needed to justify capital punishment among the summary police courts.[177] In another case, four Poles accused of adopting a "rebellious manner of speaking" (*aufrührerische Redensart*) were arrested— and subsequently shot "while trying to escape."[178]

The murder of these four Poles highlights another phrase found repeatedly throughout the police reports in which euphemism became the cover for murder. For example, the report notes four separate incidents of five, four, six, and seven individuals "shot while trying to escape." Interestingly, there is no indication that any of these individuals were merely wounded, an important omission and further evidence of the true nature and intent of the act. In fact, the report notes that, in all four cases, the individuals were executed "because of opposition, that is, attempted escape."[179] Similarly, in a report detailing the activities of Uniformed Police forces in the General Government during the first two weeks of May 1940, one finds mention of the arrest of 760 persons for "various offenses" and the execution of thirteen "while trying to escape" in addition to the shooting of five others after summary court verdicts.[180]

Furthermore, a report of June 15 lists the deaths of thirty-six persons in five separate incidents "shot while trying to escape." The report does note that, in one incident during which seven persons were shot, another four were "injured," suggesting that at least some of these escape attempts were real. In contrast, in another incident, twenty-one Jews and Poles, including a priest, died at the hands of the police while "attempting to escape."[181]

Throughout the course of the war, and especially in the Soviet Union, the use of the term "shot while trying to escape" became routine in official reports. In the case of the General Government, the euphemism offered a shortcut to the administrative process of arresting, investigating, sentencing, and then waiting for the governor general's authorization before executing. In short, it allowed SS and police forces to circumvent the normal administrative process in their prosecution of the racial policies of the Third Reich.

The Pacification of the General Government

The invasion of France and the Low Countries proved a fateful event for Poles and Jews living under the yoke of German occupation in the General Government. On May 30, 1940, Frank addressed a gathering of SS and police officials and outlined his plans for a "general pacification" action (*AB-Aktion*) within the borders of his Eastern fiefdom. He minced no words concerning the nature of this effort or its goals: "I can carry out this Polish policy only with you. You must excuse my frankness. If I had not the old National Socialist guard of fighters of the Police and the SS in this country with whom would we then carry out this policy?" He continued by discussing the objective as the "complete domination of the Polish people" and declaring: "On the 10th May the offensive in the West began, . . . [w]e must now use the moment which is at our disposal."[187]

After outlining the rationale for the action, Frank noted that he had discussed it with Krüger and with the commander in chief of the Security Police Bruno Streckenbach and that all had agreed that the war provided the opportunity "to finish off now in quick time the mass of those insurgent resistance politicians and other political suspects whom we have in our hands, and at the same time to clear away the heirs of former Polish gangsters alone." Frank acknowledged that this campaign would "cost some thousands of Poles their lives," and he gave as justification for the action a conversation with Hitler during which the Führer had discussed the need to "liquidate" the leadership class of Poland, then, and again in the future if necessary. Significantly, Frank also freely relinquished his right to review death sentences imposed during the *AB-Aktion*, placing responsibility completely in the hands of Krüger. He explained this by remarking: "This is a purely internal action for quieting the country which is necessary and lies outside the scope of normal legal trial."[183] Frank then identified the instrument for this program of extermination: "Gentlemen, we are no murderers. It is a terrible task for the policeman and SS man who is officially, or as a result of his duties, bound to carry out the execution on the basis of this measure. . . . [E]very Police and SS Chief, who has the hard duty of carrying out these sentences, must also be fully conscious of the fact that he acts here in execution of the verdict of the German nation."[184] General Franz Halder provided one indication of the success of Frank's general pacification campaign in his diary entry of August 27, 1940: "A new wave of liquidation of intellectuals and Jews is on in the East."[185]

Frank's words to his SS and police forces are eerily reminiscent of Himmler's later speech to SS and police leaders in Poznań on October 4, 1943. But his concern for his policemen appears to have been largely unnecessary. Indeed, they did not constitute a tabula rasa in terms of the lessons of brutality and atrocity but, in the course of only nine months, had become only too well schooled in them. It is significant, however, that all the police reservists operating with the police battalions had taken their oath of allegiance to Hitler, as noted in a situation report detailing the status of the Uniformed Police forces in the General Government as of May 31, 1940. In fact, Frank had personally presided over the ceremony involving reservists from the police battalion in Warsaw.[186] The fact that these ceremonies appeared to have been conducted only in the General Government, combined with the timing, seems to indicate that Himmler, Daluege, or Krüger wanted to reinforce the symbolic commitment of these reservists to the regime in the face of the large-scale pacification effort, a commitment made by regular police and SS forces years before.

Help from the Reich

A situation report detailing police actions in the first two weeks of June 1940 remarked on the initiation of the *AB-Aktion,* including the cooperation of Police Regiment Radom and the district's SD forces in the arrest of 312 persons, but noted that reports from other districts were not yet in.[187] Police forces from the Reich also became involved in the pacification effort. In an order of July 24, 1940, Daluege addressed the immediate formation of "police hunting platoons" (*Polizei-Jagdzüge*) for the conduct of "special tasks" in the General Government. Daluege called for the creation of eight special detachments (*Sonderkommandos*) composed of forty-two men each from the police districts in Berlin and Münster. These special detachments included one officer, four sergeants, twelve enlisted police troops, eighteen enlisted reservists, and seven policemen to act as drivers for the unit's vehicles. The hunting platoons were to be equally divided between the four districts of the General Government.[188]

Daluege hinted at the nature of the "special tasks" by ordering that, "in consideration of the difficult tasks which the police special detachments have to conduct in the General Government, only Police *Wachtmeister* [middle enlisted police grade] and Police *Wachtmeister* of the Reserves *who are equal to the task are to be detailed.*" Furthermore, he required that, "in particular, the members of the police special detachments must be good marksmen." Finally, he offered a clear indication of the importance that he attached to this effort by making the inspectors of the Uniformed Police in Berlin and Münster "personally responsible" for the selection of personnel involved.[189]

On August 1, Major General of the Police Heinrich Lankenau notified police officials of the requirement to establish and outfit the hunting platoons for "special tasks" in the East. In his letter, Lankenau directed various districts to provide weapons and equipment items for these formations, with each platoon receiving six machine pistols, twenty-three carbines, five binoculars, two flare guns, three wire cutters, twelve short-handled spades, three long-handled spades, and six hoes.[190] The mention of long-handled spades and hoes makes apparent the nature of the "special tasks," these items in no way constituting normal military equipment. The special care given to the selection of the men, combined with the nature of their equipment, again demonstrated the thoroughness and organization of senior police leaders in preparing forces for duties in the General Government.

The invasion of Poland provided the Uniformed Police with its baptism of fire as well as tangible proof to both Himmler and Daluege that their efforts in shaping the police into a martial instrument in the prewar period had not been in vain. Likewise, the employment of the Security Police, the SD, the Uniformed Police, and units of the SS-Verfügungstruppe in the invasion is important in several respects. First, it demonstrates Himmler's success in inserting units from the entire SS and police complex into military operations. Second, the nature and type of tasks conducted by these formations demonstrated premeditation, a preexisting intent to employ these forces at the forefront of racial policy. Finally, the integration of uniformed policemen into the Einsatzgruppen and their subsequent activities as well as the activities of the police battalions provide strong evidence of the success of Himmler's and Daluege's prewar efforts to create political soldiers within the ranks of the police.

The subsequent annexation of Polish territory and the creation of the General Government provided the police with an opportunity to demonstrate their commitment to achieving the racial objectives of the Third Reich. The German historian Martin Broszat observed: "As a result of the NSDAP's special political objective [in Poland], a system was created overlapping the state and even the Party, reaching far beyond the SS and police jurisdiction in the

Altreich [Old Reich], [a system] that repeatedly threatened to assume the character of an absolute regime of the SS and the police."[191] In truth, the experience of the police forces in Poland served as both a laboratory and a model for later campaigns in the East. If Poland had, in fact, been the organization's baptism of fire, then the campaign against the Soviet Union in 1941 proved a sanguinary confirmation ceremony.

Heinrich Himmler (*left*) with Kurt Daluege (*right*) in his field headquarters. (BA Bild 146-1974-079-118.)

Kurt Daluege conducting an inspection in East Prussia, June 27, 1941. Note the SS runes below the jacket pocket of two of the policemen on the right. (Bundesarchiv Bild 146-1985-044-258.)

Tanks of SS Police Division on the Eastern Front. (Bundesarchiv Bild 146-1985-078-20A8.)

Uniformed Police forces in action in the Soviet Union. Thousands of such actions aimed at partisans, Jews, and the local populations of the East took place during the war. (Bundesarchiv Bild 146-1993-025-03.)

A woman being interrogated by members of the Security Service (SD) and the Uniformed Police in the Soviet Union. Men, women, and children either without papers or unable to explain their presence in a given area were routinely executed, the executions hidden under a variety of euphemisms, including "bandits," "bandit helpers," "vagrants, and "beggars." (Bundesarchiv Bild 146-1993-025-19.)

Uniformed Police forces responding to a partisan attack against a rail line in the Soviet Union. Soviet partisans conducted numerous attacks against German lines of communication in the East. (Bundesarchiv Bild 146-1993-025-22.)

Daluege (*right*) greets Himmler (*left*) as he arrives for the laying of the foundation stone at the police academy in Krakau. Hans Frank, the governor general of the General Government, is standing in the background between them. (Bundesarchiv Bild 146-1993-026-28A.)

"Day of the German Police" in 1939. A policeman gives horse rides to local children during the annual winter welfare collection drive. Note the collection tin carried by the policeman and worn on his belt. The Day of the Police was one of a number of initiatives pursued by the senior SS and police leadership to demonstrate the close bond between the people and the police. (Bundesarchiv Bild 146-2000-022-16A8.)

A policeman escorts ethnic Germans from Bessarabia and the Bukowina "home into the Reich." The Uniformed Police played a key role in clearing the occupied territories of their native populations to make room for these ethnic German settlers. (Bundesarchiv Bild 146-2000-033-36.)

A Luftwaffe and police radio relay station used to coordinate air force and police operations against the partisans in the Soviet Union in 1943. Wehrmacht forces participated with the police in large-scale antipartisan operations on numerous occasions in the occupied Eastern territories. (Bundesarchiv Bild 183-1991-0206-500.)

Daluege presents members of the Uniformed Police with the "Cholm badge," an award personally sponsored by Hitler to honor Wehrmacht and police forces that held out in the Cholm pocket against Soviet forces in the winter of 1941-1942. The authorization for the policemen to wear the Cholm badge provided but one example of the union of the police with martial symbols and ideals. (Bundesarchiv Bild 183-2003-1217-500.)

The German inscription on this photograph reads: "Uniformed policemen from Austria come home." On August 24, 1938, Austrian Uniformed Police forces participated in a parade in Munich to celebrate the incorporation of Austria into the Third Reich. The police formations marched by the reviewing party in front of the Nationalist Socialist memorial to the "martyrs" of Hitler's failed "beer-hall" putsch of 1923. Attempts by senior SS and police leaders to link the traditions of the movement with the police became a consistent theme in police literature and ceremony in the prewar years. (Bundesarchiv Bild 183-2003-1217-501.)

A uniformed policeman and his dog participate in an antipartisan operation in the vicinity of the Ukrainian city of Zhitomir in September 1942. (Bundesarchiv Bild 183-B26976A.)

Daluege (*left*) visiting the police officer school in Berlin-Köpenick in January 1937. The policemen are conducting a field exercise complete with machine guns. The prewar emphasis on military training, including field maneuvers, reflected Himmler's and Daluege's desire to shape the policemen from civil servants into martial combatants. (Bundesarchiv Bild 183-C005428.)

"Day of the German Police" in 1937 in Berlin. Himmler lays a wreath at the memorial in Horst Wessel Square to honor the "martyrs" of the Party and the police who fell in battles against the parties of the Left. (Bundesarchiv Bild 183-C006788.)

Uniformed policemen clear out a hiding area used by Jews in Lublin, Poland, in December 1940. (Bundesarchiv Bild 183-H27925.)

Himmler presents awards during the track and field Police Championships held in June 1938 in Lübeck. Himmler and Daluege instituted strict standards for physical fitness within the police along with annual tests and competitions to measure athletic prowess. This "cult of the body" was directly related to other efforts to create the image of the police soldier within the green corps. (Bundesarchiv Bild 183-H29080.)

The German caption to this photograph reads: "On the Soviet Front: police in combat against the partisans." These women have been identified as partisans (*Flintenweiber*) and are being led away for interrogation. Their identification with the partisans most assuredly sealed their fate as the police executed thousands of such persons during antipartisan operations. (Bundesarchiv Bild 183-J181558.)

Captured Soviet partisans being guarded by policemen in the vicinity of Zhitomir in September 1942. (Bundesarchiv Bild 183-No123-5008.)

Himmler leading the oath of Austrian policemen as they swear fealty to Hitler in a ceremony at the "Square of Heroes" (Heldenplatz) in Vienna on March 17, 1938. The swearing of an oath to the person of Adolf Hitler by the police constituted another form of ceremony designed to tie the police to the National Socialist movement. (Bundesarchiv Bild 183-S376198.)

FIVE

CRUSADE IN THE EAST

The Führer is accomplishing an undertaking that will be the greatest in the history of the world. I know of nothing greater in one's life than to participate in this undertaking. What are the prophets of Christendom compared to this [undertaking] that we [the Uniformed Police] have to fulfill in support of the Führer's worldview.
—Kurt Daluege (January 1943)

Early in the morning of June 22, 1941, a massive artillery barrage shattered the silence along the length of the Soviet Union's western border as 3 million German troops and 500,000 from Germany's allies prepared to flood into "Stalin's Reich."[1] The scale of the German invasion was matched only by the size of Hitler's gamble in his most ambitious quest. Over 400 police officers and 11,640 police troops joined their Wehrmacht counterparts for this crusade in the East, constituting a police force approximately twice the size of the one that had entered Poland in 1939.[2] It was, however, not just the enormous scale that made this campaign unique but its brutal and atavistic nature; if Poland had provided the training ground for annihilation, then the Soviet Union offered the forum for its perfection. Daluege could claim that the campaigns of 1940 in the West, and, especially, Scandinavia, were waged against "other types of people" who were "racially related" to Germans and possessed valuable bloodlines, but not the campaigns of 1941, which were aimed at the Balkans and the Russian "colossus."[3]

The Police Formations

The opening of the campaign against the Soviet Union provided the police battalions with an opportunity to test the limits of their unique status. Prior to the attack, Hitler personally ordered the employment of police battalions to support the Wehrmacht, and the dedication of twenty-three to the opening stages offers direct evidence of the importance attached to these forces in the campaign. The nine battalions attached to the Security Divisions and the individual battalions attached to the Einsatzgruppen (Special Mission Groups) and the Organization Todt (Organization for Military Construction Projects) were fully motorized, while the remaining battalions assigned to the police regiments were only partially motorized. These formations were divided between the three Army Groups, North, Center, and South, pushing into the Soviet Union along three geographic axes of advance. The Uniformed Police forces operating with Army Group North included one police regiment of three battalions plus three police battalions attached to the Wehrmacht's Security Divisions. Similarly, the police forces in Army Group Center consisted of a police regiment of three battalions and an additional three police battalions for duty with the German army's Security Divisions, and those in Army Group South included one police regiment of three battalions and three battalions attached to the Security Divisions as well as a Special Purposes police regiment, composed of three battalions and one mounted section for operations in the Ukraine. Four companies of Police Battalion (PB) 9 assisted the Einsatzgruppen in their deadly march across the Soviet Union, and special police units, including mounted forces and armored-car and antitank detachments as well as signals sections, provided additional combat capability to the police formations.[4]

Already in April 1941, Daluege revealed the future importance of the police battalions in the coming campaign by reorganizing the reserve police battalions in an effort to increase the number of available officers and senior enlisted men as a cadre for the continued expansion of the number of these formations.[5] Of the nine police battalions placed directly at the disposal of the higher SS and police leaders (HSSPFs) during the invasion, seven were regular police battalions with numerical designations in the 300s. These "300-level" battalions consisted in large part of recruits from among the twenty thousand men mobilized from the 1909–1912 year groups in October 1939, and from their ranks emerged units that would cut a bloody swathe through the western Soviet Union in the opening stages of the campaign.[6] It is important to note that the vast majority of the police battalions' members came from these or younger year groups and were not the overaged reservists found in Christopher Browning's study of PB 101. In fact, only twenty of the approximately one hundred police battalions established during the war were composed of overaged reservists, and, even in the case of these reserve battalions, the majority of the officers and senior enlisted men came from the ranks of career policemen.[7] Not surprisingly, having undergone extensive training under the command of older career police commanders, these units proved to be ready-made instruments for the prosecution of racial policy on the Eastern Front. In fact, a report of December 2, 1941, by a German armaments inspector described the key role of the police battalions in the murder of Jews in the Ukraine during the initial months of the campaign. This official reported that there was no evidence that the Jews posed a danger to the Wehrmacht or that they were involved in widespread acts of sabotage. Still, he recounted the "organized execution [*Erschiessung*] of the Jews by formations of the Uniformed Police created expressly for this purpose."[8] Daluege later confided during a meeting of SS leaders that all the police battalions had received orders to "cleanse" their areas of the remnants of enemy forces, to secure lines of communication, to guard prisoners of war (POWs), and to protect captured stores and industrial installations. He also noted that the battalions were responsible for the "combat of criminal elements, above all political elements," in the East.[9]

The Leadership of the Police

In the war against the Soviet Union, the HSSPFs, including Hans Adolf Prütz-mann, HSSPF North; Erich von dem Bach-Zelewski, HSSPF Center; and Friedrich Jeckeln, HSSPF South, played a critical role in the prosecution of genocide. In July 1941, Himmler emphasized the authority of the HSSPFs by ordering that "all SS and police formations are explicitly [*grundsätzlich*] subordinate to the higher SS and police leaders after crossing the Reich borders."[10] Controlling all SS and police forces, including the Einsatzgruppen, the HSSPFs emerged as, in the words of one historian, "the pacesetters of the annihilation process."[11] Likewise, the police battalions that entered the Soviet Union in the summer of 1941 were led by officers and senior enlisted men who had been prepared by their backgrounds and training, as well as by the organizational culture within the police, for a war of extermination in the East. In fact, Daluege brought this message to the police battalions himself in a visit to the Eastern Front in July 1941 in which he tasked these formations with the final annihilation of Bolshevism.[12] The HSSPFs in the East quickly responded to Daluege's order, as demonstrated by the actions of Jeckeln, the HSSPF responsible for operations in the Ukraine. Using the cover of antipartisan operations, Jeckeln provided verbal orders to the commander of Police Regiment South in late July or early August "to dispose of all Jews in a particular territory or locality."[13] Jeckeln's orders were subsequently passed orally to the commanders of the police battalions and then to the respective company commanders, leaving no paper trail. Similarly, in a July 29–31 visit to the Baltics, Himmler met with Prützmann to inform him of the necessity of the "resettlement" of "criminal elements," a euphemism for mass murder.[14] The fact that Himmler personally delivered these orders indicates his effort to keep them a closely guarded secret and also demonstrates the important position of authority enjoyed by the HSSPFs. Although his orders in late July and early August certainly accelerated the killing machinery, Himmler had worked hard in the months prior to the invasion to prepare the foundation for annihilation.

Laying the Foundations for Annihilation

One of the most striking aspects of war against the Soviet Union was the lengthy and dedicated planning process conducted by Himmler to prepare his SS and police forces for the campaign. In order to avoid the problems created between SS and police forces and the Wehrmacht during the campaign in Poland, Hitler had his senior SS and police leaders draft detailed policy guidance and military orders outlining the duties and responsibilities of both military and police forces in the spring of 1941. On March 3, Hitler himself set the tone for the coming campaign in his declaration to a group of Wehrmacht commanders: "The impending campaign is more than a clash of arms; it also entails a struggle between two ideologies. . . . The Jewish-Bolshevik intelligentsia, as the oppressor in the past, must be liquidated."[15] Later that month, Field Marshal Wilhelm Keitel issued "Guidelines in Special Fields concerning Directive Number 21." Directive 21 informed Wehrmacht field commanders: "On behalf of the Führer, the Reich leader of the SS [Himmler] assumes special tasks in preparation for the political administration within the army's field of operations that arise from the final, decisive battle between two opposing political systems."[16] In a subsequent meeting with his senior military commanders at the end of the month, Hitler explicitly commented on the nature of the "special tasks" facing German forces in the Soviet Union. In a March 30 entry in his war journal, General Franz Halder revealed that Hitler described the coming campaign as a "war of extermination" and that he repeated his earlier instructions by ordering "the extermination of the Bolshevist Commissars and of the Communist intelligentsia."[17]

In conjunction with efforts to prepare the armed forces for special tasks in the East, Hitler also limited military jurisdiction by restricting the authority of military courts to examine incidents of criminal offenses involving Soviet citizens. This move essentially deprived these persons of due process and placed their fates in the hands of military and SS field units. On May 13, Keitel issued a decree suspending the jurisdiction of the courts over "enemy civilians" committing criminal offenses, thus creating a situation in which Wehrmacht, SS, and police forces literally became judge, jury, and executioner.[18]

As Wehrmacht commanders finalized their operational plans for the invasion of the Soviet Union, Himmler and Reinhard Heydrich, chief of the Security Police and Security Service (SD), developed the blueprint for the activities of SS and police forces. In a meeting with Göring on March 26, Heydrich reported on SS plans for the "solution to the Jewish question" in conjunction with the coming campaign.[19] For his part, Göring expressed his concern that German forces be made aware of the danger posed by Soviet intelligence personnel (GPU), political commissars, and Jews in order that they might know "who they had to stand against the wall." The German army High Command sent a letter to Himmler, Heydrich, and Daluege on May 6, 1941, in order to set up a meeting between SS and police leaders and the commanders of the army rear areas and the commanders of the army Security Divisions, presumably to discuss the command relationships, duties, and responsibilities of both sides in the forthcoming campaign.[20] Daluege's participation in these discussions was significant and has not received the recognition that it deserves. Once again, it offers further indirect, but still powerful, evidence of the role envisioned for the Uniformed Police in cooperation with their Security Police counterparts in the campaign against the Soviet Union.

After final negotiations with the Wehrmacht, on May 21, 1941, Himmler issued a top secret decree entitled "Special Order from the Führer" delineating the command relationship between SS and police forces and their military counterparts. The Commissar Order (*Kommissarbefehl*) of June 6, 1941, with its prescription for the execution of Communist functionaries and political commissars serving with the Red Army, including Jews in Party and state positions, provided the final link in a series of orders, decrees, and directives that paved the way for the conduct of a racial war of extermination.[21]

The Police and the Einsatzgruppen

As German forces streamed across the Soviet border on June 22, four Einsatzgruppen with the letter designations A, B, C, and D followed closely on the heels of the Wehrmacht. Assigned specific geographic areas of responsibility, Einsatzgruppe A operated in the Baltics and parts of Belorussia, Einsatzgruppe B in Belorussia, Einsatzgruppe C in northern and central Ukraine, and Einsatzgruppe D in southern Ukraine, Bessarabia, the Crimea, and the Caucasus. These groups ranged in size from almost a thousand personnel in Einsatzgruppe A to approximately five hundred in Einsatzgruppe D. The Einsatzgruppen were composed primarily of members of the Security Police (both the Gestapo and the Criminal Police), the SD, the Uniformed Police, and members of the Waffen-SS. Operating primarily in small detachments, the *Einsatzkommandos* and *Sonderkommandos* enthusiastically and methodically pursued their murderous charter, that pursuit involving actions that ranged from the execution of single individuals to the mass shootings of tens of thousands.[22]

The composition of the Einsatzgruppen in the attack on the Soviet Union epitomized the close interlinkages between all parts of Himmler's SS and police imperium by mid-1941. In fact, on April 8 Himmler met with Daluege to discuss the impending campaign and then again on April 16 with Heydrich, Daluege, General Wagner, and Hans Jüttner, the head of Himmler's SS military General Staff, or Führungsamt. This latter meeting lasted an entire afternoon and involved the senior leaders of the SS and police offices supplying troops to the Einsatzgruppen, and the activities of these formations undoubtedly constituted the central item of discussion.[23]

Reserve PB 9 was the initial Uniformed Police contingent provided to the Einsatzgruppen, serving from June to December 1941, until Reserve PB 3 replaced it in January 1942. For the initial invasion, the four companies of PB 9 were divided between the four Einsatzgruppen; however, the men were further divided into platoons and squads and then assigned to specific *Einsatzkommandos* and *Sonderkommandos,* while the company staff remained with the Einsatzgruppen headquarters staff.[24] The presence of the company commander at the headquarters provided him with an opportunity to work closely with the SS leadership of the Einsatzgruppen and to travel between the dispersed platoons on a regular basis.[25] The policemen on the company staff, including those assigned to administrative duties, also routinely participated in executions.[26]

Most of the men of the Fourth Company, assigned to Einsatzgruppe D, came from the ranks of the police reservists mobilized in 1939 and 1940. Additionally, the majority of the company came from the year groups between 1900 and 1916, with the median age falling in the year groups 1908 and 1909.[27] Although membership in the Party was more the exception than the rule for the rank and file, the age demographics of the group once again provide indirect evidence of strong proregime sentiments.[28] In preparation for their deadly duties, these men received special briefings and indoctrination prior to the attack.[29] For example, one member of the Third Company recalled a speech by the head of Einsatzgruppe C, SS-Brigadeführer Dr. Otto Rasch, discussing the "coming difficult mission."[30] Another policeman remembered the battalion being briefed by a "high-ranking police officer" in Berlin prior to the campaign and being told of its assignment to the Einsatzgruppen for "an especially important task."[31]

An examination of backgrounds of the officers in the Fourth Company, by contrast, reveals close ties, and in several cases fervent commitment, to the Party. For example, the company commander, Hans Gabel, joined the NSDAP (National Socialist German Workers' Party) and the SA in 1927. A former member of the Feldjägerkorps, he successfully entered the police officer ranks and boasted of his participation in the march into Austria, the occupation of the Sudetenland and the Czech protectorate, and the campaign in Poland. In truth, Gabel represented the ideal of the political soldier within the officer corps of the Uniformed Police, a man who embodied the concept of martial combatant and Party loyalist.[32] His background and his commitment to the mission of the killing formations were not anomalies. For example, Uniformed Police officers with reserve commissions attached to Einsatzgruppe A requested to remain with the Security Police and the SD on completion of their duties.[33]

It is certainly probable that some policemen within the rank and file found their tasks difficult and unpleasant; however, that did not prevent many of these men from executing the enemies of the Reich. Herbert Schmidt (a pseudonym), a policeman in PB 9 and a member of the Second Platoon, Third Company, remembered "having to" participate with Einsatzkommando 6 in an execution of Jews shortly after the start of the attack near Lemberg.[34] Similarly, Hermann Reuter (a pseudonym) admitted that his platoon participated with Einsatzkommando 5 in the summary execution of thirty-five persons.[35] Another policeman, Georg Bender (a pseudonym), revealed knowledge of three actions in which Jewish men, women, and children as well as "Gypsie" men, women, and children were shot in the vicinity of Nowo Ukrainka.[36] These isolated admissions, however, vastly underrated the participation of the uniformed policemen of PB 9 in the killing machinery of the Einsatzgruppen and proved to be only the tip of the iceberg. By December 1941, the unit's war diary indicated that, by itself, the battalion had taken credit for a total of fifty-two thousand victims.[37]

In postwar testimony, the commander of the Third Company, Captain of the Police Walter Kramer (a pseudonym), assigned to the headquarters of Einsatzgruppe C, contended that, sometime after the start of the killings, he traveled to Berlin to see Otto Winkelmann, the chief of staff of the Uniformed Police Operations Office, in order to request the transfer of his company from its duties. Kramer said that he informed Winkelmann of the unit's activities, divulged the "burden" (*Belastung*) placed on his men by them, and asked whether the intent was to "breed murderers."[38] In one respect, it appears highly unlikely that a captain would at his own discretion leave his unit at the front to travel to Berlin. If Kramer did, in fact, return to Berlin, it is more likely that he was directed to, in order to provide Winkelmann with details of the unit's activities. Likewise, Kramer's postwar account frames his opposition, not in terms of injustice or the moral indefensibility of the killings, but in terms of the effects on the essential "humanity" of his men, concerns expressed by Himmler and others and based on the difficult nature of large-scale face-to-face killing of unarmed men, women, and children.

Admissions of direct complicity are rare in postwar testimony, for two reasons. First, many of the former policemen remained in the ranks of the police after the war and certainly understood the danger in directly implicating themselves. They also knew what they could and should not admit. For example, many conceded that they had "heard" of executions or even that, while conducting cordon duty, they had "heard" shooting.[39] Second, these men often met in groups prior to giving testimony in order to agree on a cover story.[40] However, given their distribution among various detachments known to have participated in killing actions, it is utterly beyond belief that they remained oblivious or uninvolved.

The fact that, in the face of potential criminal prosecution, some policemen eventually admitted to involvement in murders and mass executions makes their testimony far more compelling than that of men offering outright denials. For example, Erwin Zahn (a pseudonym), a policeman with PB 3, admitted to witnessing and participating in massacres, including the execution of one hundred children from an orphanage in which the shooters primarily came from the ranks of the police. Zahn remarked: "I can say as a principle that all the squad members shot. It is possible that the one functioned as a shooter more often than the other. Great value was placed on the fact that everyone shot. We stood at the edge of the ditch and shot the victims as they were led up, women, men, and children. . . . I myself functioned as a shooter once or twice." Zahn continued: "It was clear to me that it was unjust, what was happening to the Jews; nevertheless, no one dared openly protest against it."[41] Another member of PB 3, Johann Henkel (a pseudonym), also revealed his own and his platoon's participation with Einsatzkommando 8 in the conduct of executions. Henkel admitted to taking part in one massacre of some one thousand "Jews and Russians," including men, women, and children. He stated: "I was at the time and today as well of the opinion that the shooting of women, men, and children represented an injustice, [but] no one had the possibility of evading it."[42]

Both Zahn's testimony and Henkel's are important, for a number of reasons. First, both men implicated themselves in the actions and, by doing so, validated their accounts. Second, both admitted that they realized that the murder of their victims was unjust but that protest seemed pointless. Third, both substantiated the fact that all members of their platoons participated in the shootings and that none could shirk this duty. With respect to this last point, Zahn remembered a number of members of the SS among the police reservists in his unit, and Henkel stated that the platoon leader, Lieutenant Jannicke (a pseudonym), a member of the SS, not only ensured that every man shot, but also made sure that the "regular" policemen led the way.[43] Jannicke's background and his insistence that regular policemen lead the way in the conduct of atrocity point to the intrinsic beliefs and values that had developed in the Uniformed Police officer corps as well as the importance of leadership at all levels of the SS and police in making genocide a reality.

The Police Battalions and the Einsatzgruppen

As German forces pushed into the Soviet Union, the Einsatzgruppen did not have to rely solely on the policemen of PB 9 for support for their murderous activities. They received ready and willing collaboration from the other police battalions supporting the invasion as well, collaboration that continued into 1943.[44] For example, uniformed policemen, in conjunction with Wehrmacht forces, assisted Sonderkommando 4a in the execution of 1,160 Jews in Luzk on July 2, 1941, and PB 45, PB 303, and PB 314 assisted Sonderkommando 4a in the murder of almost 34,000 Jews at a ravine in Babi Yar on September 29 and 30, 1941.[45] In Belorussia, men from PB 316 participated, with a detachment from Einsatzgruppe B, in the murder of 1,100 Jewish men in mid-July, while Reserve PB 11 assisted in pacifying the area west of Borissow.[46]

These examples represent only a small sampling of cooperative police battalion–Einsatzgruppen actions during the invasion, but they offer two insights into the nature of the organizational arrangements between the killing formations and their Uniformed Police counterparts in 1941. First, they demonstrate the close working relationship that had been established between the various branches of Himmler's SS and the police apparatus by 1941. Certainly, assistance during the prewar period and especially during the invasion and subsequent occupation of Poland had only served to strengthen that relationship. Second, they demonstrate that the police battalions entered the Soviet Union with a clear idea of the apocalyptic nature of the war and with a definite sense of the task at hand. Descriptions of visits by Himmler and Daluege and other senior SS leaders prior to a battalion's departure for the East or during its stay provide more than adequate evidence of the instructions given, even if Himmler and Daluege avoided providing written orders.

In the early stages of the war, the cooperation between the men of the Security Police and the SD and the Uniformed Police did not remain limited to the Einsatzgruppen. A platoon of policemen from Memel joined Security Police and Wehrmacht forces in the conduct of a "cleansing action" aimed primarily at Jews in the towns of Garsden, Krottingen, and Polangen just east of the German-Lithuanian border during the first week of the invasion. The policemen practiced execution procedures on June 23 before their departure for Garsden the next day, and one enlisted member of the platoon correctly guessed that the unit's mission involved the murder of Jews. Some men dropped out of the firing squad because they knew some of the 201 Jewish victims, but none of those who remained refused to shoot. Afterward, the men discussed the action among themselves and came to the conclusion that it was necessary. In the words of one participant, "Man alive, confound it, one generation has to go through this so that our children will have a better life."[47]

The Case of Police Battalion 45

The participation of the police battalions in support of the activities of the Einsatzgruppen provides one example of their involvement in the war of annihilation on the Eastern Front; however, as the activities of PB 45 demonstrate, these police formations needed no assistance in the conduct of atrocity. The battalion consisted primarily of police reservists mobilized from the Sudetenland with a mix of regular policemen. In May 1941, it received orders to move from the Reich to Poland in preparation for the coming offensive against the Soviet Union. And, in the first week of July, it began its march to the front, arriving in the Ukraine during the fourth week of July.[48] It did not take long for the battalion's men to become involved in the prosecution of racial policy as the Third Platoon of the Third Company executed an estimated ten Jews in the forest in Oleskoje in the last week of July. By the middle of August, the battalion emerged as a deadly instrument as the First and Second Companies combined in the shooting of 522 Jewish men, women, and children near Slavuta.[49] According to reports on August 22 and 24, PB 45 executed five prisoners (including three partisan women [*Flintenweiber*]), nineteen "bandits," and 598 Jews.[50]

By September, the battalion's killing activities had increased in scale dramatically. One member of the Third Company remembered the unit's participation in the execution of Jews in the towns of Dubrovka, Berdichev, and Vinnitsa. In the case of Berdichev, the battalion commander, Major Besser, and the commander of the Third Company, Captain Berentsen, supervised the execution of approximately 3,000 Jews on the grounds of the local airfield in early September. Following a routine that became standard in the East, the policemen of PB 45 gathered together the town's Jewish population and marched them in groups to the airfield while those too old or too sick to walk were ordered into trucks and driven there. The summary execution of those attempting to escape or unable to complete the march left the roadside littered with bodies. As the Jews arrived at the airfield, the Fourth Platoon of the Third Company, augmented by volunteers from other platoons, executed them in small groups, using pistols and machine pistols, a process so lengthy that only late in the evening hours could Captain Berentsen report:

"The bloody business is over!"[51] In his postwar testimony, Ferdinand Wasser (a pseudonym) insisted that he had served in a security cordon in the town during the action. Wasser alleged that the battalion's "regular" policemen acted as the most enthusiastic executioners and that "no one was forced to shoot anyone."[52]

Like many policemen interviewed after the war, Wasser identified specific individuals who had distinguished themselves by their zeal in carrying out their duties. For example, he described Herbert Kindl (a pseudonym), a senior enlisted policeman from East Prussia, as "particularly bloodthirsty" and a man who "was more an animal than a human." Wasser related a story of Kindl sitting down on the body of a naked Jewish woman as he ate a sandwich as well as his practice of grabbing children by their feet and flinging them head first into a wall. Wasser also recalled an attempt by the company's first sergeant, Fritz Forst (a pseudonym), to rape a Russian girl as well as the sadistic pleasure that Forst took in executing Jews and Slavs, including his practice of torturing prisoners by firing a pistol round upward into a victim's bent elbow, ensuring that the bullet traveled through the arm before exiting at the shoulder.[53] A police reservist from the Sudetenland, Walter Grosz (a pseudonym), also described Kindl's role in executions, but Grosz especially remembered the actions of the company's armorer, who "specialized" in the execution of children, his methods including holding them up by their feet and shooting them in the back of the head.[54]

Such testimony is so shocking in its portrayal of casual brutality that it threatens to overwhelm the ability psychologically to process it, especially as it represents only the tip of the iceberg. While their behavior might have been extreme, Kindl and Forst were not the only men who regularly participated in the conduct of mass murder. For example, Captain of the Police Berentsen also acted as a shooter during executions, as did at least two of his platoon leaders, Lieutenants Thaler and Burger (pseudonyms), the latter of whom had a reputation in the company as a "hater of Jews" (*Judenhasser*).[55] In other words, the senior leadership, both officer and enlisted, set the tone for the company. It was not just their participation in the executions but their approval and acceptance of sadistic practices that fostered an atmosphere in which brutality emerged as an organizational norm. It is important to remember, however, that PB 45 was not unique, as the actions of PB 61 under its company commander and its own "fanatical Jew hater" had proved in the occupation of Poland (see chapter 4).[56]

From Berdichev, the men of PB 45 went on to conduct executions of Jews in Vinnitsa, Faztov, Belaya Zerkov, Kiew, Pereyaslav, Poltava, and Kharkow.[57] In other words, death and atrocity were, not occasional, but constant companions of this battalion as it moved east. Its participation in the mass murder of the Jews of Kiev stands out because of the scale of that action; however, its participation in the murder of the Jews of Vinnitsa served, like the executions in Berdichev, as a bloody prelude to the events in Kiev. In Vinnitsa, the First and Third Companies, with the approval of the Wehrmacht commander of the town (*Stadtkommandant*), cooperated in rounding up and transporting the Jewish population to three giant cisterns outside the town, where they were led to the edge and shot at close range. By the end of the action, the cisterns literally overflowed with bodies.[58] The execution of Jews at Belaya Zerkov was similarly grisly. Wasser recalled:

> I have gruesome memories, especially during the execution of children, where the children were grabbed by the hair and then shot. In this process, it occurred that the top of the skull and the hair remained in the shooter's hand while the child fell into the ditch. I saw this once. In addition, I can add that, during the executions, first the children and only then the women and mothers of these children were shot. With respect to the men that were shot, for the most part it dealt with the aged [*Greise*].[59]

The actions of the men of PB 45 were distinguished, not by their extraordinariness, but by their ordinariness, by the fact that they came to represent normalcy for the police formations operating on the Eastern Front.

Massacre at Białystok

The activities of PB 309 in the city of Białystok on June 27, 1941, provide further evidence of the general organizational atmosphere established within the police battalions and the attitudes of their members. Prior to the invasion, PB 309 was one of three police battalions assigned to Wehrmacht Security Divisions in Army Group Center, PB 309 acting under the operational control of the 221st Security Division.[60] Shortly before the invasion, the division released the following instructions to prepare its men for battle: "The troops of the Red Army oppose us not only as military, but political, enemies. According to the Jewish-Bolshevist teaching, [the Red Army] will not only make use of military combat methods. The men must be prepared for this [and], if it is necessary, resort to drastic measures with the appropriate toughness and ruthlessness also with regard to the enemy population."[61]

On the morning of June 27, the battalion received orders to support its Wehrmacht counterparts in Security Regiment 2 to "cleanse the city" of any remaining Russian soldiers and "anti-German inhabitants," thereby establishing "calm, security, and order." As the Wehrmacht and police forces came into the city, they encountered no resistance; however, this did not prevent the policemen of the First and Third Companies from initiating an orgy of violence and plunder as they entered the Jewish quarter.[62] The actions of the men included the physical mistreatment and arbitrary execution of Jews as well as the looting of a local wine dealer's shop.[63] In the course of the police search of the Jewish quarter, numerous Jews, including children, fell victim.[64] By the afternoon, the policemen had rounded up at least seven hundred male Jews and locked them in the city's main synagogue. They then poured gasoline in the entrances of the synagogue and used a hand grenade to start a fire that spread to surrounding houses in the city center. Some two thousand Jews ultimately fell victim to either the fire or police bullets.[65] Afterward, the commander of PB 309, Major Ernst Weis, justified the killings as a response to resistance from "Russian soldiers and irregulars [*Freischärler*]," and he estimated the number of enemy dead at only two hundred, including Russian soldiers, irregulars, and Jews.[66]

The events in Białystok offer two insights into the activities of the police. First, the division's orders prior to the campaign framed the coming war in racial terms by equating Jews and Bolsheviks and encouraged the use of drastic measures to combat this "threat." One police officer in PB 309 even remembered a showing of the virulently anti-Semitic film *Jud Süß* during the unit's preparations in Poland as well as orders framing the impending invasion as a clash of opposing ideologies.[67] Still, the pogrom aimed at the city's Jewish population arose from the ranks of two police companies that chose to escalate the violence from mistreatment and random shootings to the premeditated massacre of hundreds. In other words, the leaders of the First and Third Companies, mere captains and lieutenants, instigated or approved of the massacre. Second, the men who perpetrated the massacre received post facto praise and recognition, not only from their battalion commander, but from the Wehrmacht division commander as well. In fact, Major Weis subsequently received a recommendation for the Iron Cross second-class for his leadership in the "cleansing actions" of June 26 and 27.[68] Not only was the acceptance of and reward for the murder of Jews a direct reflection of the values and norms present within the organizational culture of the battalion, but the actions in Białystok demonstrated the expanded boundaries of acceptable behavior within the unit. The resulting message sent to the men of PB 309 could not have been clearer, as their later activities demonstrated.

On July 3, a week after the murderous rampage, PB 309 received orders to collect and stockpile captured Russian weapons in the cities of Białowieza and Stoczek.[69] A day later, it supervised repairs to a quarter-mile stretch conducted by a 150-man "Jewish work detachment" four miles east of Białowieza on the road to Pruzhany.[70] After its actions in Białystok, little imagination is required to envision the treatment that the unit meted out to its charges. On July 5, the battalion "cleansed" a forested area near Chwojnik and hinted at the outcome by promising a report to the division's chief of staff.[71] By the second week of July, two of the battalion's companies were cooperating closely with the 350th Infantry Regiment in providing security for road and rail connections. In addition, one company remained in Białowieza in charge of a Jewish work camp (*Judenarbeitslager*) at Hajnowka.[72] This pattern of contact highlights just how closely the police were involved in the mobilization and incarceration of Jewish forced labor. But of course PB 309 was not the only battalion involved in the slaughter of Jews in the opening stages of the war. The participation of PB 307 in the massacre of Jews in the city of Brest-Litowsk during the second week of July 1941 provides another example of the rapidity with which policemen became executioners in the opening weeks of the invasion.

Massacre at Brest-Litowsk

On July 8, the HSSPF for Special Purposes, Erich von dem Bach-Zelewski, notified the 221st Security Division of his approval of the use of PB 307 in a "cleansing action" in Brest-Litowsk.[73] Not coincidentally, on the same day that Bach issued that directive he had also met with Himmler, Daluege, the commander of Police Regiment Center, Colonel Max Montua, and the commander of Army Rear Area, Center, General Max von Schenckendorff, in Białystok.[74] At this meeting Himmler had complained that too few Jews had been rounded up and had ordered the police leadership to increase their efforts. Given that the Białystok massacre followed shortly thereafter, that the Brest-Litowsk massacre followed shortly after that, and that all battalions involved were operating in Army Group Center, it appears reasonable to assume that both massacres were the direct result of Himmler's orders.[75]

Assisted by members of the 162nd Infantry Division, the police took the lead in the operation at Brest-Litowsk by closing and cordoning off areas housing the city's Jewish population early the morning of July 9. "Work-capable" Jewish males between the ages of sixteen and sixty were then identified and escorted to a central collection point, from which they were either marched or trucked to a site south of the city where, in groups of ten to twelve, they were shot by policemen using carbines. The process, which lasted from midmorning until late afternoon, was repeated for several days thereafter.[76]

A postwar investigation conducted by the state prosecutor's office in Lübeck revealed the presence of the battalion commander, Major Stahr, at the execution site,[77] apparently the result of directions given to Bach by Himmler: "Battalion commanders and company chiefs have to make special accommodations for the spiritual care of the men participating in such actions. The impressions of the day have to be blurred by having social gatherings [*Kameradschaftsabende*]. In addition, the men have to be continuously lectured about the necessity of measures caused by the political situation."[78] Apparently, the thought of mass shootings did not disturb the spiritual state of the men of PB 307 as the number of volunteers for the execution detachment exceeded the number required.[79] In fact, the availability of men willing to participate in mass murder constitutes a red thread throughout the course of the events as volunteers could always be found, whether within the ranks of the police battalions or in the Gendarmerie posts scattered throughout Poland and Russia.[80]

The massacre in Brest-Litowsk proved to be the springboard for the men of PB 307, who in the coming months murdered their way through the western Soviet Union. For example, the battalion assisted Einsatzkommando 8 in the execution of eighty persons in Starobin, a village some seventy-five miles south of Minsk, on July 29, 1941.[81] This operation appears to have involved the execution of Jewish women and children, and, at one point, a participant reported, a policeman ordered that a surviving child be taken to its mother (who already lay dead in a grave), placed on her dead body, and then shot.[82] During the rest of 1941, the battalion added to its growing total of victims, its duties mixed between securing German supply lines and combating partisans in addition to anti-Jewish actions, a pattern made all too familiar by PB 322, PB 307's sister unit.[83]

The "Shadow War"

According to one historian, the Wehrmacht's Security Divisions constituted the "backbone" of the antipartisan campaign in the Soviet Union.[84] More important, the police battalions, with their motorized formations, constituted the backbone of the Security Divisions. From the earliest days of the invasion, Wehrmacht commanders pled constantly for the assistance of the motorized battalions.[85] But few were initially available. For example, an after-action report from the 213th Security Division complaining that the division's organization and equipment were not up to the task of combating an enemy scattered in small groups across a large area specifically noted that PB 318 was the "only mobile, motorized unit" in the division.[86] Likewise, the 221st and 403rd Security Divisions indicated their concern when they temporarily lost control of their motorized police battalions in early September 1941.[87] Clearly, an army that had entered the Soviet Union largely on its feet and with its supplies largely horse drawn found motorized units to be a valuable commodity.[88] Hitler's personal intervention, resulting in the allocation of extremely scarce resources to the motorization of, not just the police formations, but the Einsatzgruppen in general, speaks volumes concerning the importance that he attached to these SS and police units.[89]

At the end of July, Himmler issued guidelines to SS mounted units operating with the Command Staff RFSS (Kommandostab Reichsführer SS) regarding the conduct of antipartisan operations and emphasizing the role of Security Police and Uniformed Police formations in assisting their SS counterparts. In order to avoid casualties, he remarked, it was necessary to use Luftwaffe aircraft to attack towns in which SS and police forces encountered particularly "stubborn resistance." To ensure the reliability of the local population, he ordered the recruitment of informers as well as the distribution of horses and foodstuffs captured by German forces but in excess of their needs. In cases where the population displayed an anti-German attitude, Himmler's solution was more direct: "If the population in a national sense is adversarial, racially and physically inferior, or even, as is often the case in swampy regions, composed of settled criminals, all those suspected of supporting the partisans are to be shot. Women and children are to be transported away, livestock and foodstuffs confiscated and secured. The villages are to be burned to the ground." Himmler ended with the warning: "Either the villages and communities form a net of support bases [*Stützpunkte*] whose inhabitants on their own accord exterminate [*totschlagen*] every partisan or marauder and inform us of everything [that happens], or they cease to exist."[90]

These guidelines offer a number of important insights into the conduct and nature of the antipartisan campaign. First and foremost, they indicate that the *Reichsführer* envisioned the campaign as a combined endeavor, one incorporating SS, Security Police, and Uniformed Police forces, a precedent established during the occupation of Poland and continued throughout the remainder of the war. Second, by calling for Luftwaffe support they pointed to a broader collaborative relationship between the SS and police complex and the German armed forces than simply cooperation with German army forces. This was not merely wishful thinking as SS and police forces repeatedly called on their counterparts in the Luftwaffe to provide support in the battle against the partisans. Finally, they reflected the brutal methods that awaited those persons and communities who opposed or were thought to oppose the German occupation.

During the occupation of the Soviet Union, the police battalions became highly skilled in the conduct of antipartisan operations aimed at both real and imagined resistance fighters and the political and racial enemies of the Third Reich. Acting on behalf of Daluege, General Winkelmann later released the fourteen-page "Guidelines for the Combat of Partisans" (originally issued by the army High Command), indicating that the document should be distributed to battalion-level units, which should immediately make it a "special object of training and discussion." The guidelines provided explicit directions on the handling of partisans: "The enemy must be *entirely wiped out*. The decision concerning the life or death of a captured partisan is difficult even for the toughest soldier. Action must be taken. He who completely disregards eventual sentiments of compassion and ruthlessly and mercilessly seizes the opportunity acts correctly."[91]

The "Guidelines for the Combat of the Partisans" was not the first Wehrmacht directive on the subject passed to the police units. For example, the police battalions operating with the 221st Security Division received instructions in a division order on August 12, 1941, to consider "*all* [Soviet] soldiers encountered west of the Beresina [River] as irregulars and to treat them accordingly."[92] The next line of the order explained what was meant by this treatment as it called for daily reports on the numbers of irregulars executed. Five weeks later, another published order distinguished between Soviet combat troops captured during battle and those who after the fighting is finished "emerge from their hiding places" to attack the German lines of communication. The former were to be taken prisoner, the latter considered irregulars and treated accordingly. However, additional directions indicated that it was the senior commander who should, on the basis of the tactical situation, decide whether captured soldiers were to be treated as prisoners or irregulars, thus allowing each commander to act according to his own judgment.[93]

When the Wehrmacht directives are compared with Himmler's guidance of July 28, it is clear that the former, although advocating atrocity, remained confined to soldiers, or at least those bearing arms or those providing direct support to combatants. In contrast, the *Reichsführer*'s guidelines clearly encompassed, not just combatants, but the racial and political enemies of the Third Reich, treating both groups as objects of extermination. For example, one Gendarmerie commander ordered the execution of "every male found wandering in the woods without [a convincing] explanation or under suspicious circumstances."[94] Still, both the Wehrmacht and the SS appear to have used antipartisan operations as a cover to eliminate a plethora of "enemies," as evidenced by a Wehrmacht report for October and November 1941 detailing the army's cooperation with SS and police forces in the execution of 10,431 of 10,940 captured partisans among whom a mere eighty-nine infantry weapons had been found.[95] In preparation for a meeting with Hitler on December 18, 1941, Himmler made the connection between the war against the partisans and the Third Reich's racial policies explicit, noting tel-egraphically: "Jewish question—to be exterminated as partisans."[96]

The Murder of Soviet POWs

In addition to combating partisans and murdering Jews, uniformed police-men became active participants in the killing of Soviet POWs. For example, during Operation "Chicken Farm," members of the Second Company of PB 306 executed several thousand POWs between September 21 and Septem-ber 28, 1941.[97] Similarly, policemen from the Gendarmerie post at Zwiahel led the execution of "former POWs."[98] In January 1942, General of the Police Adolf von Bomhard, the head of the Uniformed Police Operations Office, forwarded a copy of a Wehrmacht directive to police forces along with his own instructions concerning the importance of finding and arrest-ing escaped POWs and turning them over to the Security Police for "further handling." Bomhard also noted that, after due consideration of local condi-tions in the army rear areas, the police should take "the appropriate mea-sures in cooperation with the Einsatzgruppen" in dealing with POWs.[99] In a specific example, a Gendarmerie commander in Zhitomir ordered the exe-cution of escaped or released POWs found wandering in the forests.[100] The former case demonstrated the close cooperative relationship between the Uni-formed Police and the Security Police in the prosecution of murder, while the latter highlighted the local initiative of police commanders. In August 1942, the police received orders to shoot without warning any escaped Soviet POWs, their power to act on their own initiative in dealing with this puta-tive threat to German rule thereby being broadened.[101]

The Command Staff RFSS

In preparation for the invasion, Himmler created the Command Staff RFSS. Located in the East Prussian town of Arys, the Command Staff represented yet another marriage of forces, composed as it was of Waffen-SS and Uni-formed Police formations, again highlighting the symbiotic relationship enjoyed by the SS and the police during the first months of the campaign. Under the aegis of the Command Staff, Waffen-SS and Uniformed Police for-mations used the pretext of antipartisan operations to conduct a murderous rampage against the Soviet Union's Jewish population.[102] It was charged with acting as both a headquarters for SS and police forces and a clearinghouse for SS and police reports documenting the pacification of the Soviet Union.

Himmler's obsession with these field reports offers one indication of the importance that he attached to these units' operations. And an explanation for this obsession can be found in Himmler's regular practice of providing copies of these reports directly to Hitler, who valued them for their highly detailed accounts.

For example, a report by the First SS Brigade covering the period between July 27 and July 30 provided an overview of the brigade's mission, which was described as "the capture or annihilation of a) remnants of the 124th Soviet Infantry Division, b) armed gangs, c) irregulars, d) persons who provided encouragement to the Bolshevist system." One also learns from the report that, operating with two police battalions from Police Regiment South, the brigade executed 814 persons during the three-day period. The victims included 9 Russian soldiers in civilian attire shot as irregulars, 5 Soviet functionaries (including one woman), and 800 Jewish men and women between the ages of sixteen and sixty executed for "aiding and abetting Bolshevism and as Bolshevist irregulars."[103] A report a week later from SS Infantry Regiment 10 detailed a "cleansing action" involving the execution of 14 "agitators and Jews" and the capture of 30 prisoners, while a subsequent report noted the public hanging of 2 Jews in Zhitomir for providing "encouragement to gangs."[104]

Two separate reports, both from August 19, demonstrate that, in addition to providing support for the Waffen-SS, the police battalions had learned to murder as well as their SS counterparts did. The reports remarked on the participation of PB 303 and one company of PB 45 in the "combat of gangs" and noted the execution of 25 Jews and 16 Ukrainians by PB 314 as well as the unit's execution of 322 Jews in the town of Slavuta. The second report also referred to the use of units from Police Regiment South in antipartisan operations that resulted in the killing of 24 suspected partisans and the capture of 33 prisoners, who, after being interrogated, were shot. It also indicated the loss of 1 policeman and the wounding of 4 others.[105]

A report prepared on August 20 by Jeckeln's staff company, composed of members of both the SS and the police, detailed the execution of 514 Jews and 2 armed partisans as well as the killing by units from Police Regiment South of 212 partisans and the capture of another 19, at a cost of 1 man killed and 1 wounded.[106] A report of August 21 boasted of the execution of 367 Jews by PB 314 in a "cleansing action" to secure German supply lines.[107] And, finally, a report of August 22 recorded the execution of 5 prisoners (including 3 partisan women [*Flintenweiber*]), 19 "bandits," and 537 Jews by PB 45 and the execution on charges of "arson" of 28 Ukrainians by PB 314.[108]

These early reports are important in a number of respects. First, they highlight the close cooperation between Waffen-SS and police forces in the conduct of antipartisan operations. Second, they highlight the execution of Jews and the scale of the massacres, clearly showing that the police were not afraid to take the lead in the conduct of racial policy. Third, they present evidence— the high number of enemy killed and the low number of prisoners taken, combined with the relatively light losses experienced by the police forces—that argues that many of those killed as partisans were certainly not armed and most likely not even members of a partisan group. Fourth, they offer examples of the use of euphemism both to characterize the victims and to justify their execution. Finally, they seem to indicate a rising trend of murder and atrocity as these units became accustomed to their duties.

The last week of August proved to be an especially bloody period for the Command Staff's SS and police forces. Status reports of August 24 detailed the capture of 19 prisoners by SS Infantry Regiment 8 and 85 by SS Infantry Regiment 10 as well as the execution of 283 "Bolshevist Jews." They also indicate that the police battalions proved equally adept at killing, as demonstrated by the execution during this period of 294 Jews by PB 314, 61 Jews by PB 45, and 113 Jews by a police mounted formation. One of the reports remarked as well that the Einsatzgruppen executed 12 "bandits and irregulars" and 70 Jews.[109] On August 25, the First SS Brigade reported the execution of the 85 prisoners taken the previous day, Police Regiment South announced the execution of 1,342 Jews, and PB 304 captured and executed 8 Soviet paratroopers.[110] On August 27, the SS and police forces recorded their success by noting the capture of 145 prisoners and the execution of 98 Jews by Waffen-SS forces, but it was once again the police that led the way, their accomplishments including the capture of 23 prisoners and the execution of 1,463 Jews by Police Regiment South and the execution of 69 Jews by PB 314 and 546 Jews by Jeckeln's staff.[111]

Reading over this incomplete sampling of remaining reports from the area of the HSSPF South sent to the Command Staff RFSS in the month between July 27 and August 27, the mind numbs as numbers follow numbers in a litany that effaces the identities and human faces of those killed. These reports alone indicate that Waffen-SS formations murdered 1,294 persons, including 1,195 Jews; the police battalions 4,905, including 4,593 Jews; and Jeckeln's staff company 1,062, including 1,060 Jews. In other words, *an astounding 94 percent* of the victims were Jews. Furthermore, the SS mounted formations reported the execution of "approximately 3,000 Jews and irregulars" in the week between July 27 and August 3 alone.[112] It is important to remember that this orgy of murder proceeded independently of the deadly Einsatzgruppen march east. The routine commission of atrocities by numerous police battalions, both regular and reserve, in the rear areas of Army Group South during just the second month of the attack aptly highlights the emergence of these battalions as the "foot soldiers of annihilation."[113]

It should, therefore, come as no surprise that the commander of Police Regiment South was Colonel of the Police Hermann Franz, as previously noted a prototypical example of Himmler's ideal of the political soldier (see chapter 1). Franz, a highly decorated veteran of the Great War and a man who continued to describe himself as a "soldier" after entering the Uniformed Police in 1920, secretly joined the NSDAP in 1929 and the SS in 1940. Born in Leipzig on August 16, 1891, Franz had celebrated his fiftieth birthday in Russia amid the murderous activities of his regiment.[114] Until his transfer at the end of August, Franz directed the activities of PB 45, PB 303, and PB 314. His background and the activities of the police battalions under his command make it clear that Himmler and Daluege had chosen well in their selection of this regimental commander. Likewise, the battalions under his command proved capable instruments for enforcing racial policy.

The Case of PB 314

During August 1941, PB 314 murdered at least 1,689 persons, including 1,655 Jews, in seven separate operations.[115] In September, it cooperated with Einsatzkommando 6 in the killing of some 10,000 Jews in the city of Vinnitsa and an estimated 15,000 Jews in the city of Dnepropetrovsk.[116] Mobilized in early 1941, the battalion had moved first to a staging base in Poland and then, following the invasion, to the Soviet Union. Its home base was Vienna, and, as a postwar investigation revealed, most of its members—over 75 percent—were born between 1907 and 1914, year groups that accounted for the largest portion of the National Socialist Party's constituency.[117] Furthermore, few of the battalion's men were mobilized reservists, most having joined the Uniformed Police as "active applicants," indicating their desire to pursue a police career, a career that a great number continued within the Austrian police force after the war.[118]

Two of the men of PB 314 remembered being told of orders concerning actions to be taken against the Jewish population. One of these two, Karl Gerlach (a pseudonym), a member of the First Company, recalled being told of a secret order by an officer in his platoon: "I remember that it concerned an order with very severe measures and that toughness was also demanded from the persons [who had to carry it out]."[119] As noted earlier, the police battalions did not receive general orders to annihilate the Jews prior to the invasion; however, they had been prepared to accept that way of thinking by

their ideological indoctrination sessions as well as by the speeches and ceremonies that accompanied their departures. It is, however, possible that what
they were recalling were details passed along to them from the June 6 Commissar Order and interpreted in the light of later orders and their routine
participation in mass murder.

The testimony of Johann Lischler (a pseudonym) provides an account of
how murder became routine for the men of PB 314. After crossing into the
Soviet Union, the battalion staff and the Third Company moved into Kovel,
with the First and Second Companies divided between the nearby towns of
Lyuboml, Macijeov, and Goloby during parts of July and August. In his testimony, Lischler contended that a colleague from the First Company, Otto
Marsch (a pseudonym), discussed the "Jewish liquidation" in Macijeov conducted by his company. Marsch told Lischler of several actions involving the
mass shooting of the town's Jews, confined in a temporary camp, including
the murder of the town's Jewish council for failing to provide the established
amount of foodstuffs demanded by the company commander. Additionally,
Marsch discussed a change in execution procedures by the First Company
from shooting groups of ten with sidearms and carbines to mass shootings
using machine guns because the former process had become "too tedious"
(*zu langwierig*).[120]

For his part, Lischler described the execution of the Jews of Dnepropetrovsk over the course of a three- to four-week stay beginning in late
September 1941. The police herded the large Jewish population by the thousands into a local department store, from which they were subsequently
marched in groups to an execution site at a natural ravine near the city.[121] A
former platoon commander in the First Company, Franz Praeger (a pseudonym), also recalled the murder of the city's Jews and described his platoon's
role in the creation of a gauntlet leading to the execution site through which
the Jews were driven. Forced to leave their packed belongings in the department store, the victims had their valuables collected from them as they
approached the ravine. They then were made to stand with their backs to
the ravine, facing their executioners. The psychological distance between the
victims and their killers was, thus, further reduced as the latter could watch
the reactions of men, women, and children over the course of thousands of
executions.[122]

Praeger remembered seeing the battalion commander, Major Severth, and
his company commander, First Lieutenant of the Police Oskar Christ, at the
execution site and recalled an incident where one man insisted that he was
not a Jew, whereupon Severth or Christ ordered that the man be examined to
see if he was circumcised.[123] The First Company's zeal can, in part, be attributed to its commander. Born on March 30, 1912, in Wiesbaden, Christ proved

to be a willing killer, remembered for his arbitrary violence against both Jews and Slavs. During the executions at Dnepropetrovsk, he allegedly pulled out his pistol and fired wildly into the line of Jews, screaming that they were responsible for his brother's death, and killing several. In another instance, he shot several Russian farmers on the way to their fields without justification, murders that he subsequently defended by labeling the farmers as partisans.[124]

If Christ's commitment to the murder of Jews and Slavs appears clear, the participation of PB 314 in the entire spectrum of National Socialist racial policy in the East is equally apparent. Not only did these men murder Jews and Slavs by the thousands in cold blood using their own weapons, but they also participated in early experiments with gas vans (*Gaswagen*) during the liquidation of the Jewish ghetto in Kharkov.[125] They were extensively involved in the prosecution of antipartisan operations aimed at legitimate armed opposition as well as racial and political enemies, a campaign that routinely involved the destruction of entire villages.[126] And they rounded up forced labor for deportation to Germany and supervised the bringing in of the harvest,[127] the latter meant to ensure that the lion's share made its way into German supply channels, thereby resulting in the "calculated murder" of the indigenous population through starvation.[128] These examples demonstrate the critical role that the police played in the deaths of hundreds of thousands as they assisted in the prosecution of National Socialist racial policies, an aspect of police duties in the occupied territories that remains largely unappreciated. Furthermore, the use of local labor to harvest crops highlighted the elasticity of the terms *partisan* and *partisan helper*. For example, a police directive remarked on the need for "caution and flexibility" in the identification of "bandits" and "partisan helpers" during the harvest period, a measure aimed at ensuring the existence of a sufficient workforce for this labor-intensive activity.[129] Not only does this case demonstrate an instance where pragmatic concerns outweighed immediate security considerations, but, more important, it also showed the wide latitude given to policemen in deciding who fit the description of a partisan.

The Soviets Fight Back

On December 5, 1941, Soviet forces began a series of counteroffensives designed to relieve the pressure of the German assault on Moscow. Operating on overextended, snow-blocked supply lines in frigid weather, Wehrmacht forces suffered a major reverse.[130] Five days later, Halder noted the "critical" condition of German troops on the Russian front and the "reduced fighting strength" of German infantry forces facing the Soviet counterattack. By

December 12, reports reached Halder that some divisions "are no longer in any condition to fight," lack of supplies and Soviet pressure combining first to halt, then to throw back, the German offensive.[131]

In addition to ending the Wehrmacht's run of victories and shattering the image of the unstoppable blitzkrieg, the Soviet counteroffensive had profound implications for the men of the Uniformed Police, both the police battalions and the smaller detachments. The German High Command immediately made use of Himmler's preinvasion agreement allowing army commanders to employ police forces for "military tasks" in the event of an "urgent battlefield operation," ordering Himmler's policemen into the front lines to fill gaps caused by a shortage of troops.[132] As German lines threatened to break, police battalions from throughout the occupied territories moved into positions along the battlefront.[133] Despite facing massed Soviet forces equipped with armor and artillery, they received high marks for their combat prowess. For example, PB 323 held a twenty-kilometer sector in the area of Army Group North for eight weeks against a fully equipped Russian parachute division, resulting in the award of the Knight's Cross to the battalion's commander, Lieutenant Colonel Bernhard Griese.[134] Subsequently, Griese and a police regiment under his command played a key role in the deportation of Marseille's Jewish population and the destruction of the city's "harbor quarter" in January 1943, highlighting the ease with which police formations moved from combat to atrocity throughout the war.[135]

Between December 1941 and March 1942, thirty-one police battalions operated alone and in conjunction with the Wehrmacht to halt the Soviet drive.[136] In addition, the SS Police Division under General Alfred Wünnenberg received the responsibility for holding a defensive line along the front, with several army regiments placed under Wünnenberg's command in mid-February 1942.[137] Despite the climatic conditions and a lack of organic firepower, the police battalions, Daluege remarked, "completely proved their worth," even in the face of Soviet artillery and armor attacks.[138] One indication of their strong performance is the award of one Knight's Cross, over eight thousand Iron Crosses (first- and second-class), and twenty-two hundred combat infantry badges to the men of the police as well as "numerous commendations from army commanders and the highest army headquarters."[139] These decorations did not, however, come without a cost, as shown by police casualties between December 1941 and March 1942 (see table 2). The highest casualty rate occurred in Army Group Center, the focus of the Soviet counteroffensive, the lowest in Army Group South, whose forces participated on a much smaller scale in combat actions at the front. The toll taken on the police formations required the wholesale replacement of units in the spring of 1942.

The performance of the police battalions during the winter of 1941–1942

Table 2. Police Casualties between December 1941 and March 1942

Army Group	Officer Casualties	Troop Casualties	Percentage Casualties
Army Group North	33	1,680	24
Army Group Center	53	1,771	27
Army Group South	15	427	7
Total	101	3,878	20

Source: "Rede des Chefs der Ordnungspolizei bei der SS-Führertagung des RFSS, Der Winterkampf der Ordnungspolizei im Osten (1942)," T580, reel 217, folder 6, National Archives and Records Administration.

once again highlighted the success of Himmler's and Daluege's efforts to create both political soldiers and martial combatants within the ranks of the green corps. Still, this success proved a double-edged sword, as evidenced by a personal letter from Daluege to Himmler sharing concerns that losses experienced in combat threatened to decimate the ranks of the police battalions: "If the police regiments are to be raised to the same level as the Wehrmacht and sent to the battlefront, then it is self-evident that we receive replacements for losses just as the Wehrmacht receives them." Daluege warned: "There is hardly any possibility of refusal; otherwise we will have to disband the last active police formations in the event of further high losses."[140]

The participation of the police in the fighting likely had a number of direct effects. First, the bitter nature of the combat and the high losses inflicted and experienced by the police formations helped both intensify hatred of the adversary and frame the campaign as a war of annihilation. Second, the police battalions' help salvaging the Wehrmacht position reinforced the close relationship at the local level between the two forces. Third, the movement of the battalions into the front ranks meant, ironically, a respite for many in the occupied territories as these formations concentrated on fighting Soviet soldiers instead of killing defenseless men, women, and children. Finally, Soviet partisans in the rear areas of the German army and the areas under German civil control used this period to begin building up their strength in order to open Stalin's "second front."[141]

The Growing Partisan War

By the spring of 1942, the Soviet General Staff (Stavka) recognized the growing potential of the partisan forces, which numbered about 72,000. In order to further strengthen these forces, Soviet commandos parachuted into German occupied territories to organize partisan groups, and the Soviet air force delivered supplies and munitions. By the summer of 1942, the Soviet partisan force was "solidly established" and numbered 125,000 women and men. Operating primarily in small groups, it concentrated on interdicting German supply lines and attacking isolated garrisons.[142] By midyear, German forces were responding to the growing level of partisan activity with increased levels of brutality. For example, Josef Lücking, a former soldier, recalled: "The partisans [in Yugoslavia] used treacherous methods of fighting. . . . [W]e carried out reprisals on a 1:10 ratio: ten hostages killed for every German. The whole thing got so out of hand that in the end it was all just a matter of killing as many as possible. It was a relentless and merciless way of fighting, the likes of which I only experienced in Russia on one or two occasions."[143] And Erwin Lange (a pseudonym), a former platoon leader and battalion adjutant in PB 91, recalled that, during battles with partisans in the vicinity of Chotimsk in the summer of 1942, he could not remember a single instance in which prisoners were taken.[144] By this time, the partisan war had already evolved to such a degree that quarter was neither asked for nor given.

Lange's background offers one clue as to why no quarter was given to Soviet partisans by his platoon. Born in 1915, Lange joined the NSDAP in January 1935 and entered the police in November 1938. A performance report in 1940 described his ideological commitment as "good," remarking: "By his personal example and instruction he understands how to impress on his subordinates National Socialist philosophy [*Gedankengut*]." Lange also received two recommendations for combat decorations for "preventing attacks by bandits" and "capturing bandit helpers" during antipartisan operations in Poland and Russia. He was later promoted to captain and became a company commander of a unit tasked with combating "bandits" in Yugoslavia in 1943.[145] The fact that both Lücking and Lange fought in Russia and Yugoslavia offers two examples of the transfer of practice from one theater to the next as men conditioned by their experiences on the Eastern Front proved ready and able to apply that conditioning in other areas.

Wehrmacht and Police Cooperation

Despite jealously guarding his control of SS and police forces, Himmler placed great emphasis on maintaining a cooperative relationship between his men and Wehrmacht forces. In a directive to HSSPFs on August 2, 1941, he ordered his SS and police leaders to maintain the "greatest amity" with Wehrmacht stations and to "fulfill their wishes as far as possible."[146] By the end of the year, even small gendarmerie stations in the occupied territories continued to place importance on maintaining "close cooperation" with their Wehrmacht counterparts.[147] In some cases, this proved a difficult balancing act as Wehrmacht requests for police manpower began to exceed availability in the summer of 1941.[148]

The participation of soldiers with SS and police forces in combat at the front and during antipartisan operations points to the increasingly symbiotic relationship that had developed between the Wehrmacht and the Uniformed Police by the spring of 1942. In one respect, this relationship simply reflected a marriage of necessity, the vast landscape of the East, combined with Wehrmacht combat losses, stretching available manpower to the limit. Specifically, a battlefront extending from Finland into the Caucasus prevented a defense in depth and forced the coverage of long sectors of the front with minimal forces, and, as Halder recorded in his diary in mid-December 1941, over 24 percent of the Eastern Army (Ostheer), 775,078 men, had fallen, been wounded, or gone missing since the start of the campaign.[149] Additionally, the Soviet counteroffensive would do much to increase these losses in the coming months.

By the end of March 1942, the German army in the East was literally pleading for more police forces to support operations. In a letter of March 28, 1942, the army General Staff urgently requested additional police forces to support the suppression of the "herds of partisans" (*Partisanenherde*) in the rear area of Army Group North, in response to a "shortage of [army] forces."[150] Himmler responded to the request by flatly stating that he had no more police forces that could be sent. Furthermore, he emphasized that the army commanders needed to contact the HSSPF with their requests in a timely manner. Finally, he chided the High Command, noting the impossibility of meeting the army's demands for police and auxiliaries to fight Soviet forces at the front and partisans in the rear area as these men came from the same manpower pool and were available for only one task or the other, not both.[151]

Here one sees clear evidence of the growing reliance by the Wehrmacht on, as well as the key role played by the HSSPF in the provision of, police forces for antipartisan operations. In some respects, SS and police forces began to see themselves as superior soldiers when compared to their Wehrmacht counterparts. In fact, Bach forwarded to Himmler a copy of an order issued by General von Schenckendorff in late 1942 expressly prohibiting the evacuation of fortified positions or block houses (*Stützpunkte*) and threatening military court proceedings against soldiers who did so while still able to defend their positions, expressly noting in the accompanying note that he had not shared this order with his men as he could not "imagine that the men of the SS or police would give up a fortified position without an order to do so."[152] Himmler responded: "I am convinced that we have no need of this order for our men."[153]

In its efforts to counter the partisans, not only had the Wehrmacht come to rely on SS and police forces, but it had, in fact, borrowed a page from Himmler's book in terms of both defining and dealing with this "threat." In his study of German army reprisals in the Ukraine between October and December 1941, Truman Anderson argued: "The official presumption that Jews were the ultimate source of anti-German resistance had long since been internalized by the Ostheer (eastern army), and as a result army troops were routinely shooting groups of Jews discovered in their antipartisan patrols. Jews had also become the preferred targets of reprisal violence where available." Anderson also notes that, despite extensive cooperation with the Einsatzgruppen, the commanders in Army Group South "consistently drew a line between Soviet Jews and the Ukrainian majority" in their conduct of atrocity and reprisal.[154]

Like their counterparts in the Ukraine, the Wehrmacht forces prosecuting racial policy in Belorussia received the close attention of senior military commanders; however, the emphasis in this case focused on the role of SS and police forces. A Wehrmacht order of November 24, 1941, discussing the fate of the Jews and the Sinti and Roma cited several previous directives and noted: "As was ordered in the existing directives, the Jews must disappear from the countryside [*flaches Land*], and the Gypsies must also be annihilated." It then remarked: "The conduct of *larger* Jewish actions is not the responsibility of units of the division. These are to be conducted by civil or police authorities." It did, however, permit the use of Wehrmacht forces for the conduct of actions aimed at "smaller or larger groups of Jews" for cases involving security concerns or collective reprisals.[155] This order makes it apparent that Wehrmacht commanders not only knew about initiatives aimed at Jews and other racial enemies but also recognized the primary role of SS and police forces while reserving their own freedom of action under specific circumstances.

The cooperation between Wehrmacht and police forces had become standard operating procedure by early 1942. A report to Himmler of March 5, 1942, concerning antipartisan operations in the Ukraine mentioned the combined participation of PB 315 and army units in a three-week-long "successful annihilation action."[156] Such cooperation continued throughout the occupation period, as evidenced by a series of major antipartisan operations, and even extended to the incorporation of Luftwaffe aircraft to provide aerial reconnaissance or to bomb suspected partisan groups.[157] It was not, however, limited to the police battalions; Gendarmerie forces, having received increased responsibility for the elimination of partisans, acted alone against smaller groups but in conjunction with Wehrmacht forces against larger formations.[158] In the areas under German civil administration, Wehrmacht forces had, by the end of August 1942, become largely adjuncts, doing little more than supporting SS and police antipartisan efforts.[159]

Himmler Takes Charge of the Antipartisan Effort

During a private audience with the Duce, Benito Mussolini, in October 1942, Göring discussed the conduct of antipartisan operations in the East and explained the German practice of confiscating all livestock and foodstuffs as well as that of interning men, women, and children in work camps and burning down their villages. He then discussed the practice of lining up all the men and informing the women of the village that all would be shot unless they identified outsiders. Interestingly, he revealed: "Members of the Party carry out this task much more harshly and better [than do soldiers who are not Party members]. That's why armies that are ideologically committed, like the Germans (or the Russians) fight much harder than the others. The SS, the guard of the old fighters who have a personal connection to the Führer and constitute an elite, confirm this principle."[160]

In one respect, Göring's comments reflected a significant change in the overall command of the antipartisan efforts. His suggestion that members of the Party and the SS were best suited for this difficult duty had found its expression in Hitler's appointment in July 1942 of Himmler to head the German antipartisan effort in the areas behind the front lines. Hitler's decision identified the combat of the partisans as "primarily the task of the police" and called for the "energetic combat" of the partisan threat and its elimination by the start of the coming winter.[161] Although the Wehrmacht retained responsibility for operations against the partisans in the combat zones, Hitler's selection of Himmler clearly constituted a bureaucratic victory for the *Reichsführer* and demonstrated the increasing reliance on SS and police forces in the East.[162]

After his appointment, Himmler discussed the "so-called partisans" and informed his SS and police forces: "I am personally taking over the direction of the combat against gangs, francs-tireurs, and criminals." He also transferred regional responsibility for the antipartisan campaign to his HSSPFs.[163] Himmler's perception of the threat posed by the "so-called partisans" found its expression in one of his first postappointment actions—the prohibition on the use of the term *partisans,* either *gangs* or *gangs of robbers* to be used instead—and set the tone for his stewardship of the campaign.[164] As previously noted, the linguistic "criminalization" of these groups provided the

ostensible pretext for the actions taken to reestablish law and order and legitimized their wholesale massacre.

One indication of the nature of the campaign advocated by the *Reichsführer* can be found in a June 17, 1942, personal letter to Himmler from his
chief of staff suggesting that experience in the General Government with
"attacks by gangs" seemed to argue for a policy of "better to shoot one Pole
too many than one Pole too few."[165] To be sure, this appeared to be the motto
of the German occupation forces. In any event, Himmler organized a vast
antipartisan effort throughout the East in early August. In his instructions
to the HSSPFs, he remarked on the cooperation in the planned campaign of
the Wehrmacht, which was to conduct blocking and security operations. He
emphasized the importance of the combined efforts of the Uniformed Police
forces and the Security Police and SD forces in the effort to ensure the "annihilation of the gangs." And he reminded his SS and police leaders of the
necessity for secrecy in preparation and "tough and ruthless" measures in
the execution of the operation.[166]

Himmler's appointment was important in two respects. First, it guaran-
teed the continued close cooperation between Uniformed Police forces and
Security Police and SD forces. In late July, the HSSPF *Alpenland,* Erwin
Rösener, sent a directive to the commanders in chief of the Uniformed and
Security Police in Veldes outlining the duties of both branches in the antipartisan effort. Although the Security Police and the SD were to take the lead,
Rösener listed a number of duties reserved for the Uniformed Police, including the conduct of initial arrests, the recovery of valuables, and the cordoning off and burning down of villages and structures targeted by the Security
Police for destruction. He also gave the Uniformed Police responsibility for
"the conduct of executions, that is, the evacuation of persons designated by
the Security Police."[167] In short, the cooperation between the Uniformed and
the Security Police in the combat of the Reich's racial and political enemies
provided the template for dealing with partisan threat.

Second, Himmler's appointment guaranteed that murder and atrocity
would emerge as the institutional norms for the campaign. With Himmler's
political soldiers in charge, men tasked with upholding the racial and ideological precepts of the order and experienced in mass murder, the radicalization of the antipartisan effort was assured. One example of this
radicalization involved Hitler's order to take the "toughest measures" against
all those who joined or supported the partisans.[168] The police responded by
providing guidelines for dealing with partisans. For example, on September
15, 1942, Gendarmerie forces in the Ukraine received the following orders:
"If it is conclusively established that members of a family are active with the
bandits, then the entire family is to be made responsible and exterminated,

with agreement of the SD." The orders also allowed for the confiscation of the family's property and the burning down of its home or farm without special permission.[169] By late summer 1942, police directives broadened the category of potential victims to include persons who did not take an active role in combating or informing on partisan activities in their areas. For the police, neutrality and silence were interpreted as support for the partisan effort and punished accordingly.[170]

The Special Status of the Police Battalions

In the initial six months of the German invasion, the Uniformed Police battalions responded to Daluege's message by murdering tens of thousands of Jews, Bolsheviks, and Slavs, among others. On January 13, 1942, Daluege sent an order to police officials in the East that once again highlighted the special status of these battalions in the prosecution of National Socialist racial policy. Apparently in response to a specific request, he directed that policemen from small outposts in the occupied Eastern territories were to be used for executions only in the "most urgent individual cases." Instead, he ordered the use of the police battalions (*geschlossene Polizeiformationen*) for these actions.[171] Only three days later, in a directive entitled "Guidelines for the Combat Training of the Whole Uniformed Police Formations in the East," Daluege once again made his expectations of the police battalions clear, instructing the police battalions that the objective of combat on the Eastern Front was, not to "overcome" the enemy, but rather to ensure his "unconditional annihilation." He encouraged the development of an unreserved and firm "combat spirit" (*Kampfgeist*), and he stressed the primary object of the attack as the "ruthless annihilation of the enemy."[172]

The Face of Annihilation

By the fall of 1942, the police battalions certainly constituted the cutting edge of the process of annihilation, but they were by no means alone in their efforts. For example, Gendarmerie Battalion 1 (motorized), in cooperation with a police company, led an effort aimed at "herds of bandits" (*Banditenherde*) in the vicinity of Miedzyrzec within the General Government. The one-day operation involved the encirclement of several small villages, followed by a thorough search. The after-action report described the results: "Bandits were not found in the towns. From the group of wanted suspects, several were apprehended. Nonlocal Jews were staying in several villages and nearby forests. They were shot. During the operation, it became especially apparent that younger men and women attempted to run away and escape into the forests as the police approached. Some of these persons were arrested or shot while running away." The operation resulted in the execution of two bandits, thirteen persons who attempted to run away, and twenty-five Jews; the burning down of the farm of one partisan helper (*Helfershelfer*); the arrest of one Pole; and the rounding up of fifty-eight men and women for forced-labor duties.[173]

In the after-action report, the commander of the Gendarmerie battalion reflected on several aspects of the operation. He observed that, since the local population had displayed a fear of the police, they had obviously had a "bad conscience" (*schlechtes Gewissen*). He remarked that the attempts of the young men and women to run away demonstrated that they were not will-ing to contribute to the Reich's "construction efforts" (*Aufbauarbeit*) and that "therefore no reservations existed regarding the shooting of these ele-ments as they fled." He also suggested that unemployed young women be included in future operations to round up forced laborers as they were inclined to become friends with the bandits and provide them support. In this last case, he provided his personal opinion: "They [these young women] are under certain circumstances more dangerous than the men."[174]

The experience of the police in this operation offers several important insights into the prosecution of the antipartisan campaign. First, there were no Security Police or SD men available to participate, but this did not pre-vent these uniformed policemen from acting on their own initiative. Second, the course of the operation indicates the wide latitude and authority enjoyed by local police commanders in the prosecution of the antipartisan campaign. Third, the use of the term *herds of bandits* is reminiscent of the army's use of the phrase *herds of partisans*. This equation of the partisans with animals was deliberate, another method by which the police and the Wehrmacht dehumanized their victims in the East. Finally, this is not the only after-action report in which the suggestion that young women be used for forced-labor duties is found.

Enforcing or Dictating Racial Policy?

In the performance of their duties, Himmler's policemen were not afraid to offer suggestions, not only on improving the conduct of operations, but on further radicalizing existing policies as well. For example, Helmuth Palm (a pseudonym), a company commander in PB 310, discussed his unit's conduct of an antipartisan operation involving the encirclement and search of two

Belorussian villages in October 1942. Palm reported that the village inhabitants were gathered together and that "those that could prove beyond a doubt that they had family members working in Germany" were separated from the remaining population. The unit then executed the remaining twenty-eight men, forty women, and sixty children.[175] After the operation, Palm questioned the policy of not executing villagers whose family members were forced laborers. He complained: "The worst bandits are numbered among them." He continued: "I therefore request permission to execute the remaining families in the villages of Chmielisce and Oltusz-Lesnia."[176]

The actions of Reserve PB 133 provide another case of police alacrity in pushing the envelope of racial policy. Mobilized for duty on the Eastern Front in the summer of 1942 from their home station in Nürnberg, the unit was clearly hard at work prosecuting the Third Reich's racial policies soon after its arrival. A situation report for the period between July 25 and August 1 recorded the First Company's tally of victims for the week, including nine partisan supporters, twenty-seven beggars, seven thieves, thirteen vagrants, sixty-four Jews, two mentally ill persons, one person charged with weapons possession, and twenty-four "gypsies."[177] In other words, the victims of a recently mobilized unit with less than one month's experience in the East included the entire spectrum of racial, biological, political, and social *Untermenschen* (subhumans) reflected in National Socialist ideology. However, the company's murder of the "gypsies" had apparently exceeded the scope of its authority, as evidenced by an August 13 telegram from Lieutenant General of the Police Herbert Becker informing his subordinate police commanders: "According to the opinion of the Reich leader of the SS [Himmler], it is not permissible for the police to take action against gypsies just because they are 'gypsies.'" Becker did note, however, that this did not prevent "ruthless action" in cases involving criminal activities or support of the partisans.[178] The First Company apparently got the message that its job was to enforce, not dictate, racial policy because the unit's report for the period between August 16 and August 22 mentioned only the "arrest" of six "gypsies," their fate forwarded to regimental headquarters for final determination.[179]

The Role of Auxiliaries

Local auxiliaries under German command also assisted the police, playing a key role in operations against the partisans. One of the first initiatives pursued by SS and police leaders in the occupied Eastern territories involved the creation of auxiliary units to support the German occupation, a move supported by Hitler.[180] Already in July 1941, Himmler had authorized the immediate formation of additional auxiliary formations from the conquered territories.[181] Daluege admitted that, because of the chronic manpower shortage faced by German forces, "auxiliary forces from the occupied territories had to be included and organized, trained, and equipped for the fulfillment of police tasks." Designated as Schutzmannschaften, these units consisted primarily of volunteers and members of the former police and armed forces in their respective areas and, in some cases, released POWs.[182]

The organization of the auxiliary units proceeded on a military model with the formation of companies and battalions as well as small detachments for duty in the cities and in the countryside. In other words, the organization of the auxiliaries mirrored that of the German police in the East, ranging from battalions to small precincts and posts in cities and villages. As they were in Poland, the auxiliaries were subordinate to German police personnel, and, in fact, the lowest-ranking German policeman exercised authority over the most senior non-German auxiliary.[183] Daluege praised the auxiliary units for conducting their duties in a "courageous" and "determined" manner despite the "generally advanced age" of their men, an evaluation based in part on the high casualty rate suffered by these formations in antipartisan operations. By the end of 1941, the auxiliaries serving in the occupied Soviet territories numbered approximately 45,000.[184] One year later, these numbers exploded to some 300,000 auxiliaries, including 100,000 Ukrainians alone, an increase that coincided with a massive wave of killing aimed at the Jews and the growing partisan movement.[185]

The auxiliaries also participated in actions aimed at the Jewish population in the region. Often pogroms perpetrated by auxiliaries were instigated by German Security Police forces, who then sought to lay the blame for these "spontaneous" actions at the feet of the local populace.[186] Not all of these men were necessarily anti-Semites, but many of them came from a social background in which anti-Semitism was not an uncommon trait, and their training included political education involving virulently anti-Semitic material.[187] Social background and ideological education proved a double-edged sword as some German officials worried about maintaining discipline among men who "had lost all moral restraints" during their participation in the "liquidation of the Jewish population."[188]

In addition to ideological affinity, "material expectations provided from early on a major incentive for locals to join the ranks of auxiliary police units."[189] Such appears to have been the case for Siemion Serafimowicz, a regional Belorussian police chief described by Oswald Rufeisen as "uneducated but an exceptionally intelligent man": "He had charm, but he was also extremely violent, especially when drunk." Rufeisen also remarked: "Personally he had no special resentment toward the Jews. Neither was he a pathological murderer, as some of the others were. Once he started on what to him was an anti-Communist path he continued. Once he began, he did not look for a way out." The auxiliaries subordinate to Serafimowicz too were largely unskilled and poorly educated, but with a reputation as "social misfits."[190]

One attempt to ensure the allegiance of the auxiliaries involved the institution of a requirement for these men to take the following oath after completing four weeks of duty: "As a member of the auxiliaries, I swear to be loyal, brave, and obedient and to conscientiously fulfill my duties, especially in the battle against genocidal Bolshevism [*völkermordender Bolschewismus*]. I am prepared to give my life for this oath, so help me God."[191] The taking of this oath certainly did not guarantee allegiance, but that it was required points to the importance of ceremony and symbolism within the police, even with regard to the employment of foreign nationals. In fact, auxiliaries deserting their posts and joining the partisans proved a problem and led to orders that deserters were to be shot on the spot by the commander of the auxiliary unit or, if necessary, by an attached German policeman.

Despite the unreliability of some, the auxiliaries proved an effective instrument for supporting German efforts. For example, Ukrainian and Russian auxiliary formations received praise from Einsatzgruppe B for their assistance.[192] And Operation Winter Magic involved Uniformed and Security Police forces, Luftwaffe aircraft, a Wehrmacht antiaircraft section, and Latvian auxiliaries under German police command in a six-week operation the objective of which was the creation of a "dead zone" (*tote Zone*) within a small area of the Latvian countryside. In the course of this early 1943 operation, a senior Uniformed Police officer, Colonel Knecht, the commander of the Uniformed Police in Latvia, reminded his subordinates that executions were to be the primary responsibility of the SD. However, he allowed: "In the event that executions [are] necessary by the [auxiliary] troops because the SD is not in the vicinity, executions are to take place in houses. The bodies are to be covered with hay and straw and the houses set on fire."[193] At the end of the operation, a report concerning the actions of the Uniformed Police and the Latvian auxiliaries for the period between February 16 and March 31, 1943, detailed the killing of 77 "bandits" in combat, the capture of 9 others, the "special handling" of 875 bandits and bandit helpers, and the turning over of an additional 1,389 persons to the SD.[194] Additionally, a Security Police report noted 132 enemy casualties, 2,588 executed "bandit helpers," 22 arrests, and almost 4,000 forced deportations.[195]

In the fight against the partisans and the extermination of the Jews, the auxiliary battalions, like their German police counterparts, proved to be an effective and deadly instrument for prosecuting racial policy. One former policeman, Erwin Zahn (a pseudonym), recalled two antipartisan operations involving Auxiliary Battalion 57. In the first operation, the battalion having entered a small village, the German police officer in charge of the battalion, Lieutenant Plotz (a pseudonym), determined that the entire population— some twenty men, women, and children—belonged to the partisans. At Plotz's order, the battalion executed them all and burned down their houses and barns. In the second action, another, much larger village experienced the same fate.[196] Another policeman, Johann Henkel (a pseudonym), mentioned that the unit followed the motto: "Whoever was regarded as a Jew or suspected partisan was bumped off."[197]

The auxiliary battalions did not always work alone, Belorussian auxiliary policemen from one regional station routinely cooperating with German policemen in the murder of the local Jewish population. In such cases: "Belorussian policemen and German gendarmes used to come to a village or small town, collect all the Jewish inhabitants, and then murder them. Each killing operation resulted in ten to forty victims, depending on how many Jews resided in a specific place."[198] Oswald Rufeisen personally witnessed one such combined action in the town of Kryniczno when he was under the command of a German gendarme, Karl Schultz, a man he described as having "low intelligence, a pathological murderer and a sadist." Schultz, a baker before the war, kept a personal log of the names of his victims, except for those under the age of sixteen, whom he simply noted as "pieces" (*Stücke*). Rufeisen remembered the killings, especially the actions of one Belorussian policeman who had taken particular interest in two beautiful Jewish girls: "To my horror I saw him bend down. Next I realized that he was busy taking off the dead girl's handmade sweater. . . . The others too continued to examine the rest of the bodies impassively, methodically. When they discovered any signs of life they shot again."[199]

The actions of the auxiliaries illustrate, not just the willing participation of some segments of the indigenous populations in the murder of the Jews and the execution of their own countrymen, but, more important, the key role played by German police forces in organizing and commanding these operations. The police proved adept at taking advantage of the auxiliaries' knowledge of the local terrain, customs, and languages, as well as any existing anti-Semitic or anti-Communist prejudices, to facilitate the conduct of genocide. In this respect, one point is clear: without German guidance and encouragement, these auxiliaries might have conducted atrocity on their own, but certainly not on the scale that they eventually achieved.

By the summer of 1942, Himmler's SS and police forces had left a bloody trail of dead bodies throughout Poland and the Soviet Union. The political soldiers of the Uniformed Police had played a critical role in massacres that ranged in scale from the murderous large-scale operations of the police battalions to the smaller-scale actions conducted by gendarmes throughout the countryside of Eastern Europe. They had also cooperated extensively, not only with their counterparts in the Security Police and the SD, but with units from the Wehrmacht and the Waffen-SS as well. Despite the losses suffered by the police, Daluege lauded them for their performance in combat at the front lines and in the antipartisan campaign as well as in the prosecution of "necessary executions."[200] In a speech to SS and police leaders in early 1942, he noted that the success of the police battalions in fulfilling their duty was, "in the final analysis, the result of the National Socialist foundation [*Grundausrichtung*] of the officers and men."[201] The brutal exploitation of the occupied Eastern territories in the final years of the war provided Himmler's political soldiers with ample opportunity to demonstrate their commitment to the ideals of National Socialism and their penchant for atrocity and annihilation.

SIX

THE FACE OF OCCUPATION

We don't sleep here. Weekly three to four actions. One time Gypsies, and another time Jews, partisans, and other rabble. . . . I thank my fate that I saw this mixed race [Jews]. . . . They weren't humans, but ape-persons [*Affenmenschen*]. . . . We're moving ahead without conscience, and then "the waves close over, the world is at peace."
—Gendarmerie Sergeant Fritz Jacob (June 1942)

In the months following the invasion of the Soviet Union, SS and police formations proved their ability to prosecute the racial policies of the Third Reich against a broad range of putative racial and political enemies, including Jews, Sinti and Roma, Communists, prisoners of war (POWs), and other groups. In particular, the police battalions emerged as capable instruments for annihilation in their support to the Wehrmacht and the Einsatzgruppen; however, Himmler's policemen proved equally important in the subjugation and governance of the areas under German civil administration. In fact, the police emerged as a key tool for the consolidation and day-to-day enforcement of National Socialist rule within the occupied Eastern territories. In August 1941, Hitler remarked on his vision for the role of the police and his solution to the difficult tasks facing them in the East: "The police must certainly keep their guns ready. The men of the Party will know what to do."[1]

The Creation of Civil Administration

In July 1941, Hitler issued a decree that set the stage for the transfer of "pacified" areas in the East to German civil control under the Party's "philosopher" and chief ideologue, Alfred Rosenberg, as the head of the Reich Ministry for the Occupied Eastern Territories.[2] That decree created the Reich commissariats of the Ostland and the Ukraine, effective September 1. The former included the Baltic states of Estonia, Latvia, and Lithuania and a large part of Belorussia and was divided into four general commissariats for each of these areas. The latter consisted of a significant portion of the western Ukraine, divided into six general commissariats.[3]

In the Reich commissariats of the Ostland and the Ukraine, a Reich commissar exercised overall administrative authority. A higher SS and police leader (HSSPF) was assigned to each commissariat with command over a commander in chief of the Uniformed Police and a commander in chief of the Security Police. At the level of the general commissariats, a general commissar exercised command over an SS and police leader (SSPF) and, through him, a commander of the Uniformed Police and a commander of the Security Police.[4]

At the end of 1941, in addition to the HSSPF and four SSPFs, the organization of police forces in the four general commissariats of the Ostland included three police battalions of 1,695 men, two police companies of 304 men, and 1,330 individual duty members of the Schutzpolizei and the Gendarmerie. Police forces in the six general commissariats of the Ukraine included 1 HSSPF, 6 SSPFs, three police battalions of 2,132 men, one mounted section of 428 men, and 1,320 individual duty policemen. The total of some 3,000 German policemen in the Ostland and almost 4,000 in the Ukraine proved insufficient for the broad range of occupation tasks assigned to them, and that insufficiency helped spur the creation of indigenous auxiliary formations.[5]

The Gendarmerie in the East

Despite their relatively small size, Gendarmerie forces in the East emerged as "an agency of prime importance for the successful implementation of the 'final solution'" in the occupied territories under German civil administration from the General Government to the Reich commissariats.[6] Although in theory the Security Police retained responsibility for dealing with the racial and political enemies of the Reich, the Gendarmerie posts often took the lead because of their larger size and greater coverage, as in the case of the Gendarmerie chief Paur, who, on his own initiative, marked all Jewish prisoners for execution without the involvement of the district commissar or local Security Service (SD) office.[7] If the operations of the police battalions were notable for the scope and the scale of their killing, then the actions of the gendarmes of the small duty posts were distinguished by the cumulative effect achieved over time and especially the degree of independence displayed. The relative independence of these posts was enhanced by the fact that, in many cases, a small group of gendarmes covered a jurisdiction of hundreds of square kilometers, in areas with poor roads and rudimentary communication networks.[8]

The physical isolation of the Gendarmerie posts and their separation from higher headquarters did not prevent many of the gendarmes from becoming active and willing participants in actions aimed at Jews and in support of

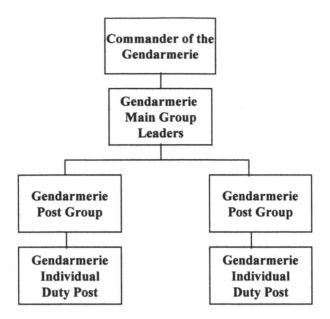

Figure 4. Organization of the Gendarmerie in the Occupied East

Source: Created by the author from organizational depiction, T580, reel 96, NARA.

antipartisan operations. In the district of Lubomil, within the General Government, the members of the Gendarmerie at the direction of the area's district commissar (*Gebietskommissar*), Bernhard Uhde, were routinely involved in the killing of local Jews during the spring and summer of 1942. Born in 1905, Uhde joined the Party in 1931 and the SA in 1935 and belonged to Rosenberg's special staff. A brutal and sadistic man, he once took several Jews, including two young girls, hostage and blackmailed the local Jewish council by demanding money in exchange for their release. After receiving the ransom, and in front of the assembled Jewish population, Uhde killed one hostage and ordered his gendarmes to execute the rest, whereupon he told his audience: "I told you that I would return those arrested. Take them."[9]

Uhde's personal involvement, including his willingness to pull the trigger himself, certainly played a key role in promoting the execution of the hostages; however, it would be a mistake to assume that, absent Uhde's involvement, they might have been spared. Consider the example of the Gendarmerie district leader Eibner, whose help in the identification and murder of local Jews was requested by a district commissar in Belorussia at the end of August 1942. Eibner subsequently reported on his efforts "to cleanse the area, especially the flat land, of Jews," an action that resulted in the shooting of 719. In addition, Eibner boasted of the success of the surrounding Gendarmerie posts in capturing and executing an additional 320 who had fled or escaped during the action. In total, gendarmes in the vicinity of Baranovitchi murdered an estimated 7,000 persons during the course of the German occupation.[10] Likewise, the Gendarmerie reports for the general commissariat Zhitomir in the Ukraine are replete with entries detailing the killing of Jews "shot while trying to escape" in the period between the summer of 1942 and the spring of 1943.[11]

The gendarmes often relied on the assistance of local auxiliaries, and, in the case of the liquidation of the Jewish ghetto in Lubomil in July 1942, uniformed policemen (both gendarmes and members of Police Battalion [PB] 314), along with Gestapo personnel and Lithuanian and Ukrainian auxiliaries, cooperated in the murder of an estimated 8,000 Jews.[12] Similarly, German gendarmes and Belorussian policemen cooperated in the liquidation of the Jewish ghetto in Mir one month later.[13] In the words of one historian: "Hunting down and shooting women and children in their hiding places had become a routine element in the work of the Gendarmerie and Schutzmannschaft at this time."[14]

The Case of Gendarmerie Battalion 1

Although most gendarmes performed their duties in small groups, such was not the case for Gendarmerie Battalion 1 (motorized), under the command of Major of the Police Schwieger. This battalion's activities in occupied Poland during August 1942 demonstrate that its men lagged behind no police formations in the prosecution of racial policy. In an operational report concerning the unit's actions from August 19 to August 22, Schwieger remarked on the use of two companies supported by mounted police forces during a sweep of the area near Leczna under a charter that he describes as follows: "They [the companies] received the assignment to conduct interrogations, searches, arrests, execution of partisans [*Banditen*], partisan helpers, persons fleeing [*flüchtende Personen*], and wandering Jews."[15] This broad charter and the open-ended description of the intended victims (with the exception of the Jews) once again highlights the significant latitude given to the police in the conduct of their duties—specifically, in determining who would live or die.

Schwieger's after-action report detailed the success of the operation, including the execution of forty-three "bandits" and partisan helpers and the burning down of five farms on the first day; the execution of thirty-three "bandits," partisan helpers, and Jews and the transfer of numerous suspects to the Security Police and SD on the second day; and, finally, the execution of one bandit and six suspicious persons "shot while trying to escape" along with the arrest of two other suspicious persons on the third day. No armed resistance was encountered, and the operation netted only seventeen bullets found at an abandoned campsite and reports of munitions cooking off during the burning down of two farms. This lack of armed resistance and the absence of weapons offers a clear indication of the specious and tenuous allegations underlying the execution of those accused of partisan activity or support.[16]

Schwieger's comments and recommendations provided a clear insight into his mentality. First, he recommended that all Jews in the area be immediately "resettled" (*umgesiedelt*) while noting that the increased numbers of "fleeing Jews" found in the area resulted from ongoing "resettlement measures" in other areas. Second, he discussed the need to employ the "most severe means" during interrogations, including the particularly effective method of shooting one suspect while standing next to another, a technique that he said loosened the tongue of an arrested Ukrainian. Third, he called for the recruitment of more informants (*V-Leute*), a call most likely prompted by the lack of armed resistance or weapons caches. Finally, although he criticized the performance of the Polish police, he praised the assistance provided by the Mounted Police Platoons (Truppenpolizei) and requested their assignment to subsequent operations. Still, he remarked on the lack of "any criminal investigative" abilities among the mounted policemen. In his mind, these men proved better soldiers than policemen.[17]

Less than a week later, Schwieger commanded a mix of Gendarmerie and mounted police forces in an antipartisan sweep northwest of Włodawa. After obtaining a list of suspects from the SD, the policemen once again moved into the field. The result of the action included the execution of eight "bandits," twenty-two partisan helpers, twelve Jews, one "wanted Communist," and two Poles "shot while fleeing." In addition, the police conducted five unspecified "reprisal measures" that apparently claimed the lives of seven persons. Once again, the haul of weapons and munitions was meager, including only one weapon and twenty-five rounds of ammunition. In his report, Schwieger again questioned the commitment of the police auxiliaries—this time the Ukrainians—to the mission. And, at the end, he actually apologized for the "relatively small" number of persons executed, a fact that he attributed to the absence of "fleeing" suspects and a difficulty in finding "incriminatory material."[18]

It is interesting that the murder of some fifty persons should constitute grounds for apology, especially given the lack of weapons found to substantiate the charges of partisan involvement. Whatever the explanation in this particular instance, however, it once again illustrated the organizational atmosphere within these units, one in which, not just murder, but mass murder emerged as a standard of reference for success. In September, Schwieger's policemen did their best to redeem themselves by killing eighty-five persons, including twenty-five Jews, and arresting one Pole and fifty-eight men fit for labor duties during two separate operations.[19] These murders yet again occurred without the battalion encountering any armed opposition. Despite the death toll achieved by the battalion in the identification and elimination of its real and imagined enemies, the fragmentary nature of the existing reports seems to indicate that this unit in fact claimed a far greater number of victims, an assertion supported by a single report from November 18, 1942, detailing the execution of ninety "fleeing persons" and the arrest and imprisonment of two hundred during a one-day operation to "cleanse" the city of Kasimierz from "resistance fighters and bandits."[20]

By the middle of November, Schwieger's gendarmes had ample opportunity to display their commitment to the process of annihilation. In December 1942, Schwieger offered a snapshot of his own worldview in a personal letter to a departing comrade. He wrote: "Through blood and race, essence and language, we are all bound together for better or worse in an inseparable community. The struggle of the community [*Kampf der Gemeinschaft*] is at the same time a struggle for each of us. The German people stand in the middle of a struggle, a struggle the likes of which hardly any people has encountered before." He continued: "You have provided proof of your readiness for action and your aggressiveness. . . . May the fortune of the soldier [*Soldatenglück*] continue to be with you."[21] Schwieger's marriage of the martial with the ideological—the outlining of a worldview and the praising of a soldier aggressive in the performance of his duties—offers insights into the organizational norms and values of more than this one specific battalion. His letter also reflected his own vision of an apocalyptic struggle in which murder and atrocity became routine means for achieving Nazi goals.

Gendarmerie and Security Police Cooperation

In spite of some doubts about their reliability, the local auxiliaries provided a vital adjunct in support of Uniformed Police operations in the East. Similarly, the Security Police forces relied heavily on the support of their uniformed counterparts as well as on auxiliaries of their own during the final years of the war. In the case of the former, an SS officer and commander of the Security Police in Belorussia observed: "If we did not receive the help of the Schupo [Schutzpolizei] and Gendarmerie, we would not know how to deal with our business."[22]

In some respects, the Gendarmerie posts acted in much the same way as their counterparts in the Reich before the war, serving as centers for collecting information on partisan activities or suspected locations of Jews in hiding, information that could then be passed to Security Police and SD posts.[23] In an October 4, 1943, directive, Himmler ordered all Gendarmerie stations within the Reich and the occupied territories to develop informant networks, an effort to support the process of information collection. In this directive, Himmler noted that gendarmes were "duty bound" to develop and use informants in support of antipartisan operations (*Bandenbekämpfung*), especially in the East. Furthermore, he directed that these informants be made available to the Security Police and SD as well in order to ensure the "closest cooperation" between the two organizations.[24] Still, the iron law of economy of force often meant that the German gendarmes and their indigenous auxiliaries were the only forces routinely in place capable of conducting antipartisan and anti-Jewish actions, an everyday reality clearly recognized by the leadership of the Security Police. In fact, the absence of Security Police and SD personnel during antipartisan operations led a commander of a motorized Gendarmerie battalion to complain—and request such assistance during "large-scale operations" in order to facilitate "criminal evaluation" (*kriminalistische Auswertung*).[25]

A sergeant in the Gendarmerie, Fritz Jacob, expressed the practical manifestation of the relationship between the uniformed policemen and the Security Police and SD personnel in a letter to Lieutenant General of the Police Rudolf Querner of June 21, 1942. In discussing actions taken against Jews, partisans, and "other rabble," Jacob wrote: "It is nice that we now have an SD field office here with which I work excellently." He continued: "We don't practice vigilante justice here. However, in places where actions demand immediate reprisal, one establishes contact with the SD, and the just judgment is immediately administered. Using the methods of normal jurisdiction, it would be impossible to exterminate an entire family if only the father was the guilty party."[26]

Another example shows how Gendarmerie forces played a key role in supporting the partial "liquidation" of the Jewish ghetto in Stolpce (Stolbsty) after an initial SD action on September 23, 1942, that resulted in the execution of 750 Jews, mostly women and those unable to work. Despite the efforts of the SD, an estimated 850 Jews successfully avoided capture and went into hiding in the ghetto. During the following week, Gendarmerie forces scoured the ghetto and captured and executed 488 of them, mostly women and children.[27] The cooperation of the Gendarmerie proved critical to the success of the SD's efforts.

Senior SSPFs worked hard to strengthen the relationship between the Uniformed and the Security Police in the East. For example, SS General Odilo Globocnik met with officers from the Gendarmerie, the Schutzpolizei, the SS, and the Security Police in order to discuss the employment of a motorized Gendarmerie battalion in a planned action in the region of Zamosc. The purpose of the operation involved the arrest of "suspects" from surrounding communities not listed on village population lists (*Einwohnerlisten*) and demanded the "closest cooperation" between the Gendarmerie and the Security Police. Additionally, the preparatory orders noted that partisans and their helpers were to be "handled" according to the Führer's orders (i.e., executed).[28] In some cases, the Security Police needed to rein in the zeal of their uniformed counterparts, too quick to execute partisans and, thereby, eliminating sources of intelligence, by reminding them of the need to prevent escape attempts "and, as a consequence, the necessity to shoot prisoners trying to escape."[29]

Finding the Right Men

Despite the extensive reliance on gendarmes and individual duty Schutzpolizei in the East, Daluege did worry about the qualifications of *reservists* from both the Gendarmerie and the Schutzpolizei. In an October 1942 letter to Major General of the Police Otto Winkelmann, Bomhard's successor as head of the Uniformed Police Operations Office, he expressed reservations concerning the "military training" of the reservists, referring specifically to their qualifications to train auxiliaries and ethnic German police forces to the standard established by Himmler. He therefore ordered Winkelmann to transfer unqualified reservists back to the Reich and to identify "combat-proven men" as their replacements.[30] Daluege's directive offers two important insights concerning the views of the police leadership on duty in the occupied East. First, Daluege certainly realized that not all his reservists met the standards for duty in the East, and he was determined to improve the quality of his police forces serving there. Second, the emphasis on finding "combat-proven men" once again highlights the importance placed by Daluege on using policemen with a martial background in the East, men prepared to face the difficult duties awaiting them.

Not coincidentally, Daluege's letter came at the same time that Himmler issued a directive addressing the suitability of police personnel for duty in the East. In his directive, Himmler warned that policemen convicted of "impermissible interaction" with indigenous peoples or "improper conduct" in the occupied territories would be identified as "unsuited for duties in the East." Himmler did, however, offer these policemen a chance to redeem themselves at a different duty station in the East. In cases where a final determination was made by the *Reichsführer* against a policeman, the remark "unsuited for duties in the East" was added to his personnel file, precluding the opportunity for further promotion.[31]

In a related July 1942 measure, Himmler prohibited the transfer of police and SD personnel married or related to Polish nationals who had not become German citizens to the annexed Polish territories and the General Government.[32] Later, the effects of regional influences emerged as a concern for both Himmler and Daluege. In March 1943, Daluege sent out a directive ordering that all police commanders within the annexed Polish territories conduct a review as to whether any of their men had family ties to persons in Poland. Daluege's order came as a response to a case in which Himmler rejected a policeman's marriage application despite the ethnic German background of the bride to be. The reason for the refusal involved the accusation that the woman remained "under the sway" of Polish influence, a fact substantiated by her fiancé's failure to speak to her in German as well as his failure to instill in her a German spirit and a National Socialist attitude. In this case, Daluege not only blamed the individual policeman but also warned of consequences for his superiors, who had failed to teach (*erziehen*) him properly or to provide him with "special ideological schooling."[33]

The fact that a single incident involving a German policeman and an ethnic German woman generated such a strong reaction from Himmler and Daluege again demonstrates both men's intense interest in the activities of their policemen in the East. For Himmler and Daluege, these men were not just German policemen but representatives of a specific worldview. They were missionaries, with a responsibility to act as models of the German master race and propagators of the National Socialist message among the elect, whether German or ethnic German.

Mischlinge *in the Police*

Certainly one group that did not qualify as the "right men" were those persons identified as *Mischlinge,* or of "mixed Jewish blood" as defined in the Nuremberg racial laws of 1935. This group included persons with two Jewish grandparents (*Mischlinge* of the first degree) and those with one Jewish grandparent (*Mischlinge* of the second degree). In the Nazi racial hierarchy, the *Mischlinge* occupied a precarious position between "Aryan Germans" and Jews.[34] In contrast to the Wehrmacht, with which as many as 150,000 *Mischlinge* are estimated to have served, the SS and police leadership moved to reduce the number of persons of "mixed Jewish blood" serving in the police.[35]

Although, technically, *Mischlinge* were not Jews, the Uniformed Police Office for Administration and Legal Issues addressed the subject of *Mischlinge* within the ranks of the police administration in the summer of 1939. The number of *Mischlinge* in administrative positions, in fact, turned out to be quite small, with fourteen in the Schutzpolizei, five in the Community Police, and only one in the Gendarmerie. The preferred method of dealing with these men was forced retirement.[36] In one case, a veteran of the Great War and former policeman, H. J. von Gundlach, appealed to General of the Police Rudolf Querner in August 1939 requesting his help in gaining reentry into the officer ranks of the military. Gundlach, a man with one Jewish grandparent, complained to Querner that he was merely the "victim of his father's sins."[37]

Even the incredible strain caused by three years of war on the manpower of the police and the resulting mobilization of tens of thousands of police reservists did not result in a major change in policy. For example, Himmler prohibited the entry of police reservists with two Jewish grandparents or married to women with two Jewish grandparents into the ranks of the green corps. While an exception was made for police reservists with one Jewish grandparent or married to women with one Jewish grandparent, they were prohibited from filling any supervisory positions.[38] If tens of thousands of *Mischlinge* could fight for the Wehrmacht and the Third Reich, such was not the case with Himmler's political soldiers.

Standardizing Behavior

No organizational culture can guarantee that all members of the organization will think and act the same. The greater the isolation of a unit from its parent organization and the smaller its size, the more likely there is to be divergence from organizational norms, values, and procedures. This fact might help explain why Himmler and Daluege chose to emphasize the special role of the police battalions during the war. Likewise, Himmler's early concerns about the Community Police and Daluege's reservations about the police reservists highlight a similar issue. Many reservists, especially older reservists operating in remote outposts, had not been adequately trained, problem areas including lack of military experience, token socialization within the police corps, and minimal exposure to existing ideological initiatives. Daluege attempted to address the first of these problem areas by ensuring the assignment of policemen with military experience to duty in the East. Likewise, age restrictions for duty in the occupied territories, combined with a continued emphasis on ideological instruction, proved ways of addressing the second and third problem areas. Finally, the willingness of the senior SS and police leadership to hold police commanders personally responsible for transfers to the East of unqualified or ill-suited policemen sent a powerful message to both these police commanders and their subordinates. Despite these efforts, however, behavior among these men, especially the gendarmes, did vary substantially.

Examples of Gendarmerie Behavior

The range of behavior exhibited by gendarmes in the East extended from direct opposition to the conduct of atrocity, to dutiful obedience, and into the realm of enthusiastic, if not sadistic, support for the most brutal treatment of the local populations. In the case of opposition, a Gendarmerie noncommissioned officer prevented mobilized ethnic German auxiliaries from conducting actions against the local population in the Polish city of Pelplin in October 1939. When told that the auxiliaries were acting on Himmler's orders, this gendarme replied that this did not "interest him in the slightest" as he took his orders from the town's mayor. In the end, however, both the mayor and his gendarme received the message as to whose authority was greater when the auxiliaries returned the next day with SD support and undertook their bloody duties.[39] Such obstinacy should be seen, not as the rule, but as the exception among those operating in the East. In the end, the organization's goals trumped the authority of the gendarme, no doubt providing a clear object lesson to anyone contemplating taking a similar principled stance.

Reinhold Hein, the head of a Gendarmerie post in the Belorussian town of Mir, provides another example, this time of a policeman perhaps best described as the model of the "obedient civil servant." Hein exercised "absolute control" over the actions taken by the twelve German and indigenous policemen within his jurisdiction. Described as a man "with a strong sense of discipline supported by an equally strong sense of duty," he "tried to follow commands without inflicting unnecessary pain . . . [and] abhorred the use of sadistic methods that served no other purpose except to hurt."[40] Still, while Hein may not have been a sadist, he was a murderer.

A career policeman in his late forties, Hein arrived in Mir in the wake of a rampage by Wehrmacht soldiers that resulted in the murder of fifteen hundred of the town's Jews. It was not the killing of the Jews that appeared to bother Hein; rather, it was the haphazard and unorganized manner in which the murders were committed. In fact, Hein took pride in the fact that "when he was responsible for an Aktion the Jews were led to their graves in an orderly fashion! They were shot in an equally orderly fashion. There was no mess." During his stay in Mir, Hein's gendarmes, supported by the local police, conducted numerous actions aimed at the region's Jewish population as well as the partisan movement, most actions against Jews involving the murder of between ten and forty victims. In comparing the two types of operations, Oswald Rufeisen remembered a clear distinction between those against Jews and those against partisans. According to Rufeisen, three gendarmes, including Hein, regularly avoided participation in anti-Jewish actions, while all willingly joined in operations "against partisans or those accused of partisan collaboration."[41]

In reality, this distinction often proved illusory as Jews found during antipartisan sweeps fell victim to the police. For example, gendarmes in the vicinity of Zhitomir in the Ukraine "routinely reported ex post facto the shooting of small numbers of Jews found hiding in the forest and fields."[42] Likewise, Hein supervised and directed anti-Jewish actions even if he made an effort to avoid direct participation in the killing of defenseless persons. His men also remained diligent in tracking down and executing Jews, including four men and two women who were found in the woods in the wake of a Gendarmerie anti-Jewish action. In this case, Hein reported: "They were summarily shot on the spot and properly buried in an especially suitable location."[43] Ultimately, Hein remained true to the organization's values by enforcing the established practice of murder and atrocity. In this respect, his actions mirrored a mentality that demanded toughness and a lack of compassion but rejected sadism or taking pleasure in the infliction of pain, a mentality identified by one historian as a common attribute among the SD leadership corps.[44]

Still, some policemen enjoyed the conduct of atrocity. As discussed in the previous chapter, Karl Schultz displayed particular enthusiasm in the prosecution of anti-Jewish actions. (The fact that Schultz was Hein's deputy might explain in part Hein's tendency to absent himself from such actions.) Schultz was, in fact, the archetype of the "willing executioner." For example, he expressly reserved the right to shoot four "ravishing teenage girls" as they stood side by side at the conclusion of an operation involving the murder of some 40 men, women, and children. Likewise, some three weeks after the partial "liquidation" of the ghetto in Stolpce (Stolbsty) on October 11, 1942, he felt "compelled" to organize—*on his own authority*—"a one-time action" supported by Latvian auxiliaries that resulted in the execution of 350 of the ghetto's remaining Jews. In his report on the action, he dryly observed: "Children as well as those incapable of work are no longer present [in the ghetto]."[45] Schultz repeatedly demonstrated his commitment to the enforcement of racial policy and proved willing to use his own initiative in the murder of Jews. However, not only Schultz, but other members of the Gendarmerie post as well emerged as "eager" killers.[46]

The case of Ernst Schmidt (a pseudonym) provides another example of a gendarme who became routinely involved in murder and atrocity in the General Government. Born in 1907, Schmidt entered the Reichswehr in 1925 and remained in the military until his voluntary transfer to the Gendarmerie in 1938. In late 1940, he received orders to report to the Gendarmerie post in the town of Tyszowce to take charge of some ten to twelve gendarmes and a number of Polish policemen.[47] The postwar testimonies of Polish survivors demonstrate that Schmidt was a brutal man who killed without cause and without compunction. For example, Morris Trost remembered over a hundred Jews who had been detailed by the Gendarmerie for various street-cleaning details being "arbitrarily" shot by Schmidt. Trost also witnessed Schmidt's execution of a Jewish man returning from services still wearing his prayer shawl as well as the murder of a man who had stepped outside his front door without the Star of David displayed on his clothing.[48]

Other survivors remembered Schmidt's enthusiasm for killing Jews of all ages, especially during Jewish holidays. Schmidt and his gendarmes also organized the large-scale deportation of some two thousand of Tyszowce's Jews to the death camp at Belzec in May 1942. During this action, the police killed some one hundred Jews, and Schmidt personally executed the eight members of the Jewish council. Later that year, in October, another witness testified that Schmidt and his policemen murdered approximately three hundred Jews from the town of Komarow.[49] Even among his colleagues, Schmidt earned a reputation as "a very brutal man" (*ein sehr scharfer Mann*).[50]

It is clear that both Schultz and Schmidt enjoyed their work. They were men who used positions of responsibility to murder routinely and with little or no provocation. Their actions exemplify the extent to which the boundaries of acceptable and desired behavior had been distorted even among isolated gendarmes operating in small groups and with great autonomy. In these men, the message of annihilation transmitted in ideological indoctrination and in the organizational values of the police found fertile soil. The senior SS and police leadership could only applaud their zeal and dedication, a fact made manifest in the nomination of Schmidt to receive a specially inscribed book during Julfest ceremonies in December 1942.[51]

The Schupo War Criminals of Stryj

Not only gendarmes manning small posts but members of the Schutzpolizei also operated in small groups in selected towns throughout the occupied East. For example, some twenty uniformed policemen established a precinct post in the Galician town of Stryj early in October 1941. Interviews conducted in 1947 with eleven of these men show that they constituted a largely homogeneous group. All were Austrians, and ten of the eleven had been career policemen. In fact, eight of the eleven entered the police before 1928. The oldest was born in 1895, the youngest in 1905, and the remaining nine men during the seven-year period between 1896 and 1903.[52] According to one policeman, Johann Schaffner, only three of the twenty policemen assigned to Stryj *were not* members of the NSDAP. Furthermore, Schaffner testified that the majority of the seventeen Party members wore the honor chevron awarded to "old fighters."[53]

The arrival of these men in Stryj proved an ill omen for the Jewish population in the town and the surrounding vicinity as these Austrian policemen initiated a campaign that would eventually leave several thousand murdered Jews in its wake. After forcing the town's Jewish council to provide the furnishings for the police station, these policemen initially assumed normal police duties, including the control of the black market as well as the regulation of local trade. Still, as Police Sergeant Max Preuer recalled, even the regulation of trade provided some of the men ample opportunity to display their brutality, especially against the local Jewish population. Preuer testified: "[Police Sergeant] Venhoda proved himself especially aggressive in the execution of his duties and committed acts of violence which disgusted me. . . . [Police Sergeant] Garber replaced me in the trade supervision. Garber proved himself a zealous national socialist [*sic*] and was employed for various special actions by Klarmann [the post commander]."[54]

During their stay in Stryj, Garber and Venhoda proved their "zealousness" in the conduct of their duties by routinely participating in the execution of local Jews. Born on November 1, 1897, Alexander Garber entered the Austrian police in 1920 and was remembered by several of his former colleagues for both his brutality and his commitment to National Socialism. Even before the war, Garber benefited from the Nazis' anti-Jewish actions, taking possession in 1938 of an apartment in Vienna formerly owned by a Jew.[55] Born on June 15, 1901, Franz Venhoda entered the Viennese police force in 1923 and joined the NSDAP in 1932.[56] By 1943, both Garber and Venhoda, along with their police colleagues, had taken part in numerous special actions.

The nature of the "various special actions" soon became apparent as these policemen, often assisted by Ukrainian auxiliaries, initiated several large-scale "liquidations" of Jews between 1942 and 1943. According to Garber, the first mass execution took place in April 1942 in the nearby forest of Holobutow, the SD participating. Garber recalled: "The Jews, who had first to strip, were taken to opposite sides of the pit in groups of 20, and had to stand at the edge of the pit with their backs to us. I, and the above mentioned men, then fired with Russian machine pistols, some of us also with Russian carbines, at the people standing in front of us at a distance of about 6 metres [*sic*], aiming at their heads. . . . In this way, about 300 women, children and men were liquidated by us in the first action."[57] This first killing action provided only a small taste of what was to come.

From mid-1942 until the end of 1943, the Austrian policemen in Stryj killed the area's Jews in a number of planned operations. For example, in October 1942, the police rounded up the Jewish population of Stryj and drove them into the town's small synagogue. Police Sergeant Johann Kranzler remembered: "About 1,000 persons were crowded into the synagogue and due to lack of space they had to stand up, pressed tight against each other. When the action was completed the synagogue was locked and they remained there for three days in this inhuman condition."[58] Those who survived this ordeal subsequently perished at the hands of the police in the Holbutow forest. A few months later, the police turned their attention to the local Jewish hospital. In this action, the police had orders to "deliver the Jews who were fit for transport to the Stryj prison"; however, the Jews apparently discerned the true objective of the action and attempted to flee. Police Sergeant Christament admitted: "The Jews fled from their beds and we stood them up in the hospital yard and shot them down. Those who were unable to run due to their health condition, were shot in their beds by [Lieutenant] Klarmann. . . . I clearly remember that this was not the only action in the hospital but that it had been preceded by several earlier ones."[59]

In early 1943, the German authorities established a ghetto in Stryj, an area surrounded by a wooden fence. The concentration of the town's Jews did not stop the killing as the police continued to conduct raids into the ghetto in support of the Security Police. Preuer recalled one such action: "Inside the ghetto, Klarmann's special trusties, namely Hick, Scheiflinger, Garber, Christamen [*sic*], Heinrich, Zeman, Tibes and Bischinger were engaged in driving the Jews together . . . assisted by the Ukrainian militiamen. The arrested people were grossly mistreated and beaten. I myself saw how Zeman beat an arrested person with a stick, or some hard object. Garber and Hick behaved with particular brutality in this action and screamed like wild men."[60]

The decision to completely "liquidate" the town's Jewish ghetto provided additional opportunities for the policemen. Police Sergeant Garber testified:

"It happened quite often that our post was informed that there were some Jews in hiding. We were ordered to find them and liquidate them on the spot. . . . We got the people out of their hiding places, so called bunkers, drove them together against some wall in the ghetto and blindly shot them." He continued: "Later, liquidations were also carried out in the Jewish cemetery. The Jews were arrested in the ghetto, taken to the prison and when a large enough contingent was collected, transported to the Jewish cemetery. . . . In Holobutow about 2,000 Jews were liquidated and in the Jewish cemetery 1,500."[61]

The murders conducted by the policemen in Stryj offer several insights into the activities of a small group of men who enjoyed great autonomy. First, the age of these men appears to have had little affect on their actions as a group ranging in age roughly from thirty-eight to forty-eight found common cause in the murder of Jews. Second, both regulars and reservists answered the call, including the unit's driver, Zeman, a police sergeant in the reserves who viciously beat a Jew with a stick during one action. Third, the unit's leadership clearly played a role in facilitating the men's action. Police Sergeant Johann Schaffner cited the influence of the precinct commander, Lieutenant Klarmann, as being particularly important.[62] Likewise, Klarmann's second in command was a member of the SS and an "old fighter" who had entered the Party in July 1932.[63] Fourth, Schaffner also emphasized in his testimony the importance of "enthusiastic" National Socialists such as Venhoda, Christament, and Garber in shaping the behavior of the group.[64] In this respect, the large percentage of Party members within the unit appears to have helped shape its atmosphere and organizational values as it did its part in support of National Socialist racial policy.

The actions of the policemen assigned to the precinct post at Stryj were not exceptional, as demonstrated by the murderous activities of the policemen of another precinct post in the Polish city of Kolomea. As was that in Stryj, the precinct post in Kolomea was manned by a small detachment of Austrian policemen. In the period between November 1941 and February 1943, these policemen, on their own, and in cooperation with the Security Police, "carried out systematic weekly shootings." By the end of the German occupation, German police forces and Ukrainian auxiliaries killed an estimated sixty thousand Jews over the course of numerous operations, including the murder of four hundred children from the Kolomea ghetto, an operation led by the precinct commander Captain Hertl. One member of the unit also remembered Hertl using a horsewhip on defenseless Jews as they were assembled for transport. He further remarked: "We Schutzpolizei men always shouted at the Jews, using gross expressions, such as 'Jewish pig.'"[65] Once again, the example of the unit's leader established the organizational norms for a group of men who routinely employed casual brutality and racial epithets in support of their murderous charter.

The Case of PB 310

The actions of the men of PB 310 during occupation duties in the East provide another demonstration of the inherent ruthlessness of the German antipartisan campaign and of the enthusiasm and effort displayed by the men who prosecuted it. PB 310 was one of twelve police battalions mobilized during August and September 1940 expressly for duty outside the Reich. Its first tour of duty in the East was spent in the Radom district of the General Government between October 1940 and August 1941. It remained in the General Government until it received orders in February 1942 to proceed to the Eastern Front south of Leningrad as an emergency force to stem the Soviet winter offensive. The unit arrived in the Belorussian city of Kobrin in August 1942 and, one month later, received orders to prosecute antipartisan operations within the district of Wolhynien-Podolien in conjunction with Operation Triangle.[66]

On September 22, the battalion commander, Major of the Police Bruno Holling, issued orders to his companies to "annihilate" the "bandit-contaminated" villages of Borki, Borysowka, and Zablocie. Early the next morning, the entire Tenth Company, supported by a platoon from the Ninth Company, set out for the village of Borki. This phase of the operation "proceeded without a hitch" except for a problem caused by some farmers who proved reluctant to relinquish their *panje*-wagons (two-wheeled horse-drawn carts) to support the operation; however, the company "took the necessary measures to ensure the punishment" of these obstinate peasants and obtained the carts.[67]

On the unit's arrival on the village outskirts, the officer in charge of the action, Lieutenant of the Police Müller, found that the map of the village did not show a number of outlying houses. Therefore, he ordered the unit to conduct a pincer movement instead of the planned encirclement. In his after-action report, Müller subsequently boasted: "By this maneuver I achieved the complete seizure of all the village inhabitants and their successful movement to the collection point." At the collection point, the policemen began the task of questioning the 809 gathered villagers and determined that only 104 could be classified as "politically reliable," a verdict that sealed the fate of the remaining 705, including 203 men, 372 women, and 130 children, who were shot in small groups at close range at a nearby execution site between 9:00 A.M. and 6:00 P.M. In his report, Müller observed that the "executions proceeded smoothly and the procedure proved itself as entirely appropriate."[68]

The pride of accomplishment expressed by Müller, combined with the rationale offered and, especially, the murder of children, provides a clear example of just how far the boundaries of the permissible and desirable had expanded by the end of 1942. The victims were not the Reich's "Jewish arch-enemy," just simple peasants whose "political reliability" could not be guaranteed, a determination left solely to the police. And it is clear that the police could have chosen to spare more persons than they did instead of following the policy of "better one Russian too many, than one too few." After two years in the East, these men could stand next to their victims with pistols and machine pistols and commit cold-blooded murder on a large scale with a sense of accomplishment in the task.

The actions of the men of the Eleventh Company on September 23 in support of Operation Triangle complemented that of their counterparts. Captain of the Police Helmuth Palm (a pseudonym), the company commander, led his men in a mission to "destroy the village of Zablocie and to shoot its inhabitants." Supported by a platoon from the Ninth Company, the unit reached Zablocie at 2:00 A.M. and by 5:30 A.M. had gathered the inhabitants together in the village school. After learning of a small group of houses four miles away, Palm sent a detachment to round up these additional families and bring them to Zablocie. The arrival of men from the SD and the subsequent interrogations led to the release of five of the families. The policemen divided the remaining 284 men, women, and children into three groups and executed them. Palm reported that, except for a single escape attempt, the executions proceeded according to plan. His description of the attitude of the condemned offers an indication of his own beliefs: "The majority of the village inhabitants on account of their guilty consciences and not unaware of their own responsibility calmly met their *well-deserved* fate."[69]

In the end, the executions appeared to bother Palm far less than the problems associated with transporting the village's confiscated livestock and grain supplies. The seizure of seven hundred cows, four hundred pigs, four hundred sheep, seventy horses, and eighty thousand kilograms of grain stretched the capability of the ninety-three available *panje*-wagons to the limit. In the last line of his report, Palm worried about the lack of qualified personnel to handle the care of the cows, especially the milk cows,[70] a concern that appears grotesque in contrast to an absolute indifference to the murder of almost three hundred people. However, from Palm's perspective and that of the Third Reich, these Russian peasants were, indeed, worth less than the livestock in their possession. In fact, confiscated livestock and grain supplies provided a valuable addition to the limited German resources. In a July 1941 directive to the HSSPFs, Himmler made this point clear by prohibiting the wholesale slaughter of captured livestock during "cleansing and clearing actions" and ordering its delivery to designated farms for breeding purposes.[71]

Major Holling's final report on the operation provides another glimpse into the mentality of the battalion's leadership. A member of the SS since 1939, Holling complained of poor maps and too few men, the latter resulting in the exclusion of several outlying farmhouses from the operation. Holling conjectured that these isolated farmhouses were exactly those most likely to be used by the partisans. He did not, however, extend this line of reasoning to its logical conclusion: that the vast majority of those executed were most probably, not partisans, but innocent farmers. Instead, he complained about the inadequate preparations made for feeding the confiscated cows and the late notification of the district officials responsible for the transport of the livestock. Once again, the lives of captured cows (a total of 1,470) proved a greater concern than the deaths of people (a total of 1,163).[72] There was also something important missing from the report. Despite the detailed inventory of confiscated goods, no mention was made of captured weapons, a further indication of the absence of partisan activity among those executed.

In the weeks after the conclusion of Operation Triangle, the actions of Palm's company paint a chilling portrait of routine atrocity and steadfast commitment to enforcing the racial policy of the Third Reich. For example, Palm reported the arrest and subsequent execution of a woman and four children, labeled *Ostmenschen* (lit. "East People"), found "wandering" in the forest on October 1, 1942.[73] In Palm's worldview, the fact that a woman and four children were *Ostmenschen* provided sufficient justification for their murder. In truth, Palm constituted the archetype of Himmler's and Daluege's vision for the police. Born in 1915, he joined the Hitler Youth in 1931, the SS in 1933, and the NSDAP in 1935. A graduate of the *SS-Junkerschule*, he also completed an SS training course at Dachau before the war.[74] Palm was a true believer, and his company report entries for October 5 and 6 further demonstrate the unit's casual disregard of and disdain for the lives of the Slavic *Untermenschen* (subhumans). On October 5, a combined second and third platoon patrol led to the arrest of "11 men, 41 women, and 64 children (all *Ostmenschen*)" and the subsequent execution of one man, eleven women, and fifteen children in a forest near Kamienica on the same day. The next day's report laconically noted: "The remaining *Ostmenschen* taken into custody during the previous day's action in Kamienica were executed. 10 men, 30 women, and 49 children were shot."[75]

The most chilling aspect of these actions is, not the clinical description of the cold-blooded murder of sixty-four children, but the fact that, by this time, the killing of innocents had become routine. In fact, the men of Palm's company killed an additional forty men, forty-seven women, and twenty-eight children between October 7 and October 9, and the term *Ostmenschen* appears four times in the entries for this three-day period.[76] Similarly, a situation report for the period between October 12 and October 18 demonstrated the full extent of the company's participation in the National Socialist war of annihilation in the East. During this period, these policemen executed a man and a woman on the grounds that they were "Soviet citizens"; eight men and nine women as "bandit helpers"; seven men and nine women labeled *Ostmenschen*; and one Jew without identification papers. The report also remarked that "all available men from the company were detailed to a special action [*Sonderaktion*] in the city of Brest" on October 15 and returned to their stations the following day.[77] What the report failed to mention was that, on October 15 and 16, police and auxiliary units executed thousands of Jews in the Brest ghetto and took more than ten thousand to the train station to be further transported to execution sites in the area of Brona-Gora.[78] The men of the Eleventh Company proved that they were "equal opportunity killers" willing to prosecute their duties in the name of a worldview that legitimized the murder of those listed as Soviet citizens, bandit helpers, *Ostmenschen,* and Jews.

If Palm set the standards for his men, he was not the only person responsible for influencing their actions. The words and deeds of Police Sergeant Helmuth Schmidt (a pseudonym) provide additional insight into the organizational atmosphere within the company. Born in 1911, Schmidt entered the SA and the NSDAP in 1933 and joined the battalion in September 1940. In postwar testimony, Schmidt's brother-in-law, Fritz Lange (a pseudonym), recounted that, while at home on leave during the war, and after having had several drinks, Schmidt told Lange that he had participated in the execution of Jews in Poland. Reacting to Lange's profession of disbelief, Schmidt reportedly exclaimed: "The Jews were not people but a danger to the German *Volk.*" Lange also recalled his brother-in-law's stories of how mothers often pleaded for their children's lives—and, in particular, the story of how Schmidt had purposefully executed the child of one such mother so that she might watch it die. Schmidt then told Lange: "We know no mercy."[79]

Similarly, Schmidt's former wife testified that she overheard him state that "earlier [before the war] he couldn't hurt a fly" but that "now he could shoot a Jew in the head while eating a sandwich." For her part, the ex-wife rationalized Schmidt's actions as the result of stress brought on by the war: "My husband was OK earlier, I mean before the war; only after the war did I recognize that he had become sadistic."[80] It is difficult to believe that the man who bragged to his brother-in-law of his reputation as the "Terror of Lemberg" was an unwilling tool of racial policy.[81] Whether brought on by the rigors of war or the culture of the police, or both, Schmidt's conversion to an instrument of genocide was complete.

Party Membership and Mass Murder

Statistics from October 1940 on Party and SS membership within PB 310 show that Palm and Schmidt were not alone. The battalion's staff, four companies, and hunting platoon counted 232 NSDAP members, 15 SS members, 15 SA members, 11 National Socialist Driving Corps members, 140 National Socialist Welfare Organization members, 3 National Socialist Flying Corps members, and 1 Hitler Youth member. In other words, the overwhelming majority of the battalion had a direct tie to a Party organization, and some 40 percent belonged to the NSDAP.[82] A January 1941 survey showed a slight decline (to 219) in Party members across the entire battalion.[83] In contrast, an October 1941 list shows 49 SS members in the First, Second, and Third Companies, a more than threefold increase when these three companies are considered alone.[84] Finally, an age profile of the battalion's men indicated that the vast majority were born between 1905 and 1915, a generational cohort especially attracted to the NSDAP.[85]

A comparison of the policemen from Stryj with the men of PB 310 seems to imply that Party membership, not age, was a stronger indicator of commitment to National Socialist policy. One study even cited a significant correlation between Party membership and the perpetration of crimes.[86] Still, age and experience did matter. For example, 25 percent of the men from the middle-aged rank and file of Reserve PB 101 were Party members, while 63 percent of the battalion's career senior noncommissioned officers were Party members and 20 percent SS members.[87] In this case, the role of the unit's officers and senior enlisted personnel proved important in establishing the organizational expectations, norms, and standards guiding the expected behavior of the group.

Daluege, in fact, remarked on the overrepresentation of the police within the Party on several occasions.[88] Likewise, the thorough penetration of the police officer corps by Party members—by the end of 1941, 66 percent of all regular and 67 percent of all reserve Uniformed Police officers belonged to the Party—provides an additional measure for evaluating the nature of the organizational environment established within the police. Furthermore, 30 percent of the regular and 7 percent of the reserve police officers held membership in the SS.[89] In the end, Party affiliation was not a prerequisite for mass murder, but it did serve as a concrete expression of an individual's allegiance to the regime and its worldview.

The Case of PB 133

As the men of PB 310 murdered their way through Belorussia, the men of Reserve PB 133 played an important part in the destruction of the Jews of Galicia. Mobilized in Nuremberg during the war, the battalion, under the command of the Security Police and with the assistance of Ukrainian auxiliaries, participated in the massacre of two thousand Jews, including men, women, and children, in the town of Nadworna on October 6, 1941. Conducted under the direction of the chief of the Stanislawow Security Police, Hans Krüger, the killings were intended to be a dress rehearsal (*Probeaktion*) for operations aimed at eliminating the Galician Jews.[90] Less than a week later, these same forces, including individual duty policemen, cooperated in a large-scale massacre of the Jews of Stanislawow. The shootings on this "Bloody Sunday" began at noon and lasted well into the night, under the glare of truck headlights, until the Germans finally gave up and sent the remaining Jews back to the town's ghetto, having murdered at least ten thousand. The next day, a group of men from PB 133 returned to the execution site—the Jewish cemetery—and finished off the wounded who had climbed out of the mass graves but been unable to go further.[91] In the following weeks, PB 133 proved an important resource for the district's Security Police leadership as it embarked on a campaign that cut through Galicia's Jewish population.[92]

These massacres set the tone for the battalion's stay in the East. Once more, leadership played an important role in establishing objectives and standards. Ernst Lederer, the commander of the First Company, was born in 1913 and became a businessman after earning his *Abitur*. Lederer joined the SS in 1933 and attended the *SS-Junkerschule* in 1937 in preparation for duty with the SD. He transferred from the SD to the Uniformed Police in the summer of 1940. A man of action, Lederer received special recognition for his activities during the invasion of Poland and, on his arrival in the General Government, led a *Jagdkommando* (hunting platoon) before assuming command of the First Company.[93] In one respect, Lederer's biography is strikingly similar to Palm's, and his transfer from the SD to the police provides a specific example of the interlocking nature of Himmler's SS and police complex.

The actions during the summer and fall of 1942 of PB 133, especially those of Lederer's company, provide additional evidence of these men's role in and commitment to the enforcement of racial policy. A series of weekly reports for the period from July 25 to September 12, 1942, illustrates the degree to which the First Company became involved in the elimination of the full spectrum of the Reich's putative racial enemies. For example, the unit reported the execution of 147 persons the week of July 25–August 1, including 69

Jews, 27 beggars, 24 "Gypsies," 13 vagrants, 9 partisan sympathizers (*Helfershelfer*), 7 thieves, 2 mentally ill persons, and 1 person found with a weapon. In the same time period, the company arrested 19 persons, including 9 political suspects, 6 forced laborers, 2 persons with weapons, 1 vagrant, and 1 POW.[94]

This report is interesting in several respects. First, it was the execution of these "Gypsies" that led to the restatement of Himmler's policy discussed in the previous chapter. Second, the spectrum of those killed runs almost the full range of the racial, political, and social enemies of the Reich. The murder of the Jews in the summer of 1942 is not surprising as the decision for a "Final Solution" to the Jewish question had been made many months earlier. Likewise, the execution of partisan sympathizers was to be expected; however, the murder of vagrants, beggars, and the purportedly mentally ill once again demonstrates that the policemen conducting these patrols made a conscious decision to kill when they did not have to. Third, the fact that some policemen chose to arrest persons for the same "offenses" underlines the fact that the police could choose between executing, arresting, and even possibly ignoring. In the cases of weapons possession, it is unclear what types of weapons or munitions were recovered, a fact that may help explain the disparity in treatment.

During the following week, August 2–8, Lederer reported that his company executed three beggars, five "asocial" persons (four women and a child), and seven Jews. In addition, the report noted the arrest of thirty-three persons, including ten Jews, five "asocial" persons, five black marketeers, four POWs, three beggars, two thieves, two partisan sympathizers, one political suspect, and one vagrant. Five of those arrested were turned over to the Security Police, one was turned over to the Labor Office, and nineteen were released.[95] The others presumably remained in jail or were executed. Once again, that "beggars" or "asocial" persons might be executed or arrested or even possibly released points to the significant latitude enjoyed by the individual police patrols. Still, the willingness to release persons is less significant than is the rationale for executions and arrests, also pointing to significant latitude accorded policemen at the unit level.

During the next month, the First Company executed thirty-three persons, including twelve Jews, six partisans (*Banditen*), five vagrants, four mentally ill persons, two beggars, one thief, and one POW. In comparison, it arrested fifty-nine persons and released fifteen, including several persons sent to the Labor Office for forced labor.[96] By mid-September 1942, the men of PB 133 were clearly experienced in the conduct of murder. Their participation in the massacres of Jews in late 1941, combined with their battalion's actions against the racial, political, and social enemies of the Reich (covered in the fragmentary reports for the summer of 1942), offer another indication of the routine nature of the killing and the broad range of victims encompassed. In postwar testimony, one police officer reflected: "The police battalions did nothing other than massacre Jews and round up people for forced labor in Germany."[97] Certainly, the men of PB 133 and PB 310 fulfilled these duties, but they also widened their scope well beyond the murder of Jews.

PB 91 Returns to the East

During the first months of 1941, PB 91, the unit involved in the massacre of the Jewish community in Ostrów (see chapter 4 above), prepared to return to the East. After its employment in the initial campaign against Poland, the battalion had conducted security duties on the Norwegian and Swedish border from June 1940 until January 1941, afterward returning to the Reich to reconstitute. In Germany, it received a number of reservists to augment its ranks and underwent a period of "intensive training" before an October 1941 deployment to the Soviet Union. Despite the large influx of new reservists, numerous policemen who had served with the unit in Poland and Norway remained with it.[98]

After their return to the East, the men of PB 91 once again became active participants in support of the Third Reich's racial policies against the Jews. Despite the introduction of reservists, the battalion's leadership remained firmly in the hands of regular policemen. For example, Captain of the Police Wilhelm Ahrens took over the command of the Third Company in late 1941. Born on May 19, 1911, in Hamburg, Ahrens joined the police in April 1932 and rose through the enlisted ranks before receiving his commission as a lieutenant in August 1936. A member of the NSDAP since May 1937 and the SS since June 1940, he participated with police forces in the occupation of the Sudetenland and the invasion of Poland.[99]

As a career policeman with combat experience and ties to the Party and the SS, Ahrens offered another example of the ideal police commander prized by Himmler and Daluege. In fact, he provided proof of his commitment during an action in the Krynki ghetto aimed at eliminating "old and infirm Jews" (*alte und gebrechliche Juden*) in the spring of 1942. After receiving his orders, Ahrens notified his men of a "confiscation and search action" planned for the following day. Likewise, the First Company prepared for a similar action in the Grodno ghetto. The men of the Third Company assembled early the next morning and climbed aboard trucks for the journey to

Krynki, some twenty-five miles west of their station in Volkovysk. The field kitchen traveled with the unit and provided coffee to the men after their arrival. Ahrens then reportedly informed his platoon leaders of the objective of the action, including orders to search the entire Jewish ghetto for food stores and "scarce goods" (*Mangelwaren aller Art*) as well as to execute all old and infirm ghetto inhabitants. The platoon leaders were given the option of either executing these "useless bread eaters" (*unnütze Brotesser*) in their apartments or handing them over to an execution squad.[100]

On reaching the town, Ahrens informed the ghetto commandant as well as the Jewish council of his mission and ordered the latter to assist his men in their search for foodstuffs and scarce goods. The company entered the ghetto through the main gate, and Ahrens established his command post just inside the gate. The policemen "swarmed" into the apartments, and shortly there-after came the sounds of "heavy shooting" as the policemen executed Jews in their homes and on the streets.[101] One policeman testified that Police Sergeant Wilhelm Gelb (a pseudonym) especially "distinguished" himself during the operation. Gelb's reported actions included an incident where an old Jew told him that he was sick, whereupon Gelb ordered the man to turn around and shot him in the head on the spot.[102] Ahrens ordered that the thirty Jews brought to the collection point be locked in the synagogue (next to the main gate) and that a bundle of hand grenades be tossed in.[103]

It is important to note that the action, originally aimed at the old and the infirm, escalated into a free-for-all that claimed the lives of numerous Jews. In fact, the ghetto commandant complained that the action had cost him some of his best craftsmen.[104] In other words, some policemen chose to kill when they did not have to. While the scale of the action at Krynki pales in comparison to that of other massacres, it does serve to demonstrate the cumulative effects of National Socialist occupation policies. Five, ten, fifty, or more persons killed by one unit on a given day eventually totaled tens of thousands, a total reaching hundreds of thousands, and perhaps even a million or more, when the actions of all police units in the East are taken into account.

On June 18, 1942, PB 91 was assigned to the 221st Security Division to assist in antipartisan operations. At first, in order to familiarize the men with their new area of operations, the unit performed security and patrol duties, including the patrol of roads and rail lines to prevent sabotage. On July 1, a quick-reaction force composed of policemen from PB 91 became involved in a firefight that resulted in the capture of forty-four partisans and the killing of four. But, despite its stated mission of combating partisans, it was not long before the unit once again took the lead in anti-Jewish actions. For example, it conducted a "raid against Jews" on account of "suspected support of the partisans and weapons possession" in the town of Chotimsk in mid-July. During the action, the policemen shot twenty-four Jews during "breakout attempts."[105]

Later that summer, PB 91 participated in the extermination of the Jewish population in the Chotimsk ghetto. During this operation, the policemen rounded up some one hundred Jewish men, women, and children and transported them by truck to a nearby forest, where they were forced to dig their own graves and then shot by men from the Third Company.[106] When questioned after the war as to why the men of PB 91 acted as they did, one former member of the unit, Alfred Metzger (a pseudonym), replied: "A bad spirit [*Geist*] ruled the company. The company was brutalized [by its experiences], especially the senior noncommissioned officers from the area of Saarbrücken. That's how I assessed it."[107] While Metzger's response is not phrased in terms of the existence of an organizational atmosphere within the company that established the killing of Jews and other "undesirables" as the group norm, such an atmosphere is, in fact, what it reflects. Two decades after the event, Metzger clearly recognized that this was a "bad spirit." Likewise, his comment about the role of the senior noncommissioned officers (*Unterführer*) in establishing an attitude of brutalization within the company once again highlights the important contribution by all levels of police leadership in establishing brutality and atrocity as group standards.

Murder in the Countryside

As the police battalions continued their bloody work, the men of the Gendarmerie and their auxiliary proxies remained key actors in the continuing slow but steady march of annihilation through the countryside. By late 1942 and early 1943, numerous police reports noted the increasing strength of partisan activity. For example, a report by the SS and police district leader in Borrisow (Belorussia), a lieutenant in the Gendarmerie, in late November 1942 observed: "The attacks and raids by armed bandits within the Gendarmerie district continued without change during this reporting period."[108] A March 1943 report remarked on the "active bandit activity" and the "depressed atmosphere" among the local populace brought on by recent German military reverses, including the loss of the Sixth Army at Stalingrad.[109] And reports from a mounted police formation operating in the General Government remarked on the increased partisan activity as well as the increase in the size of partisan forces caused by the flight of Jews to them.[110]

In response to the increasing partisan activity and fears of a further loss of support among the local population, police forces increased the pressure on those communities suspected of partisan collaboration. For example, a commander of the Gendarmerie issued the following instructions to his posts in early 1943: "When villages or estates are evacuated and burned down for preventive purposes, the inhabitants are all to be taken away together if their 'special treatment' (execution) does not take place then and there with the consent of the *Gebietskommissar*. Every leader of a unit must realize that all the inhabitants who escape after the destruction of their estate become new members of the partisans [*Banden*] and therefore contribute largely to endangering the pacification of the area."[111] By May 1943, the burning down of villages and the "special treatment" of the inhabitants was a well-established practice. In the town of Saslawl in the district of Minsk, a local official notified the *Gebietskommissar* that, on May 1, 1943, three villages were destroyed by German police forces and that, during the operation, the "majority of the population was shot" and all the homes burned down. An attachment to the letter listed thirteen villages from the area subject to the same treatment, the "number of liquidated inhabitants" totaling 1,419, the number of farms destroyed 317.[112]

The routine conduct of murder by policemen was a fixture, not just in the occupied Soviet Union, but, as previously seen, in the annexed Polish territories as well. For example, the reports of a Gendarmerie post in the district of Oppeln (Opole) in Silesia contain repeated entries concerning Poles being "shot while trying to escape." The list of victims includes "long-sought criminals," farmers, "asocials," black marketeers, forced laborers, and smugglers.[113] From these reports, it is clear that the phrase *shot while trying to escape* was no more than a euphemism meant to justify murder. These gendarmes proved especially lethal in the period between June 20 and June 26, 1943. They began by killing three Poles during three separate "escape attempts." But they most clearly demonstrated their commitment to the enforcement of racial policy when, on June 26, 1943, they conducted an action "on the orders" of the Criminal Police that was aimed at the "mentally ill" (*Geisteskranke and Schwachsinnige*) and resulted in the arrest of eighty-eight persons, who were subsequently "led away" (*abgeführt*).[114] That no destination was specified, and that there is no indication that they were handed over to the Criminal Police, strongly suggests that *led away* was simply another euphemism for murder.

The arrest and execution of the eighty-eight allegedly mentally ill persons is important in several respects. First, that this was an action conducted on the orders of the Criminal Police once again demonstrates the close cooperative relationship enjoyed by the Uniformed Police and their Security Police counterparts. Second, given the unlikelihood of eighty-eight mentally ill persons being found in such a small rural area, it appears that the gendarmes conducting the action themselves determined who was to be labeled as "mentally ill." Third, these gendarmes were career policemen, not reservists, born between 1896 and 1910, and under the command of the fifty-one-year-old Lieutenant of the Gendarmerie Hermann Degen (a pseudonym).[115]

Postwar testimony from Polish survivors of the German occupation underlines the casual brutality of these gendarmes and the broad scope of their authority. For example, Stanislaw Majchrzak recalled the arrest of his brother one evening in March 1942 and the notification the following day that the family could pick up the body. On reaching the Gendarmerie post, the father was told that his son had been shot because he "resisted"; however, on inspection, the corpse showed "numerous injuries" from blunt force trauma but no evidence of a bullet wound.[116] Katarzyna Idzikowska recalled the arrest in December 1942 of her brother, who had just returned on a pass after two years of forced labor in the Reich. The following day, she went to the Gendarmerie post to bring her brother some food and was told that he had been "transported away." She left the post but then decided to return to find out where her brother had been taken. In response to her question, a gendarme threatened: "Beat it, or you'll be shot too."[117]

Antipartisan Operations in Southeast Europe

Two introductory comparisons between the occupation forces in the East and those in Southeast Europe can usefully be made. As in the East, in Southeast Europe Wehrmacht and police forces cooperated closely in the prosecution of antipartisan operations and the extermination of the region's Jewish population. Also as in the East, in Southeast Europe the regular influx of seasoned troops guaranteed a core of men experienced in enforcing racial policy. The result was deadly. For example, on December 17, 1941, Reserve PB 93, operating near Veldes, Yugoslavia, reported killing 45 men and 3 women in combat with the partisans and an additional 140 men and 1 woman who were summarily executed or shot during escape attempts.[118] And, earlier that year, soldiers and policemen had combined to murder more than one thousand persons in Serbia alone during the two-month period July–August. Atrocities committed in Serbia followed a familiar pattern, and, despite the absence of an "explicit racial motive" with respect to the Serbian people, German actions between 1941 and 1943 incorporated elements "on the level with the annihilation of the Jews that permit a comparison with the practice of the murder of the Jews in the East."[119]

A farewell order of February 13, 1942, from Lieutenant General of the Police Georg Schreyer, the outgoing commander in chief of the Uniformed

Police *Alpenland* (Salzburg), offered one indication of the nature of police operations in Southeast Europe. Schreyer thanked the men of the Uniformed Police for their efforts in the pacification of Slovenia (Yugoslavia) and attributed this success to the "offensive spirit and sacrifice [*Opfermut*] of the courageous [police] battalions." He then reminded the men of their lost comrades and identified their sacrifice as symbolizing the duty to fight for the Führer and the *Volk* "until the last enemy is annihilated."[120] Schreyer's evaluation of the state of the partisan threat proved too optimistic, but his exhortation surely continued to resonate with the men long after his departure.

At the end of June 1942, Himmler, in coordination with Wehrmacht authorities, planned a series of large-scale antipartisan operations throughout Southeast Europe aimed at the "total cleansing" (*Gesamt-Bereinigung*) of the region. On the afternoon of June 25, Himmler met with Daluege to discuss the organization of an antipartisan operation in Slovenia, Operation Enzian.[121] On the same day, the *Reichsführer* charged the HSSPF *Alpenland,* Erwin Rösener, with overall command of the operation, but selected Major General of the Police Karl Brenner, Schreyer's successor as commander in chief of the Uniformed Police in Salzburg, to lead the operation in the field. Once again Himmler chose well as Brenner was the man who had approved the massacre at Ostrów in November 1939. Scheduled to last four weeks, the operation involved numerous police battalions, including PB 93, PB 171, PB 181, PB 316, PB 322, Police Mountain Regiment 18, a motorized Gendarmerie company, and Wehrmacht forces. In addition, Himmler ordered Security Police and SD forces to supplement the Uniformed Police by developing intelligence estimates on the location and strength of partisan forces.[122]

In order to increase the capabilities of the police formations, Himmler directed the transfer of mortars, flame throwers, and artillery to the battalions and the creation of police "artillery companies." The trend of improved firepower continued throughout the war and made Himmler's "political soldiers" an increasingly versatile and lethal force.[123] Himmler also ordered the HSSPFs to consult with Daluege and provide him with a projected start date for the operation by July 1.

In guidance that he issued to his SS and police forces concerning the operation, Himmler revealed: "The action has the [objective] of rendering harmless all elements of the population who willingly furnish the gangs with persons, food, weapons, or shelter. The men of a guilty family, in many cases even the entire clan, are always to be executed." He continued: "The women of these families are to be arrested and brought to a concentration camp. The children are to be taken from their home . . . and I expect a separate report on the number and racial value of these children."[124] A situation report of

July 11, 1942, provided one indication of the practical manifestation of this guidance by detailing the burning down of the villages of Gradisce and Koreno and the execution of all males over the age of fifteen, allegedly in response to accusations of supporting the partisans. The police "resettled" the remaining women and children to other areas.[125] The police forces in Southeast Europe did not, however, limit themselves to simple antipartisan operations as they routinely participated in the conduct of reprisal actions against the local population, as noted in a police activity report detailing the summary execution of 144 "Communist violent criminals" (*kommunistische Gewaltverbrecher*).[126]

The actions of the police formations in Southeast Europe demonstrate that murder and atrocity were not simply the tools of policemen locked in an apocalyptic struggle with "Jewish-Bolshevist" enemies on the Eastern Front. Far more, the actions of gendarmes and individual duty Policemen in Poland, combined with the actions of police battalions throughout Eastern Europe, reveal a consistent pattern of thought and behavior in the prosecution of National Socialist policy. The SS and police leadership and, indeed, Hitler himself continued to rely on the commitment of these forces to the "cleansing" of the occupied territories. And the murderous activity continued even as Hitler's Reich began to contract and the police forces fell back into Germany. On German soil, many of these battalions, organized into Combat Groups (Kampfgruppen), joined Wehrmacht units battling Soviet forces in the East and American and British forces in the West. For example, the policemen of Kampfgruppe II engaged American forces for nineteen days in a bitter battle for control of the imperial city of Aachen in October 1944.[127]

In the wake of the battle for Aachen, the commander of the unit, Colonel of the Police Fuchs, praised his policemen for fighting "shoulder to shoulder" with the soldiers of the Wehrmacht while inflicting "considerable bloody losses" on the enemy and earning the respect of their adversaries. In his final order to his men, Fuchs declared that the Americans had learned one lesson in the battle for the city: "The German man fights and falls, but he does not capitulate as he will rather die than become a slave."[128] These were indeed ironic words coming from a police force that had made so many Europeans into slaves. Even as the remains of the First Reich crashed down around them, these men still found time to murder eighty men and women by the end of October 1944.[129] In the last three months of the year, their victims included Poles, Russians, French POWs, Belgians, Dutch, a Greek, an Italian, three German "half Jews" (*Halbjuden*), and ten German citizens (*Reichsdeutsche*), most on charges of plundering, attempted escape, incitement, or resistance.[130] The picture of policemen in the role of soldiers fighting heroically in the final defense of the Reich offers one final illustration of the soldierly ideal espoused within the green corps during the life of the Third Reich, but it was once again a picture painted in the blood of its victims, the ultimate testament to Himmler's efforts in creating his legions of political soldiers.

CONCLUSION

Despite the immensity of their crimes, the police battalions and the men of the Uniformed Police escaped the reach of Nuremberg, and, unlike their SS counterparts in the Gestapo and the Security Service (SD), the Ordnungspolizei were not identified by the Allies as a criminal organization. This omission is all the more surprising when one considers the availability of evidence, ranging from classified radio intercepts to the analysis of the police prepared by British military intelligence during the war.[1] In fact, a British intelligence analysis of the German police *in April 1945* described the police battalions as "among the most nazified [*sic*], fanatical and brutal German field units. Their participation in 'punitive' actions has made them a terror of Norway, Poland, Yugoslavia, Greece, Czechoslovakia and Italy."[2]

As subsequent investigations in the 1950s and 1960s revealed, many of the men who served as policemen in the East and participated in the horrific crimes described in the previous chapters returned to duty as policemen in the Federal Republic of Germany and in Austria. Considering that these men were mobilized from specific cities and regions during the war and that, after the war, they continued their service in law enforcement, it is reasonable to conclude that many of them remained in contact with each other and cooperated in establishing cover stories as their crimes came to light during the postwar period.[3] Their position in German law enforcement allowed them to receive word from friends or contacts concerning possible investigations, and their own experience in the legal system made them clearly aware of the rules of evidence and testimony. This is especially evident in the thousands of interviews conducted by state prosecutors as person after person either claims to have known nothing about any murders or admits only to "having heard about such things." Still, when confronted with wartime reports or accusations of witnesses, some admitted having "witnessed" the conduct of genocide, and a few even admitted to participating.

What is striking about these investigations from the researcher's perspective is the fact that so few former policemen provided the impetus or initial information to begin investigations of their former units. Those who had murdered men, women, and children or seen them murdered on a routine basis apparently could continue to rationalize their actions or those of their

colleagues decades after the war. Not only were these men able to free themselves from feelings of shame or guilt, but some even managed to mytholo-
gize their wartime service. For example, Hermann Franz, a convinced Nazi
and commander of a police regiment that prosecuted a series of murderous
activities in the Soviet Union in the summer of 1942, published a history of
the Police Mountain Regiment in 1963. As is to be expected, Franz's account
tells of heroic soldiers in "military service" against dangerous partisans and
an "atheistic Bolshevistic ideology." Despite his best efforts, Franz's ideology also seeps through in phrases such as "combat against gangs" [*Bandenkampf*] and a reference to a commander's "highest commandment" being
the preservation of "precious German blood."[4] Likewise, the choice of Adolf
von Bomhard, the head of the Uniformed Police Operations Office from
1936 to 1942—a man who had direct knowledge of and access to the reporting of genocide in Poland and the Soviet Union and sent personal instructions to the police formations concerning cooperation with the
Einsatzgruppen and taking the "appropriate measures" for dealing with
Soviet prisoners of war—to write the book's foreword is bitterly ironic.[5]
    Franz was not the only senior ranking member of the police to attempt to
rewrite history after the war. Dr. Heinrich Lankenau, the former commander
in chief of the Uniformed Police in Münster and in the Netherlands, published
a work devoted to the air-raid duties of the police inside Germany. Lankenau's story focuses on the activities of heroic policemen and air-defense volunteers as they seek to save German families buried under the rubble by Allied
bombs. In this story, the police emerge as heroes driven by their duty to save
German victims, a theme with contemporary resonance for those familiar with
the recent debate concerning Jörg Friedrich's *Der Brand*.[6] Not surprisingly,
Lankenau devotes little attention to police activities in the East other than to
remark on the "extensive and great responsibility" associated with the "new
tasks" of governing the occupied territories.[7] Neither does he discuss his membership in the SS or his role in a series of executions involving Polish forced
laborers.[8] In Lankenau's account, "ideals"—"duty," "comradeship," "military service"—take pride of place, not their practical expression, as evidenced
in countless acts of murder and atrocity in the occupied territories.[9]

Reality versus Rhetoric

In one respect it is not surprising that the concepts of comradeship, duty, and
martial service should find their way into the writings of these men, for these
were, indeed, the organizational values on which they had built their professional identities during the Third Reich. The words of Franz and Lankenau

offered vibrant echoes of the past. In May 1942, the commander of the Gendarmerie in Zhitomir, Major of the Police von Bredow, reminded his gendarmes: "The highest commandment is comradeship. . . . We are not commissars with all their evil vices. We are soldiers of Prussian rearing and stand before a task that demands from us our greatest efforts. We only must learn in this task with which the Führer charged us here in the Ukraine to see something very important and beautiful, something on which depends the fate of Germany for the coming centuries."[10]

The creation of a martial identity tied to the ideological precepts of the Third Reich remained a focus for the training of the police throughout the war, the established ideal being the political soldier. In late September 1944, a ten-thousand-man replacement draft for the police began its training, training that had as its explicit goal "the education of the man as a politically and militarily schooled, field-qualified combatant."[11] Even as Allied bombers pounded German cities into rubble and Allied armies advanced into the Reich, the ideal of a "politically and militarily schooled" police soldier remained the standard. This standard held especially for the midlevel leadership of the police as evidenced by a trip taken by General of the Police Adolf von Bomhard to Poland at the end of November 1944. The purpose of this visit to the crumbling Eastern Front primarily involved the evaluation of a police major for promotion to lieutenant colonel and the examination of a police lieutenant colonel concerning his suitability for transfer to the Uniformed Police Operations Office in Berlin. Bomhard's personal report to the acting head of the Uniformed Police, Alfred Wünnenberg, demonstrates the importance placed by the senior police leadership on the selection of the right man for the job even as the Third Reich crumbled around them.[12] Indeed, it took "political soldiers" to prosecute the type of war envisioned by Hitler, Himmler, Heydrich, and Daluege on the Eastern Front—men who may not have always enjoyed their tasks but who nonetheless felt that they were making an important contribution to the Führer's vision and the creation of a new German empire. Hitler, in turn, praised the SS and police formations for their "energetic and vigorous action" in the pacification of the occupied territories.[13]

Atrocity as a Standard of Warfare?

In truth, acts of atrocity have accompanied warfare since time immemorial. Thucydides tells of the fate of the Melians, who after refusing to yield to Athenian demands suffer the execution of their men and the enslavement of their women and children.[14] Likewise, John Dower offered a view of the racial hatreds and acts of atrocity, on both sides, that accompanied the battles in the Pacific during World War II.[15] Finally, the massacre of Vietnamese civilians at My Lai offers a more contemporary example of atrocity. Did the actions of German policemen on the Eastern Front constitute simply a continuation of an inevitable trend toward brutalization and murder in the course of warfare? While murder and outrage do, indeed, accompany war, the Athenians did decide to spare the Mytilenes during the war with Sparta. Similarly, while racial prejudices certainly played a role in individual actions in the war in the Pacific, Roosevelt and Truman did not send orders or create an institutional policy promoting and condoning the slaughter of all Japanese men, women, and children in the field. Finally, despite the lenient sentence ultimately given to Lieutenant William L. Calley Jr., he was charged, stood trial, and was convicted of murdering twenty-two civilians at My Lai.[16]

The difference is that the Uniformed Police formations and policemen who served in the occupied Eastern territories during World War II embarked on a premeditated campaign of annihilation sanctioned from the highest levels of political, civil, and military leadership. The very structure and premise on which Hitler's "racial state" rested promoted the creation of an apocalyptic mind-set in which "toughness and ruthlessness" became the acceptable and preferred standard for dealing with conquered populations and especially the European Jews. In turn, the police accepted their murderous mission as a "necessary evil" in the course of creating a German empire.[17] In this sense, Himmler's SS and policemen existed in an organizational environment that created a "new moral order," one in which principles of exclusion and enmity such as anti-Semitism and anti-Bolshevism reigned supreme.[18]

Killing Eye to Eye

In his study of Police Battalion (PB) 101, Christopher Browning discussed the experiment by Stanley Milgram concerning the willingness of "naïve volunteer subjects" to inflict pain on fellow human beings when given orders from an "authority figure" and placed in a position of power over the "victim."[19] Certainly, Browning is correct in using this model to point out the effect of authority figures and disparate power relationships in influencing human behavior. However, does Milgram's model then account for the behavior of German policemen?

In the case of the police battalions and individual duty policemen on the Eastern Front, it appears that there may be some grounds for making this comparison; however, there are also important differences between the two situations. First, the policemen were not naive volunteers but, in most cases, and especially within the officer corps and senior enlisted ranks, experienced professionals whose choice of law enforcement as a career routinely faced them with hostile situations and violent behavior. Second, the men of the police generally knew beforehand the murderous nature of the actions that they were about to undertake. While some former policemen contended that the first killing may have come as a surprise, the many subsequent actions certainly did not. Likewise, the fact that the killings became an open secret within the units and that some units passed around photographs of killings to new arrivals also calls into question the supposed lack of cognizance of these men as they loaded onto trucks and drove to a local Jewish ghetto, prison, or nearby town.[20] Admittedly, some men experienced a period of desensitization, but this period often proved to be very short. Third, these men routinely killed their victims while standing next to them and after looking into their eyes. The standard procedure for mass killings at the side of an open pit meant that the uniforms and boots of the shooters literally became covered with the blood and body matter of their victims. Stated another way, how much compliance would Milgram have received if his naive volunteers had been asked to kill up close and for an extended period of time? As Milgram found, and as Browning noted, as the level of active participation and physical contact required between the "perpetrator" and the "victim" increased, so too did the refusal of the former to administer punishment to the latter.[21]

The purpose of the preceding discussion is not to discount the influence of authority figures completely. However, Milgram's model does not explain the numerous examples of gendarmes serving at isolated outposts in the East who on their own initiative routinely and enthusiastically killed even when they had a choice not to. Nor does it explain the behavior of men like Helmuth Palm, whose suggestions for operations were intended to increase the number of murdered, all in accordance with the motto: "One Pole or Russian too many is better than one too few."

The End of Individual Responsibility and the Totality of Organizational Culture?

As Browning's study of PB 101 clearly demonstrated, not all policemen chose to kill. In fact, there are examples of policemen who attempted to prevent killing, as the case of Gendarmerie Sergeant Hahn in Poland in October 1939 demonstrated. The fact that Hahn was subsequently overruled does not negate the fact that he attempted to prevent murder.[22] Likewise, Gendarmerie Sergeant Karl Karner received orders to participate in a "special mission" (*Sondereinsatz*) involving the arrest of a priest and a former mayor from an area under German control. Watching his prisoners pack their bags, he remarked: "I can't watch these types of things over the long run." Karner's superior described him as a "conscientious and sober man . . . who is not ready for the demands of a special mission"—and decided to transfer him without prejudice.[23]

The cases of Hahn and Karner demonstrate that, despite the efforts of Himmler and Daluege to instill their own vision of the "political soldier" in the police, not all policemen were willing to accept the extreme implications of this philosophy. Still, the organization rendered futile Hahn's efforts and reassigned Karner so that he could still play a role. In the end, when there was killing to be done, there were always more than enough volunteers.[24]

Proving the Negative

The case of Gendarmerie Sergeant Karner raises an important point. Not every man was able to withstand the psychological strain of repeatedly being involved in murder, a fact recognized by Himmler and Daluege. In the end, policemen always had the choice of refusing to participate in murder.[25] At worst, this refusal led to some further additional duty, possibly verbal abuse by an officer, and snide comments from one's colleagues. It did not, however, carry with it the danger of execution or incarceration, as so many policemen claimed during postwar investigations. There is not a *single* documented case of a policeman being shot or imprisoned for refusing to kill Jews in cold blood.[26] Likewise, of the literally millions of pages of documents recovered from Himmler's and Daluege's headquarters, there is not one mention of either man discussing a problem within the ranks of the police concerning a refusal to murder or an inability to find policemen willing to kill.[27] This is significant, especially when one considers Himmler's penchant for becoming involved in any problem, great or small, within his SS and police empire, including such mundane issues as the prevention of sexually transmitted diseases.[28] Given the attention that Himmler devoted to a marriage application rejected because the policeman's ethnic German fiancée remained "under the sway" of Polish influence, certainly policemen objecting to murder or refusing to kill would have received his attention had the issue been of any concern.[29] In the end, lack of evidence is not proof that it does not exist; it is, however, worth noting its implications for the general course of police behavior.

Ideology and Anti-Semitism

Despite their best efforts, the SS and police leadership was unable to establish a uniform and homogeneous body of members; however, they did succeed in creating an organizational culture within the police, one built on the pillars of anti-Semitism and anti-Bolshevism, that progressively broadened the boundaries of acceptable and desired behavior. Himmler's rant against the danger posed by Jewish-Bolshevism during the ceremony appointing him as chief of the Police and Daluege's "statistical evidence" tying the Jews to the majority of the crimes committed in Germany offer but two examples. Likewise, a directive preventing policemen from staying in a Berlin hotel because it was frequented by Jews or the prohibition on incarcerating Latvians with Jews on "ideological and racial political grounds" offer two seemingly minor but telling examples of the practical manifestations of this culture beyond the conduct of mass killings.[30]

Equipped with a new conception of crime and a vision of their role in ensuring the health of the peoples' community, the police emerged as an instrument par excellence for the conduct of murder and atrocity. The statement of a policeman from PB 322, made in response to a question as to why his unit had killed Jews, captures the organizational mind-set: "Because it was preached to us at every training session, that one needed to exterminate this race. They were guilty of all the evil in the world and also for the outbreak of the war."[31] So does that of Kurt Möbius, another policeman: "Although I am aware that it is the duty of the police to protect the innocent, I was however at the time convinced that the Jewish people were not innocent but guilty. I believed all the propaganda that Jews were criminals and subhuman. . . . The thought that one should oppose or evade the order to take part in the extermination of the Jews never entered my head either."[32]

Similar examples abound. Writing a letter home in early July 1941, a member of Reserve Police Battalion 105 warned: "The Jews are free game. . . . One can only give the Jews some well intentioned advice: Bring no more children into the world. They no longer have a future."[33] Three years later, another policeman wrote to his hometown police commander in Oldenburg discussing the pleasure that he and his colleagues received from getting news from their old precinct. This policeman then boasted: "The comrades Sgt. Schulze, Wilken, and Sgt. of the Reserves Wemken and Stöver were very active in the cleansing of Hungary of the Jews. Riding the trains for days on end with the purpose of guarding the transports was the task and really did a number on my waistline [*hat stark am Fett gezehrt*]. But here we still have good provisions in the form of bacon, butter, and eggs." He then remarked:

"Comrade Sergeant Wiemers is a platoon leader and with comrades Janacek, Kühl, Müller K., Uhlenhut, Bohle, Eisenhauer, and Osterthun is currently in the Carpathians for a special mission. I myself was attached to a special unit [*Sondereinsatzkommando*] of the SD and have traveled throughout most of Hungary with this unit."[34] Here again we see a man capable of discussing the mass murder of the Hungarian Jews and his waistline in the same paragraph. This matter-of-fact approach to genocide—exemplified, as previously seen, by men like Police Sergeant Helmuth Schmidt, the "Terror of Lemberg," who "could shoot a Jew in the head while eating a sandwich"—is, perhaps, the most striking aspect uncovered by this research.[35]

The Strategy of Cumulative Annihilation

The previous chapters have offered numerous examples of atrocities, but, for each example that I have given, I have been forced to set aside five, ten, even twenty others. Some—like SS General Jürgen Stroop, infamous for his role in the crushing of the Warsaw ghetto uprising, discussing the handing over of the operation in May 1943 to his deputy, Major of the Police Otto Bundtke—record large-scale actions: "That man Bundtke had a tough job believe me. . . . The Jewish insurgents realized that our troops had been substantially reduced, and they gave us a very hard time. . . . Bundtke suffered losses—quite a few, in fact—but in the end he liquidated nearly all the Jewish resistance points."[36] Others—like an October 28, 1942, diary entry for the First Company of PB 310—record small-scale actions: in this case the capture by a police hunting platoon of three Jews and their execution after a short interrogation, a process repeated with three other Jews the following day.[37]

Likewise, the previous chapters have discussed many different police units, both large and small. Of course other examples remain: for example, PB 41 and a report of November 11, 1942, detailing, under the title "Overview of Success" (*Erfolgsübersicht*), the killing of 12 "bandits," 13 partisan helpers, and 391 Jews; or PB 67 and a report detailing the execution of 77 "bandits" and 74 Jews on December 3 and 4, 1942.[38] In the end, the total number of those who fell victim to the Uniformed Police may never be known, but the figure certainly runs into the hundreds of thousands, if not a million or more. For every large-scale massacre like those at Babi Yar and Kamenez-Podolsk, there were hundreds, if not thousands, of small-scale ghetto-clearing operations and executions during rail transports and antipartisan operations, all of which contributed to a cumulative strategy of annihilation.

"Ideological Soldiers" or *"Ordinary Men"?*

Historians should rightly be wary of treating the complexities of human motivation reductively and finding one single explanation for events so monstrously beyond human comprehension. However, to argue that organizational culture and the ideology underpinning it provided the environment that facilitated annihilation is not to paint the world of the police in simplistic Manichaean terms. Instead, it is to recognize that the impetus for genocide came from within an organization that established and promoted its own values, beliefs, and standards for behavior, that created an environment in which persecution, exploitation, and murder became both acceptable and desirable attributes of a police corps charged with preserving the German *Volk* and locked in an apocalyptic battle against the internal and external enemies of the Reich. In a January 1943 speech commemorating the tenth year of National Socialist rule, Daluege boasted of Himmler's success in building a "police combat troop of the National Socialist movement." He then exclaimed: "For Adolf Hitler, this corps of the SS and the police represents his struggle for a greater Germany, Europe, and the world. Its [the corps'] task is the annihilation of the eternal enemies of all folkish [*völkisch*] and racially conscious nations."[39] If annihilation was the goal, then the men of the Uniformed Police more than met their quota—the ultimate testament to Himmler's and Daluege's efforts to create a corps of "political soldiers."

NOTES

Unless an English-language source is noted, translations are mine. The following abbreviations have been used in the notes:

BArch = Bundesarchiv;
BDC = Berlin Document Center;
IMT = International Military Tribunal;
NARA = National Archives and Records Administration;
USHMMA = U.S. Holocaust Memorial Museum Archive;
ZStl = Zentrale Stelle der Landesjustizverwaltungen.

Introduction

1. "Auswärtiger Einsatz [War Diary of the Third Company of Police Battalion 322, December 24, 1941]," RG 48.004M, reel 2, frame 200851, U.S. Holocaust Memorial Museum Archive (hereafter USHMMA).

2. Heiner Lichtenstein, *Himmler's grüne Helfer: Die Schutz- und Ordnungspolizei im "Dritten Reich"* (Cologne: Bund, 1990), 61.

3. "Auswärtiger Einsatz [War Diary of the Third Company of Police Battalion 322, December 24, 1941]," RG 48.004M, reel 2, frames 200851–200852, USHMMA.

4. Konrad Kwiet, "Auftakt zum Holocaust: Ein Polizeibataillon im Osteinsatz," in *Der Nationalsozialismus: Studien zur Ideologie und Herrschaft*, ed. Wolfgang Benz, Hans Buchheim, and Hans Mommsen (Frankfurt a.M.: Fischer Taschenbuch, 1993), 191.

5. Ibid., 193.

6. "Auswärtiger Einsatz [War Diary of the Third Company of Police Battalion 322, June 7, 1941]," RG 48.004M, reel 2, frames 200743–200744, USHMMA.

7. "Auswärtiger Einsatz [War Diary of the Third Company of Police Battalion 322, June 28, 1941]," RG 48.004M, reel 2, frame 200751, USHMMA.

8. Andrej Angrick, Martina Voigt, Silke Ammerschubert, and Peter Klein, "Da hätte man schon Tagebuch führen müssen," in *Die Normalität des Verbrechens: Bilanz und Perspektiven der Forschung zu den nationalsozialistischen Gewaltverbrechen*, ed. Helge Grabitz, Klaus Bästlein, and Johannes Tuchel (Berlin: Druckhaus Hentrich, 1994), 372 n. 33.

9. "Auswärtiger Einsatz [War Diary of the Third Company of Police Battalion 322, July 6, 7, and 8, 1941]," RG 48.004M, reel 2, frame 200758, USHMMA.

10. Angrick et al., "Da hätte man schon Tagebuch führen müssen," 334.

11. Ibid., 331, 334–335.

12. "Der Befehlshaber des rückw. Heeres-Gebietes Mitte, Ia, Korpsbefehl Nr. 26 [July 10, 1941]," RH 26-221, file 12a, Bundesarchiv (hereafter BArch).

13. War Diary of Police Battalion 322 [July 9, 1941], RG 48.004M, reel 2, frame 200906, USHMMA.

14. For a more complete discussion of the activities of the Einsatzgruppen, see Helmut Krausnick, *Hitlers Einsatzgruppen: Die Truppen des Weltanschauungskrieges, 1938–1942* (Frankfurt a.m.: Fischer Taschenbuch, 1981).

15. "Auswärtiger Einsatz [War Diary of the Third Company of Police Battalion 322, July 10, 13, and 14, 1941]," RG 48.004M, reel 2, frames 200761–200762; and War Diary of Police Battalion 322 [July 9, 1941], RG 48.004M, reel 2, frame 200906, USHMMA.

16. War Diary of Police Battalion 322 [July 17, 1941], RG 48.004M, reel 2, frame 200911, USHMMA.

17. "Auswärtiger Einsatz [War Diary of the Third Company of Police Battalion 322, July 26, 1941]," RG 48.004M, reel 2, frame 200781, USHMMA.

18. Bernhard Daenekas, "Verbrechen deutscher Polizeieinheiten im Zweiten Weltkrieg—aus der Sicht eines Ermittlungsbeamten," *Archiv für Polizeigeschichte* 4 (1993): 23.

19. "Auswärtiger Einsatz [War Diary of the Third Company of Police Battalion 322, August 10, 1941]," RG 48.004M, reel 2, frame 200796, USHMMA. See also Kwiet, "Auftakt," 201–202.

20. War Diary of Police Battalion 322 [August 10, 15, 1941], RG 48.004M, reel 2, frames 200935 and 200937; and "Auswärtiger Einsatz [War Diary of the Third Company of Police Battalion 322, August 14, 1941]," RG 48.004M, reel 2, frame 200798, USHMMA. The company's war diary entry indicates that this action took place on August 14, while the battalion's diary lists the event under the entry for August 15.

21. "Auswärtiger Einsatz [War Diary of the Third Company of Police Battalion 322, August 15, 1941]," RG 48.004M, reel 2, frame 200799, USHMMA.

22. "9./III.Pol.Btl. Rgt. Mitte, Betrifft: Tagesmeldung [September 1, 1941]," RG 48.004M, reel 2, frame 201227, USHMMA; and "Auswärtiger Einsatz [War Diary of the Third Company of Police Battalion 322, September 1, 1941]," RG 48.004M, reel 2, frames 200806–200807, USHMMA.

23. "III./Pol/Rgt.Mitte, Betrifft: Judenaktion der 8. Kompanie in Krassnopolje am 22.10.1941 [October 26, 1941]," RG 48.004M, reel 2, frames 201328–201335, USHMMA.

24. War Diary of Police Battalion 322 [October 16–17 and 22, 1941], RG 48.004M, reel 2, frames 200997 and 200100, USHMMA.

25. See Robert Gellately, *Backing Hitler: Consent and Coercion in Nazi Germany* (New York: Oxford University Press, 2001); and Gregory Wegner, *Anti-Semitism and Schooling under the Third Reich* (New York: Routledge Falmer, 2002). For one man's view of this issue, see Victor Klemperer, *I Will Bear Witness: A Diary of the Nazi Years, 1933–1941*, trans. Martin Chalmers (New York: Random House, 1998), and *I Will Bear Witness: A Diary of the Nazi Years, 1942–1945*, trans. Martin Chalmers (New York: Random House, 1999).

26. Christopher R. Browning, *The Final Solution and the German Foreign Office: A Study of Referat D III of Abteilung Deutschland, 1940–43* (New York: Holmes & Meier, 1978), 185.

27. Peter Hayes, *Industry and Ideology: IG Farben and the Nazi Era* (Cambridge: Cambridge University Press, 2001), xxvi.

28. Alfred Mierzejewski, "A Public Enterprise in the Service of Mass Murder: The Deutsche Reichsbahn and the Holocaust," *Holocaust and Genocide Studies* 15 (spring 2001): 41.

29. Yaacov Lozowick, *Hitler's Bureaucrats: The Nazi Security Police and the Banality of Evil,* trans. Haim Watzman (London: Continuum, 2000), 8.

30. Rudolf Höss, *Commandant of Auschwitz: The Autobiography of Rudolf Höss,* trans. Constantine Fitz Gibbon (Cleveland: World, 1959), 85.

31. Michael Thad Allen, *The Business of Genocide: The SS, Slave Labor, and the Concentration Camps* (Chapel Hill: University of North Carolina Press, 2002).

32. See Christopher R. Browning, *Ordinary Men: Reserve Police Battalion 101 and the Final Solution in Poland* (New York: Harper Collins, 1992).

33. Daniel J. Goldhagen, *Hitler's Willing Executioners: Ordinary Germans and the Holocaust* (New York: Knopf, 1996), 277, 416. A more thoughtful examination of this issue is provided by Jürgen Matthäus, "Ausbildungsziel Judenmord? Zum Stellenwert der 'weltanschaulichen Erziehung' von SS und Polizei im Rahmen der 'Endlösung,'" *Zeitschrift für Geschichtswissenschaft* 47 (1999): 673–699.

34. See, e.g., Klaus-Michael Mallmann, "Der qualitative Sprung im Vernichtungsprozeß: Das Massaker von Kamenez-Podolsk Ende August 1941," *Jahrbuch für Antisemitismusforschung* 10 (2001): 241, and "'. . . Mißgeburten, die nicht auf diese Welt gehören': Die deutsche Ordnungspolizei in Polen, 1939–1941," in *Genesis des Genozids: Polen, 1939–1941,* ed. Klaus-Michael Mallmann and Bogdan Musial (Darmstadt: Wissenschaftliche Buchgesellschaft, 2004), 71–89; and Klaus-Michael Mallmann, Volker Rieß, and Wolfram Pyta, eds., *Deutscher Osten, 1939– 1945: Der Weltanschauungskrieg in Photos und Texten* (Darmstadt: Wissenschaftliche Buchgesellschaft, 2003). I would like to thank Michael Mallmann for giving me a draft copy of "Mißgeburten" prior to its publication.

35. Jürgen Matthäus, Konrad Kwiet, Jürgen Forster, and Richard Breitman, *Ausbildungsziel Judenmord? "Weltanschauliche Erziehung" von SS, Polizei und Waffen-SS im Rahmen der "Endlösung"* (Frankfurt a.M.: Fischer Taschenbuch, 2003), 85.

36. Edgar H. Schein, *Organizational Culture and Leadership* (San Francisco: Jossey-Bass, 1985), 6.

37. Ibid., 223–243.

38. Stephen J. Harrison, "Police Organizational Culture: Using Ingrained Values to Build Positive Organizational Improvement," *Public Administration and Management: An Interactive Journal* 3, no. 2 (1998), http://www.pamij.com/harrison.html (accessed October 27, 2004).

39. International Military Tribunal (hereafter IMT), *Trials of the Major War Criminals before the International Military Tribunal,* vol. 29 (Nuremberg: Secretariat of the Military Tribunal, 1948), pp. 227–228.

40. "Geschäftsverteilung u. Geschäftsverkehr d. Chefs der Deutschen Polizei im Reichsministerium des Innern, RdErl. des RFSSuChdDtPol. im RMdI v. 26.6.1936, O/S Nr. 3/36 [June 26, 1936]," T580, reel 95, NARA.

41. For a detailed description of the activities of the Security Police and SD, see George C. Browder, *Foundations of the Nazi Police State: The Formation of SIPO and SD* (Lexington: University Press of Kentucky, 1990); and Michael Wildt, *Generation des Unbedingten: Das Führungskorps des Reichssicherheitshauptamtes* (Hamburg: Hamburger Edition, 2003).

42. Friederich Wilhelm, *Die Polizei im NS-Staat: Die Geschichte ihrer Organisation im Überblick* (Paderborn: Ferdinand Schöningh, 1997), 23–24, 85–87.

43. "Entwurf eines am 27. April 1939 vor dem Deutschen Gemeindetag zu haltenden Vortrages des Reichsführers SS und Chef der Deutschen Polizei über die Gemeindepolizei und das Feuerlöschwesens [April 1939]," T580, reel 37, NARA. See also "Disposition zum Vortrag General Daluege, Die Ordnungspolizei," T580, reel 216, file 5, NARA; and "Der Chef der Ordnungspolizei [September 5, 1939]," T580, reel 96, NARA.

44. Tom Segev, *Soldiers of Evil: The Commandants of the Nazi Concentration Camps,* trans. Haim Watzman (New York: McGraw-Hill, 1987), 73. See also Robert Lewis Koehl, *The Black Corps: The Structure and Power Struggles of the Nazi SS* (Madison: University of Wisconsin Press, 1983), 48.

45. Bernd Wegner, *Hitlers politische Soldaten: Die Waffen-SS, 1933–1945,* 4th ed. (Paderborn: Ferdinand Schöningh, 1982), 79. See also Segev, *Soldiers of Evil,* 95–96; and Charles W. Sydnor Jr., *Soldiers of Destruction: The SS Death's Head Division, 1933–1945* (Princeton, N.J.: Princeton University Press, 1977). In addition to their responsibilities in the concentration camps, the Death's Head units also provided combat formations for duty at the front as part of the Waffen-SS.

46. Max Domarus, ed., *Hitler: Reden und Proklamationen, 1932–1945,* 2 vols. (Wiesbaden: R. Löwit, 1973), 1:881. Hitler admitted this desire in a directive dealing with the SS dated August 17, 1938.

47. Speech by Kurt Daluege during the state ceremony naming Heinrich Himmler as chief of the German police [June 18, 1936], T580, reel 216, file 3, National Archives and Records Administration (hereafter NARA).

48. Speech by Heinrich Himmler during the state ceremony naming him as chief of the German police [June 18, 1936], T580, reel 216, file 3, NARA.

49. Gerd Rühle, *Das Dritte Reich: Dokumentarische Darstellung des Aufbaues der Nation, das vierte Jahr* (Berlin: Hummelverlag, 1937), 272.

50. "Der Weg der Ordnungspolizei von SS-Gruppenführer, General der Polizei, Kurt Daluege [January 23, 1939]," T580, reel 216, file 5, NARA.

51. Claudia Koonz, *The Nazi Conscience* (Cambridge, Mass.: Harvard University Press, 2003), 6.

52. Stefan Klemp, *Freispruch für das "Mord-Bataillon": Die NS-Ordnungspolizei und die Nachkriegsjustiz* (Münster: Lit Verlag, 1998), 23–24.

53. Ernst Klee, Willi Dreßen, and Volker Rieß, eds., *"The Good Old Days": The Holocaust as Seen by Its Perpetrators and Bystanders,* trans. Deborah Burnstone (New York: Free Press, 1991), 220–221. Testimony given by Möbius in 1961.

54. Melita Maschmann, *Fazit: Kein Rechtfertigungsversuch* (Stuttgart: Deutsche Verlags–Anstalt, 1963), 61. Maschmann discusses these feelings as part of her reaction to the violence committed against Jews and Jewish businesses during the "Night of Broken Glass" (Kristallnacht).

55. Mallmann, Rieß, and Pyta, eds., *Deutscher Osten,* 137.

56. Stephan Linck, "'. . . schon allein wegen des Schmutzes . . .' Wie Polizisten über ihren Einsatz schreiben: Das Mitteilungsblatt der Schutzpolizei Flensburg, 1944/45," *Archiv für Polizeigeschichte* 9 (1998): 52.

57. *Vossische Zeitung* (Berlin), March 18, 1933.

58. "Der Kommandeur der Gendarmerie Shitomir, Kommandobefehl Nr. 27/43 [April 12, 1943]," RG 53.002M, fond 658, reel 5, file 3, USHMMA.

59. Paul Kohl, *Der Krieg der Wehrmacht und der deutschen Polizei, 1941–1944* (Frankfurt a.M.: Fischer Taschenbuch, 1995), 233–234.

60. IMT, *Trials of the Major War Criminals before the International Military Tribunal,* vol. 22 (Nuremberg: Secretariat of the Military Tribunal, 1948), p. 232.

61. Rolf Giesen, *Nazi Propaganda Films: A History and Filmography* (Jefferson, N.C.: McFarland, 2003), 137–139.

62. "Der Kommandeur der Gendarmerie Shitomir, Kommandobefehl Nr. 27/43 [April 12, 1943]," RG 53.002M, fond 658, reel 5, file 3, USHMMA.

63. "Der Kommandeur der Ordnungspolizei b. SS- u. Polizeiführer Weißruthenien, Tagesbefehl Nr. 17 [August 14, 1943]," RG 53.002M, fond 389, reel 3, file 1, USHMMA.

64. Linck, "'. . . schon allein wegen des Schmutzes . . . ,'" 52.

65. Letter from HSSPF Rösener to Polizei-Einsatzstab Südost [February 20, 1942], 503 AR-Z 9/1965, file 2, p. 298, ZStl.

66. "Chef der Sicherheitspolizei und des SD, Nr. 1042 II/41-1515, Betr.: Photographieren von Exekutionen [April 16, 1942]," RG 06.025.63, KGB Archive Box 59, USHMMA. Himmler issued this prohibition on November 12, 1941.

67. "Rede des Chefs der Ordnungspolizei bei der SS-Führertagung des RFSS, Der Winterkampf der Ordnungspolizei im Osten" (captured German documents microfilmed at the Berlin Document Center), T580, reel 217, file 6, NARA. See also "Der Chef der Ordnungspolizei, Vortrag über den Kräfte- und Kriegseinsatz der Ordnungspolizei im Jahre 1941," T580, reel 96, NARA.

68. Peter Longerich, *Politik der Vernichtung: Eine Gesamtdarstellung der nationalsozialistischen Judenverfolgung* (Munich: Piper, 1998), 306–307, 662.

69. Klaus-Michael Mallmann, "Der Einstieg in den Genozid: Das Lübecker Polizeibataillon 307 und das Massaker in Brest-Litowsk Anfang Juli 1941," *Archiv für Polizeigeschichte* 10 (1999): 83.

70. Edward B. Westermann, "'Ordinary Men' or 'Ideological Soldiers'? Police Battalion 310 in Russia, 1942," *German Studies Review* 21 (February 1998): 51.

71. Michael H. Kater, *The Nazi Party: A Social Profile of Members and Leaders, 1919–1945* (Cambridge, Mass.: Harvard University Press, 1983), 141.

72. Browning, *Ordinary Men,* 48.

73. Klemp, "*Mord-Bataillon,*" 30. Average age is based on the year 1940.

74. Longerich, *Vernichtung,* 306.

75. Jürgen Matthäus, "What about the 'Ordinary Men'? The German Order Police and the Holocaust in the Occupied Soviet Union," *Holocaust and Genocide Studies* 10 (fall 1996): 134–150.

76. Klaus-Michael Mallmann, "Vom Fußvolk der 'Endlösung': Ordnungspolizei, Ostkrieg und Judenmord," *Tel Aviver Jahrbuch für deutsche Geschichte* 26 (1997): 365.

77. Raul Hilberg, *The Destruction of the European Jews,* 3 vols., rev. ed. (New York: Holmes & Meier, 1985), 2:466.

78. Georg Tessin, "Die Stäbe und Truppeneinheiten der Ordnungspolizei," in *Zur Geschichte der Ordnungspolizei,* by Hans-Joachim Neufeldt, Jürgen Huck, and Georg Tessin (Koblenz: Schriften des Bundesarchivs, 1957), pt. 2, pp. 15–16.

79. "Res. Pol. Batl. 122, Lagebericht für die Zeit vom 1. bis 15. Juli 1942 [July 16, 1942]," R 20, file 10, pp. 3–4, BArch; and "II./Pol. Regiment 14, Lagebericht für die Zeit vom 16. bis 31. August 1942 [September 1, 1942]," R 20, file 10, pp. 6–7, BArch. See also Westermann, "'Ordinary Men' or 'Ideological Soldiers'?" 48.

80. Donald M. McKale, *Hitler's Shadow War: The Holocaust and World War II* (New York: Cooper Square, 2002).

81. IMT, *Trials,* vol. 29, pp. 103, 104–105.

82. IMT, *Trials of the Major War Criminals before the International Military Tribunal,* vol. 32 (Nuremberg: Secretariat of the Military Tribunal, 1948), pp. 279–282.

83. "Der Führer, OKW/WFst/Op. Nr. 00281/42g.K. [August 18, 1942]," RW 4, file 554, BArch.

84. Mallmann, "Fußvolk," 373.

85. Mallmann, Rieß, and Pyta, eds., *Deutscher Osten,* 139.

86. Testimony of Walter S., V 205 AR-Nr. 512/1963, file 1, pp. 26–27, Zentrale Stelle der Landesjustizverwaltungen (hereafter ZStl).

87. Hilberg, *Destruction,* 3:301.

88. IMT, *Trials,* vol. 32, pp. 471–475, 478. Documents 3710-PS, 3713-PS.

Chapter 1. Taking Charge of the Police

1. Michael Burleigh, *The Third Reich: A New History* (New York: Hill & Wang, 2000), 151. See also Gerhard Weinberg, ed., *Hitler's Second Book: The Unpublished Sequel to Mein Kampf by Adolf Hitler,* trans. Krista Smith (New York: Enigma, 2003), 48–49.

2. Wolfgang J. Mommsen, *Imperial Germany, 1867–1918: Politics, Culture, and Society in an Authoritarian State,* trans. Richard Deveson (London: Arnold, 1995), 23–24. Mommsen correctly notes that this process was driven in large part by the desire of the German state of Prussia to maintain its preeminent role within the new German nation.

3. Thomas Nipperdey, *Deutsche Geschichte, 1866–1918,* vol. 2, *Machtstaat vor der Demokratie* (Munich: C. H. Beck, 1992), 128.

4. Ibid., 126.

5. Raymond Fosdick as quoted by Brian Chapman, *Police State* (New York: Praeger, 1970), 48.

6. Alf Lüdtke, *Police and State in Prussia, 1815–1850* (New York: Cambridge University Press, 1989), 70.

7. Jonathan Sperber, *Rhineland Radicals: The Democratic Movement and the Revolution of 1848–1849* (Princeton, N.J.: Princeton University Press, 1991), 377.

8. Hsi-Huey Liang, *The Berlin Police Force in the Weimarer Republic* (Berkeley: University of California Press, 1970), 27–29. See also Sperber, *Rhineland Radicals,* 88–91.

9. Nipperdey, *Machtstaat vor der Demokratie,* 127–128.

10. Thomas Diembach, "Vom Spazierstock zur Automatikpistole: Die Bewaffnung der Kriminalpolizei im Kaisserreich," *Archiv für Polizeigeschichte* 14 (2003): 46–48.

11. Charles I. Bevans, ed., *Treaties and Other International Agreements of the United States of America, 1776–1949* (Washington, D.C.: U.S. Government Printing Office, 1969), 116.

12. Harold J. Gordon Jr., "Police Careers in the Weimar Republic," in *Proceedings of the Citadel Symposium on Hitler and the National Socialist Era, 24–25 April*

1980, ed. Michael B. Barrett (Charleston, S.C.: Citadel Development Foundation, 1982), 161; Browder, *Foundations*, 36.

13. Peter Leßmann, *Die preußische Schutzpolizei in der Weimarer Republik: Streifendienst und Straßenkampf* (Düsseldorf: Droste, 1989), 1.

14. Liang, *Berlin Police*, 6.

15. Hans-Joachim Neufeldt, "Entstehung und Organisation des Hauptamtes Ordnungspolizei," in Neufeldt, Huck, and Tessin, *Zur Geschichte*, pt. 1, p. 5.

16. Gordon, "Police Careers," 164.

17. Frederick E. Blachly and Miriam E. Oatman, *The Government and Administration of Germany* (Baltimore: Johns Hopkins University Press, 1928), 413. See also Browder, *Foundations*, 38.

18. Gordon, "Police Careers," 163. See also Neufeldt, "Entstehung und Organisation," 5; and Tonis Hunold, *Polizei in der Reform: Was Staatsbürger und Polizei voneinander erwarten könnten* (Düsseldorf: Econ, 1968), 225–226. Neufeldt is somewhat less sanguine about the degree of influence exerted by the federal subsidy on the state police than is Gordon, and Hunold highlights the extremely slow and difficult progress in standardizing the states' police organizations.

19. Liang, *Berlin Police*, 9.

20. Neufeldt, "Entstehung und Organisation," 5. See also Blachly and Oatman, *Government and Administration*, 413.

21. Dan Bar-On, *Legacy of Silence: Encounters with Children of the Third Reich* (Cambridge, Mass.: Harvard University Press, 1989), 91; and Karin Hartewig, "'Eine sogenannte Neutralität der Beamten gibt es nicht': Sozialer Protest, bürgerliche Gesellschaft und Polizei im Ruhrgebiet, 1918–1924," in *"Sicherheit" und "Wohlfahrt": Polizei, Gesellschaft und Herrschaft im 19. und 20. Jahrhundert*, ed. Alf Lüdtke (Frankfurt a.M.: Suhrkamp, 1992), 315.

22. Hartewig, "'Eine sogenannte Neutralität der Beamten gibt es nicht,'" 314–316.

23. Eric D. Kohler, "The Crisis in the Prussian Schutzpolizei, 1930–32," in *Police Forces in History*, ed. George L. Mosse (London: Sage, 1975), 135, 148.

24. I. L. Hunt, *American Military Government of Occupied Germany, 1918–1920*, vol. 1, *Report of the Officer in Charge of Civil Affairs Third Army and American Forces in Germany* (n.p., 1920), 22.

25. Liang, *Berlin Police*, 41–42. See also Hajo Holborn, *A History of Modern Germany, 1840–1945* (Princeton, N.J.: Princeton University Press, 1969), 528–532.

26. Liang, *Berlin Police*, 41, 59. See also Hartewig, "'Eine sogenannte Neutralität der Beamten gibt es nicht,'" 322.

27. Hunold, *Polizei in der Reform*, 29–30.

28. Liang, *Berlin Police*, 70.

29. Hermann Graml, "Die Wehrmacht im Dritten Reich," *Vierteljahrshefte für Zeitgeschichte* 45 (July 1997): 365–366.

30. Siegfried Zaika, *Polizeigeschichte: Die Exekutive im Lichte der historischen Konfliktforschung—Untersuchungen über die Theorie und Praxis der preußischen Schutzpolizei in der Weimarer Republik zur Verhinderung und Bekämpfung innerer Unruhen* (Lübeck: Verlag für polizeiliches Fachschrifttum Georg Schmidt-Römhild, 1979), 81–100. In addition to the police forces involved, the Reichswehr provided a field artillery battery equipped with mortars to support the police.

31. Zaika, *Polizeigeschichte*, 128–132.

32. Ian Kershaw, *Hitler, 1889–1936: Hubris* (New York: Norton, 1998), 431.

33. Zaika, *Polizeigeschichte,* 89.

34. Leßmann, *Schutzpolizei,* 231–233.

35. Liang, *Berlin Police,* 55.

36. Leßmann, *Schutzpolizei,* 252–253.

37. See generally ibid., 231–234, 240–247 (quotations from 231, 232, and 241, respectively).

38. Richard Bessel, "Militarisierung und Modernisierung: Polizeiliches Handeln in der Weimarer Republik," in Lüdtke, ed., *"Sicherheit" und "Wohlfahrt,"* 324, 329, 343.

39. Ulrich Herbert, "Ideological Legitimization and Political Practice of the Leadership of the National Socialist Secret Police," trans. Maike Bohn, in *The Third Reich between Vision and Reality,* ed. Hans Mommsen (Oxford: Berg, 2001), 99.

40. Koehl, *The Black Corps,* 10.

41. Lothar Danner, *Ordnungspolizei Hamburg: Betrachtungen zu ihrer Geschichte 1918 bis 1933* (Hamburg: Deutsche Polizei, 1958), 11.

42. Leßmann, *Schutzpolizei,* 349–351, 365.

43. Ibid., 351.

44. Ibid., 365, 371–373. Only two Social Democratic police presidents remained in office until 1933 in Prussia.

45. Kohler, "Crisis," 149–150.

46. Jürgen Siggemann, *Die kasernierte Polizei und das Problem der inneren Sicherheit in der Weimarer Republik* (Frankfurt a.M.: Rita G. Fischer, 1980), 209.

47. Leßmann, *Schutzpolizei,* 365–369. Leßmann quotes Grzesinski and Otto Braun in making this assessment.

48. Jürgen Matthäus, "'Warum wird über das Judentum geschult?'" in *Die Gestapo im Zweiten Weltkrieg: "Heimatfront" und besetztes Europa,* ed. Gerhard Paul and Klaus-Michael Mallmann (Darmstadt: Primus, 2000), 102.

49. Jürgen W. Falter, *Hitlers Wähler* (Munich: C. H. Beck, 1991), 242, 244. Falter notes, however, that the evidence concerning the voting patterns of civil servants in support of the Nazi Party is a very complicated issue.

50. Danner, *Ordnungspolizei,* 217, 224.

51. Hermann Franz file, former collection of the Berlin Document Center (hereafter BDC), RG 242, SSO 219, frame 618, NARA. This is a letter from the *Kreisleitung* of the NSDAP in Plauen on April 13, 1938, confirming Franz's membership.

52. "Personalangaben," RG 242, SSO 219, frames 632–633, 637–638, NARA. See also "Der Chef der Ordnungspolizei, O-Kdo.P II(2a)Fra.VI 76 r. [June 26, 1940]," RG 242, SSO 219, frame 659, NARA.

53. "Nationalsozialistische Deutsche Arbeiterpartei, Gau Sachsen [June 28, 1932]," T580, reel 95, NARA.

54. Kershaw, *Hubris,* 319. See also Hans Kehrl, ed., *Jahrbuch der deutschen Polizei, 1936* (Leipzig: Breitkopf & Härtel, 1936), 30.

55. Richard Bessel, "Die 'Modernisierung' der Polizei im Nationalsozialismus," in *Norddeutschland im Nationalsozialismus,* ed. Frank Bajohr (Hamburg: Ergebnisse, 1993), 377.

56. Danner, *Ordnungspolizei,* 216–217, 222–223.

57. Falter, *Wähler,* 248.

58. Danner, *Ordnungspolizei,* 216–217, 222–223.

59. "Nationalsozialistische Deutsche Arbeiterpartei, Gauleitung Groß-Berlin, Betrifft: Reichsbund ehemaliger Polizeibeamter e.V. Berlin [January 24, 1933]," T580, reel 95, NARA. The Reichsbund had changed its name to the "Notgemeinschaft ehemaliger Schutzpolizeibeamter" and was seeking official recognition by the NSDAP. The organization counted 250 members in Berlin, 300 in Breslau, and 50 in Stettin.

60. Browder, *Foundations,* 46.

61. Leßmann, *Schutzpolizei,* 371–373, 376.

62. "Reichsinnenminister Dr. Frick, Kameraden von der Leitung der deutschen Polizei [June 18, 1936]," T580, reel 216, file 3, NARA. See also untitled and undated biographical report on Kurt Daluege, T580, reel 219, file 57, NARA.

63. Heinz Höhne, *The Order of the Death's Head: The Story of Hitler's SS,* trans. Richard Barry (New York: Coward-McCann, 1969), 82–83, 90.

64. Herbert Michaelis and Ernst Schraepler, eds., *Das Dritte Reich: Die Zertrümmerung des Parteienstaates und die Grundlegung der Diktatur,* vol. 9 of *Ursachen und Folgen vom deutschen Zusammenbruch 1918 und 1945 bis zur staatlichen Neuordnung Deutschlands in der Gegenwart* (Berlin: Dokumenten Verlag Dr. Herbert Wendler, 1964), 18–19, 38–39.

65. Ibid., 38–39.

66. Heiko M. Pannbacker, "Die Polizei im Bild der 'Polizei'—die Preußische Schutzpolizei zwischen Weimarer Republik und Drittem Reich in Selbstdarstellungen," *Archiv für Polizeigeschichte* 7 (1996): 26.

67. "Die Stellung und Aufgaben der Polizei im Dritten Reich [October 18, 1935]," T580, reel 216, file 3, NARA.

68. Leßmann, *Schutzpolizei,* 386, 388.

69. *Vossische Zeitung* (Berlin), March 6, 1933, morning edition.

70. Peter Padfield, *Himmler: Reichsführer SS* (New York: Henry Holt, 1990), 126.

71. Leßmann, *Schutzpolizei,* 386, 388.

72. *Völkischer Beobachter* (Berlin), February 14, 1933.

73. *Völkischer Beobachter* (Berlin), February 17, 1933.

74. *Vossische Zeitung* (Berlin), March 6, 1933.

75. *Völkischer Beobachter* (Berlin), February 17, 1933.

76. Elke Fröhlich, *Die Tagebücher von Joseph Goebbels: Sämtliche Fragmente,* pt. 1, vol. 2 (Munich: K. G. Saur, 1987), 375. Diary entry of February 15, 1933.

77. Karl D. Bracher, Wolfgang Sauer, and Gerhard Schulz, *Die nationalsozialistische Machtergreifung* (Cologne: Westdeutscher, 1960), 435.

78. Prussian ministerial directive "IIb II51b Nr. 6/33 [February 28, 1933]," T580, reel 97, NARA.

79. "Vortrag vor den Reichsstatthaltern, Oberpräsidenten und Regierungspräsidenten [June 26, 1939]," T580, reel 216, file 5, NARA. Göring's efforts related to both the Uniformed and the Political Police. For his thoughts on the latter, see "Der Preußische Minister des Innern, I 1000/49 [February 21, 1933]," T580, reel 95, NARA.

80. "Der Preußische Minister des Innern, Sonderabteilung Daluege, Tgb. Nr. SD 2717. Ha. K [June 15, 1933]," T580, reel 220, file 61, NARA.

81. Letter from Daluege to Göring [January 10, 1934], R 19, file 390, pp. 5–6. In addition to those employed in official positions, Daluege noted that 579 SS men, 221 SA men, 26 Stahlhelm men, and 35 male and 18 female Party members were receiving pay (*Lohnempfänger*).

82. Letter from *Ministerialdirigent* Hans Kehrl to Daluege [April 10, 1936], former collection of the BDC, ORPO A 422 (Hans Kehrl), BArch. This prohibition was subsequently modified by allowing the NSDAP *Gauleiter* (district leader) to approve promotions for these individuals, thus allowing the Party to exert control over this process.

83. *Völkischer Beobachter* (Berlin), March 15, 1933. It is important to note that the incorporation of these SA and SS men into the Bavarian police preceded the creation of the Bavarian Hilfspolizei in April 1933.

84. Letter from Martin Bormann to Daluege [December 10, 1935], R 19, file 423, BArch.

85. Letter from Daluege to Martin Bormann [January 18, 1936], R 19, file 423, BArch.

86. "Partei-Statistik, Band I, Parteimitglieder, Stand 1. Januar 1935," former collection of the Library of the BDC, RG 242, reel B-007, frames 865–866, NARA.

87. Gerd Rühle, *Das Dritte Reich: Dokumentarische Darstellung des Aufbaues der Nation* (Berlin: Hummelverlag, 1934), 104–106.

88. "Der Reichsminister des Innern, Nr. I A 5000/12.5 [May 12, 1933]," T580, reel 94, NARA.

89. "Der Reichsminister des Innern, Nr. I A 5205/12.5 II. Ang. [May 24, 1933]," T580, reel 94, NARA.

90. Michaelis and Schraepler, eds., *Das Dritte Reich,* 86.

91. Höhne, *Order of the Death's Head,* 103–104 (quotation from 103).

92. Wilhelm, *Polizei im NS-Staat,* 74, 90–92. Although important, the transfer of most police civil servants to the Reich budget in April 1937 and in April 1940 did not prevent either Daluege or, later, Himmler from exercising command prerogatives over these forces in the natural extension of the first and second "Coordination Laws."

93. *Deutschland-Bericht der SOPADE* (Frankfurt a.M.: Petra Nettlebeck, 1980), 757.

94. "Vortrag vor den Reichsstatthaltern, Oberpräsidenten und Regierungspräsidenten [June 26, 1939]," T580, reel 216, NARA.

95. *Deutschland-Bericht der SOPADE,* 757.

96. *Vossische Zeitung* (Berlin), March 17, 1933, morning edition.

97. *Deutschland-Bericht der SOPADE,* 757.

98. Ulrich Herbert, *Best: Biographische Studien über Radikalismus, Weltanschauung und Vernunft, 1903–1989* (Bonn: J. H. W. Dietz, 1996), 122–128. The case of Hessen offers a view into two contrasting styles pursued by Nazi officials in the co-optation of the police. In the first case, after his appointment to head the Hessian police, the National Socialist Werner Best sought to maintain continuity by keeping specialists with "national sympathies" in their positions while promoting young National Socialists as the next generation of leadership. In contrast, Sprenger sought the immediate "cleansing" of the police through the appointment of Party members of long-standing in spite of their lack of law enforcement experience or training.

99. "Die Stellung und Aufgaben der Polizei im Dritten Reich [October 18, 1935]," T580, reel 216, file 3, NARA. See also "Entwurf eines am 27. April 1939 vor dem Deutschen Gemeindetag zu haltenden Vortrages des Reichsführers SS und Chef der Deutschen Polizei über die Gemeindepolizei und das Feuerlöschwesen [April 1939]," T580, reel 37, NARA; and "Entwurf, Vortrag des Reichsführers SS und Chef

der Deutschen Polizei vor dem Deutschen Gemeindetag über Fragen der Gemeindepolizei [May 5, 1939]," T580, reel 37, NARA.

100. "Erlaß des Kommissars des Reiches, Einberufung und Verwendung von Hilfspolizei [February 22, 1933]," T175, reel 14, frames 2516670–2516688, NARA.

101. Martin Broszat, *The Hitler State: The Foundation and Development of the Internal Structure of the Third Reich*, trans. John W. Hiden (London: Longman, 1981), 79.

102. Leßmann, *Schutzpolizei*, 393.

103. Herbert, *Best*, 124.

104. "OSAF, Chef Nr. 583/33 IV. Ang., Einberufung und Verwendung von Hilfspolizei in Bayern," T580, reel 96, file 467, NARA. This manning strength also
included a suggestion for Hilfspolizei manpower levels of up to 100 percent for police
and Gendarmerie forces in areas outside the control of the state police administrations. This initial suggestion was subsequently lowered to 20 percent in areas under
the jurisdiction of the state police administration and 75 percent in other areas. See
"Durchführungsbestimmungen über Einberufung und Verwendung von Hilfs-
polizeibeamten in Bayern," T580, reel 97, file 467, NARA.

105. *Vossische Zeitung* (Berlin), March 14, 1933, evening edition, and March 9,
1933, evening edition.

106. *Vossische Zeitung* (Berlin), March 24, 1933, evening edition.

107. *Vossische Zeitung* (Berlin), August 6, 1933, morning edition.

108. *Vossische Zeitung* (Berlin), March 9, 1933, evening edition, and March 11,
1933, morning edition.

109. "Der Preußische Minister des Innern, II 1272/29.4.33 [May 29, 1933],"
T580, reel 220, file 62, NARA.

110. "Der Preußische Minister des Innern, Sonderabteilung Daluege, Tgb.Nr. S.D.
2712, IIa.K. [June 15, 1933]," T580, reel 220, file 61, NARA.

111. "Auflösung der Hilfspolizei, RdErl. d. MdI. v. 2.8.1933 II C I 59 Nr. 89/33
[August 2, 1933]," T580, reel 97, NARA.

112. Leßmann, *Schutzpolizei*, 396.

113. "Nr. 2401g 255, Staatsministerium des Innern [December 22, 1933]," T580,
reel 97, NARA.

114. Bracher, Sauer, and Schulz, *Machtergreifung*, 72.

115. Rühle, *Das Dritte Reich* (1934), 112–113. The protection of veterans of the
First World War provided the major exception in this legislation.

116. "Weitere Durchf.-Best. d. MdJ. zu [para.] 6 des Ges. zur Wiederherstellung
des Berufsbeamtentums in der Fass. des Ges. v. 23.6.1933 [June 30, 1933]," T580,
reel 220, file 62, NARA.

117. "Der Preussische Minister des Innern, Sonderabteilung Daluege, Tgb.Nr. S.D.
2717. Ha.K. [June 15, 1933]," T580, reel 220, file 61, NARA. Report marked
"Eigenhändig!" and "Streng Vertraulich!"

118. Schein, *Organizational Culture*, 235.

119. Carl Severing, *Mein Lebensweg*, vol. 2 (Cologne: Greven, 1950), 83–84.

120. Liang, *Berlin Police*, 79 (quotation), 80.

121. *Vossische Zeitung* (Berlin), March 23, 1933, morning edition.

122. Pannbacker, "Die Polizei im Bild der 'Polizei,'" 26.

123. *Vossische Zeitung* (Berlin), August 1, 1933, morning edition.

124. "Ansprache des Generalleutnants der Landespolizei Daluege an die Kommandeure der Schutzpolizei [April 25, 1935]," T580, reel 96, NARA.

125. *Völkischer Beobachter* (Berlin), October 5, 1933.

126. Willy Hansen, "Zwischen Selbstdarstellung und Propaganda-Aktion: 'Verkehrserziehungswochen' und 'Tag der Deutschen Polizei' als Beispiele der polizeilichen Öffentlichkeitsarbeit im NS-Staat," in *Wessen Freund und wessen Helfer? Die Kölner Polizei im Nationalsozialismus,* ed. Harald Buhlan and Werner Jung (Cologne: Emons, 2000), 244–245.

127. Kehrl, ed., *Jahrbuch,* 40–42. See also Helmuth Koschorke, ed., *Die Polizei—einmal anders!* (Munich: Zentralverlag der NSDAP, 1937), 56.

128. *Die Polizei: Dein Freund, dein Helfer: Ein Leseheft für die deutsche Jugend* (Breslau: Ferdinand Hirt, 1936), 20, 23–25, 30, 39, 94.

129. Koschorke, ed., *Die Polizei—einmal anders!* 11.

130. Hansen, "Zwischen Selbstdarstellung und Propaganda-Aktion," 249, 256.

131. "Willst Du zur Polizei?" T580, reel 95, NARA.

132. "(Vortrag des Generalleutnant der L.P. Kurt Daluege, Befehlshaber der deutschen Polizei, vor den Mitgliedern der Reichspressekonferenz) [July 20, 1935]," T580, reel 216, file 3, NARA. These statistics are based on Daluege's numbers for 1934.

133. Hansen, "Zwischen Selbstdarstellung und Propaganda-Aktion," 249–250, 256.

134. Giles MacDonogh, *Berlin: A Portrait of Its History, Politics, Architecture, and Society* (New York: St. Martin's, 1997), 43.

135. Herbert, *Best,* 169, 171.

136. Severin Roeseling, "Konkurrenz, Arbeitsteilung, Kollegialität—Zum Verhältnis von Polizei und Gestapo in Köln," in Buhlan and Jung, eds., *Wessen Freund und wessen Helfer?* 200–201.

137. Herbert, *Best,* 169.

138. Robert Gellately, *The Gestapo and German Society: Enforcing Racial Policy, 1933–1945* (Oxford: Clarendon, 1990), 72, 75.

139. Heinz Wagner, "Die Polizei im Faschismus," in *Strafjustiz und Polizei,* ed. Udo Reifner and Bernd-Rüdeger Sonnen (Frankfurt a.M.: Campus, 1984), 172.

140. Roeseling, "Zum Verhältnis von Polizei und Gestapo in Köln," 209. The "Second Gestapo Law" of November 30, 1933, once again reinforced the requirement that Prussian police authorities support the Gestapo in its investigations.

141. "Herrn Ministerialdirektor Daluege durch die Hand des Herrn Ministerialrats Fischer [June 26, 1933]," T580, reel 95, NARA. This letter is marked "Eilt sehr!" and "von Hand zu Hand."

142. Karl-Heinz Heller, "The Remodeled Praetorians: The German Ordnungspolizei as Guardians of the 'New Order,'" in *Nazism and the Common Man: Essays in German History (1929–1939),* ed. Otis Mitchell (Lanham, Md.: University Press of America, 1981), 46.

143. Zaika, *Polizeigeschichte,* 172–173.

144. "Geheime Staatspolizei, Staatspolizeistelle Würzburg, BNr. 6570 A, Betreff: Überführung der Fahnen des ehem. NSDFB (Stahlhelm) in das Stahlhelm-Museum Magdeburg [December 29, 1937]," T580, reel 97, NARA.

145. Roeseling, "Zum Verhältnis von Polizei und Gestapo in Köln," 211–212.

146. "Gendarmeriekreisführer des Landkreis Lauterbach, Betreffend: Hamsterkäufe [September 22, 1939]," T580, reel 109, NARA.

147. Reinhard Rürup, ed., *Topography of Terror: Gestapo, SS, and Reichssicherheitshauptamt on the "Prince Albrecht Terrain"* (Berlin: Willmuth Arenhövel, 1989),

46–47. See also Wilhelm, *Polizei im NS-Staat,* 54–58; Roeseling, "Zum Verhältnis von Polizei und Gestapo in Köln," 213; and Bessel, "Die 'Modernisierung' der Polizei," 375.

148. *Völkischer Beobachter* (Berlin), March 3, 1933.

149. Pannbacker, "Die Polizei im Bild der 'Polizei,'" 22–23.

150. Roeseling, "Zum Verhältnis von Polizei und Gestapo in Köln," 211.

151. *Völkischer Beobachter* (Berlin), July 25, 1933.

152. "Geheimes Staatspolizeiamt, II B. Nr. [October 9, 1933]," T175, reel 229, frame 2767552, NARA. The instructions did request that inmates be handled in a "tactful" manner in order to promote their reintegration into society. The fact that the instructions were limited to "followers" and "low-level functionaries" supports the view that the National Socialist leadership felt that these were persons who had been misled or made poor decisions and could, therefore, be "rehabilitated." See also "Der Regierungspräsident, Schleswig, 25. Sept. 1933-I.P.P.-6-, Abschrift. Der Preussische Minister des Innern. Berlin, den 19.Sept.1933. Nr. II G 1946/19.9.33, Schnellbrief, Betrifft: Nachprüfung des gemäss [paragraph] 1 der Norverordnung [*sic*] vom 28. Februar 1933 erlassenen Schutzhaftanordnungen [September 25, 1933]," T175, reel 229, frames 2767459–2767461, NARA.

153. "Staatsministerium des Innern, Nr. 2557 a. 52, An die Regierungen, Betreff: Auskünfte über die politische Zuverlässikeit von Personen [July 20, 1935]," T580, reel 115, NARA.

154. Roeseling, "Zum Verhältnis von Polizei und Gestapo in Köln," 219–220.

155. Bessel, "Die 'Modernisierung' der Polizei," 379.

156. Hansjörg Riechert, "Die Polizei des Dritten Reiches im Dienst der Rassenhygiene," *Archiv für Polizeigeschichte* 5 (1994): 70–71.

157. "Der Regierungspräsident, Schleswig, 25. Sept. 1933-I.P.P.-6-, Abschrift. Der Preussische Minister des Innern. Berlin, den 19.Sept.1933. Nr. II G 1946/19.9.33, Schnellbrief, Betrifft: Nachprüfung des gemäss [paragraph] 1 der Norverordnung [*sic*] vom 28. Februar 1933 erlassenen Schutzhaftanordnungen [September 25, 1933]," T175, reel 229, frames 2767459–2767461, NARA. The letter also noted that some city and community administrations had applied for "protective custody" in order to clear their welfare roles of the mentally incompetent and addicts.

158. Anthony Read and David Fisher, *Kristallnacht: The Unleashing of the Holocaust* (New York: Peter Bedrick, 1989), 65.

159. Matthäus et al., *Ausbildungsziel Judenmord?* 42.

160. Matthäus, "Ausbildungsziel Judenmord?" 677. See also Bessel, "Die 'Modernisierung' der Polizei," 379.

161. IMT, *Trials,* vol. 29, pp. 255–258. See also Heller, "Praetorians," 59.

162. "Preussische Geheime Staatspolizei, Der Stellvertretende Chef, B.Nr. 255/35 I D, Betrifft: Weitergabe von Anweisungen des Geheimen Staatspolizeiamts an die Kreispolizeibehörden [August 15, 1936]," T175, reel 229, frame 2767310, NARA; "Der Chef der Sicherheitspolizei, S V 1 Nr. 282/37, Betr.: Weitergabe von Erlassen an die Landräte und Ortspolizeiverwaltungen [March 18, 1937]," T175, reel 229, frame 2767328, NARA; and "Geheime Staatspolizei, Geheimes Staatspolizeiamt, B.Nr. 80/37 I D, Betrifft: Weitergabe von generellen Runderlassen an die Kreis- und Ortspolizeibehörden [March 19, 1937]," T175, reel 229, frame 2767330, NARA.

163. Werner Best, *Die Deutsche Polizei* (Darmstadt: L. C. Wittich, 1940), 95.

164. Herbert, *Best,* 161.

165. Letter from Kurt Daluege to Reinhard Heydrich [June 23, 1937], R 19, file 390, pp. 57–58, BArch.
166. Letter from Adolf von Bomhard to Kurt Daluege [July 3, 1937], BDC file A 439, Oto Roettig, BArch.
167. Letter from Kurt Daluege to Reinhard Heydrich [December 7, 1937], T580, reel 221, file 63, NARA. See also "Der Regierungspräsident, PS. 3581, Betr.: Verhältnis von Sicherheitsdienst und Ordnungspolizei [November 29, 1937]," T580, reel 221, file 63, NARA.
168. Letter from Kurt Daluege to Reinhard Heydrich [January 20, 1941], T580, reel 220, file 62, NARA.
169. "Gend.-Station Münnerstadt, empf. 15.III 1936, Nr. 565, An den Herrn Vorstand des Bezirks-Amt Bad Kissingen mit folg. Berichte [*sic*] in Rückvorlage [March 15, 1936]," T580, reel 106, NARA. The report noted that no detrimental information had been found concerning the activities of the local Augustinian order. For example, the clergy returned the "Hitler salute" when greeted with it, and their "political behavior" was commented on positively in interviews with "old Party members."
170. "Nr. 7734, Betreff: Versetzung von Geistlichen [July 29, 1938]," T580, reel 106, NARA; and "Gendarmerieposten Ebenhausen Mfr., empf. 9.10.1938, Nr. 1544 [October 6, 1938]," T580, reel 106, NARA.
171. "Geheime Staatspolizei, Staatspolizeistelle Würzburg, BNr.4854 A, Bn/Hi, Betreff: Feststellung von kath. Geistlichen, die Kinder erzeugt haben [September 22, 1937]," T580, reel 106, NARA. Reports from Gendarmerie stations in Steinach a.d. Saale, Ebenhausen, and Bad Kissingen were all negative.
172. "Betreff: Erhebungen, I. An die Gendarmeriestationen [April 9, 1936]," T580, reel 106, NARA; and "Gendarmerie-Station Ebenhausen, An das Bezirksamt Kissingen, Betreff: Erhebungen [April 24, 1936]," T580, reel 106, NARA.
173. "I. Fernspruch der Gestapo Würzburg vom 30.3.1938, 14.40 Uhr, Betr. Wochenschrift 'Durchbruch' [March 30, 1938]," T580, reel 106, NARA; and "I. Fernspruch der Gestapo Würzburg vom 30.3.1938, 17.15 Uhr [March 30, 1938]," T580, reel 106, NARA.
174. "Der Landrat, I. An die Geheime Staatspolizei, Staatspolizeistelle Würzburg, Betreff: Vertrieb minderwertigen Unterhaltungsschrifttums [July 2, 1941]," T580, reel 106, NARA; and "Kriminal-Polizei Bad Kissingen, Betreff: Vertrieb von minderwertigen Unterhaltungsschrifttums [June 16, 1941]," T580, reel 106, NARA. The July report notes that Gendarmerie personnel confiscated copies of two additional novels in addition to those listed.
175. *Vossische Zeitung* (Berlin), March 11, 1933.
176. Matthäus, "'Warum wird über das Judentum geschult?'" 104–105.
177. Wolfgang Benz, "Der Rückfall in die Barbarei: Bericht über den Pogrom," in *Der Judenpogrom 1938: Von der "Reichskristallnacht" zum Völkermord*, ed. Walter Pehle (Frankfurt a.M.: Fischer Taschenbuch, 1988), 23.
178. Matthäus, "'Warum wird über das Judentum geschult?'" 104–105.
179. Christian Zentner and Friedemann Bedürftig, eds., *The Encyclopedia of the Third Reich*, trans. Amy Hackett (New York: Macmillan, 1991), 515.
180. Read and Fisher, *Kristallnacht*, 65–66. See also Gerhard Schoenberner, *Der gelbe Stern: Die Judenverfolgung in Europa, 1933–1945* (Frankfurt a.M.: Fischer Taschenbuch, 1992), 21.

181. Frederic Zeller, *When Time Ran Out: Coming of Age in the Third Reich* (Sag Harbor, N.Y.: Permanent, 1989), 137–140.

182. Ruth Andreas-Friederich, *Berlin Underground, 1938–1945*, trans. Barrows Mussey (New York: Paragon, 1947), 18.

183. Bernt Engelmann, *In Hitler's Germany: Everyday Life in the Third Reich* (New York: Schocken, 1986), 128–129.

184. Read and Fisher, *Kristallnacht*, 76.

185. "Vortrag über die Deutsche Ordnungspolizei [September 2, 1940]," T580, reel 96, NARA.

186. Rühle, *Das Dritte Reich* (1937), 268. See also Browder, *Foundations*, 226.

187. Browder, *Foundations*, 226.

188. Ibid., 229. In January 1937, Frick sent Himmler a letter complaining that he had been bypassed in the review of a draft law, a situation that he had expressly addressed in a circular decree of November 28, 1936. See "Der Reichs- und Preußische Minister des Innern, I A 75/5170 [January 25, 1937]," T175, reel 229, frame 2767327, NARA.

189. Untitled report [June 18, 1936], T580, reel 216, NARA.

190. Neufeldt, "Entstehung und Organisation," 33.

191. "Vortrag vor den Reichsstatthaltern, Oberpräsidenten und Regierungspräsidenten [June 26, 1939]," T580, reel 216, file 5, NARA.

192. "Der Weg der Ordnungspolizei von SS-Gruppenführer, General der Polizei, Kurt Daluege [January 23, 1939]," T580, reel 216, file 5, NARA.

193. "Der Chef der Ordnungspolizei, Vortrag über Kräfte- und Kriegseinsatz der Ordnungspolizei im Jahre 1941, [1942]," T580, reel 96, NARA. The overwhelming majority of these men, 8,451, were mobilized from the Gendarmerie for duty with the German Military Police (Feldgendarmerie).

194. "Ansprache des Chefs der Ordnungspolizei, General der Polizei Daluege, anlässlich der Dienstbesprechung der Kommandeure der Gendarmerie am 16. Januar 1941," T580, reel 216, file 6, NARA. See also "Vortrag vor den Reichsstatthaltern, Oberpräsidenten und Regierungspräsidenten [June 26, 1939]," T580, reel 216, file 5, NARA; and "Die Ordnungspolizei jederzeit einsatzbereit [February 13, 1941]," T580, reel 216, file 2, NARA.

195. Tessin, "Stäbe und Truppeneinheiten," 13.

Chapter 2. Building a Martial Identity

1. Gerhard Weinberg, *Germany, Hitler, and World War II: Essays in Modern German and World History* (Cambridge: Cambridge University Press, 1995), 32.

2. Adolf Hitler, *Mein Kampf*, trans. Ralph Manheim (Boston: Houghton Mifflin, 1962), 231.

3. Weinberg, *Germany, Hitler, and World War II*, 35.

4. Max Domarus, ed., *Hitler: Speeches and Proclamations, 1932–1945: The Chronicle of a Dictatorship*, vol. 3, *The Years 1939–1940*, trans. Mary Fran Gilbert (Wauconda, Ill.: Bolchazy-Carducci, 1997), 1441.

5. Wolfram Wette, "NS-Propaganda und Kriegsbereitschaft der Deutschen bis 1936," in *Francia: Forschungen zur westeuropäischen Geschichte*, ed. Institut Historique

Allemand (Munich: Artemis, 1978), 589–590. For an overview of this theme in film, see Giesen, *Nazi Propaganda Films,* 41–47, 51–92.

6. H. W. Koch, *The Hitler Youth: Origins and Development, 1922–1945* (New York: Dorset, 1975), 119.

7. Wette, "NS-Propaganda," 589.

8. See Jay W. Baird, *To Die for Germany: Heroes in the Nazi Pantheon* (Bloomington: Indiana University Press, 1990).

9. Richard J. Overy, *Goering: The "Iron Man"* (London: Routledge & Kegan Paul, 1984), 164.

10. Claudia Koonz, *Mothers in the Fatherland: Women, the Family, and Nazi Politics* (New York: St. Martin's, 1987), 89.

11. William L. Shirer, *Berlin Diary: The Journal of a Foreign Correspondent, 1934–1941* (New York: Knopf, 1942), 19.

12. William E. Dodd, *Ambassador Dodd's Diary, 1933–1938,* ed. William E. Dodd Jr. and Martha Dodd (New York: Harcourt, Brace, 1941), 127.

13. *Völkischer Beobachter* (Berlin), May 18, 1933.

14. Max Domarus, ed., *Hitler: Speeches and Proclamations, 1932–1945: The Chronicle of a Dictatorship,* vol. 1, *The Years 1932–1934,* trans. Mary Fran Gilbert (Wauconda, Ill.: Bolchazy-Carducci, 1990), 380, 383.

15. Office of U.S. Chief of Counsel for Prosecution of Axis Criminality, *Nazi Conspiracy and Aggression,* vol. 1 (Washington, D.C.: U.S. Government Printing Office, 1946), 320–321, 341. This cooperation was later formalized in an agreement between the Wehrmacht and the Hitler Youth of August 11, 1939.

16. Koch, *Hitler Youth,* 119.

17. Johannes Steinhoff, Peter Pechel, and Dennis Showalter, *Voices from the Third Reich: An Oral History* (Washington, D.C.: Regnery Gateway, 1989), xxxvii–xxxviii.

18. Günter de Bruyn, *Zwischenbilanz: Eine Jugend in Berlin* (Frankfurt a.M.: Fischer Taschenbuch, 1992), 142–143.

19. Elizabeth Harvey, *Women and the Nazi East: Agents and Witnesses of Germanization* (New Haven, Conn.: Yale University Press, 2003), 76–77.

20. Wildt, *Generation des Unbedingten,* 137–142. Wildt makes this argument for those born between 1900 and 1910 who eventually joined the leadership ranks of the Reich Security Main Office, but this phenomenon applied to many of the men who entered the Uniformed Police as well.

21. Gilmer W. Blackburn, *Education in the Third Reich: A Study of Race and History in Nazi Textbooks* (Albany: State University of New York Press, 1985), 97, 95.

22. Peter Merkl, *The Making of a Stormtrooper* (Princeton, N.J.: Princeton University Press, 1980), 70.

23. Koch, *Hitler Youth,* 238.

24. Bernd Weisbrod, "Violence and Sacrifice: Imagining the Nation in Weimar Germany," in Mommsen, ed., *Third Reich,* 14.

25. Horst Friedrich, "Eine bewegte Gedenkstätte: Das 'Ehrenmal der gefallenen Gendarmen' der ehemaligen Gendarmerieschule Bad Ems," *Archiv für Polizeigeschichte* 8 (1997): 58.

26. Wilhelm Deist, Manfred Messerschmidt, Hans-Erich Volkmann, and Wolfram Wette, *Ursachen und Voraussetzungen des Zweiten Weltkrieges* (Frankfurt a.M.: Fischer Taschenbuch, 1989), 44. It is necessary to point out that, in this case, *the*

Führer principle refers, not to the person of Adolf Hitler, but rather to the concept of a strong central leader.

27. "Rede des Vertreters des Reichsführers SS, Chef der deutschen Polizei, Chef der Ordnungspolizei, General Daluege im Kameradschaftsbund Deutscher Polizeibeamten [August 26, 1937]," R 19, file 380, BArch.

28. Robert G. L. Waite, *The Vanguard of Nazism: The Free Corps Movement in Postwar Germany, 1918–1923* (Cambridge, Mass.: Harvard University Press, 1952), 264, 267, 270.

29. Peter von Heydebreck, *Wir Wehr-Wölfe: Erinnerungen eines Freikorpsführers* (Leipzig: K. F. Koehler, 1931), 82, 205–206.

30. Waite, *Vanguard of Nazism,* 279.

31. See Nigel H. Jones, *Hitler's Heralds: The Story of the Freikorps, 1918–1923* (New York: Dorsett, 1987); and Waite, *Vanguard of Nazism.* In his study of the leadership of the Reich Security Main Office, Michael Wildt emphasizes the connection between this group of men and their participation in nationalist organizations, including the Freikorps. See also Wildt, *Generation des Unbedingten,* 53–67.

32. "Ansprache des General Daluege bei der Einweihung des Ruhrkämpfer-Ehrenmals in Bochum [April 17, 1937]," R 19, file 380, BArch.

33. Merkl, *Stormtrooper,* 205–206.

34. Bruce Campbell, *The SA Generals and the Rise of Nazism* (Lexington: University Press of Kentucky, 1998), 148–149.

35. Hans-Ulrich Wehler, *The German Empire, 1871–1918,* trans. Kim Traynor (Oxford: Berg, 1985), 153.

36. Kohler, "Crisis," 132; and Lüdtke, *Police and State in Prussia,* 70–71.

37. Bessel, "Militarisierung und Modernisierung," 324, 329, 343.

38. Campbell, *SA Generals,* 11.

39. Thomas Köhler, "Anstiftung zur Versklavung und Völkermord," in *Im Auftrag: Polizei, Verwaltung, und Verantwortung,* ed. Alfons Kenkmann and Christoph Spieker (Essen: Klartext, 2001), 155.

40. Detlev Peukert, *Inside Nazi Germany: Conformity, Opposition, and Racism in Everyday Life,* trans. Richard Deveson (New Haven, Conn.: Yale University Press, 1987), 205.

41. Erich Gritzbach, ed., *Hermann Göring: Reden und Aufsätze* (Munich: Zentralverlag der NSDAP, 1939), 17–18. Göring repeated this anti-Marxist message to Prussian police officers in mid-March 1933, stating that "every available means" would be used to fight those (i.e., Marxists) who tried to prevent the unity of the German people. See *Vossische Zeitung* (Berlin), March 17, 1933.

42. *Vossische Zeitung* (Berlin), March 18, 1933.

43. *Völkischer Beobachter* (Berlin), April 20, 1933.

44. "RdErl d. MdI v. 28.2.1933, IIb II51b Nr. 6/33," T580, reel 97, NARA.

45. Rühle, *Das Dritte Reich* (1934), 113.

46. "Deutsches Nachrichtenbüro, Die Verbundenheit der SA mit der Polizei von Polizeigeneral Kurt Daluege [April 28, 1934]," T580, reel 220, file 61, NARA.

47. Domarus, ed., *Hitler: The Years 1939–1940,* 1442. Speech to the Reichstag on January 30, 1939.

48. "Der Preußische Minister des Innern, Sonderabteilung Daluege, Tgb. Nr. S.D. 2717. Ha. K. [June 15, 1933]," T580, reel 220, file 61, NARA. Marked "Eigenhändig!" and "Streng Vertraulich!"

49. Hermann Graml, *Reichskristallnacht: Antisemitismus und Judenverfolgung im Dritten Reich* (Munich: Deutscher Taschenbuch Verlag, 1988), 22–29. See also Benz, "Barbarei," 20, 33–34.

50. Kehrl, ed., *Jahrbuch,* 32.

51. "Der Preuss. Ministerpräsident, Landespolizei, Org. 2 (G.L. Pol.), Berlin [June 30, 1934]," T580, reel 84, file 402. See also Höhne, *Order of the Death's Head,* 126.

52. "Der Preuss. Ministerpräsident, Landespolizei, Befehl and die L. P. J. Südost [June 30, 1934]," T580, reel 84, file 402, NARA. This order was passed orally to the Landespolizei.

53. Höhne, *Order of the Death's Head,* 119; and Bracher, Sauer, and Schulz, *Machtergreifung,* 962. See also Pannbacker, "Die Polizei im Bild der 'Polizei,'" 22.

54. *Deutschland-Bericht der SOPADE,* 302.

55. Herbert, *Best,* 144.

56. Letter from Heinrich Himmler to Kurt Daluege, July 16, 1934, Kurt Daluege file, former collection of the BDC (emphasis added).

57. Herbert, "Ideological Legitimization," 104.

58. "Der Reichswehrminister, Nr. 340/35 L II a [March 23, 1935]," T580, reel 219, file 219, NARA. Less than two months later, von Blomberg was appointed the Reich war minister.

59. "Der Führer und Reichskanzler [June 17, 1936]," T580, reel 219, file 57, NARA.

60. Erich Radecke, "Die Landespolizei als Kadertruppe für die Wehrmacht," *Archiv für Polizeigeschichte* 2 (1991): 43.

61. "Vortrag vor den Reichsstatthaltern, Oberpräsidenten und Regierungspräsidenten [June 26, 1939]," T580, reel 216, NARA. Daluege noted that the total size of the Reich Uniformed Police forces decreased over the course of the year from 123,000 to approximately 83,000. In addition, the police lost 120 of 160 training bases, 1,600 vehicles, and 90 percent of their armory stocks.

62. IMT, *Trials,* vol. 29, p. 227. Lecture by Himmler on the "Nature and Purpose of the SS and the Police" in January 1937.

63. "Der Oberste SA-Führer, Ch. Nr. 1461/33, Betreff: SA-Feldpolizei [August 11, 1933]," T580, reel 96, NARA.

64. "Stellung und Aufgaben der Polizei im Dritten Reich [October 1935]," T580, reel 216, file 3, NARA. Speech presented by Daluege to the members of the training course for police civil servants.

65. Ibid.

66. "Der Oberste SA-Führer, Ch. Nr. 1547/33, Betreff: Feldjägerkorps in Preussen [October 7, 1933]," T580, reel 96, NARA. The effective date of establishment was retroactive to October 1.

67. "Der Oberste SA-Führer, Ch. Nr. 3049 [February 27, 1934]," T580, reel 96, NARA. Himmler subsequently required SS members in the FJK to withdraw from the SS, allowing for their readmittance only after their "honorable discharge" from the FJK. See "Der Reichsführer- SS, Abt. II P Nr. 2 2327, Betrifft: Feldjägerkorps in Preussen [February 19, 1934]," T580, reel 96, NARA.

68. "SA der NSDAP, Der Führer der Gruppe Hansa, Standort-Befehl Nr. 14/35 [March 8, 1935]," T580, reel 96, NARA.

69. "SA der NSDAP, Der Führer der Gruppe Hansa, Besondere Anordnung!, Feldjägerkorps [February 27, 1934]," T580, reel 96, NARA.

70. "Der Oberste SA-Führer, VI Nr. 10004/34, Betreff: Feldjägerkorps [January 11, 1934]," T580, reel 96, NARA. Röhm subsequently prohibited members of the FJK from wearing the police star.

71. "Der Preussische Ministerpräsident [June 30, 1934]," T580, reel 96, NARA. See also "Feldjägerabteilung IIIb, Tgb.-Nr. III/pers./5504/35 Dr. R./Stan., Betrifft: Eingliederung in die Schutzpolizei [April 30, 1935]," T580, reel 96, NARA; "SA der NSDAP, Der Oberste SA-Führer, Führungsamt, F 2 Nr. 19239, Betrifft: Feldjäger-korps [May 23, 1935]," T580, reel 96, NARA; and Wilhelm, *Polizei im NS-Staat*, 51–52. The final organizational incorporation of the FJK occurred on April 1, 1936, and included 3,159 men.

72. Untitled report prepared by Hans Kehrl, an official with the Prussian and Reich Interior Ministries, in late 1935, T580, reel 220, file 61, NARA.

73. "Ansprache des Generalleutnants der Landespolizei Daluege an die Kom-mandeure der Schutzpolizei [April 25, 1935]," T580, reel 216, file 3, NARA. See also "Die neue Gestaltung der deutschen Polizei; Die Aufgaben des eingegliederten Feld-jägerkorps," *Deutsche Allgemeine Zeitung*, May 10, 1935.

74. "Stellung und Aufgaben der Polizei im Dritten Reich [October 1935]," T580, reel 216, file 3, NARA. Speech presented by Daluege to the members of the training course for police civil servants. Daluege discussed the probationary period in an answer drafted for a radio interview of May 8, 1935. See "Entwurf für das Zweige-spräch am Mikrophon [May 8, 1935]," T580, reel 216, file 3, NARA.

75. "Ansprache des Generalleutnants der Landespolizei Daluege an die Kom-mandeure der Schutzpolizei [April 25, 1935]," T580, reel 216, file 3, NARA.

76. Broszat, *Hitler State*, 78.

77. "Entwurf für das Zweigespräch am Mikrophon [May 8, 1935]," T580, reel 216, file 3, NARA.

78. "Stellung und Aufgaben der Polizei im Dritten Reich, Von Generalleutnant der Landespolizei Kurt Daluege [October 18, 1935]," T580, reel 216, file 3, NARA.

79. Werner Zwingelberg, "Die Erziehung des Polizeibeamten zum National-sozialisten," in Kehrl, ed., *Jahrbuch*, 23. See also Dieter Schenk, *Auf dem rechten Auge blind: Die braunen Wurzeln des BKA* (Cologne: Kiepenheuer & Witsch, 2001); and Wildt, *Generation des Unbedingten*, 415.

80. Rudolf Querner, "Schutzpolizei einst und jetzt!" in Kehrl, ed., *Jahrbuch*, 58.

81. "Entwurf eines am 27. April 1939 vor dem Deutschen Gemeindetag zu hal-tenden Vortrages des Reichsführers SS und Chef der Deutschen Polizei über die Gemeindepolizei und das Feuerlöschwesen [April 1939]," T580, reel 37, NARA. See also "Entwurf, Vortrag des Reichsführers SS und Chef der Deutschen Polizei vor dem Deutschen Gemeindetag über Fragen der Gemeindepolizei [May 5, 1939]," T580, reel 37, NARA.

82. "Entwurf, Vortrag des Reichsführers SS und Chef der Deutschen Polizei vor dem Deutschen Gemeindetag über Fragen der Gemeindepolizei [May 5, 1939]," T580, reel 37, NARA.

83. Helmuth Koschorke, "Von der 'Knüppelgarde' zur Volkspolizei!" in Kehrl, ed., *Jahrbuch*, 32–34.

84. Kershaw, *Hubris*, 252, 289, 343. See also Ian Kershaw, *Hitler: 1936–1945, Nemesis* (New York: Norton, 2000), 283.

85. Domarus, ed., *Hitler: The Years 1939–1940*, 1471–1472.

86. Stephan Linck, *Der Ordnung verpflichtet: Deutsche Polizei 1933–1949, der*

Fall Flensburg (Paderborn: Ferdinand Schöningh, 2000), 44. Linck contends that Fulda was a German nationalist, not a National Socialist; however, the practical effect of this distinction appears to have been nominal with respect to police actions aimed at the putative enemies of the Third Reich.

87. As quoted in Edward B. Westermann, "Shaping the Police Soldier as an Instrument for Annihilation," in *The Impact of Nazism: New Perspectives on the Third Reich and Its Legacy*, ed. Alan Steinweis and Daniel Rogers (Lincoln: University of Nebraska Press, 2003), 129. Original citation: "Der Kommandeur der Gendarmerie Shitomir, Kommandobrief Nr. 3/42 [May 5, 1942]," RG 53.002M, fond 658, reel 5, file 2, USHMMA.

88. "Vortrag vor den Reichsstatthaltern, Oberpräsidenten und Regierungspräsidenten [June 26, 1939]," T580, reel 216, NARA.

89. "Der Polizeibeamte, Bürgerkrieg wird vorbereitet! Wir decken auf: Militärische Uebungen der Schutzpolizei [February 1931]," T580, reel 95, NARA. This article appeared in a monthly paper published by a Communist group supporting "Red" members within the lower and middle ranks of the Uniformed Police.

90. *Deutschland-Bericht der SOPADE*, 58–60, 86, 341, 809.

91. "Landespolizei-Inspektion Brandenburg (Sitz Berlin), Kommandantur Berlin (T), IIa Nr. 152/33 geh. [November 11, 1933]," T405, reel 1, frame 4827829, NARA; and "Wehrkreiskommando III (3. Division), Abtlg. Ia op Nr. 188/33 g.Kdos [August 31, 1933]," T405, reel 1, frames 4827844–4827849, NARA. It is important to note the classification of these reports as *geheim* (secret) and *geheime Kommandosache* (top secret). The need for secrecy involved the prohibition in Article 162 of the Versailles Treaty on "military training" for "gendarmes and employees of the local or municipal police." See Lawrence Martin, ed., *The Treaties of Peace, 1919–1923*, vol. 1 (New York: Carnegie Endowment for International Peace, 1924), 96.

92. "Eröffnung der Polizeisportschule, Rede des Chefs der Ordnungspolizei General Daluege [January 19, 1937]," R 19, file 380, BArch.

93. "Eröffnung der Polizeifünfkampf-Meisterschaften in Plauen [1937]," R 19, file 380, BArch. Opening speech delivered by Daluege. See also Rühle, *Das Dritte Reich* (1937), 275.

94. "Eröffnungsansprache zu den Polizeimeisterschaften in Frankfurt am Main [1937]," R 19, file 380, BArch; and "Eröffnung der Polizeifünfkampf-Meisterschaften in Plauen [1937]," R 19, file 380, BArch. Both opening speeches delivered by Daluege.

95. Rühle, *Das Dritte Reich* (1937), 272. See also "Der Reichs- und Preussische Minister des Innern, O-VuR. Org. R. 74/36 [October 9, 1936]," R 1501, reel 5628, frame 505, BArch.

96. "Einstellung von Militäranwärtern in die Schutzpolizei des Reiches und der Gemeinden [May 5, 1939]," T175, reel 227, frame 2766036, NARA. The status as full-time civil servant (*Beamte*) became official on the completion of a six-month probationary period.

97. Rühle, *Das Dritte Reich* (1937), 272.

98. "Willst Du zur Polizei? [1939]," former collection of the Library of the BDC, RG 242, reel 168, frames 772, 776, NARA.

99. Koschorke, ed., *Die Polizei—einmal anders!* 34. See also Pannbacker, "Die Polizei im Bild der 'Polizei,'" 26.

100. "Ansprache des Generalleutnants der Landespolizei Daluege an die Kom-

mandeure der Schutzpolizei [April 25, 1935]," T580, reel 220, file 61, NARA. See also "Willst Du zur Polizei?" T580, reel 95, NARA.

101. Letter from Daluege to Ministerialdirigent Bracht [May 5, 1936], former collection of the BDC, ORPO A 422 (Hans Kehrl), BArch. See also "Auszug aus der Rede des Gen. vor den Höheren SS- und Pol. Führern am 23.I.39, Der Weg der Ordnungspolizei [January 23, 1939]," T580, reel 216, file 5, NARA. Hitler also approved a new parade uniform for the police.

102. Koschorke, "Von der 'Knüppelgarde' zur Volkspolizei!" 29, 33. See also "Der Reichsführer SS und Chef der Deutschen Polizei im Reichsministerium des Innern, Betrifft: Verleihung des Verwundetenabzeichens [November 24, 1939]," T175, reel 227, frame 2766161, NARA.

103. The 1996 suicide of a senior U.S. Navy officer stemming in part from allegations of his wearing a combat device that he had not earned offers a perfect illustration of the importance attached to combat decorations and awards within military-type organizations.

104. *Der märkische Adler* (Berlin), September 28, 1934. The Kurmark primarily encompassed the area of the mark of Brandenburg.

105. Letter from Martin Bormann to Daluege [December 10, 1935], R 19, file 423, BArch.

106. Memorandum to State Secretary Hans Pfundtner [November 2, 1936], file 5628, frame 423, BArch.

107. "Der Stellvertreter des Führers, Betrifft: Zugehörigkeit von uniformierten Polizeibeamten zur SA; dort..Zch. [*sic*] 5727 n.f.D. [July 29, 1938]," T580, reel 95, NARA.

108. Kehrl, ed., *Jahrbuch*, 60–61.

109. Kehrl, ed., *Jahrbuch*, 65–67, 74–81.

110. Padfield, *Himmler*, 204.

111. *Der Deutsche Polizeibeamte*, June 1, 1937.

112. Kehrl, ed., *Jahrbuch*, 63–64.

113. Bracher, Sauer, and Schulz, *Machtergreifung*, 430. See also Gritzbach, ed., *Hermann Göring*, 18.

114. Kehrl, ed., *Jahrbuch*, 60–61.

115. "Ausbildung der Ordnungspolizei (Auszugsweise für Gendarmerie) [January 12, 1937]," former collection of the Library of the BDC, RG 242, reel 170, frames 1528–1529, NARA. Gendarmerie personnel were held to the Wehrmacht physical fitness standard only until their fortieth birthday.

116. "Der Reichsführer SS und Chef der Deutschen Polizei im Reichsministerium des Innern, O.-Kdo.A (3) Nr. 111/37 [October 10, 1937]," T580, reel 95, NARA.

117. Kershaw, *Nemesis*, 46–50.

118. "Der Reichsführer SS und Chef der Deutschen Polizei im Reichsministerium des Innern, O.-Kdo.A (3) Nr. 111/37 [October 10, 1937]," T580, reel 95, NARA. The discussion of exercises using *Abteilungsverbände* (duty sections) provided the rough equivalent to battalion strength. See Tessin, "Stäbe und Truppeneinheiten," 9.

119. "Der Chef der Ordnungspolizei [January 12, 1938]," R 19, file 460, pp. 19–20, 26, NARA. Daluege incorrectly identifies the title as *Fallschirmtruppen und Infanterie* instead of *Fallschirmtruppen und Luftinfanterie*.

120. "Programm für die Inspekteur-Besprechung [May 30–31 and June 1, 1938]," R 19, file 460, p. 64, BArch.

121. Pannbacker, "Die Polizei im Bild der 'Polizei,'" 26.

122. Tessin, "Stäbe und Truppeneinheiten," 9.

123. "Vortrag vor den Reichsstatthaltern, Oberpräsidenten und Regierungspräsidenten [June 26, 1939]," T580, reel 216, NARA. See also Tessin, "Stäbe und Truppeneinheiten," 9.

124. Wolfgang Kopitzsch, "Polizeieinheiten in Hamburg in der Weimarer Republik und im Dritten Reich," in *Die Deutsche Polizei und ihre Geschichte: Beiträge zu einem distanzierten Verhältnis,* ed. Peter Nitschke (Hilden: Deutsche Polizeiliteratur, 1996), 143–144.

125. Letter from Major General of the Police Karl Pfeffer-Wildenbruch to Kurt Daluege [November 26, 1938], file of Karl Pfeffer-Wildenbruch, former collection of the BDC. See also Letter from Kurt Daluege to Karl Pfeffer-Wildenbruch [November 29, 1938], file of Karl Pfeffer-Wildenbruch, former collection of the BDC.

126. "Vortrag vor den Reichsstatthaltern, Oberpräsidenten und Regierungspräsidenten [June 26, 1939]," T580, reel 216, NARA. Some 900 policemen remained in Austria for the "reorganization" of the police there, while some 3,500 policemen remained in the Sudetenland for the same purpose. See also Tessin, "Stäbe und Truppeneinheiten," 11.

127. "Entwurf, Vortrag des Reichsführers SS und Chef der Deutschen Polizei vor dem Deutschen Gemeindetag über Fragen der Gemeindepolizei [May 5, 1939]," T580, reel 37, NARA.

128. "Auszug aus der Rede des Gen. vor den Höheren SS- und Pol. Führern am 23.I.39, Der Weg der Ordnungspolizei [January 23, 1939]," T580, reel 216, file 5, NARA.

129. Letter from Lieutenant Colonel of the Uniformed Police Dr. Hartmann in Madrid to Daluege [May 21, 1940], T580, reel 221, file 63, NARA. The letter notes that the original request had been made in November 1939. Hartmann's letter was forwarded by the chief of the Operations Office Adolf von Bomhard to Daluege.

130. Supreme Headquarters Allied Expeditionary Force Evaluation and Dissemination Section, *The German Police* (London: n.p., 1945), 27.

131. Report to Daluege from Major der Schutzpolizei Kummetz [May 19, 1937], R 19, file 414, BArch.

132. Letter from Daluege to Himmler [March 9, 1938], R 19, file 414, BArch.

133. Letter from Himmler to Martin Bormann [January 24, 1939], R 19, file 414, BArch.

134. "Vortrag vor den Reichsstatthaltern, Oberpräsidenten und Regierungspräsidenten [June 26, 1939]," T580, reel 216, NARA.

135. Neufeldt, "Entstehung und Organisation," 73.

136. Supreme Headquarters, *The German Police,* 27. See also "Ansprache des Chefs der Ordnungspolizei General der Polizei Daluege anlässlich der Eröffnung der Kolonial-Polizeischule in Oranienburg [April 28, 1941]," R 19, file 382, BArch. See also Gerhard Weinberg, *World in the Balance: Behind the Scenes of World War II* (Hanover: University Press of New England, 1981), 127.

137. Letter from Daluege to Lieutenant General of the Police Adolf von Bomhard [July 3, 1940], R 19, file 414, BArch.

138. Christopher Browning, *The Origins of the Final Solution: The Evolution of Nazi Jewish Policy, September 1939–March 1942* (Lincoln: University of Nebraska Press, 2004), 81–89.

139. Neufeldt, "Entstehung und Organisation," 73. For a discussion of Hitler's ambitions for German empire, see Norman Goda, *Tomorrow the World: Hitler, Northwest Africa, and the Path toward America* (College Station: Texas A&M University Press, 1998).

140. "Vortrag vor den Reichsstatthaltern, Oberpräsidenten und Regierungspräsidenten [June 26, 1939]," T580, reel 216, NARA. See also Tessin, "Stäbe und Truppeneinheiten," 12–13.

141. "Nr. 20 15.3.41 Tag der Deutschen Polizei, 1941, Rundfunkansprache über Einsatz der Ordn.Polizei," R 19, file 382, BArch.

142. "Ansprache des Chefs der Ordnungspolizei, General der Polizei Daluege, anläßlich der Dienstbesprechung der Kommandeure der Gendarmerie [January 16, 1941]," T580, reel 216, file 6, NARA.

143. Tessin, "Stäbe und Truppeneinheiten," 13–14.

144. "Der Chef der Ordnungspolizei, Vortrag über Kräfte- und Kriegseinsatz der Ordnungspolizei im Jahre 1941 [February 1942]," T580, reel 96, NARA.

145. "Ansprache des Chefs der Ordnungspolizei, General der Polizei Daluege, anläßlich der Dienstbesprechung der Kommandeure der Gendarmerie [January 16, 1941]," T580, reel 216, file 6, NARA.

146. Examples of this practice can be seen in the January 15 and July 15, 1941, issues of *Die Deutsche Polizei*.

147. "Der Chef der Ordnungspolizei [September 19, 1939]," T580, reel 221, file 63, NARA.

148. "Der Reichsführer SS und Chef der Deutschen Polizei, O-Kdo. O Nr. 150/39, Betrifft: Aufstellung von Ausbildungs-Bataillonen [October 31, 1939]," R 19, file 304, pp. 25–31, BArch; and "Der Chef der Ordnungspolizei, Vortrag über Kräfte- und Kriegseinsatz der Ordnungspolizei im Jahre 1941 [February 1941]," T580, reel 96, NARA. In contrast, see Tessin, "Stäbe und Truppeneinheiten," 15. Tessin states that Himmler received Hitler's approval for 9,000 men from the 1918–1920 year groups (ages twenty-one to twenty-three in 1939) and 17,000 men from the 1909–1912 year groups (ages thirty to thirty-three in 1939) for duty with the police, with younger men from the 1918–1920 year groups entering the ranks of the police battalions.

149. "Der Reichsminister des Innern, Pol.O.-Kdo. G 4 (P 1a) Nr. 28/39, Betr.: Verstärkung der Polizei durch ungediente Wehrpflichtige [October 11, 1939]," Verschiedenes 301 Bt, file 153, pp. 293–294, ZStl. See also Tessin, "Stäbe und Truppeneinheiten," 14; and Longerich, *Vernichtung*, 307. This practice continued into 1941, with the secretary of the NSDAP, Martin Bormann, restating the requirement for political evaluations from the responsible party organizations for every applicant to the police battalions and the SS Police Division. See "Reichsverfügungsblatt, Anordnung A28/41, Betr.: Politische Beurteilung von Rekruten der SS-Polizeidivision und der Polizeibataillone [June 10, 1941]," T580, reel 97, NARA.

150. Tessin, "Stäbe und Truppeneinheiten," 14. The primary financial enticement for applying for duty with the police included the guarantee that individuals completing twelve years of service would enter the permanent ranks of the civil service (*Beamte auf Lebenszeit*).

151. Longerrich, *Vernichtung*, 307.

152. "Der Chef der Ordnungspolizei [April 27, 1940]," T580, reel 219, files 59–60, NARA.

153. Ibid.

154. "Vortrag über die Deutsche Ordnungspolizei [September 2, 1940]," T580, reel 96, NARA. Querner describes the creation of "garrisoned police companies" (*Polizeikompanien*) from the youngest year groups.

155. "Pol.O-Vu.R. Reich, Begründung [1940]," R 1501, file 5628, frame 115, BArch.

156. Untitled memo addressed to Himmler with the salutation "Lieber Heinrich" [March 7, 1940], T580, reel 219, files 59–60, NARA. Daluege also wanted to discuss Göring's decision to terminate the Wehrmacht's responsibility for the feeding (*Verpflegung*) of the police.

157. "Der Reichsführer SS und Chef der Deutschen Polizei im Reichsministerium des Innern, O.Kdo. O (1) Nr. 354/39, Betrifft: Aufgaben der Pol.Bataillone in den besetzten Ostgebieten [November 29, 1939]," RG 15.011M, reel 21, file 279, USHMMA.

158. Memorandum from Daluege to Lieutenant General of the Police Adolf von Bomhard [March 21, 1940], T580, reel 221, file 63, NARA.

159. "Der Reichsführer SS und Chef der Deutschen Polizei im Reichsministerium des Innern, O-Kdo. WE (1) Nr. 104/1940, Betr.: Richtlinien für die Durchführung der weltanschaulichen Erziehung der Ordnungspolizei während der Kriegszeit [June 2, 1940]," RG 15.011M, reel 11, file 155, USHMMA.

160. "Der Befehlshaber der Ordnungspolizei beim Generalgouverneur in Polen, Ic/18 03, Betr.: Weltanschauliche Erziehung der Ordnungspolizei [June 25, 1940]," RG 15.011M, reel 11, file 155, USHMMA.

161. "Der Chef der Ordnungspolizei, Der Aufbau der Ordnungspolizei für den Kriegseinsatz [August 20, 1940]," T580, reel 96, NARA.

162. Ibid.

163. Ibid.

164. "Der Chef der Ordnungspolizei, Die Verstärkung der Polizei für ihre Friedensaufgaben [August 20, 1940]," T580, reel 96, NARA. The ratio within the Reich (including the Sudetenland) was 1:475 with the inclusion of the 91,500-man Police Reserve.

165. Letter from Rudolf Querner to Kurt Daluege [September 14, 1939], Rudolf Querner file, former collection of the BDC. Querner provides a perfect example of the "military-minded" policeman. Born on October 6, 1893, he served as an officer in the Great War and won the Iron Cross first- and second-class.

166. "Der Reichsführer SS und Chef der Deutschen Polizei im Reichsministerium des Innern, O.-Kdo.P I (1a) Nr. 379/39 [September 7, 1939]," T175, reel 227, frame 2766094, NARA.

167. "Deutsche Polizei im besetzten Polen—ein Leserbrief aus dem Jahr 1939," *Archiv für Polizeigeschichte* 10 (1999): 28–29.

168. Klaus-Michael Mallmann, "'. . . Mißgeburten, die nicht auf diese Welt gehören': Die Ordnungspolizei im besetzten Polen, 1939–1941" (n.p., 2003), 8. Mallmann is citing the War Diary of PB 310, R 20, file 83, BArch.

169. *SS: Unter Sigrune und Adler* (Krakau: Buchverlag Ost, 1940), 56, 58. I would like to thank Ray Brandon for providing me with a copy of this work.

170. Linck, "'. . . schon allein wegen des Schmutzes . . . ,'" 52.

171. Hanns Wirth and Fritz Göhler, *Schutzpolizei im Kampfeinsatz: Handbuch der Taktik des Polizeibataillons,* 2d ed. (Berlin: E. S. Mittler & Sohn, 1942), 160.

172. Hans Richter, *Einsatz der Polizei: Bei den Polizeibataillonen in Ost, Nord, West*, 2d ed. (Berlin: Zentralverlag der NSDAP, 1942), 8, 14–18, 21, 29, 105. The second edition of this work came out only a year after the first, and the total number of copies printed reached twenty-seven thousand.

173. Helmuth Koschorke, *Polizei greift ein! Kriegsberichte aus Ost, West und Nord* (Berlin: Franz Schneider, 1941). A copy of this book's cover appears in Thomas Köhler, "Helmuth Koschorke: 'Wenn ich an die letzten beiden Tage denke, packt mich der Ekel. Juden, Juden und nochmals Juden,'" in Kenkmann and Spieker, eds., *Im Auftrag*, 157.

174. See *Die Deutsche Polizei*, June 1, 1941, July 15, 1941, and August 15, 1941. The June and July editions carried these stories on the front page.

175. *Die Deutsche Polizei*, July 15, 1941.

176. *Die Deutsche Polizei*, February 15, 1944, front cover. A copy of this page appears in Kenkmann and Spieker, eds., *Im Auftrag*, 80.

177. "Deutsche Künstler und die SS, Hermann Geiseler, Polizei-Gebirgsjäger in Oberkrain, Nr. 9414," from the author's personal collection.

178. A reproduction of this poster appears in Buhlan and Jung, eds., *Wessen Freund und wessen Helfer?* 278.

179. "Der Kommandeur der Gendarmerie Shitomir, Kommandobefehl Nr. 23/42 [July 20, 1942]," RG 53.002M, fond 658, reel 5, file 2, USHMMA.

Chapter 3. Instilling the SS Ethic

1. "Vortrag über die Deutsche Ordnungspolizei [September 2, 1940]," T580, reel 96, NARA.

2. Wegner, *Hitlers politische Soldaten*, 11.

3. Richard Bessel, *Political Violence and the Rise of Nazism: The Storm Troopers in Eastern Germany, 1925–1934* (New Haven, Conn.: Yale University Press, 1984), 66.

4. IMT, *Trials*, vol. 29, pp. 122–123, 149–165. Document 1919-PS.

5. Ibid., vol. 29, pp. 145, 149–151. Document 1919-PS.

6. Helmut Krausnick, Hans Buchheim, Martin Broszat, and Hans-Adolf Jacobsen, *Anatomy of the SS State*, trans. Richard Barry, Marian Jackson, and Dorothy Long (New York: Walker, 1968), 321–322.

7. Sydnor, *Soldiers of Destruction*, 278–279.

8. Wegner, *Hitlers politische Soldaten*, 203, 341–343.

9. "Der Chef der Ordnungspolizei, O.-Kdo. G2(01) Nr. 6IX/40 (g), Lagebericht [January 28, 1940]," T580, reel 96, NARA.

10. "Aus dem Lagebericht (Zwischenbericht) des Kommandeurs der Ordnungspolizei für den Distrikt Warschau, Ia 1508, Tgb.Nr.217/40 geh. vom 27.9.40 [September 27, 1940]," T580, reel 213, frames 574–575, NARA.

11. "Höhere SS u. Polizeiführer Ost Krakau, nr. 977 5.9.41 1045=gei=, Der Höhere SS und Polizeiführer Ost, 6154/41 [September 5, 1941]," Collection of the Polish Main Commission, Warsaw, Kommandeur der Sicherheitspolizei Radom, vol. 173, p. 76. I would like to thank Dieter Pohl for providing me with a copy of this document.

12. "Sicherheitspolizei, Kriminalkommissariat Bilgoraj, Tgb.Nr.2380/42 [December 15, 1942]," RG 15.066M, reel 2, file 25, USHMMA.

13. "Der Kommandeur der Ordnungspolizei im Distrikt Lublin, Betr.: Zusammenarbeit mit den Dienststellen des Kdrs.d.Sipo.u.SD in der Bandenbekämpfung [February 12, 1943]," RG 15.011M, reel 7, file 87, USHMMA.

14. Karl-Heinz Heller, *The Reshaping and Political Conditioning of the German Ordnungspolizei, 1933–1945: A Study of Techniques Used in the Nazi State to Conform Local Police Units to National Socialist Theory and Practice* (Ann Arbor, Mich.: University Microfilms, 1971), 24–25.

15. "Die Stellung und Aufgaben der Polizei im Dritten Reich [October 18, 1935]," T580, reel 216, file 3, NARA.

16. "Vertraulich, An die Hauptreferenten von IIIC [September 25, 1935]," R 19, file 390, pp. 29–30, BArch.

17. Gerd Rühle, *Das Dritte Reich: Das fünfte Jahr* (Berlin: Hummelverlag, 1938), 34.

18. "Der Chef der Ordnungspolizei, Inspekteur-Besprechung am 9. Dezember 1937 [January 12, 1938]," R 19, file 460, p. 25, BArch. The expected increase came from the projected end of the probationary period for some 250 Party "candidates" (*Anwärter*).

19. Domarus, ed., *Hitler: Reden und Proklamationen,* 1:463.

20. Werner Roediger, "Welche Bedeutung hat der neue Eid für den Offizier der Schutzpolizei?" in Kehrl, ed., *Jahrbuch,* 52. See also Kenkmann and Spieker, eds., *Im Auftrag,* 53. Kenkmann and Spieker include a photograph of uniformed policemen taking the oath in Cologne in 1940.

21. "Ansprache des General Daluege bei der Einweihung des Ruhrkämpfer-Ehrenmal in Bochum [April 17, 1937]," R 19, file 380, BArch.

22. Domarus, ed., *Hitler: Reden und Proklamationen,* 2:720.

23. Koehl, *The Black Corps,* 48. See also Domarus, ed., *Hitler: Reden und Proklamationen,* 2:720.

24. "Die Polizei [1938–1939?]," T580, reel 95, NARA. This is a six-page report detailing many aspects of the organization and function of both the Uniformed and the Security Police.

25. Herbert, *Best,* 168.

26. Rühle, *Das Dritte Reich* (1938), 34.

27. Koschorke, ed., *Die Polizei—einmal anders!* 11.

28. "Vortrag vor den Reichsstatthaltern, Oberpräsidenten und Regierungspräsidenten [June 26, 1939]," T580, reel 216, NARA. See also "Merkblatt für die Nachwuchswerbung der Ordnungspolizei [September 1938]," Kurt Daluege file, former collection of the BDC. The "Merkblatt" from September 1938 remarks that future police applicants will come "mainly" (*hauptsächlich*) from the ranks of the SS.

29. Domarus, ed., *Hitler: Reden und Proklamationen,* 1:881.

30. Speech by Kurt Daluege during the state ceremony naming Heinrich Himmler as the chief of the German police [June 18, 1936], T580, reel 216, file 3, NARA.

31. Rühle, *Das Dritte Reich* (1937), 269.

32. "Der Führer, Berlin den 16. Januar 1937," T580, reel 219, file 57, NARA. See also "Der Weg der Ordnungspolizei von SS-Obergruppenführer, General der Polizei, Kurt Daluege, Chef der Ordnungspolizei [January 23, 1939]," T580, reel 216, file 5, NARA. Hitler signed the authorization for the wearing of the SS runes on January 16, 1937, but the first award of the device did not take place until May 10, 1937.

33. Ingo Löhken, *Die Polizei-Uniformen in Preussen, 1866–1945* (Freidberg: Podzun-Pallas, 1986), 52.

34. Krausnick et al., *Anatomy of the SS State*, 206–207. Contrary to the postwar assertions of some policemen that SS-rank parity was established for all members of the police, SS rank was given only to policemen *after* their voluntary application for and acceptance into the ranks of the SS.

35. IMT, *Trials*, vol. 29, pp. 228, 233.

36. Ibid., vol. 29, p. 101. Himmler made this statement in a speech to the officer corps of the SS Bodyguard Company "Adolf Hitler" on September 7, 1940.

37. Wegner, *Hitlers politische Soldaten*, 142. This contrasts with Robert Koehl's assertion: "There is virtually no sign of movement from the *Verfügungstruppen, Totenkopfverbände,* and the officer candidate schools into the police." See Koehl, *Black Corps*, 331.

38. IMT, *Trials*, vol. 29, pp. 230–231, 233, 234.

39. "Merkblatt für die Nachwuchswerbung der Ordnungspolizei (Herausgegeben vom RFSS und Chef der Deutschen Polizei im Reichsministerium des Innern) [September 1938]," R 19, file 390, p. 62, BArch. See also "BdO. Iib 3115/17.3., Betrifft: Werbung für die Waffen-SS und Polizei [March 18, 1942]," T175, reel 227, frame 2765683, NARA.

40. Heller, *Reshaping and Political Conditioning*, 93.

41. "Merkblatt für die Nachwuchswerbung der Ordnungspolizei (Herausgegeben vom RFSS und Chef der Deutschen Polizei im Reichsministerium des Innern [September 1938]," R 19, file 390, p. 62, BArch.

42. "Der Reichsführer SS und Chef der Deutschen Polizei im Reichsministerium des Innern, O-Kdo. P I (1) Nr. 208/38 [September 22, 1938]," T580, reel 95, NARA.

43. *Das Polizeibataillon 307 (Lübeck) "im Osteinsatz" 1940–1945* (Essen: Schmidt-Römhild, 2002), 13.

44. IMT, *Trials*, vol. 29, p. 210.

45. "Der Reichsführer-SS, SS-Personalkanzlei, Tgb.Nr. 34/38, Betrifft: Aufnahme von Angehörigen der uniformierten Ordnungspolizei in die SS [February 21, 1938]," T580, reel 95, NARA. See also "SS-Oberabschnitt Main, Abt. VI Az. 9b D/I, Betr.: Aufnahme von Polizeiangehörigen als SS Führer in die SS [August 22, 1939]," T580, reel 95, NARA; and "73. SS Standarte, Abt. VI Az. 9b, Betr.: Aufnahme von Angehörigen der uniformierten Ordnungspolizei in die Schutzstaffel der NSDAP [January 9, 1939]," T580, reel 95, NARA.

46. "Der Reichsführer SS und Chef der Deutschen Polizei im Reichsministerium des Innern, O-Kdo.P I (1a) Nr.178 III/38, Betrifft: Aufstellung von SS-Polizei-Einheiten [July 27, 1939]," T175, reel 227, frames 2766077–2766079, NARA. A *Sturm* would be created with approximately fifty members, and plans also included the creation of *Sturmbanne* composed of two to four *Stürme* in areas with greater numbers of SS members in the police.

47. "Merkblatt für den Eintritt von Angehörigen der SS-Verfügungstruppe als Polizeiwachtmeister in die Schutzpolizei [January 1938]," T580, reel 88, file 437, NARA; and "Der Chef des SS-Hauptamtes Versorgungs- und Fürsorgeamt-SS, XII Az.: VT 25 e/6.4.38, Betrifft: Unterbringung der zum 1.10.1938 ausscheidenden SS-VT-Angehörigen [April 6, 1938]," T580, reel 88, file 437, NARA. Some restrictions applied for the former SS-VT men, including that they be unmarried and not over the age of twenty-five. Duty involved opportunities to join the Uniformed Police, the Customs Service (Zollgrenzdienst), and the Border Police (Grenzpolizei).

48. "Der Reichsführer-SS und Chef der Deutschen Polizei im Reichsministerium

des Innern, O-Kdo.P II(1a)34c Nr.72/39, Betr.: Einstellung von Angehörigen der SS-VT. in die Schutzpolizei [July 28, 1939]," T580, reel 95, NARA. See also "Fürsorge- und Versorgungsamt-SS, Berlin, Abt.Kanzlei Az.: B1/1 K/N, Betr.: Übernahme von Angehörigen der SS-V.T. in die Ordnungspolizei [August 3, 1939]," T580, reel 95, NARA. These men were to receive their police training in groups composed solely of former members of the SS-VT.

49. Heller, *Reshaping and Political Conditioning*, 94.

50. "Rd. Erl. von 12.11.40 ueber Aufnahme von Angehoerigen der Schutzpol. des Reichs und der Gemeinden der Gend. und der Feuerschutzpol. [November 12, 1940]," T580, reel 95, NARA.

51. Wegner, *Hitlers politische Soldaten*, 225. Many of these men were probably associated with the SS Police Division, but this still provides an important insight into the symbiotic relationship between the two organizations concerning transfer of personnel in both directions.

52. "Zahlenmäßige und statistische Unterlagen zur Besprechung der Befehlshaber und Inspekteure der Ord.-Polizei vom 1.-4. Februar 1942," T580, reel 96, NARA. In contrast, approximately 9 percent of the entire German population held membership in the NSDAP. See Kater, *The Nazi Party*, 73.

53. "Abschrift, Kommando der Schutzpolizei, S. IIb. 3040/16.6., Betr.: Übernahme in die SS [June 17, 1942]," UdSSR, file 412, p. 791, ZStl. See also "Der Höhere SS- und Polizeiführer West, Tgb. Nr.: 500/42, Betr.: Aufnahme von Wachtm. (SB) und Meister der Ordnungspolizei in die Schutzstaffel der NSDAP [June 25, 1942]," UdSSR, file 412, p. 793, ZStl.

54. Peter Witte, Michael Wildt, Martina Voigt, Dieter Pohl, Peter Klein, Christian Gerlach, Christoph Dieckmann, and Andrej Angrick, eds., *Der Dienstkalender Heinrich Himmlers, 1941/42* (Hamburg: Christians, 1999), 201.

55. "Der Chef des Amtes für Verwaltung und Recht [October 9, 1942]," T580, reel 95, NARA.

56. Witte et al., eds., *Dienstkalender*, 201.

57. Wegner, *Hitlers politische Soldaten*, 294–295.

58. From an order by Hitler on February 24, 1943, RG 53.002M, fond 389, reel 3, file 1, USHMMA.

59. IMT, *Trials*, vol. 29, pp. 104–105. Himmler made this statement in a speech to the officer corps of the SS Bodyguard Company "Adolf Hitler" on September 7, 1940.

60. Isabel Heinemann, *"Rasse, Siedlung, deutsches Blut": Das Rasse- und Siedlungshauptamt der SS und die rassenpolitische Neuordnung Europas* (Göttingen: Wallenstein, 2003), 96. See also Matthäus et al., *Ausbildungsziel Judenmord?* 37.

61. Heinemann, *"Rasse, Siedlung, deutsches Blut,"* 97–101. See also Heller, *Reshaping and Political Conditioning*, 101–102.

62. Matthäus et al., *Ausbildungsziel Judenmord?* 46–47.

63. Heinemann, *"Rasse, Siedlung, deutsches Blut,"* 100. Heinemann notes that the transfer of these duties was not intended to denote a degradation in the importance of the RuSHA but was far more a function of the organization's lack of adequate financial resources to continue the program, an obstacle not faced by the SS Training Office.

64. "Der Weg der Ordnungspolizei von SS-Gruppenführer, General der Polizei, Kurt Daluege [January 23, 1939]," T580, reel 216, file 5, NARA.

65. Heller, *Reshaping and Political Conditioning*, 111.

66. "Betr.: Weltanschauliche Schulung der Ordnungspolizei," R 19, file 308, p. 86, BArch.

67. "Vorläufiges Merkblatt für die Durchführung der weltanschaulichen Monatsschulung [1940?]," T175, reel 224, frames 2762244–2762250, NARA.

68. Ibid., frames 2762247, 2762249. In addition, each lecturer was required to fill out a detailed report concerning the effectiveness of his lecture, questions from and discussion by the participants, and suggestions for improvement.

69. Matthäus et al., *Ausbildungsziel Judenmord?* 54–55. The two hours of ideological instruction constituted slightly over 4 percent of the forty-six hours of total instruction given per week.

70. "NSDAP, Der Stellvertreter des Führers, Stabsleiter, Braunes Haus, III P-Su/Ha, Betrifft: Abgabe politischer Beurteilungen über Offiziere der Schutzpolizei [April 22, 1937]," R 19, file 423, BArch.

71. "Dienstanweisung für den Chef des Schulungsamtes SS und Pol. [October 17, 1939]," T175, reel 227, frame 2766104.

72. Heller, *Reshaping and Political Conditioning*, 126–127.

73. "Der Reichsführer S.S. und Chef der Deutschen Polizei im Reichsministerium des Innern, O-Kdo. WE (1) Nr. 104/1940, Betr.: Richtlinien für die Durchführung der weltanschaulichen Erziehung der Ordnungspolizei während der Kriegszeit [June 2, 1940]," RG 15.011M, reel 11, file 155, USHMMA.

74. Matthäus, "'Warum wird über das Judentum geschult?'" 114.

75. Heinemann, *"Rasse, Siedlung, deutsches Blut,"* 94–96.

76. "'Politischer Informationsdienst,' RdErl. d. RFSSuChDtPol. im RmdI. v. 28.9.1940 [September 28, 1940]," RG 15.011M, reel 11, file 156, USHMMA.

77. Ibid.

78. "Der Befehlshaber der Ordnungspolizei beim Generalgouverneur, Betr.: Politischer Informationsdienst [December 6, 1940]," RG 15.011M, reel 11, file 152, USHMMA. The word *immediately* has been underlined twice by hand in the original. This letter was passed along by the office of the senior commander of the Uniformed Police in the district of Lublin on December 12, 1940, to his subordinate units.

79. "Der Kommandeur der Ordnungspolizei im Distrikt Lublin, Ic 18 00 [December 22, 1940]," RG 15.011M, reel 11, file 151, USHMMA.

80. "Politischer Informationsdienst, Folge 1, Charakterliche Bewährung [October 10, 1940]," T175, reel 229, frames 2767973–2767974, NARA.

81. "Politischer Informationsdienst, Folge 8, Der Einsatz für den biologischen Sieg [February 10, 1941]," T175, reel 229, frame 2768001, NARA.

82. Browning, *Origins*, 484 n. 87.

83. Heller, *Reshaping and Political Conditioning*, 186–187, 203–206, 158, 207.

84. "Gendarmerie-Hauptmannschaft Zamosc, Ic 1802, Bericht über die Durchführung der weltanschaulichen Erziehung der Ordnungspolizei in der Zeit vom 21. Januar bis 20. März 1942 [March 14, 1942]," RG 15.011M, reel 11, file 159, USHMMA.

85. "Kommandeur der Gendarmerie im Distrikt Lublin, Abt. I a 1810/42, Betrifft: Weltanschauliche Schulung [September 28, 1942]," RG 15.011M, reel 11, file 159, USHMMA.

86. "Der Kommandeur der Ordnungspolizei im Distrikt Lublin, Abt. I c/18 06,

Betr.: Weltanschauliche Schulung der Pol.-Verwaltungs-Beamten [September 30, 1942]," RG 15.011M, reel 11, file 157, USHMMA.

87. "Kommandeur der Gendarmerie im Distrikt Lublin, Abt. I c 18 10, Betrifft: Weltanschauliche Erziehung [March 20, 1943]," RG 15.011M, reel 11, file 159, USHMMA.

88. "Einglied. des Kameradschaftsbundes Deutscher Pol.-Beamten in den Reichsbund d. Deutschen Beamten, RdErl. d. RuMdI zgl. i.R.v.PrMPräs. (LP.) v. 29.1.1935-III BI 1511/35 II. [January 29, 1935]," T580, reel 95, NARA.

89. "Satzung des Kameradschaftsbundes Deutscher Polizeibeamten (im Reichsbund der Deutschen Beamten e.V.) e.V. [1935?]," T580, reel 95, NARA.

90. "NS.-Rechtswahrerbund Reichsdienststelle, Betr.: Organisationszugehörigkeit der Polizeibeamten [March 30, 1939]," T580, reel 95, NARA. This document is marked "for official use only!" and "not intended for publication!"

91. Matthäus et al., *Ausbildungsziel Judenmord?* 45 n. 34.

92. "Der Reichsführer SS und Chef der Deutschen Polizei im Reichsministerium des Innern, O.-Kdo.A (3) Nr.111/37, Betrifft: Ausbildung der Wachtmeister (SB) und Meister (SB) der Ordnungspolizei [October 10, 1937]," T580, reel 95, NARA.

93. *Die Deutsche Polizei*, May 1, 1937, BArch.

94. *Die Deutsche Polizei*, November 15, 1937, RG242, reel 170, frame 533, NARA. The anti–Comintern Pact between Nazi Germany and Japan—signed in November 1936—stipulated that neither party would provide support to the Soviet Union should either be attacked by the Soviet Union. Italy joined the pact in 1937.

95. Matthäus et al., *Ausbildungsziel Judenmord?* 59.

96. *Die Deutsche Polizei*, July 15, 1941, BArch.

97. *Die Deutsche Polizei*, October 1, 1941, BArch.

98. "Der Kommandeur der Gendarmerie Shitomir, Kommandobefehl Nr. 27/43 [April 12, 1943]," RG 53.002M, fond 658, reel 5, file 3, USHMMA.

99. Matthäus et al., *Ausbildungsziel Judenmord?* 60.

100. William L. Combs, *The Voice of the SS: A History of the SS Journal "Das Schwarze Korps"* (New York: Peter Lang, 1986), 20.

101. Matthäus et al., *Ausbildungsziel Judenmord?* 38.

102. "Der Reichsführer SS und Chef der Deutschen Polizei im Reichsministerium des Innern, O-Kdo P I (1a) Nr.168 III/39, Betrifft: Aushängekästen für 'Das Schwarze Korps'. [October 28, 1939]," T175, reel 227, frame 2766127, NARA.

103. Combs, *Voice of the SS,* 107, 70 (see also 31, 41–42, 304).

104. Ibid., 129–138, 376–377.

105. Roland Schoenfelder, Karl Kasper, and Erwin Bindewald, *Vom Werden der deutschen Polizei* (Leipzig: Breitkopf & Härtel, 1937), 273.

106. Ibid., 303–305.

107. Helmuth Koschorke, *Polizeireiter in Polen* (Berlin: Franz Schneider, 1940), 23, 49, 5–6, 12.

108. Ibid., 44–47.

109. Koschorke, *Polizei greift ein!* 49.

110. Ibid., 13, 16, 21.

111. Richter, *Einsatz der Polizei,* [p. ii].

112. Richter, *Einsatz der Polizei,* 17–18, 21, 23, 29–30, 31.

113. Ibid., 38. For another insightful discussion of themes in police literature, see Köhler, "Völkermord," 130–157.

114. "Die Ordnungspolizei jederzeit einsatzbereit [February 13, 1941]," T580, reel 216, file 2, NARA.

115. Hans Richter, *Ordnungspolizei auf den Rollbahnen des Ostens: Bildbericht von den Einsätzen der Ordnungspolizei im Sommer 1941 im Osten, ergänzt durch kurze Erlebnisberichte* (Berlin: Zentralverlag der NSDAP, 1943), 7, 10–12. Richter died in an accident on the Eastern Front on July 27, 1941, and this work appeared posthumously under his name.

116. Köhler, "Völkermord," 151.

117. "Der Reichsführer SS und Chef der Deutschen Polizei im Reichsministerium des Innern, O-Kdo.II WE (4) Nr. 577-3/1941, Betr.: Truppenbetreuung 'Spiel für Kameraden' [December 6, 1941]," R 19, file 333, pp. 37–38, BArch. See also "Auswärtiger Einsatz [War Diary of the Third Company of Police Battalion 322, September 19, 1941 and September 21, 1941]," RG 48.004M, reel 2, frames 200816–200817, USHMMA.

118. Heller, *Reshaping and Political Conditioning,* 140.

119. Matthäus et al., *Ausbildungsziel Judenmord?* 64.

120. Ibid., 61–62, 64.

121. "Auswärtiger Einsatz [War Diary of the Third Company of Police Battalion 322, July 26, August 15, October 1–2, and December 9–10, 1941]," RG 48.004M, reel 2, frames 200781, 200799, 200824–200825, 200847, USHMMA.

122. "Auswärtiger Einsatz [War Diary of the Third Company of Police Battalion 322, December 9, 1941]," RG 48.004M, reel 2, frame 200846, USHMMA.

123. "Polizei-Einsatzstab Südost, Ch.d.St., Veldes, Tagesbefehl Nr. 5, Betr.: A) Bekanntgabe eines Befehls RFSSuChdDtPol. [January 9, 1942]," 503 AR-Z 9/1965, file 1, p. 280, ZStl.

124. "Der Höhere SS- und Polizeiführer Russland Mitte [September 5, 1941]," NS 19, reel 1671, frames 129–130, BArch.

125. Richter, *Einsatz der Polizei,* 19, 24.

126. "Kommandeur der Gendarmerie im Distrikt Lublin, Abt. I c 18 10, Betrifft: Weltanschauliche Erziehung [March 20, 1943]," RG 15.011M, reel 11, file 159, USHMMA.

127. Witte et al., eds., *Dienstkalender,* 183, 189, 193–195, 224–225, 245.

128. Klee, Dreßen, and Rieß, eds., *"The Good Old Days,"* 80.

129. IMT, *Trials,* vol. 29, p. 151. Document 1919-PS. In practice, such retirements did, in fact, occur. Take, e.g., the case of Erwin Schulz, the head of Einsatzkommando 5, who, after receiving orders to kill Jews not involved in work as well as their families, requested a transfer back to his teaching position at the police academy in Charlottenburg. Schulz later reported: "I personally experienced no disadvantage whatsoever as a result of my intervention." See Klee, Dreßen, and Rieß, eds., *"The Good Old Days,"* 85–86.

130. Richard Breitman, *The Architect of Genocide: Himmler and the Final Solution* (New York: Knopf, 1991), 213.

131. Wagner, "Die Polizei im Faschismus," 162.

132. Neufeldt, "Entstehung und Organisation," 21.

133. Wilhelm, *Polizei im NS-Staat,* 84. See also Ruth Bettina Birn, *Die Höheren SS- und Polizeiführer: Himmlers Vertreter im Reich und in den besetzten Gebieten* (Düsseldorf: Droste, 1986), 81. In the state of Prussia, the inspector of the Uniformed Police was subordinated to the state president (*Oberpräsidenten*).

134. Rühle, *Das Dritte Reich* (1938), 35.

135. Krausnick et al., *Anatomy of the SS State,* 213–216.

136. Hans Buchheim, "Die Höheren SS- und Polizeiführer," *Vierteljahrshefte für Zeitgeschichte* 11 (October 1963): 379.

137. "Der Weg der Ordnungspolizei [January 23, 1939]," T580, reel 216, file 5, NARA.

138. Birn, *Die Höheren SS- und Polizeiführer,* 350–351 (quotation), 352.

139. Krausnick et al., *Anatomy of the SS State,* 216.

140. "Dienstanweisung für die Höheren SS- und Polizeiführer [December 18, 1939]," T580, reel 95, NARA. The letter begins with the personal salutation "Dear Berger!"

141. Krausnick et al., *Anatomy of the SS State,* 220.

142. "Der Reichsführer-SS, Tgb.Nr. 36/156/43 g. [June 15, 1943]," T580, reel 95, NARA.

143. "Der Reichsminister für die besetzten Ostgebiete, Nr. 945/43 g [July 20, 1943]," T580, reel 37, NARA.

Chapter 4. Baptism of Fire

1. Czelaw Madajczyk, *Die Okkupationspolitik Nazideutschlands in Polen, 1939–1945* (Cologne: Pahl-Rugenstein, 1988), 18–19.

2. Martin Broszat, *Nationalsozialistische Polenpolitik, 1939–1945* (Stuttgart: Deutsche Verlags–Anstalt, 1961), 19–21.

3. Charles Burdick and Hans-Adolf Jacobsen, *The Halder War Diary, 1939–1942* (Novato, Calif.: Presidio, 1988), 31.

4. Kershaw, *Nemesis,* 223.

5. "Der Chef der Ordnungspolizei, Der Aufbau der Ordnungspolizei für den Kriegseinsatz [August 20, 1940]," T580, roll 96, NARA. By September 1, 1939, the entire Uniformed Police maintained a stock of only 290 heavy machine guns and 190 light machine guns. Only a year later, the number of heavy machine guns had almost quadrupled, to 1,100, and the number of light machine guns had increased nine times, to 1,736. During the course of the war, the firepower of the police formations expanded to include heavy mortars, artillery pieces, and even armored tanks, reflecting the increased reliance on these forces in a variety of missions.

6. "Disposition zum Vortrag General Daluege, Die Ordnungspolizei," T580, reel 216, file 5, NARA. See also "Der Chef der Ordnungspolizei [September 5, 1939]," T580, reel 96, NARA.

7. "Der Chef der Ordnungspolizei [September 5, 1939]," T580, reel 96, NARA. In the letter, Daluege directed higher SS and police leaders to begin negotiations with formations of the Party for the delivery of the needed equipment items.

8. Elisabeth Wagner, ed., *Der General Quartiermeister: Briefe und Tagebuchaufzeichnungen des Generalquartiermeisters des Heeres General der Artillerie Eduard Wagner* (Munich: Günter Olzog, 1963), 127. The head of the Uniformed Police Operations Office (Kommandoamt), Lieutenant General of the Police Adolf von Bomhard, accompanied Daluege to this meeting.

9. "Der Reichsführer SS, z.Zt. Führerhauptquartier, AR/666/iy [September 13, 1939]," T580, reel 37, NARA.

10. Michael Howard, *The Franco-Prussian War: The German Invasion of France, 1870–1871* (New York: Dorset, 1961), 251.

11. John Horne and Alan Kramer, "German 'Atrocities' and Franco-German Opinion, 1914: The Evidence of German Soldiers' Diaries," *Journal of Modern History* 66 (March 1994): 17.

12. Alfred M. de Zayas, *The Wehrmacht War Crimes Bureau, 1939–1945* (Lincoln: University of Nebraska Press, 1989), 140–141. See also Christian Streit, *Keine Kameraden: Die Wehrmacht und die sowjetischen Kriegsgefangenen, 1941–1945* (Bonn: J. H. W. Dietz, 1991), 106–108.

13. "Vortrag über die Deutsche Ordnungspolizei [September 2, 1940]," T580, reel 96, NARA.

14. "Die Ordnungspolizei jederzeit einsatzbereit [Februrary 13, 1941]," T580, reel 216, file 2, NARA. See also Arnold Lissance, ed., *The Halder Diaries: The Private War Journals of Colonel General Franz Halder,* 2 vols. (Boulder, Colo.: Westview, 1976), 1:54; and Tessin, "Stäbe und Truppeneinheiten," 33.

15. "Oberfeldkommandantur 530, Stabsquartier [September 12, 1939]," T580, reel 96, NARA.

16. "Oberfeldkommandantur 530, St. Qu., II a Nr. 68/39 geh. [December 23, 1939]," T580, reel 96, NARA.

17. Edward B. Westermann, "'Friend and Helper': German Uniformed Police Operations in Poland and the General Government, 1939–1941," *Journal of Military History* 58 (October 1994): 648.

18. "Vortrag über die Deutsche Ordnungspolizei [September 2, 1940]," T580, reel 96, NARA.

19. *SS: Unter Sigrune und Adler,* 16–17.

20. "Vortrag über die Deutsche Ordnungspolizei [September 2, 1940]," T580, reel 96, NARA.

21. Krausnick, *Einsatzgruppen,* 41.

22. Alexander B. Rossino, *Hitler Strikes Poland: Blitzkrieg, Ideology, and Atrocity* (Lawrence: University Press of Kansas, 2003), 12.

23. Krausnick, *Einsatzgruppen,* 29.

24. Włodzimierz Borodziej, *Terror und Politik: Die Deutsche Polizei und die Polnische Widerstandsbewegung im Generalgouvernement, 1939–1944* (Mainz: Philipp von Zabern, 1999), 26.

25. Rossino, *Poland,* 14.

26. Krausnick, *Einsatzgruppen,* 35.

27. Rossino, *Poland,* 15–16. Rossino notes that the lists of special suspects (*Sonderfahndungslisten*) contained the names of some sixty-one thousand Polish Christians and Jews designated by the Security Police as "anti-German elements."

28. Rossino, *Poland,* 14. See also Mallmann, "'Mißgeburten'" (2004), 71.

29. Mallmann, "'Mißgeburten'" (2004), 21.

30. Krausnick, *Einsatzgruppen,* 42.

31. Mallmann, "'Mißgeburten'" (2004), 72.

32. Rossino, *Poland,* 90.

33. Westermann, "'Friend and Helper,'" 646.

34. Klemp, "*Mord-Bataillon,*" 36.

35. Reinhard Henkys, *Die nationalsozialistischen Gewaltverbrechen: Geschichte und Gericht* (Stuttgart: Kreuz, 1964), 90. See also Klemp, "*Mord-Bataillon,*" 36.

36. "Der Chef der Ordnungspolizei, Berlin [September 5, 1939]," T580, reel 96, NARA.

37. Mallmann, "'Mißgeburten'" (2004), 73.

38. Personal letter from Walter von Keudell to SS-Gruppenführer Friedrich Wilhelm Rediess [September 15, 1939], T580, reel 96, NARA. See also Zentner and Bedürftig, *Encyclopedia*, 496–497.

39. Klemp, *"Mord-Bataillon,"* 31–35.

40. "Der Befehlshaber der Ordnungspolizei beim Chef der Zivilverwaltung beim Militärbefehlshaber Posen, Ia Tgb. Nr. 491/39, Betrifft: Berichterstattung [October 19, 1939]," Verschiedenes 301, file 153, pp. 118–119, ZStl.

41. "Der Befehlshaber der Ordnungspolizei beim Chef der Zivilverwaltung beim Militärbefehlshaber Posen, Ia Tgb. Nr. 491/39, Betrifft: Berichterstattung [October 19, 1939]," Verschiedenes 301, file 153, pp. 118–119, ZStl. See also Klemp, *"Mord-Bataillon,"* 36.

42. Klemp, *"Mord-Bataillon,"* 36–37.

43. "Der Befehlshaber der Ordnungspolizei beim Chef der Zivilverwaltung beim Militärbefehlshaber Posen, Ia Tgb. Nr. 491/39, Betrifft: Berichterstattung [October 19, 1939]," Verschiedenes 301, file 153, p. 120, ZStl.

44. For examples of the German depiction of Polish actions in Bromberg, see Rolf Bathe, *Der Feldzug der 18 Tage: Chronik des Polnischen Dramas* (Berlin: Gerhard Stalling, 1939), 29–44; and Koschorke, *Polizeireiter,* 40–50.

45. Rossino, *Poland,* 62.

46. Ibid., 64.

47. Mallmann, "'Mißgeburten'" (2004), 74.

48. "Der Reichsführer SS und Chef der Deutschen Polizei im Reichsministerium des Innern, O-Kdo. O Nr. 150/39, Betrifft: Aufstellung von Ausbildungs-Bataillonen [October 31, 1939]," R 19, file 304, p. 25. See also "Gedenkrede zur Ehrenfeier für den gefallenen Generalleutnant der Polizei SS-Gruppenführer Arthur Mülverstedt [1941]," T580, reel 216, file 6, NARA.

49. "Pol.-Regiment 4, Bericht vom 10.10.39., Betr.: Berichterstattung an den Chef der Ordnungspolizei [October 10, 1939]," T580, reel 96, NARA.

50. Rossino, *Poland,* 154–156.

51. "Verordnung über Waffenbesitz vom 12. September 1939," T501, reel 229, frame 568, NARA. This directive appeared above the signature of General Walther von Brauchitsch, the commander in chief of the army.

52. Mallmann, "'Mißgeburten'" (2004), 73.

53. "Kommandantur Warschau, Abt. I a, An Polizeiregiment Warschau [November 13, 1939]," T580, reel 96, NARA. In the case of the Jewish merchant, his complaints after being cheated by the soldier led to his being punched in the face. As a crowd gathered around the scene, one Pole remarked: "Why are you all laughing? Wait a couple of days; then the Germans will treat the Poles exactly as they are now treating the Jews."

54. Rossino, *Poland,* 77 (see also 259 n. 38). Himmler issued the directive first on September 3 and then again on September 7, providing clear evidence of the importance that he attached to it.

55. "Der Reichsführer SS und Chef der Deutschen Polizei im Reichsministerium des Innern, O-Kdo. O (1) 1 Nr. 275/40, Betrifft: Behandlung polnischer Offiziere [April 30, 1940]," R 19, file 304, pp. 86–87, BArch.

56. Reinhard Rürup, *Der Krieg gegen die Sowjetunion, 1941–1945* (Berlin: Argon, 1991), 122. In this order, Reichenau noted: "The primary goal of the campaign against the Jewish-Bolshevist system is the complete destruction of the power structure and the extermination of the Asiatic influence in the European cultural center." This statement provides one of the clearest expressions of the racial and apocalyptic nature of the war against the Soviet Union.

57. Mallmann, "'Mißgeburten'" (2004), 73.

58. Werner Roehr, *Nacht über Europa: Die Faschistische Okkupationspolitik in Polen* (Cologne: Pahl-Rugenstein, 1989), 346–352.

59. "Vortrag über die Deutsche Ordnungspolizei [September 2, 1940]," T580, reel 96, NARA.

60. "Der Befehlshaber der Ordnungspolizei beim Chef der Zivilverwaltung beim Militärbefehlshaber Posen, Ia Tgb. Nr. 327/39 [October 14, 1939]," T580, reel 96, NARA.

61. "Der Reichsführer SS und Chef der Deutschen Polizei im Reichsministerium des Innern, O.-Kdo. O (4) Nr. 250/39, Betr.: Bereitstellung von Kräften der Gend. des Einzeldienstes für einen weiteren Einsatz im Osten [September 20, 1939]," R 19, file 304, pp. 13–14, BArch.

62. Personal letter from Daluege to Adolf von Bomhard [April 27, 1940], T580, reel 219, file 59, NARA. See also "Der Landrat des Kreises Stopnica, Betr.: Lagebericht [October 30, 1939]," T501, reel 229, frame 443, NARA; and "Der Reichsführer SS und Chef der Deutschen Polizei im Reichsministerium des Innern, O.-Kdo. Ig-Ia Nr. 820/42 (g.), Betr.: Erfassung von Offizieren, Unterführern und Männern der Ordnungspolizei in Standorten mit ständig erhöhter Alarmbereitschaft [November 1, 1942]," RG 15.011M, reel 20, file 271, USHMMA.

63. Letter from Rudolf Querner to Kurt Daluege, September 14, 1939, Rudolf Querner file, former collection of the BDC. Querner provides a perfect example of the "military-minded" policeman. Born on October 6, 1893, he served as an officer in the First World War and won the Iron Cross, both first- and second-class. He was also a self-described "career officer" despite his demobilization from the army in 1919. See Birn, *Die Höheren SS- und Polizeiführer*, 342.

64. Westermann, "'Friend and Helper,'" 643–661. See also Alexander B. Rossino, "Nazi Anti-Jewish Policy during the Polish Campaign: The Case of Einsatzgruppe von Woyrsch," *German Studies Review* 24 (February 2001): 35–53.

65. "Deutsche Polizei im besetzten Polen," 28.

66. Mallmann, "'Mißgeburten'" (2004), 73.

67. "Tagebuch [September 1939]," R 19, file 403, pp. 6–12, BArch.

68. "Der Kommandierende General des XVIII. Armeekorps [September 21, 1939]," T580, reel 96, NARA.

69. "SS Polizei Division [undated]," T580, reel 97, NARA. See also Koehl, *Black Corps*, 195, 205.

70. "Gedenkrede zur Ehrenfeier für den gefallenen Generalleutnant der Polizei SS-Gruppenführer Arthur Mülverstedt [1941]," T580, reel 216, file 6, NARA.

71. "Der Chef der Ordnungspolizei, Kdo. I O (3) 1 Nr. 256/42, Betr.: Unterstellung der SS-Pol.-Division und ihrer Ersatz-Einheiten unter die Waffen-SS und Durchführungsbestimmungen hierzu [September 4, 1942]," R 20, file 1, pp. 13–15, BArch.

72. "[Merkblatt] für den Eintritt als Freiwilliger in die SS-Polizei Division und für den späteren Übertritt in die Polizei [undated]," T580, reel 97, NARA.

73. Wegner, *Hitlers politische Soldaten,* 120–121, 127.

74. "Der Reichsführer SS und Chef der Deutschen Polizei im Reichsministerium des Innern, Hauptamt SS-Gericht, R/G XIV/1 [November 20, 1939]," T580, reel 96, NARA. This measure also applied to senior SS leaders, members of the SS-VT, SS Death's Head formations, and members of the *Junkerschulen* and was given the effective date of October 17, 1939. In addition, members of the Security Police operating in Poland were also placed under SS legal jurisdiction. It was not until September 1, 1942, that this measure was changed to include *all* members of the Uniformed Police serving in the East. See "Der Reichsführer-SS, Hauptamt SS-Gericht, Nr. Ia/102 Tgb.Nr. 392/41 [July 30, 1942]," T580, reel 96, NARA.

75. Personal note from Daluege to Himmler, March 7, 1940, T580, reel 219, file 59, NARA. Daluege begins this note with the familiar salutation "Dear Heinrich," providing one indication of the close relationship between these two men.

76. Letter from Chief of the German Uniformed Police Kurt Daluege to Police General Adolf von Bomhard, March 21, 1940, T580, reel 221, ordner 63, NARA. On April 27, 1940, Daluege wrote a letter to von Bomhard reminding him that the selection of officers and senior noncommissioned officers for the training battalions was the "first priority." He also complained to von Bomhard that, in two cases, the candidates submitted had been found completely unsuitable and that he expected disciplinary measures to be taken against the officers who recommended them. See letter from Daluege to von Bomhard, April 27, 1940, T580, reel 219, file 59, NARA.

77. "Die Ordnungspolizei jederzeit einsatzbereit! [Februrary 13, 1941]," T580, reel 216, file 2, NARA. This information is in a speech by Daluege.

78. "Entwurf für die Rundfunkansprache zum 'Tag der Deutschen Polizei' [March 15, 1941]," R 19, file 382, BArch.

79. For examples, see the testimonies of Heinrich D. (b. November 7, 1891) and Wilhelm E. (b. October 10, 1893), V 205 AR-Nr. 512/1963, file 1, pp. 47–48, ZStl.

80. "Der Reichsführer SS- und Chef der Deutschen Polizei im Reichsministerium des Innern, O.Kdo O (1) 1 Nr.5/40, Schnellbrief [January 5, 1940]," T580, reel 96, NARA.

81. "Der Chef des Kommandoamtes, O-Kdo. I o (3) Nr. 24/43, Betr.: Einsatz von Polizeiverwaltungsbeamten [January 13, 1943]," R 19, file 102, p. 94, BArch. Lieutenant General of the Police Otto Winkelmann even inquired as to whether it was possible to ensure that police administrative officials serving in the occupied territories be restricted to the year groups 1901 and later.

82. "Partei-Statistik, Band I, Parteimitglieder, Stand 1. Januar 1935," former collection of the Library of the BDC, RG 242, reel B-007, frames 915–916, NARA.

83. Kater, *The Nazi Party,* 139–148.

84. "Der Reichsführer SS und Chef der Deutschen Polizei im Reichsministerium des Innern, O-Kdo. O (1) 1 Nr. 808/40, Betrifft: Verwendung der im Heimatgebiet vorhandenen Polizei-Battalione [November 21, 1940]," R 19, file 304, p. 145, BArch.

85. "Fernspruch, Betr.: Austausch älterer Pol.-Reservisten in den Pol.-Regimentern gegen jüngere Pol.-Reservisten des Einzeldienstes [November 26, 1942]," RG 15.011M, reel 20, file 275, USHMMA. See also "Der Chef der Ordnungspolizei, KdO g I Org. (3) 23/44 (g.), Betr.: Austausch von ehem. Jugoslawien Gendarmen und Polizei-Reservisten der slowenischen Volksgruppe in Kärnten, Oberkrain und Untersteiermark [April 15, 1944]," Verschiedenes 301 Cd, file 163, p. 228; and "Bericht

über die von Oberstlt.d.Gend Kuhn (Org. 4) und Maj.d.SchP. Degener (Org. 3) durchgeführte Dienstreise nach Kroatien [March 31, 1944]," Verschiedenes 301 Cd, file 163, p. 219, ZStl.

86. "Der Reichsführer SS- und Chef der Deutschen Polizei im Reichsministerium des Innern, O-Kdo I O (4) Nr. 249/42, Betr.: Bereitstellung von Pol.-Wachtm. (SB) der Reserve, die bei der Gendarmerie d.E. Dienst versehen, für einen Einsatz mit der Gendarmerie im Osten [May 5, 1942]," R 19, file 304, pp. 199–200, BArch. Daluege also agreed to allow the use of men over the age of forty-five in "exceptional" cases, but only if the men were volunteers and met the necessary physical and training requirements. The report also noted that, if possible, these men should also receive tactical training, including the searching of houses and forests, the "cleaning out" of a "criminal nest" (*Verbrechernest*), and search and arrest procedures.

87. "Nachweisung über die im Distrikt Lublin eingesetzten Meister [1942]," 208 AR-Z 80/60, file 2, pp. 344–347, ZStl.

88. *Das Recht des Generalgouvernements* (Krakau: Burgverlag, 1940), 29.

89. Madajczyk, *Okkupationspolitik*, 24.

90. *Das Recht des Generalgouvernements*, 33.

91. Borodziej, *Terror und Politik*, 33.

92. *Das Recht des Generalgouvernements*, 33. See also Borodziej, *Terror und Politik*, 42.

93. "Vortrag über die Deutsche Ordnungspolizei [September 2, 1940]," T580, reel 96, NARA.

94. "Die Ordnungspolizei jederzeit einsatzbereit! [Februrary 13, 1941]," T580, reel 216, file 2, NARA. This information is in a speech by Daluege.

95. Testimony of Josef-Aleksander Kielar, 208 AR-Z 30/62, file 1, p. 217, ZStl.

96. Testimony of Jan Krawczyk, 208 AR-Z 30/62, file 1, p. 219, ZStl.

97. "Der Befehlshaber der Ordnungspolizei beim Chef der Zivilverwaltung beim Militärbefehlshaber Posen, Ia Tgb. Nr. 327/39 [October 14, 1939]," T580, reel 96, NARA.

98. "Vortrag über die Deutsche Ordnungspolizei [September 2, 1940]," T580, reel 96, NARA. In addition, the Maritime and Waterway Protection Police (Wasserschutzpolizei) lost 35 officers and 650 men to the German navy (Kriegsmarine) for duty in the Naval Police. See also "Nr. 205 VPS, Der Kommandeur der Gendarmerie bei dem Regierungspräsidenten, Betr.: Verwendung der Polizei-Reserve im Gend.-Einzeldienst [April 16, 1940]," T580, reel 96, NARA.

99. "Der Reichsführer SS und Chef der Deutschen Polizei im Reichsministerium des Innern, O-Kdo. O (4) Nr. 489/40, Betr: Einsatz der Gendarmerie des Einzeldienstes im Generalgouvernement [November 11, 1940]," R 19, file 304, pp. 138–141, BArch.

100. "Der Chef der Ordnungspolizei, Der Aufbau der Ordnungspolizei für den Kriegseinsatz [August 20, 1940]," T580, reel 96, NARA; "Der Chef der Ordnungspolizei, Vortrag über den Kräfte- und Kriegseinsatz der Ordnungspolizei im Jahre 1941 [1942]," T580, reel 96, NARA.

101. "Der Chef der Ordnungspolizei, Vortrag über den Kräfte- und Kriegseinsatz der Ordnungspolizei im Jahre 1941 [1942]," T580, reel 96, NARA.

102. "Der Oberbefehlshaber Ost, Ic/Ac, B.Nr.991/39 geh., Betr.: Vorgänge in Ostrow Maz. am 9.11.39 [December 7, 1939]," Verschiedenes 301 Bt, file 153, pp. 26–27, ZStl.

103. Testimony of Polizeiobermeister Josef K., February 16, 1960, 211 AR-Z 350/59, file 1, p. 124, ZStl. See also Mallmann, "'Mißgeburten'" (2004), 79.

104. Testimony of Polizeihauptkommissar Otto F., February 22, 1960, 211 AR-Z 350/59, file 1, p. 141, ZStl.

105. Testimony of Polizeiobermeister Josef K., February 16, 1960, 211 AR-Z 350/59, file 1, pp. 124–126, ZStl. K. says that Hoffmann did not share the nature of the mission with him, a very unlikely story given his position within the company staff.

106. Ibid., pp. 115, 26. This information comes from background material accumulated by the federal prosecutor's office.

107. Testimony of Otto F., February 22, 1960, 211 AR-Z 350/59, file 1, pp. 170–172, ZStl.

108. Ibid., p. 143. Interestingly, Kirschner was a member of both the NSDAP and the SS. See also Mallmann, "'Mißgeburten'" (2004), 79, in which is provided an account of one policeman who tore an infant from its mother's arm and shot it while holding it in front of him.

109. Testimony of Ernst T., February 5, 1960, 211 AR-Z 350/59, file 1, p. 101, ZStl.

110. Testimony of Wilhelm M., 211 AR-Z 350/59, file 1, p. 40, ZStl.

111. "Der Oberbefehlshaber Ost, Vortragsnotizen für Vortrag Oberost beim Oberbefehlshaber des Heeres am 15.2 in Spala [February 6, 1940]," 208 AR-Z 30/62, file 1, pp. 20–21, ZStl. It was noted in the orders that the commendation was to be passed along to all members of the battalion.

112. "Der Chef der Ordnungspolizei, O.Kdo. O (1) 1 Nr. 403/39 [December 13, 1939]," T580, reel 96, NARA.

113. "Der Oberbefehlshaber Ost, Vortragsnotizen für Vortrag Oberost beim Oberbefehlshaber des Heeres am 15.2 in Spala [February 6, 1940]," 208 AR-Z 30/62, file 1, pp. 12–13, ZStl.

114. Wagner, ed., *Der General Quartiermeister,* 103, 134–135.

115. Burdick and Jacobsen, *Halder War Diary,* 57.

116. Lissance, ed., *The Halder Diaries,* 1:97.

117. For Wehrmacht actions in Poland, see Rossino, *Poland,* 154–185. For the campaign in Russia, see Omer Bartov, *The Eastern Front, 1941–1945: German Troops and the Barbarisation of Warfare* (New York: Macmillan, 1986).

118. "Der Oberbefehlshaber Ost, Vortragsnotizen für Vortrag Oberost beim Oberbefehlshaber des Heeres am 15.2 in Spala [February 6, 1940]," 208 AR-Z 30/62, file 1, pp. 13–14, ZStl.

119. "Der Reichsführer SS, Tgb. Nr. I 2885/39 geh. [November 29, 1939]," T580, reel 88, file 437, NARA.

120. "Betrifft: Säuberungsaktion östlich der Weichsel [December 7, 1939]," T580, reel 88, file 437, NARA.

121. *SS: Unter Sigrune und Adler,* 5.

122. "Der Höh. SS-u. Pol.-Fhr Ost, Betr. Verhältnis Wehrmacht, SS und Polizei [December 24, 1939]," RG 15.011M, reel 20, file 271, USHMMA.

123. "Oberbefehlshaber Ost, Chef des Generalstabes, Oi Qu 858/40g [April 9, 1940]," RH 1, file 58, p. 80, BArch. I would like to thank Peter Hoffmann for bringing this document to my attention.

124. "Oberbefehlshaber Ost, Chef des Generalstabes, Oi Qu 858/40g [April 9, 1940]," RH 1, file 58, p. 83, BArch.

125. Ibid., pp. 83–84.

126. "Der Reichsführer SS und Chef der Deutschen Polizei im Reichsministerium des Innern, O-Kdo. WE (1) Nr. 104/1940, Betr.: Richtlinien für die Durchführung der weltanschaulichen Erziehung der Ordnungspolizei während der Kriegszeit [June 2, 1940]," RG 15.011M, reel 11, file 155, USHMMA.

127. IMT, *Trials,* vol. 29, p. 358. Document 2233-PS.

128. Browning, *Ordinary Men,* 39.

129. Testimony of Wilhem H., 211 AR-Z 350/59, file 1, pp. 35–36, ZStl.

130. Henkys, *Gewaltverbrechen,* 90–91.

131. *The Black Book of Poland* (New York: G. P. Putnam's Sons, 1942), 176–177.

132. "Der Oberbefehlshaber Ost, Vortragsnotizen für Vortrag Oberost beim Oberbefehlshaber des Heeres am 15.2 in Spala [February 6, 1940]," 208 AR-Z 30/62, file 1, p. 16, ZStl. See also *The Black Book of Poland* 165.

133. Testimony of Ernst J., 211 AR-Z 350/59, file 1, p. 59, ZStl.

134. Ibid.

135. "Der Kommandeur der Gendarmerie, Shitomir, Kommandobefehl Nr. 18/42 [June 6, 1942]," RG 53.002M, fond 658, reel 5, file 2, USHMMA.

136. Browning, *Ordinary Men,* 39.

137. "Der Chef der Ordnungspolizei, O-Kdo. g 2 (o1) Nr. 6 XI/40(g.), Lagebericht [May 31, 1940]," T501, reel 212, frame 1014, NARA.

138. Harvey, *Women and the Nazi East,* 152.

139. Michael Burleigh, *Germany Turns Eastwards: A Study of Ostforschung in the Third Reich* (Cambridge: Cambridge University Press, 1988), 178.

140. Browning, *Ordinary Men,* 40.

141. Henkys, *Gewaltverbrechen,* 90.

142. "Der Chef der Ordnungspolizei, O-Kdo. g 2 (o1) Nr. 6 IX/40(g.), Lagebericht [May 15, 1940]," T580, reel 96, NARA.

143. Wojciech Zyśko, ed., *Zeszyty Majdanka,* vol. 5, *Z Dziakalności Niemieckies Policji w Dystrykcie Lubelskim w Pierwszym Okresie Okupacji* (Lublin: Wydawnictwo Lubelskie, 1971), 224–225.

144. "Der Chef der Ordnungspolizei, O-Kdo. g 2 (o1) Nr. 6 XI/40(g.), Lagebericht [June 15, 1940]," T501, reel 212, frame 1125, NARA. See also Zyśko, *Policji,* 233.

145. "Der Chef der Ordnungspolizei, O-Kdo. g 2 (o1) Nr. 6 XIV/40(g.), Lagebericht [June 28, 1940]," T501, reel 213, frame 95, NARA. See also Zyśko, *Policji,* 223.

146. "Der Oberbefehlshaber Ost Rüstungsinspektion Oberost [June 14, 1940]," T501, reel 212, frames 1138–1139, NARA.

147. Zyśko, *Policji,* 239.

148. "Der Kommandeur der Gendarmerie im Distrikt Lublin, Abt. Ia, Betr.: Einsatz von weiteren 140 000 Arbeitskräften aus dem Generalgouvernement im Altreich [September 17, 1942]," RG 15.011M, reel 21, file 279, USHMMA.

149. "Der Chef der Ordnungspolizei, O-Kdo. g 2 (o1) Nr. 6 II/40(g.), Lagebericht [January 28, 1940]," T580, reel 96, NARA.

150. "Der Chef der Ordnungspolizei, O-Kdo. g 2 (o1) Nr. 6 IX/40(g.), Lagebericht [May 15, 1940]," T501, reel 212, frame 908, NARA.

151. "Der Chef der Ordnungspolizei, O-Kdo. g 2 (o1) Nr. 6 XI/40(g.), Lagebericht [May 31, 1940]," T501, reel 212, frame 1008, NARA.

152. Hilberg, *Destruction,* 1:221–223.

153. "Der Chef der Ordnungspolizei, O-Kdo. g 2 (o1) Nr. 6 XI/40(g.), Lagebericht [May 31, 1940]," T501, reel 212, frame 1016, NARA.

154. Hilberg, *Destruction,* 1:223.
155. Mallmann, "'Mißgeburten'" (2004), 80.
156. Klemp, *"Mord-Bataillon,"* 42. See also Hilberg, *Destruction,* 1:227.
157. Klemp, *"Mord-Bataillon,"* 45, 48–49.
158. Testimony of Philipp K., 211 AR-Z 350/59, file 1, p. 185, ZStl (emphasis added).
159. Zyśko, *Policji,* 220, 222.
160. "Der Chef der Ordnungspolizei, O-Kdo. g 2 (01) Nr. 6 IX/40(g.), Lagebericht [May 15, 1940]," T501, reel 212, frames 895–896, NARA.
161. Zyśko, *Policji,* 234. From a report by the First Company of PB 314 dated March 22, 1941.
162. IMT, *Trials,* vol. 29, p. 361. Document 2233-PS.
163. Mallmann, "'Mißgeburten'" (2004), 74.
164. "Der Chef der Ordnungspolizei, O-Kdo. g 2 (01) Nr. 6 II/40(g.), Lagebericht [January 28, 1940]," T580, reel 96, NARA.
165. Browning, *Origins,* 31.
166. "Der Chef der Ordnungspolizei, O.-Kdo. g 2 (01) Nr. 6 II/40(g.) [January 28, 1940]," T580, reel 96, NARA; and "Der Chef der Ordnungspolizei, Der Aufbau der Ordnungspolizei für den Kriegseinsatz [August 20, 1940]," T580, reel 96, NARA.
167. Dieter Pohl, "Ukrainische Hilfskräfte beim Mord an den Juden," in *Die Täter der Shoah: Fanatische Nationalsozialisten oder ganz normale Deutsche?* ed. Gerhard Paul (Göttingen: Wallstein, 2002), 207.
168. Borodziej, *Terror und Politik,* 34.
169. Pohl, "Ukrainische Hilfskräfte," 211–219. See also Browning, *Ordinary Men,* 52.
170. *Das Recht des General Gouvernements,* 35–36.
171. "Der Inspekteur des Sonderdienstes, Der Sonderdienst im Generalgouvernement [June 1, 1944]," T501, reel 229, frame 65, NARA.
172. Breitman, *Architect,* 235.
173. IMT, *Trials,* vol. 29, p. 361. Document 2233-PS.
174. Hans Frank, *Hans Frank's Diary,* ed. and trans. Stanisław Piotrowski (Warsaw: Drukarnia Uniwersytetu im A. Mickiewicza, 1961), 224–225.
175. Browning, *Origins,* 34–35.
176. "III./Polizei-Regiment-Mitte, Bericht vom 16.2. bis 28.2.1942 [March 1, 1942]," RG 48.004M, reel 2, frame 201479, USHMMA.
177. "Der Chef der Ordnungspolizei, O.-Kdo. g 2 (01) Nr. 6 II/40(g.) [January 28, 1940]," T580, reel 96, NARA.
178. "Der Chef der Ordnungspolizei, O.-Kdo. g 2 (01) Nr. 6 II/40(g.) [January 28, 1940]," T580, reel 96, NARA.
179. "Der Chef der Ordnungspolizei, O.-Kdo. g 2 (01) Nr. 6 IX/40(g.), Lagebericht [May 15, 1940]," T501, reel 212, frames 898, 904, NARA.
180. "Der Chef der Ordnungspolizei, O.-Kdo. g 2 (01) Nr. 6 XI/40(g.), Lagebericht [May 31, 1940]," T501, reel 212, frames 1010, 1016, NARA. During the same period in the Reich district Wartheland, police forces arrested 1,130 persons with the intention of bringing them before the summary court, but not before shooting five outright for attempted escape or "opposition" (*Widerstand*).
181. "Der Chef der Ordnungspolizei, O.-Kdo. g 2 (01) Nr. 6 XII/40(g.), Lagebericht [June 15, 1940]," T501, reel 212, frames 1121, 1124, 1126, 1128, 1130, NARA.
182. Frank, *Hans Frank's Diary,* 227.

183. IMT, *Trials of the Major War Criminals before the International Military Tribunal*, vol. 12 (Nuremberg: Secretariat of the Military Tribunal, 1947), p. 38. Testimony of Hans Frank on April 18, 1946, before the International Military Tribunal.

184. Frank, *Hans Frank's Diary*, 228–229.

185. Lissance, *The Halder Diaries*, 1:565.

186. "Der Chef der Ordnungspolizei, O.-Kdo. g 2 (01) Nr. 6 XII/40(g.), Lagebericht [June 15, 1940]," T501, reel 212, frame 1121, NARA.

187. "Der Chef der Ordnungspolizei, O.-Kdo. g 2 (01) Nr. 6 XIV/40(g.), Lagebericht [June 30, 1940]," T501, reel 213, frame 82, NARA.

188. "Der Reichsführer SS- und Chef der Deutschen Polizei im Reichsministerium des Innern, O-Kdo. O (3) 1 Nr. 81/40, Betr.: Aufstellung von Pol.-Jagdzügen (Pol.-Jgd.-Zg.) zum Einsatz im Generalgouvernement [July 24, 1940]," T580, reel 97, NARA. Police Regiments Warsaw and Radom received two platoons each.

189. "Der Reichsführer SS- und Chef der Deutschen Polizei im Reichsministerium des Innern, O-Kdo. O (3) 1 Nr. 81/40, Betr.: Aufstellung von Pol.-Jagdzügen (Pol.-Jgd.-Zg.) zum Einsatz im Generalgouvernement [July 24, 1940]," T580, reel 97, NARA (emphasis added).

190. "BdO. 1a P. Sch. (9), Betr.: Aufstellung von Pol.-Jagdzügen zum Einsatz im Generalgouvernement [August 1, 1940]," T580, reel 97, NARA.

191. Broszat, *Polenpolitik*, 57.

Chapter 5. Crusade in the East

1. Gerhard Weinberg, *A World at Arms: A Global History of World War II* (Cambridge: Cambridge University Press, 1994), 264.

2. Edward B. Westermann, "Himmler's Uniformed Police on the Eastern Front, 1941–1942," *War in History* 3 (1996): 309.

3. "Die Ordnungspolizei jederzeit einsatzbereit! [February 13, 1941]," T580, reel 216, file 2, NARA. Speech by Daluege to the NSKK. See also "Nr.20 15.3.41 Tag der Deutschen Polizei, 1941, Rundfunkansprache über Einsatz der Ordn.Polizei [March 15, 1941]," R 19, file 382, BArch. Draft text of a radio address prepared for Daluege.

4. "Der Chef der Ordnungspolizei, Vortrag über den Kräfte- und Kriegseinsatz der Ordnungspolizei im Jahre 1941 [February 1942]," T580, reel 96, NARA. See also "Rede des Chefs der Ordnungspolizei bei der SS-Führertagung des RFSS, Der Winterkampf der Ordnungspolizei im Osten [1942]," T580, reel 217, file 6, NARA.

5. "Der Reichsführer SS und Chef der Deutschen Polizei im Reichsministerium des Innern, O-Kdo. I O (3) 1 Nr. 90/41, Betrifft: Umgliederung von Res.Pol.-Batl [April 26, 1941]," R 19, file 304, pp. 174–175, BArch. The completion date for this action was May 5, 1941.

6. Longerich, *Vernichtung*, 307. Police battalions in this group include the notorious units 307, 309, 310, and 322. For a more detailed demographic breakdown of a 300-level battalion, see Westermann, "'Ordinary Men' or 'Ideological Soldiers'?" 41–68.

7. Longerich, *Vernichtung*, 306, 307. Of the fifty-two reserve police battalions in existence at the beginning of 1941, thirty-one came from the ranks of the twenty-six-thousand-man replacement force released to the police in October 1939. See ibid., 662 n. 42. For example, in Reserve PB 61, ten of thirteen officers, or 76 percent,

belonged to the SS, and nine of thirteen, or 69 percent, held party membership. See Klemp, *"Mord-Bataillon,"* 29–30.

8. IMT, *Trials,* vol. 32, p. 73.

9. "Rede des Chefs der Ordnungspolizei bei der SS-Führertagung des RFSS, Der Winterkampf der Ordnungspolizei im Osten [1942]," T580, reel 217, file 6, NARA.

10. "Berlin RMDI Nr 494 10/7 1817 [July 10, 1941]," NS 19, file 1671, frame 14, BArch.

11. Mallmann, "Der qualitative Sprung im Vernichtungsprozeß," 241.

12. War diary of the Police Training Battalion-Vienna (PB 322) [July 9, 1941], RG 48.004M, reel 2, frame 200906, USHMMA.

13. Richard Breitman, *Official Secrets: What the Nazis Planned, What the British and Americans Knew* (New York: Hill & Wang, 1998), 63.

14. Breitman, *Official Secrets,* 59. See also Witte et al., eds., *Dienstkalender,* 188–189.

15. Jürgen Förster, "Operation Barbarossa as a War of Conquest and Annihilation," in *The Attack on the Soviet Union,* ed. Research Institute for Military History, trans. Dean S. McMurry, Ewald Osers, and Louise Wilmot (Oxford: Clarendon, 1998), 482.

16. Krausnick, *Einsatzgruppen,* 100–101. See also Förster, "Operation Barbarossa," 496–497 and Klein, ed. *Einsatzgruppen,* 365.

17. Lissance, ed., *The Halder Diaries,* 2:846.

18. Förster, "Operation Barbarossa," 496–507.

19. Peter Klein, ed., *Die Einsatzgruppen in der besetzten Sowjetunion, 1941/42: Die Tätigkeits- und Lageberichte des Chefs der Sicherheitspolizei und des SD* (Berlin: Druckhaus Hentrich, 1997), 367–368. This quote comes from a special report prepared for Himmler in the wake of Heydrich's meeting with Göring on March 26, 1941.

20. "Oberkommando des Heeres, Gen.St. d H/Gen.Qu, Abt.K.Verw. (Qu 4 B/org.), Nr. II/525/41 g.K., Betr.: Unterweisung über den vorgesehenen Einsatz [May 6, 1941]," NS 19, file 2818, fiche 1, frame 1, BArch.

21. Förster, "Operation Barbarossa," 501–502.

22. Krausnick, *Einsatzgruppen,* 121–178.

23. Klein, ed., *Einsatzgruppen,* 20–21.

24. Testimony of Hans K., 204 AR-Nr. 2356/1965, file 5, p. 613, ZStl. See also testimony of Georg H., 202 AR 165/61, file 1, p. 32, ZStl; and testimony of Gottfried K., 204 AR-Nr. 2356/1965, file 1, p. 198, ZStl.

25. Testimony of Walter K., 204 AR-Nr. 2356/1965, file 1, p. 81, ZStl.

26. Testimonies of Gottfried K., and Willi S., 204 AR-Nr. 2356/1965, file 1, pp. 210–212, 217, 247, ZStl.

27. Andrej Angrick, *Besatzungspolitik und Massenmord: Die Einsatzgruppe D in der südlichen Sowjetunion, 1941–1943* (Hamburg: Hamburger Edition, 2003), 394. I would like to thank Andrej Angrick for providing me with a personal copy of what will certainly become the standard work on Einsatzgruppe D.

28. Wildt, *Generation des Unbedingten,* 137–142.

29. Browning, *Ordinary Men,* 183.

30. Testimony of Hans K., 204 AR-Nr. 2356/1965, file 2, p. 128, ZStl. SS-Brigadeführer and Major General of the Police Dr. Otto Rasch was a man with two doctoral degrees. Hans K. contends that Rasch did not provide specifics of the forthcoming mission but did warn the men about the consequences of not following

orders. This type of testimony offers an example of a classic postwar defense strategy, members of the killing units never admitting to being told what actions they were about to commit or to being directly involved in executions, but noting at the same time that they had been threatened with severe consequences for not following orders that had yet to be given.

31. Testimony of Walter L., 204 AR-Nr. 2356/1965, file 1, p. 193, ZStl.

32. Angrick, *Besatzungspolitik,* 395–396.

33. IMT, *Trials of the Major War Criminals before the International Military Tribunal,* vol. 37 (Nuremberg: Secretariat of the Military Tribunal, 1949), p. 677. Document 180-L.

34. Testimonies of Herbert S. and Walter K., 204 AR-Nr. 2356/1965, file 2, pp. 84–85, 128, ZStl.

35. Testimony of Hermann R., 204 AR-Nr. 2356/1965, file 2, p. 159, ZStl.

36. Testimony of Georg B., 204 AR-Nr. 2356/1965, file 2, p. 175, ZStl.

37. Mallmann, Rieß, and Pyta, eds., *Deutscher Osten,* 132.

38. Testimony of Walter K., 204 AR-Nr. 2356/1965, file 1, pp. 86–87, ZStl.

39. Testimony of Erwin Z., 202 AR 165/61, file 1, p. 60, ZStl. See also testimony of Johannes F., 204 AR-Nr. 2356/1965, file 2, p. 33, ZStl. The statement of "having heard rumors of" (*vom Hörensagen*) executions appears repeatedly throughout the postwar testimony of men with the police battalions.

40. Klemp, *"Mord-Bataillon,"* 15.

41. Testimony of Erwin Z., 202 AR 165/61, file 1, pp. 61–62, ZStl. Interestingly, Zahn apparently realized the degree to which he had implicated himself and subsequently refused to sign the official copy of the protocol prepared following the interview.

42. Testimony of Johann H., 202 AR 165/61, file 1, pp. 77–78, ZStl.

43. Testimony of Erwin Z., 202 AR 165/61, file 1, p. 62, ZStl; testimony of Johann H., 202 AR 165/61, file 1, pp. 77–78, ZStl.

44. French L. MacLean, *The Field Men: The SS Officers Who Led the Einsatzkommandos—the Nazi Mobile Killing Units* (Atglen, Pa.: Schiffer Military History, 1999), 18–19.

45. Dieter Pohl, "Die Einsatzgruppe C," in Klein, ed., *Einsatzgruppen,* 73, 75.

46. Christian Gerlach, "Kontextualisierung der Aktionen eines Mordkommandos-die Einsatzgruppe B," in *Täter im Vernichtungskrieg: Der Überfall auf die Sowjetunion und der Völkermord an den Juden,* ed. Wolf Kaiser (Berlin: Propyläen, 2002), 88, 92.

47. Matthäus, "German Order Police," 135–136.

48. Investigation overview prepared by the German state prosecutor's office on September 10, 1968, 204 AR-Z 1251/65, file 2, pp. 370–373, ZStl. See also testimonies of Fritz F. and Ferdinand W., 204 AR-Z 1251/65, file 1, pp. 2, 28, ZStl.

49. Investigation overview prepared by the German state prosecutor's office on September 10, 1968, 204 AR-Z 1251/65, file 2, pp. 374–375, ZStl.

50. "Fernschreiben [August 22, 1941]," CSSR (Russland), file 147, p. 13, ZStl. See also investigation overview prepared by the German state prosecutor's office on September 10, 1968, 204 AR-Z 1251/65, file 2, pp. 374–375, ZStl.

51. Testimony of Fritz F., 204 AR-Z 1251/65, file 1, pp. 9, 2, 28, 7–8, 10, ZStl.

52. Testimony of Ferdinand W., 204 AR-Z 1251/65, file 1, pp. 31–32, ZStl.

53. Ibid., pp. 32, 33, 39.

54. Testimony of Walter G., 204 AR-Z 1251/65, file 1, pp. 46, 48, 51, ZStl.

55. Testimonies of Fritz F., and Ferdinand W., 204 AR-Z 1251/65, file 1, pp. 6, 19, 27, 33, ZStl.

56. Klemp, *"Mord-Bataillon,"* 23.

57. Testimony of Ferdinand W., 204 AR-Z 1251/65, file 1, p. 31, ZStl.

58. Testimony of Fritz F., 204 AR-Z 1251/65, file 1, pp. 13–15, ZStl. See also testimony of Ferdinand W., 204 AR-Z 1251/65, file 1, p. 33, ZStl.

59. Testimony of Ferdinand W., 204 AR-Z 1251/65, file 1, p. 35, ZStl.

60. "Sich.-Division, Abt Ia Nr. 444/41 geh. [June 19, 1941]," RH 26-221, file 11a, BArch.

61. Mallmann, Rieß, and Pyta, eds., *Deutscher Osten,* 70.

62. Testimony of Hubert H., 205 AR-Z 20/60, file 3, p. 862, ZStl., as cited in Mallmann, Rieß, and Pyta, eds., *Deutscher Osten,* 72.

63. Mallmann, Rieß, and Pyta, eds., *Deutscher Osten,* 70.

64. *Das Polizeibataillon 307 (Lübeck) "im Osteinsatz,"* 21.

65. Browning, *Ordinary Men,* 11.

66. *Das Polizeibataillon 307 (Lübeck) "im Osteinsatz,"* 21. See also Mallmann, Rieß, and Pyta, eds., *Deutscher Osten,* 71.

67. Testimony of former Lieutenant of the Police Heinrich Schneider, 205 AR-Z 20/60, file 2, pp. 463, 465, ZStl, as cited in Mallmann, Rieß, and Pyta, eds., *Deutscher Osten,* 71.

68. Mallmann, Rieß, and Pyta, eds., *Deutscher Osten,* 74.

69. "Sich. Division 221, Abt Ia [July 3, 1941]," RH 26-221, file 12a, BArch.

70. "Sich.-Division 221, Abt Ia [July 4, 1941]," RH 26-221, file 12a, BArch.

71. "Sich Division, Abt Ia, Betr.: Versprengte Truppen [July 5, 1941]," RH 26-221, file 12a, BArch.

72. "Sich. Division 221, Abt. Ia, Divisionsbefehl für den Einsatz der Sich. Division 221 im erweiterten rückw. Heeres-Geb. [July 11, 1941]," RH 26-221, file 12a, BArch.

73. "Der Höhere SS. u. Polizeiführer z.b.V. beim Befehlshaber d. rückw. H.-G. Mitte, Betr.: Säuberungsaktion in Brest [July 8, 1941]," RH 26-221, file 12a, BArch.

74. Witte et al., eds., *Dienstkalendar,* 183.

75. Angrick et al., "Da hätte man schon Tagebuch führen müssen," 334.

76. *Das Polizeibataillon 307 (Lübeck) "im Osteinsatz,"* 22–23.

77. Ibid., 23–24.

78. Browning, *Origins,* 258.

79. *Das Polizeibataillon 307 (Lübeck) "im Osteinsatz,"* 23–24.

80. Mallmann, "Der qualitative Sprung im Vernichtungsprozeß," 253; Klemp, *"Mord-Bataillon,"* 97; and Nechama Tec, *In the Lion's Den: The Life of Oswald Rufeisen* (Oxford: Oxford University Press, 1990), 120–121.

81. "Standorte, Pol. Batl. 307 [n.d.]," MfS-HA IX/11, RHE 48/76 SU, folder 1, pp. 000132–000149, Die Bundesbeauftragte für die Unterlagen des Staatssicherheitsdienstes der ehemaligen DDR. I would like to thank Ray Brandon for providing me with copies of these files.

82. *Das Polizeibataillon 307 (Lübeck) "im Osteinsatz,"* 17.

83. "Standorte, Pol. Batl. 307 [n.d.]," MfS-HA IX/11, RHE 48/76 SU, folder 1, pp. 000077, 000131–000132, Die Bundesbeauftragte für die Unterlagen des Staatssicherheitsdienstes der ehemaligen DDR. See also *Das Polizeibataillon 307 (Lübeck) "im Osteinsatz,"* 16–17.

84. Ben Sheperd, "Hawks, Doves, and Tote Zonen: A Wehrmacht Security Division in Central Russia, 1943," *Journal of Contemporary History* 37 (July 2002): 350.

85. "Der Befehlshaber des rückw. Heeres-Gebietes 102, Ia Br. B. Nr. 284/geh., Korpsbefehl Nr. 18 Betr.: Höh. SS- u. Polizei Führer [June 24, 1941]," RH 26-221, file 12b, BArch. See also "Der Befehlshaber des rückw. Heeres-Gebietes Mitte, Betr.: Abschnittseinteilung, diesseitiges Schreiben v. 18.8.41 [August 18, 1941]," RH 26-221, file 13b, BArch; "Der Befehlshaber des rückw. Heeres-Gebietes Mitte, Ia, Korpsbefehl Nr. 44 [August 23, 1941]," RH 26-221, file 13b, BArch; "SSD Fernschreiben 1 [August 20, 1941]," RH 26-221, file 13b, BArch; and "Heeresgruppe Mitte, Ib Nr. 1563/41 geh., Betr.: Rückw. Heeresgebiet und rückw. Armeegebiet [August 26, 1941]," RH 26-221, file 13b, BArch.

86. "Auszug aus dem Erfahrungsbericht der Sich. Div. 213 [September 1941]," RH 26-221, file 13a, BArch.

87. "Der Befehlshaber des rückw. Heeres-Gebietes Mitte, Ia [September 9, 1941]," RH 26-221, file 13a, BArch.

88. Weinberg, *World at Arms*, 264. For an excellent analysis of German motorized vs. horse-drawn capabilities, see Richard L. DiNardo, *Mechanized Juggernaut or Military Anachronism? Horses and the German Army of World War II* (New York: Greenwood, 1991).

89. "Der Chef des Kommando-Amtes [January 12, 1938]," R 19, file 460, p. 37, BArch. See also "Pol. O-VuR. Reich, Begründung [1940]," R 1501, file 5628, p. 11, BArch.

90. "Kommandostab RFSS, Abt. Ia, Tgb.-Nr. Ia 18/0/41 geh., Betrifft: Richtlinien für die Durchkämmung und Durchstreifung von Sumpfgebieten durch Reitereinheiten [July 28, 1941]," CSSR (Russland), file 147, pp. 59a–59d, ZStl.

91. "Der Chef der Ordnungspolizei, Kdo. I-Ia (1) 5 Nr. 5/41 [November 17, 1941]," T175, reel 3, frame 2503434, NARA.

92. "Sich-Division 221, Abt Ia, Divisionsbefehl [August 12, 1941]," RH 26-221, file 13b, BArch.

93. "Der Befehlshaber des rückw. Heeres-Gebietes Mitte, Ia, Korpsbefehl Nr. 54 [September 19, 1941]," RH 26-221, file 13a, BArch. These instructions followed on the heels of guidelines issued by the army High Command on September 13, 1941.

94. "Der Kommandeur der Gendarmerie, Zhitomir, Kommandobefehl Nr. 18/42 [June 6, 1942]," RG 53.002M. fond 658, file 2, USHMMA.

95. Streit, *Kameraden*, 107–108.

96. Witte et al., eds., *Dienstkalender*, 294.

97. Lichtenstein, *Himmlers grüne Helfer*, 178.

98. Martin Dean, "The German Gendarmerie, the Ukrainian Schutzmannschaft, and the 'Second Wave' of Jewish Killings in Occupied Ukraine: German Policing at the Local Level in the Zhitomir Region, 1941–1944," *German History* 14 (1996): 181.

99. "Der Chef der Ordnungspolizei, Kdo. I g Ia (1) Nr. 127/41 (g.) [January 5, 1942]," UdSSR, file 245 Ac, p. 572, ZStl.

100. "Der Kommandeur der Gendarmerie, Zhitomir, Kommandobefehl Nr. 18/42 [June 6, 1942]," RG 53.002M. fond 658, file 2, USHMMA.

101. "Tagesbefehl Nr. 13, Waffengebrauch der Polizei gegenüber flüchtigen Kriegsgefangenen [August 28, 1942]," RG 53.002M, fond 389, reel 3, file 1, USHMMA.

102. Yehoshua Büchler, "Kommandostab Reichsführer-SS: Himmler's Personal Murder Brigades in 1941," *Holocaust and Genocide Studies* 1 (1986): 14.

103. "1. SS-Brigade, Tätigkeitsbericht für die Zeit vom 27.7.41/12.00 Uhr-30.7.41/12.00 Uhr [July 30, 1941]," CSSR (Russland), file 147, pp. 1–2, ZStl.

104. "1. SS-Brigade, Tätigkeitsbericht für die Zeit vom 6.8.41/12.00 Uhr-10.8.41/12.00 Uhr [August 1941]," CSSR (Russland), file 147, p. 3, ZStl; and "Funkspruch, 1.SS-Brig [August 9, 1941]," CSSR (Russland), file 147, p. 4, ZStl.

105. "Fernschreiben, von Pol.Praes.Berlin [August 19, 1941]," CSSR (Russland), file 147, p. 7, ZStl; and "Fernschreiben [August 19, 1941]," CSSR (Russland), file 147, p. 8, ZStl.

106. "Fernschreiben [August 20, 1941]," CSSR (Russland), file 147, p. 10, ZStl.

107. "Fernschreiben [August 21, 1941]," CSSR (Russland), file 147, p. 14, ZStl.

108. "Fernschreiben [August 22, 1941]," CSSR (Russland), file 147, p. 13, ZStl.

109. "Fernschreiben [August 24, 1941]," CSSR (Russland), file 147, pp. 17, ZStl; and "Funkspruch [August 24, 1941]," CSSR (Russland), file 147, p. 19, ZStl.

110. "Fernschreiben [August 25, 1941]," CSSR (Russland), file 147, p. 22, ZStl.

111. "Funkspruch [August 27, 1941]," CSSR (Russland), file 147, p. 25, ZStl; and "Fernschreiben [August 27, 1941]," CSSR (Russland), file 147, p. 24, ZStl.

112. "Kommandostab RF-SS, Abt Ia, Betrifft: Bericht des Kdo.Stabes RF-SS über die Tätigkeit für die Zeit vom 28.7. bis 3.8.1941 einschl. [August 6, 1941]," CSSR (Russland), file 147, p. 77, ZStl.

113. Mallmann, "Fußvolk," 355.

114. Former collection of the BDC, Hermann Franz (16.8.91). See also Hermann Franz file, RG 242, SSO 219, frames 618, 632–633, NARA. Franz was also a several-time champion of the police pentathlon competition in the state of Saxony.

115. State prosecutor's overview of police atrocity, 204 AR-Z 1251/65, file 1, pp. 1–5, 253, ZStl.

116. Browning, *Origins,* 292. See also letter of German State Prosecutor [May 11, 1965], State prosecutor's overview, 204 AR-Z 1251/65, file 1, p. 6, ZStl.

117. "Verzeichnis der namentlich bekannten Angehörigen des Pol. Rgt. Süd (Pol. Rgt. bzw. SS-Pol-Rgt 10), die aus Österreich stammen, früher dort wohnhaft waren oder dort ihren Heimatsstandort hatten und für die der Aufenthalt noch nicht ermittelt wurde," 204 AR-Z 1251/65, file 1, pp. 139–178, ZStl.

118. Examples include testimonies of Alfred S., Ferdinand W., Johann P., Josef S., Johann L., Anton M., Johann S., Franz H., and Werner F., 204 AR-Z 1251/65, file 1, pp. 31, 33, 37, 45, 51, 62, 65, 73, 81, ZStl.

119. Testimonies of Johann L., and Karl G., 204 AR-Z 1251/65, file 1, pp. 52, 94, ZStl.

120. Testimony of Johann L., 204 AR-Z 1251/65, file 1, pp. 52–53, ZStl.

121. Ibid., p. 53.

122. Testimony of Franz P., 204 AR-Z 1251/65, file 1, pp. 58–59, ZStl.

123. Ibid., pp. 59–60.

124. Letter from the German State Prosecutor's Office [May 11, 1965], 204 AR-Z 1251/65, file 1, p. 18, ZStl.

125. Testimonies of Franz P. and Anton M., 204 AR-Z 1251/65, file 1, pp. 60, 62, ZStl.

126. Testimonies of Franz H., Alfred K., and Johann P., 204 AR-Z 1251/65, file 1, pp. 74–75, 78–80, ZStl.

127. Testimonies of Johann L. and Karl S., 204 AR-Z 1251/65, file 1, pp. 52, 104, ZStl.

128. See Christian Gerlach, *Kalkulierte Morde: Die deutsche Wirtschafts- und Vernichtungspolitik in Weißrußland, 1941 bis 1944* (Hamburg: Hamburger Edition, 1999). Daluege later highlighted the key role played by the police battalions in the expropriation of foodstuffs in the occupied East and praised the efforts of one police regiment that alone confiscated 900,000 tons of produce (see "Der Chef der Ordnungspolizei, Dienstbesprechung der Befehlshaber und Inspekteure der Ordnungspolizei im Januar 1943 in Berlin [February 1, 1943]," T175, reel 3, frame 2503392, NARA).

129. "II./Pol. 25, Sonderanordnung, Betrifft: Konzentrisches Säuberungsverfahren [August 25, 1942]," RG 15.011M, reel 2, file 276, USHMMA.

130. David Glantz, *Barbarossa: Hitler's Invasion of Russia, 1941* (Stroud: Tempus, 2001), 185–203.

131. Lissance, ed., *The Halder Diaries,* 2:1344, 1349.

132. Krausnick, *Einsatzgruppen,* 119.

133. "Rede des Chefs der Ordnungspolizei bei der SS-Führertagung des RFSS, Der Winterkampf der Ordnungspolizei im Osten [1942]," T580, reel 217, file 6, NARA.

134. "Der Chef der Ordnungspolizei, Bericht des Chefs der Ordnungspolizei, SS-Oberst-Gruppenführer und Generaloberst Daluege, Kräfte- und Kriegseinsatz der Ordnungspolizei im Kriegsjahre 1942 [February 1, 1943]," T175, reel 3, frame 2503384, NARA.

135. Ahlrich Meyer, *Die deutsche Besatzung in Frankreich, 1940–1944: Widerstandsbekämpfung und Judenverfolgung* (Darmstadt: Wissenschaftliche Buchgesellschaft, 2000), 115–127.

136. "Der Chef der Ordnungspolizei, Vortrag über den Kräfte- und Kriegseinsatz der Ordnungspolizei im Jahre 1941 [February 1942]," T580, reel 96, NARA.

137. "Der Chef der Ordnungspolizei, Bericht des Chefs der Ordnungspolizei, SS-Oberst-Gruppenführer und Generaloberst Daluege, Kräfte- und Kriegseinsatz der Ordnungspolizei im Kriegsjahre 1942 [February 1, 1943]," T175, reel 3, frame 2503390, NARA.

138. "Rede des Chefs der Ordnungspolizei bei der SS-Führertagung des RFSS, Der Winterkampf der Ordnungspolizei im Osten [1942]," T580, reel 217, file 6, NARA.

139. "Der Chef der Ordnungspolizei, Bericht des Chefs der Ordnungspolizei, SS-Oberst-Gruppenführer und Generaloberst Daluege, Kräfte- und Kriegseinsatz der Ordnungspolizei im Kriegsjahre 1942 [February 1, 1943]," T175, reel 3, frame 2503384, NARA; "Rede des Chefs der Ordnungspolizei bei der SS-Führertagung des RFSS, Der Winterkampf der Ordnungspolizei im Osten [1942]," T580, reel 217, file 6, NARA. By the end of 1941, the total included 1 Knight's Cross, almost 800 Iron Crosses, more than 1,000 War Service Crosses, 308 wound badges, and 201 combat infantry badges.

140. Personal letter from Daluege to Himmler [December 8, 1942], R 19, file 390, p. 87, BArch.

141. Alexander Dallin, *German Rule in Russia, 1941–1945: A Study of Occupation Policies* (Boulder, Colo.: Westview, 1981), 209. See also "Rede des Chefs der Ordnungspolizei bei der SS-Führertagung des RFSS, Der Winterkampf der Ordnungspolizei im Osten [1942]," T580, reel 217, file 6, NARA.

142. Leonid D. Grenkevich, *The Soviet Partisan Movement, 1941–1944* (London: Frank Cass, 1999), 205, 207–208.

143. Steinhoff, Pechel, and Showalter, *Voices,* 269–270.

144. Testimony of Erwin L., 208 AR-Z 30/62, file 1 p. 108, ZStl.

145. Ibid., pp. 41–43, 52, 55–56.

146. "Der Reichsführer SS und Chef der Deutschen Polizei im Reichsministerium des Innern, O.-Kdo. G 2 (o 1) Nr. 259/41 (g.), Betr.: 'SS- und Polizeistandortführer' in den rückwärtigen Heeresgebieten als Beauftragte der Höheren SS- und Polizeiführer [August 2, 1941]," R 19, file 333, p. 5, BArch.

147. "Der Kommandant in Weissruthenien des Wehrmachtbefehlshaber Ostland, Befehl Nr. 21 [November 18, 1941]," RG 53.002M, file 698, USHMMA.

148. "Der Kommandeur der Ordnungspolizei im Distrikt Lublin, Ia 1002 [July 18, 1941]," RG 15.011M, reel 21, frame 279, USHMMA.

149. Lissance, ed., *The Halder Diaries*, 2:1355. The number excludes medical casualties.

150. "Oberkommando des Heeres, Gen St d H/Gen Qu, Abt. K.Vers. (Qu 4 B), Nr. II/519/42 g.Kdos., Betr.: Partis. Bekämpfung bei H.Gr. Nord [March 28, 1942]," NS 19, reel 1671, frame 155, BArch.

151. "Der Reichsführer-SS, Tgb. Nr. 1167/42 geh. Rs. [March 31, 1942]," NS 19, reel 1671, frame 156, BArch. This letter is marked "Geheime Reichssache" and was limited to six controlled copies.

152. "Der Kommandierende General der Sicherungstruppen und Befh. im Heeres-gebiet Mitte, Ia Br. B. Nr. 632/42 g. Kdos., Grundlegender Befehl Nr. 1 [October 30, 1942]," NS 19, reel 1671, frames 161–163, BArch.

153. "Der Höhere SS- u. Polizeiführer Rußland Mitte, Abtlg. Ia Tgb. Nr. 1196/42 g.Rs., Betr.: Abschrift eines Befehls [November 2, 1942]," NS 19, reel 1671, frame 164, BArch.

154. Truman Anderson, "Incident at Baranivka: German Reprisals and the Soviet Partisan Movement in Ukraine, October–December 1941," *Journal of Modern History* 71 (September 1999): 602, 621.

155. "Der Kommandant in Weissruthenien des Wehrmachtbefehlshaber Ostland, Abt. Ia, Befehl Nr. 24 [November 24, 1941]," RG 53.002M, file 698, USHMMA.

156. "+RVST BLN NR 889 5/3 1518, Betr.: Lage im Reichskommissariat Ukraine [March 5, 1942]," NS 19, reel 1671, frame 11, BArch.

157. "Einsatzbericht d. Torn.Fu. B I vom 8.6.43 bis 10.6.1943 [June 10, 1943]," RG 15.011M, reel 21, frame 278, USHMMA. See also "Der Reichsführer-SS, Kommandostab, Abt. Ia, Tgb.Nr. Ia 490/42 g.Kdos, Netr.: Unterdrückung der Banden-tätigkeit in Weißruthenien [August 7, 1942]," NS 19, reel 1671, frame 88, BArch.

158. "Der Kdeur.d.Gend.Shitomir, Gend.Hauptmschft.Mosyr, Haupt-mannschaftsbefehl Nr. 3 [September 15, 1942]," RG 53.002M, fond 658, reel 5, file 3, USHMMA.

159. "Der Reichminister für die besetzten Ostgebiete, II 1 d 963/42 GRs, Betr.: Verstärkte Bekämpfung des Bandenunwesens in den besetzten Ostgebieten [August 25, 1942]," NS 19, reel 1671, frame 110, BArch.

160. IMT, *Trials of the Major War Criminals before the International Military Tribunal*, vol. 35 (Nuremberg: Secretariat of the Military Tribunal, 1949), p. 408. Document 729-D.

161. "Oberkommando der Wehrmacht, Nr. 0025 2/42 g.K./WFST/Qu(II), Betr.: Partisanenbekaempfung [July 23, 1942]," NS 19, file 1671, pp. 81–82, BArch. See also "Der Reichminister für die besetzten Ostgebiete, II 1 d 963/42 GRs, Betr.: Verstärkte Bekämpfung des Bandenunwesens in den besetzten Ostgebieten [August 25, 1942]," NS 19, reel 1671, frame 110, BArch.

162. Personal letter from von dem Bach to Himmler [September 5, 1942], NS 19, reel 1671, frames 118–119, BArch.

163. "Kommandostab RF-SS, Abt. Ia, TgbNr. Ia 567/42 geh., Betr.: Führung in der Bandenbekämpfung [July 28, 1942]," NS 19, reel 1671, frame 77, BArch.

164. "Befehlshaber der Ordnungspolizei, Alpenland, Befehlsstelle Veldes, Tagesbefehl Nr. 27 [July 31, 1942]," RG 48.004M, reel 2, frames 201615–201616, USHMMA.

165. "Der Reichsführer SS, Chef des SS-Hauptamtes, VS-Nr. 2140/42, Entwurf [June 17, 1942]," Kurt Daluege file, former collection of the BDC. In this letter, Berger asked for permission to comb German prisons for convicted poachers in order to create a special antipartisan detachment modeled after the notorious Sonderkommando Dirlewanger.

166. "Der Reichsführer-SS, Kommandostab, Abt. Ia, Tgb.Nr. Ia 490/42 g.Kdos, Betr.: Unterdrückung der Bandentätigkeit in Weißruthenien [August 7, 1942]," NS 19, reel 1671, frames 87–88, BArch. See also "Der Reichsführer-SS, Kommandostab, Abt. Ia, Tgb.Nr. Ia 491/42 g.Kdos, Betr.: Unterdrückung der Bandentätigkeit in Bialystock [sic] [August 7, 1942]," NS 19, reel 1671, frames 90–91, BArch.

167. "Der Höhere SS- und Polizeiführer im Wehrkreis XVIII, Befehlsstelle Veldes [July 27, 1942]," RG 48.004M, reel 2, frames 201605–201606, USHMMA.

168. "Der Reichminister für die besetzten Ostgebiete, II 1 d 963/42 GRs, Betr.: Verstärkte Bekämpfung des Bandenunwesens in den besetzten Ostgebieten [August 25, 1942]," NS 19, reel 1671, frame 110, BArch.

169. "Der Kdeur.d.Gend.Shitomir, Gend.Hauptmschft.Mosyr, Hauptmannschaftsbefehl Nr. 3 [September 15, 1942]," RG 53.002M, fond 658, reel 5, file 3, USHMMA.

170. "Sicherungsabschnitt Mitte, Ia, Befehl Nr. 1, Anlage 5 [August 13, 1942]," RG 15.011M, reel 2, file 276, USHMMA.

171. "Der Chef der Ordnungspolizei, Betr.: Heranziehung des Einzeldienstes der Ordnungspolizei zur Durchführung von Exekutionen [January 13, 1942]," RG 06.025.63, KGB Archive Box 59, USHMMA. I would like to thank Dieter Pohl for bringing this document to my attention.

172. Westermann, "Himmler's Uniformed Police on the Eastern Front," 326.

173. "1. Gend.-Btl. (mot.), Einsatzbericht über den Einsatz des 1.Gend.-Batl. (mot.) am 19.9.1942 im Raume Drelow, 10 km südostwärts Miedzyrzec [September 20, 1942]," RG 15.011M, reel 21, file 276, USHMMA.

174. Ibid.

175. Westermann, "'Ordinary Men' or 'Ideological Soldiers'?" 59.

176. "II./Pol. 15, Ergebnisbericht über die Aktion in den Dörfern Chmielisce und Oltusz-Lesnia [October 24, 1942]," UdSSR, folder 412, pp. 847–848, ZStl.

177. Westermann, "'Ordinary Men' or 'Ideological Soldiers'?" 61.

178. Ibid.

179. Ibid.

180. "Der Reichminister für die besetzten Ostgebiete, II 1 d 963/42 GRs, Betr.: Verstärkte Bekämpfung des Bandenunwesens in den besetzten Ostgebieten [August 25, 1942]," NS 19, reel 1671, frame 111, BArch.

181. Browning, *Origins,* 274.

182. "Der Chef der Ordnungspolizei, Vortrag über den Kräfte- und Kriegseinsatz der Ordnungspolizei im Jahre 1941 [February 1942]," T580, reel 96, NARA. See also Pohl, "Ukrainische Hilfskräfte," 210.

183. Tessin, "Stäbe und Truppeneinheiten," 56. See also Tec, *Oswald Rufeisen*, 85.

184. "Der Chef der Ordnungspolizei, Vortrag über den Kräfte- und Kriegseinsatz der Ordnungspolizei im Jahre 1941 [February 1942]," T580, reel 96, NARA. At the end of 1941, Daluege estimated that there were a total of 31,652 auxiliaries in the *Reichkommissariat Ostland* and 14,452 in the *Reichkommissariat Ukraine*.

185. Browning, *Origins*, 274–275. See also Pohl, "Ukrainische Hilfskräfte," 211.

186. Ronald Headland, *Messages of Murder: A Study of the Reports of the Einsatzgruppen of the Security Police and the Security Service, 1941–1943* (Rutherford, N.J.: Fairleigh Dickinson University Press, 1992), 59. See also Pohl, "Ukrainische Hilfskräfte," 212.

187. Dean, "German Gendarmerie," 179.

188. Browning, *Origins*, 274.

189. Ibid., 274. See also Browning, *Ordinary Men*, 158.

190. Tec, *Oswald Rufeisen*, 64–65, 80.

191. "Der Reichsführer SS und Chef der Deutschen Polizei im Reichsministerium des Innern, O.-Kdo. I O (1) Nr. 443/42, Betr.: Vereidigung der Schutzmannschaft [August 31, 1942]," R 19, file 304, p. 222, BArch. See also Dean, "German Gendarmerie," 179.

192. "Polizeilicher Lagebericht für die Zeit vom 1. bis 15.9.1942 [September 1942]," RG 53.002M, fond 658, reel 5, file 1, USHMMA.

193. Ruth Bettina Birn, "'Zaunkönig' an 'Uhrmacher': Große Partisanenaktionen 1942/43 am Beispiel des 'Unternehmens Winterzauber,'" *Militärgeschichtliche Zeitschrift* 60 (2001): 104–105, 111.

194. "Der Höhere SS- und Polizeiführer für das Ostland und Rußland Nord, Führungsstab, IA, Befehl über Abschluß des Unternehmens 'Winterzauber' [March 30, 1943]," UdSSR, file 245 Af, pp. 161–164, 191, ZStl. The high number of transferred persons is a direct reflection of the orders given to the policemen at the start of the operation.

195. Birn, "'Zaunkönig' an 'Uhrmacher,'" 115. Birn also discusses another report listing 137 enemy combatant deaths, 51 arrests, and 1,807 executions of "suspects." While acknowledging the role of the German police leadership, Birn emphasizes the role of the auxiliaries in the executions conducted by the police forces.

196. Testimony of Erwin Z., 202 AR 165/61, file 1, pp. 62–63, ZStl.

197. Testimony of Johann H., 202 AR 165/61, file 1, p. 80, ZStl.

198. Tec, *Oswald Rufeisen*, 89.

199. Tec, *Oswald Rufeisen*, 94–95.

200. "Der Chef der Ordnungspolizei, Vortrag über den Kräfte- und Kriegseinsatz der Ordnungspolizei im Jahre 1941 [February 1942]," T580, reel 96, NARA.

201. "Rede des Chefs der Ordnungspolizei bei der SS-Führertagung des RFSS, Der Winterkampf der Ordnungspolizei im Osten [1942]," T580, reel 217, file 6, NARA.

Chapter 6. The Face of Occupation

1. Henry Picker, *Hitlers Tischgespräche im Führerhauptquartier* (Frankfurt a.M.: Ullstein, 1993), 62.

2. Norbert Müller, ed., *Die faschistische Okkupationspolitik in den zeitweilig besetzten Gebieten der Sowjetunion (1941–1944)* (Berlin: Deutscher Verlag der Wissenschaften, 1991), 164–166.

3. Dallin, *German Rule*, 85–86, 91–94.

4. "Der Chef der Ordnungspolizei, Vortrag über den Kräfte- und Kriegseinsatz der Ordnungspolizei im Jahre 1941 [February 1942]," T580, reel 96, NARA.

5. Ibid.

6. Matthäus, "German Order Police," 136.

7. Dean, "German Gendarmerie," 180. See also Wendy Lower, "Der 'reibungslose' Holocaust? Nazi Implementation of the Holocaust in Ukraine, 1941–1944," in *Networks of Nazi Persecution: Bureaucracy, Business, and the Organization of the Holocaust*, ed. Gerald Feldman and Wolfgang Seibel (New York: Berghahn, 2004). I would like to thank Wendy Lower for providing me with a copy of her manuscript prior to its publication.

8. Picker, *Hitlers Tischgespräche*, 62. See also Tec, *Oswald Rufeisen*, 74, 85.

9. "Abschlussbericht der Zentralestelle der Landesjustizverwaltungen," 204 AR-Z 1251/65, file 1, pp. 223–226, ZStl.

10. "An den Kommandeur der Gendarmerie Weißruthenien in Minsk, Betrifft: Bereinigung des Gebiets von Juden [August 26, 1942]," UdSSR, file 245c, p. 90, ZStl. See also Matthäus, "German Order Police," 138, 148.

11. Dean, "German Gendarmerie," 184–185.

12. "Abschlussbericht der Zentralestelle der Landesjustizverwaltungen," 204 AR-Z 1251/65, file 1, pp. 220–225, 253–254, ZStl.

13. Tec, *Oswald Rufeisen*, 161.

14. Dean, "German Gendarmerie," 185.

15. "1. Gendarmerie-Batallion (mot.), Einsatzbericht über den Einsatz des 1.Gend-Batl.(mot.) in der Zeit vom 19. bis 22.8.1942 im Sicherungsabschnitt Leczna [August 23, 1942]," RG 15.011M, reel 21, file 276, USHMMA.

16. Ibid.

17. Ibid.

18. "1. Gend-Batl (mot.), Einsatzbericht über den Einsatz des 1.Gend.-Batl. (mot.) in der Zeit vom 26. bis 28.8.1942 im Sicherungsabschnitt nordwestl. Wlodawa [August 29, 1942]," RG 15.011M, reel 21, file 276, USHMMA. The total of those killed given for the second day of this action is forty-three, although only thirty-five persons are listed. It therefore seems likely that seven persons were killed during the five reprisal measures listed on the same day.

19. "Funktrupp a (mot), Zugwachtm.Windelen, Bericht über den Einsatz des gr. Pol.-Funktrupp a (mot) vom 19.9.42 [September 22, 1942]," RG 15.011M, reel 21, file 277, USHMMA; and "1. Gend.-Btl (mot.), Ereignismeldung [September 30, 1942]," RG 15.011M, reel 21, file 276, USHMMA.

20. Untitled activity report by a police signals section attached to Gendarmerie Battalion 1 [November 18, 1942], RG 15.011M, reel 21, file 277, USHMMA.

21. "Der Kommandeur des I.Gend.-Batl.(mot.) [December 8, 1942]," RG 15.011M, reel 20, file 275, USHMMA.

22. Matthäus, "German Order Police," 138.

23. Dean, "German Gendarmerie," 187.

24. "Der Reichsführer SS und Chef der Deutschen Polizei im Reichsministerium des Innern, O.-Kdo. G 2 (o 4) Nr. 25II/43 (g), Betr.: Beschäftigung von Vertrauensleuten bei der Gendarmerie [October 4, 1943]," T175, reel 277, frames 5488979–5488980, NARA. Himmler also noted that informants who provided political information only should be handed over to the Security Police.

25. "1. Gend-Batl (mot.), Einsatzbericht über den Einsatz des 1.Gend.-Batl. (mot.) in der Zeit vom 26. bis 28.8.1942 im Sicherungsabschnitt nordwestl. Wlodawa [August 29, 1942]," RG 15.011M, reel 21, file 276, USHMMA.

26. Personal letter from Fritz Jacob to Querner [June 21, 1942], Rudolf Querner file, former collection of the BDC.

27. "Abschrift, Betrifft: Judenaktion in Stolpce [October 18, 1942]," UdSSR, file 245c, p. 79, ZStl.

28. "Der Kommandeur der Ordnungspolizei im Distrikt Lublin, Ia, Betr: Besprechung am 27.1.1943, 09.00 Uhr, beim SS- und Polizeiführer Lublin [January 27, 1943]," 208 AR-Z 80/60, file 2, p. 349, ZStl.

29. Matthäus, "German Order Police," 143.

30. Letter from Daluege to Winkelmann [October 8, 1942], T580, reel 221, file 63, NARA.

31. "Der Reichsführer-SS und Chef der Deutschen Polizei im Reichsministerium des Innern, O-VuR. PBG. 4409/41, Betr.: Vermerk 'Ungeeignet für den Osteinsatz' [October 8, 1942]," Verschiedenes, file 117, pp. 132–133, ZStl.

32. "Der Reichsführer-SS und Chef der Deutschen Polizei im Reichsministerium des Innern, O-VuR. PBG. 4315/41, Betr.: Verwendung von polnisch versippten Pol.- und SD Angehörigen in den eingegliederten Ostgebieten und im Generalgouverne-ment [July 20, 1942]," R 19, file 74, p. 131, BArch.

33. "Der Kommandeur der Ordnungspolizei im Distrikt Lublin, II a/b [March 13, 1943]," RG 15.011M, reel 20, file 274, USHMMA. This document contains an order forwarded under Daluege's signature with the following subject line: "Ver-wendung von polnisch versippten Angehörigen der Ordnungspolizei in den eingegliederten Ostgebieten und im Generalgouvernment [March 8, 1943]."

34. Hilberg, *Destruction*, 1:72. Several additional factors pertained to *Mischlinge* that might result in their classification as Jews, including religious observance and marriage to a Jew.

35. Bryan Mark Rigg, *Hitler's Jewish Soldiers: The Untold Story of Nazi Racial Laws and Men of Jewish Descent in the German Military* (Lawrence: University Press of Kansas, 2002), 1. For a detailed demographic discussion of the *Mischlinge* in Nazi Germany, see Jeremy Noakes, "The Development of Nazi Policy towards the Ger-man-Jewish 'Mischlinge,' 1933–1945," in *Holocaust: Critical Concepts in Histori-cal Studies,* vol. 1, *Hitler, Nazism, and the "Racial State,"* ed. David Cesarani (London: Routledge, 2004), 239–311.

36. "Referat O.-VuR.5, Zu O.-VuR P BG 2161/38 [June 3, 1939]," R 19, file 74, p. 1, BArch.

37. Personal letter from H. J. G. to Rudolf Querner, August 28, 1939, former collection of the BDC, ORPO A 417 (H. J. von Gundlach), BArch. It is clear from this letter that Gundlach sought to reenter the officer ranks to participate in the loom-ing war with Poland.

38. "Der Kommandeur der Ordnungspolizei im Distrikt Lublin, II b, 20 02 [November 18, 1942]; Abschrift, Der Reichsführer SS und Chef der Deutschen Polizei im Reichsministerium des Innern, O-Kdo. I RV(1) 1 nr. 456/42, Betr.: Jüdisch Ver-sippte in der Polizei-Reserve [October 27, 1942]," RG 15.011M, reel 20, file 275, USHMMA. In addition, *Mischlinge* of the second degree accepted for duty within the police were required to sign a statement affirming that they had only one Jewish grandparent.

39. Browning, *Origins,* 33.

40. Tec, *Oswald Rufeisen,* 74–75, 85.

41. Ibid., 89, 102.

42. Lower, "Der 'reibungslose' Holocaust?" 250.

43. "Gend.-Außenposten 'Mir', Gend.-Kreis Baranowitschi, Generalbezirk Weißruthenien, Betr.: Ergreifung 6 geflüchteter Juden und standrechtliche Erschiessung derselben [October 1, 1942]," UdSSR, file 245c, p. 86, ZStl.

44. Wildt, *Generation des Unbedingten,* 156.

45. "Abschrift, Betrifft: Judenaktion in Stolpce [October 18, 1942]," UdSSR, file 245c, p. 79, ZStl. This report is signed by Hauptwachtmeister der Schutzpolizei Schultz, who, given the rank, location, and date, appears to have been Karl Schultz.

46. Tec, *Oswald Rufeisen,* 93, 103, 121–122. Rufeisen noted that the gendarmes came from across Germany, including one man from Holland, and that most were over forty years old.

47. Testimony of Morris Trost, 208 AR-Z 80/60, file 1, p. 35, ZStl; and testimony of Ernst S., 208 AR-Z 80-60, file 2, p. 415, ZStl. See also State prosecutor's letter on the investigation of former gendarmes [March 7, 1961], 208 AR-Z 80/60, file 1, pp. 256–257, ZStl.

48. Testimony of Morris Trost, 208 AR-Z 80/60, file 1, pp. 36–37, ZStl.

49. Report prepared by the state prosecutor summarizing the testimony of twenty individual eyewitnesses interviewed during a trip to Israel, 208 AR-Z 80/60, file 1, pp. 123–127, ZStl.

50. Testimony of Franz R., 208 AR-Z 80/60, file 1, pp. 92–93, ZStl.

51. Report of the German state prosecutor, dated March 7, 1961, 208 AR-Z 80/60, file 1, pp. 256–257, ZStl.

52. *The Schupo War Criminals of Stryj* (n.p., n.d.), 1–42. Copies of the testimonies of the former members of the police post in Stryj conducted by the State Police of Vienna in 1947. Holding of the USHMM library in Washington, D.C. The testimonies place the number of policemen at the post in Stryj between sixteen and twenty.

53. Ibid., 32. Testimony of Johann Schaffner, October 15, 1947.

54. Ibid., 21. Testimony of Max Preuer, October 15, 1947.

55. Ibid., 6, 9, 12, 22, 28, 30, 33–34.

56. Ibid., 37. Testimony of Franz Venhoda, October 8, 1947.

57. Ibid., 7. Testimony of Alexander Garber, October 16, 1947.

58. Ibid., 12. Testimony of Johann Kranzler, October 18, 1947.

59. Ibid., 4–5. Testimony of Josef Christament, October 17, 1947.

60. Ibid., 22. Testimony of Maximilian Preuer, October 15, 1947.

61. Ibid., 7–8. Testimony of Alexander Garber, October 16, 1947.

62. Ibid., 34. Testimony of Johann Schaffner, October 15, 1947.

63. Ibid., 16. Testimony of Johann Pflamitzer, October 3, 1947.

64. Ibid., 34. Testimony of Johann Schaffner, October 15, 1947.

65. Tuviah Friedman, ed., *Schupo-Kriegsverbrecher in Kolomea* (Vienna: Jewish Historical Documentation Center, 1990), 3, 10, 18.

66. Westermann, "'Ordinary Men' or "Ideological Soldiers'?" 47–48.

67. Kohl, *Krieg,* 230–231, 233–234.

68. Ibid., 233–234.

69. UdSSR, file 412, p. 836, ZStl (emphasis added). The police executed an additional five persons found hiding in the village.

70. Ibid., p. 837.

71. "Fernschreiben, Führer-Hauptquartier [July 26, 1941]," T580, reel 19, files 59–60, NARA.

72. UdSSR, file 412, pp. 597–598, 762, ZStl.

73. UdSSR, file 412, pp. 944–945, ZStl.

74. Westermann, "'Ordinary Men'" or 'Ideological Soldiers'?" 56.

75. "11./Pol. 15, Lage- und Tätigkeitsbericht der 11./Pol. 15 für die Zeit vom 5.10. bis 11.10.42 [October 11, 1942]," UdSSR, file 412, pp. 844–846, ZStl.

76. Ibid.

77. "Lage- und Tätigkeitsbericht der 11. Pol. 15 für die Zeit vom 12. bis 18.10.42," UdSSR, file 412, ZStl.

78. Kohl, *Krieg,* 276 n. 16.

79. Testimony of Fritz L., 204 AR-Z 12/61, file 1, pp. 2–5, ZStl.

80. Testimony of Schmidt's ex-wife, 204 AR-Z 12/61, file 1, pp. 29–30, ZStl.

81. Testimony of Fritz L., 204 AR-Z 12/61, file 1, pp. 2–5, ZStl.

82. "Zahlenmässige Nachweisung über die Zugehörigkeit zur NSDAP und Gliederungen der Partei [October 1940]," UdSSR, file 412, p. 691, ZStl.

83. "Polizei-Bataillon 310, II a/b, 20 20/41, Betr. Erfassung der Mitglieder der NSDAP [January 12, 1941]," UdSSR, file 412, p. 823, ZStl.

84. "Verwaltung, Betrifft: Namentliche Listen der SS Angehörigen [October 21, 1941]," UdSSR, file 412, pp. 796–805, ZStl.

85. Westermann, "'Ordinary Men' or 'Ideological Soldiers'?" 51. See also Kater, *The Nazi Party,* 141. In his social profile, Kater found that National Socialism held its "greatest attraction" for those born between 1905 and 1912.

86. Michael Mann, "Were the Perpetrators of Genocide 'Ordinary Men' or 'Real Nazis'? Results from Fifteen Hundred Biographies," *Holocaust and Genocide Studies* 14 (winter 2000): 331–366.

87. Browning, *Origins,* 231.

88. See Kater, *The Nazi Party,* 73.

89. "Zahlenmässige und statistische Unterlagen zur Besprechung der Befehlshaber und Inspekteure der Ord.-Polizei vom 1.-4. Februar 1942," T580, reel 96, NARA.

90. Thomas Sandkühler, *"Endlösung" in Galizien: Der Judenmord in Ostpolen und die Rettungsinitiativen von Berthold Beitz, 1941–1944* (Bonn: J. H. W. Dietz, 1996), 149–150. See also Browning, *Origins,* 349–350.

91. Browning, *Origins,* 349. See also Sandkühler, *"Endlösung" in Galizien,* 151–152.

92. Browning, *Origins,* 350.

93. Sandkühler, *"Endlösung" in Galizien,* 443–444.

94. "Sicherungsbezirk Nord, Res.-Pol.-Batl. (mot) 133, 1. Kompanie [August 1, 1942]," UdSSR, file 410, p. 536, ZStl. The nine "partisan sympathizers" included five Jews who are included in both categories in the figures presented above.

95. "Res.-Pol.-Batl. (mot) 133, 1. Kompanie [August 8, 1942]," UdSSR, file 410, p. 533, ZStl.

96. "5./Pol. 24 [August 15, 1942]," UdSSR, file 410, p. 528, ZStl; "Sicherungsbezirk Nord, 5./Pol. 24 [August 22, 1942]," UdSSR, file 410, p. 526, ZStl; and "Sicherungsbezirk Nord, 5./Pol. 24 [September 12, 1942]," UdSSR, file 410, p. 525, ZStl. The two reports covering the period August 22–September 5, 1942, are not available.

97. Dieter Pohl, *Nationalsozialistische Judenverfolgung in Ostgalizien, 1941–1944: Organisation und Durchführung eines staatlichen Massenverbrechens* (Munich: R. Oldenbourg, 1997), 276.

98. "Wesentliches Ergebnis der Ermittlungen und Voruntersuchung," 205 AR-Nr. 512/1963, file 8, pp. 955, 962–963, ZStl.

99. "Wesentliches Ergebnis der Ermittlungen und Voruntersuchung," 205 AR-Nr. 512/1963, file 8, pp. 951–953, ZStl.

100. "Wesentliches Ergebnis der Ermittlungen und Voruntersuchung," 205 AR-Nr. 512/1963, file 8, pp. 968–970, ZStl. See also testimony of Willy K., V 205 AR-Nr. 512/1963, file 1, p. 200, ZStl; testimony of Hubert R., V 205 AR-Nr. 512/1963, file 1, p. 33, ZStl; and testimony of Otto K., V 205 AR-Nr. 512/1963, file 2, p. 119, ZStl.

101. "Wesentliches Ergebnis der Ermittlungen und Voruntersuchung," 205 AR-Nr. 512/1963, file 8, pp. 969–970, ZStl.

102. Testimony of Lothar H., V 205 AR-Nr. 512/1963, file 1, p. 183, ZStl.

103. "Wesentliches Ergebnis der Ermittlungen und Voruntersuchung," 205 AR-Nr. 512/1963, file 8, pp. 969–972, ZStl.

104. "Wesentliches Ergebnis der Ermittlungen und Voruntersuchung," 205 AR-Nr. 512/1963, file 8, pp. 972, ZStl.

105. "221. Sich.-Division, Kriegstagebuch Nr. 5 für die Zeit vom 18.6. bis 31.12.1942," RH 26-221, file 37, BArch. War diary entries for June 18–25 and July 1–12, 1942.

106. Testimony of Albert M., V 205 AR-Nr. 512/1963, file 2, p. 151, ZStl. M. says that he was part of the escort detachment transporting Jews to the killing site but that he neither did any shooting himself nor saw the actual shootings.

107. Testimony of Albert M., V 205 AR-Nr. 512/1963, file 2, p. 153, ZStl.

108. "SS und Pol.-Gebietsführer Borissow (Pleszenice), Lagebericht für den Monat November [November 22, 1942]," UdSSR, file 245d, p. 50, ZStl.

109. "SS und Pol.-Gebietsführer Borissow (Pleszenice), Lagebericht für den Monat März 1943 [March 17, 1943]," UdSSR, file 245d, p. 55, ZStl.

110. Wojciech Zyśko, *Zeszyty Majdanka*, vol. 6, *Eksterminacyjna Działalność Truppenpolizei w Dystrykcie Lubelskim w Latach, 1943* (Lublin: Wydawnictwo Lubelskie, 1972), 156–166.

111. Dean, "German Gendarmerie," 188, quoting Command Order 11/43 (February 1, 1943).

112. "Der Kreisälteste in Saslawl, Gebiet Minsk-Land [May 24, 1943]," UdSSR, file 245d, pp. 67–68, ZStl.

113. Activity reports for "Gendarmerie Kreis Blachstadt, Regierungsbezirk Oppeln [November 1942 and January, April, June 1943]," 205 AR-Z 32/81, file 1, pp. 59–62, 64, 67–68, ZStl.

114. Activity report for "Gendarmerie Kreis Blachstadt, Regierungsbezirk Oppeln [June 30, 1943]," 205 AR-Z 32/81, file 1, p. 64, ZStl.

115. State prosecutor's list of Gendarmerie members, 205 AR-Z 32/81, file 2, pp. 383–389, ZStl. A listing of the policemen serving in the Gendarmerie posts in this area identifies only three of the thirty as reservists.

116. Testimony of Stanislaw Majchrzak, 205 AR-Z 32/81, file 1, pp. 131–133, ZStl.

117. Testimony of Katarzyna Suchanksa (née Idzikowska), 205 AR-Z 32/81, file 1, pp. 149–151, ZStl.

118. "Der Stellvertreter des Befehlshabers der Ordnungspolizei Alpenland in Veldes, Tgb. Nr. 662/41, Betrifft: Nachweisung der beim Gegner eingetretenen Verluste [December 17, 1941]," 503 AR-Z 9/1965, file 1, p. 305, ZStl.

119. Walter Manoschek, "Kriegsverbrechen und Judenvernichtung in Serbien, 1941–1942," in *Kriegsverbrechen im 20. Jahrhundert,* ed. Wolfram Wette and Gerd R. Ueberschär (Darmstadt: Primus, 2001), 126–127, 131.

120. "Polizei-Einsatzstab-Südost, Veldes, Sonderbefehl [February 13, 1942]," 503 AR-Z 9/1965, file 2, p. 301, ZStl.

121. Witte et al., eds., *Dienstkalender,* 466.

122. "Geheime Kdo.-Sache, Der RFSS, Kommando Stab RFSS, Tgb. Nr. Ia 323/42 g.Kdos., Befehl für die Unterdrückung der Bandentätigkeit in den Gebieten Oberkrain und Untersteiermark [June 25, 1942]," 503 AR-Z 9/1965, file 1, p. 18, ZStl.

123. "Der Chef der Ordnungspolizei, KdO I O (3) 1 Nr. 467/43, Betr.: Aufstellung einer Pol.-Gesch.-Batterie beim Befehlshaber der Ordnungspolizei in Kroatien [August 31, 1943]," Verschiedenes 301, file 163, pp. 62–63, ZStl. See also "Der Chef der Ordnungspolizei, KdO I O (3) 1 Nr. 454/43, Betr.: Aufstellung der Pol.-Inf.-Geschützkomp 'Alpenland' [August 6, 1943]," Verschiedenes 301, file 163, p. 54, ZStl.

124. "Der Reichsführer-SS, Kdo.Staf [sic] RF-SS, Richtlinien für die Durchführung der Aktion gegen Partisanen und sonstige Banditen in Oberkrain und Untersteiermark [June 25, 1942]," 503 AR-Z 9/1965, file 1, p. 20, ZStl.

125. "Der Höhere SS und Polizeiführer Alpenland, Befehlshaber der Ordnungspolizei, Befehlsstelle Veldes, Lage am 11. Juli 1942 [July 11, 1942]," 503 AR-Z 9/1965, file 1, p. 6, ZStl.

126. Police activity report entry [October 2, 1942], 503 AR-Z 9/1965, file 1, p. 11, ZStl.

127. "Kampfgruppe II, Fuchs, Kampfgruppenbefehl Nr. 15 [October 23, 1944]," T175, reel 224, frame 2763006, NARA. See also "Kampfgruppe III, Ia, Betr: Einsatz des IV. Batl. [January 1, 1945]," T175, reel 224, frames 2762976–2762977, NARA; and "Funkspruch" of Kampfgruppe I [February 12, 1945], T175, reel 224, frame 2762946, NARA.

128. "Kampfgruppe II, Fuchs, Kampfgruppenbefehl Nr. 15 [October 23, 1944]," T175, reel 224, frame 2763006, NARA.

129. "Der Höhere SS- und Polizeiführer West, Führungsstab [30.10.1944]," T175, reel 224, frames 2763017–2763019, NARA.

130. Undated five-page list containing names of eighty persons executed between September 21 and December 22, 1944, T175, reel 224, frames 2762927–2762931, NARA.

Conclusion

1. See Breitman, *Official Secrets*; and Supreme Headquarters, *The German Police,* 21. Breitman's work exposed the availability to contemporary political and military leaders of captured police intercepts detailing the participation of the police battalions in the conduct of genocide.

2. Supreme Headquarters, *The German Police,* 21.

3. Michael Okroy, "'Man will unserem Batl. was tun . . .': Der Wuppertaler Bia-

lystok-Prozeß 1967/68 und die Ermittlungen gegen Angehörige des Polizeibataillons 309," in Kenkmann and Spieker, eds., *Im Auftrag,* 301–317.

4. Hermann Franz, *Gebirgsjäger der Polizei: Polizei-Gebirgsjäger-Regiment 18 und Polizei-Gebirgsartillerieabteilung 1942 bis 1945* (Bad Nauheim: Hans-Henning Podzun, 1963), 16, 19, 57, 79.

5. "Der Chef der Ordnungspolizei, Kdo.I g Ia (1) Nr. 127/41 (g.), Abschrift einer Verfügung des OKW [January 5, 1942]," UdSSR, file 245 Ac, p. 572, ZStl.

6. Jörg Friedrich, *Der Brand: Deutschland im Bombenkrieg, 1940–1945* (Berlin: Propyläen, 2002).

7. Heinrich Lankenau, ed., *Polizei im Einsatz während des Krieges in Rheinland-Westfalen* (Bremen: H. M. Haunschild, 1957), 16.

8. Christoph Spieker, "Export von Münster nach Den Haag: BdO Dr, Heinrich Lankenau (1891–1983)," in Kenkmann and Spieker, eds., *Im Auftrag,* 183.

9. Lankenau, *Polizei im Einsatz,* 5, 17, 20.

10. "Der Kommandeur der Gendarmerie Shitomir, Kommandobrief Nr. 3/42 [May 5, 1942]," RG 53.002M, fond 658, reel 5, USHMMA.

11. "Der Chef der Ordnungspolizei, Kdo. I Ausb. (3) 2 Nr. 261/44, Betr.: Ausbildung des 10,000 Mann-Ersatzes [September 23, 1944]," R 19, file 308, pp. 234–236, BArch.

12. "Report from Adolf von Bomhard to Alfred Wünnenberg [December 6, 1944]," R 19, file 281, pp. 45–51, BArch.

13. Picker, *Hitlers Tischgespräche,* 375.

14. Robert B. Strasser, ed., *The Landmark Thucydides: A Comprehensive Guide to the Peloponnesian War* (New York: Free Press, 1996), 357.

15. John Dower, *War without Mercy: Race and Power in the Pacific War* (New York: Pantheon, 1986).

16. Spencer Tucker, ed., *The Encyclopedia of the Vietnam War: A Political, Social, and Military History* (Oxford: Oxford University Press, 1998), 280–281. Calley's initial life sentence was subsequently reduced to twenty years by the Court of Military Appeals. He was paroled by President Nixon in 1974.

17. Mallmann, "Der qualitative Sprung im Vernichtungsprozeß," 253.

18. For one analysis of this process, see Koonz, *The Nazi Conscience.*

19. Browning, *Ordinary Men,* 171–176.

20. Testimony of Johann P., 204 AR-Z 1251/65, file 1, p. 38, ZStl.

21. Stanley Milgram, *Obedience to Authority: An Experimental View* (New York: Harper & Row, 1974), 36. Milgram's study found that 70 *percent* of "perpetrators" defied the experimenter when they sat next to the "victim" and were forced to place the victim's hand on the shock plate.

22. Browning, *Origins,* 33.

23. "Der Kommandeur der Gendarmerie beim Chef der Zivilverwaltung in der Untersteiermark, Betr.: Karner, Karl, Gend.Meister, Verhalten [May 29, 1941]," Verschiedenes, file 167, p. 367, ZStl.

24. Mallmann, "Der qualitative Sprung im Vernichtungsprozeß," 253.

25. Browning, *Ordinary Men,* 2, 56.

26. For a more detailed examination of this question, see David H. Kitterman, "Those Who Said 'No!': Germans Who Refused to Execute Civilians during World War II," *German Studies Review* 11 (May 1988): 241–254.

27. I would like to thank Klaus-Michael Mallmann for sharing this insight during a conversation at the University of Stuttgart.

28. "Der Höhere SS- und Polizeiführer West, Betrifft: Verhütung von Geschlechtskrankheiten," T175, reel 224, frame 2762919, NARA.

29. "Der Kommandeur der Ordnungspolizei im Distrikt Lublin, II a/b [March 13, 1943]," RG 15.011M, reel 20, file 274, USHMMA. This document contains an order forwarded under Daluege's signature with the following subject line: "Verwendung von polnisch versippten Angehörigen der Ordnungspolizei in den eingegliederten Ostgebieten und im Generalgouvernment [March 8, 1943]."

30. "Der Kommandeur der Orpo b. SS- u. Polizeiführer Weissruthenien, Tagesbefehl No. 16 [July 31, 1943]," RG 53.002M, reel 3, fond 389, file 1, USHMMA.

31. Testimony of Erich H., as cited in Mallmann, Rieß, and Pyta, eds., *Deutscher Osten*, 137.

32. Klee, Dreßen, and Rieß, eds., *"The Good Old Days,"* 220–221.

33. Browning, *Origins*, 260.

34. Letter (*Feldpost*) from a policeman to his home unit commander in Oldenburg [August 6, 1944], Verschiedenes 301Ch, file 167, pp. 178–179, ZStl.

35. Testimony of Schmidt's ex-wife, 204 AR-Z 12/61, file 1, pp. 29–30, ZStl.

36. Kazimierz Moczarski, *Conversations with an Executioner,* ed. Mariana Fitzpatrick (Englewood Cliffs, N.J.: Prentice-Hall, 1981), 172.

37. "9./Pol. 15, Betr.: Wochenbericht für die Zeit vom 26.10-1.11.1942 [November 1, 1942]," UdSSR, file 412, pp. 841–842, ZStl.

38. "I./Pol.22, Ia 12 39a, Zwischenbericht [November 11, 1942]," RG 15.011M, reel 21, file 276, USHMMA; and "II./Pol-Regt. 22, I a 15 30, Zwischenbericht [December 4, 1942]," RG 15.011M, reel 21, file 276, USHMMA.

39. "Zum 10. Jahrestage der nationalsozialistischen Revolution, SS und Polizei im großdeutschen Freiheitskampfe [January 30, 1943]," T580, reel 216, file 2, NARA.

BIBLIOGRAPHY

Archives and Research Centers

U.S. Holocaust Memorial Museum Archive, Washington, D.C.

RG 06.025.63. *Selected Central Records of the Federal Security Service of the Russian Federation.*
RG 15.011M. *Der Kommandeur der Gendarmerie im Distrikt Lublin.*
RG 15.066M. *Gouverneur des Distrikts Lublin.*
RG 48.004M. *Records of the Military Historical Institute, Prague.*
RG 53.002M. *Selected Records of the Belarus Central State Archive, Minsk.*

Zentrale Stelle der Landesjustizverwaltungen, Ludwigsburg, Germany

Case Investigations

202 AR 165/61.
204 AR-Z 12/61.
204 AR-Z 1251/65.
204 AR-Nr. 2356/1965.
205 AR-Nr. 512/1963.
205 AR-Z 20/60.
205 AR-Z 32/81.
V 205 AR-Nr. 512/1963.
208 AR-Z 80/60.
208 AR-Z 30/62.
211 AR-Z 350/59.
503 AR-Z 9/1965.

Document Collections (Folder Identification)

CSSR.
UdSSR 245 Ac.
UdSSR 245 Af.
UdSSR 245c.
UdSSR 245d.
UdSSR 410.
UdSSR 412.
Verschiedenes 117.
Verschiedenes 167.

Verschiedenes 301.
Verschiedenes 301 Bt.
Verschiedenes 301 Cd.
Verschiedenes 301 Ch.

BUNDESARCHIV, BERLIN

NS 19. *Persönlicher Stab Reichsführer-SS.*
R 19. *Chef der Ordnungspolizei, Hauptamt Ordnungspolizei.*
R 20. *Chef der Bandenkampfverbände, Truppen und Schulen der Ordnungspolizei.*
R 1501. *Reichsministerium des Innern.*

BUNDESARCHIV-MILITÄRARCHIV, FREIBURG

RH-1. *Adjutantur des Chefs der Heeresleitung/Oberbefehlshaber des Heeres.*
RH 26-221. *Oberkommando des Heeres/Sicherungs-Division 221.*
RW 4. *Oberkommando der Wehrmacht/Wehrmachtführungsstab.*

NATIONAL ARCHIVES AND RECORDS ADMINISTRATION,
COLLEGE PARK, MARYLAND

T175. *Records of the Reichsführer SS and Chief of the German Police.*
T405. *German Air Force Reports: Luftgaukommandos, Flak, Deutsche Luftwaffen-mission in Rumänien.*
T501. *Records of German Field Commands: Rear Areas, Occupied Territories, and Others.*
T580. *Captured German Documents Microfilmed at the Berlin Document Center.*

DIE BUNDESBEAUFTRAGTE FÜR DIE UNTERLAGEN DES STAATSSICHERHEITSDIENSTES
DER EHEMALIGEN DDR, BERLIN

Document Collection

MfS-HA IX/11, RHE 48/76 SU.

Unpublished Documents

Hunt, I. L. *American Military Government of Occupied Germany, 1918–1920.* Vol. 1, *Report of the Officer in Charge of Civil Affairs Third Army and American Forces in Germany.* N.p., 1920. A copy is held by the Air University library at Maxwell A.F.B.
Klaus-Michael Mallmann. " '. . . Mißgeburten, die nicht auf diese Welt gehören': Die Ordnungspolizei im besetzten Polen, 1939–1941." N.p., 2003.
The Schupo War Criminals of Stryj. n.p., n.d.
Supreme Headquarters Allied Expeditionary Force Evaluation and Dissemination Section, G-2 (Counter Intelligence Sub-Division). *The German Police.* London: n.p., 1945.

Published Documents

Deutschland-Bericht der SOPADE. Frankfurt a.M.: Petra Nettlebeck, 1980.
International Military Tribunal. *Trials of the Major War Criminals before the International Military Tribunal*. Vol. 12. Nuremberg: Secretariat of the Military Tribunal, 1947.
————. *Trials of the Major War Criminals before the International Military Tribunal*. Vol. 22. Nuremberg: Secretariat of the Military Tribunal, 1948.
————. *Trials of the Major War Criminals before the International Military Tribunal*. Vol. 29. Nuremberg: Secretariat of the Military Tribunal, 1948.
————. *Trials of the Major War Criminals before the International Military Tribunal*. Vol. 32. Nuremberg: Secretariat of the Military Tribunal, 1948.
————. *Trials of the Major War Criminals before the International Military Tribunal*. Vol. 35. Nuremberg: Secretariat of the Military Tribunal, 1949.
————. *Trials of the Major War Criminals before the International Military Tribunal*. Vol. 37. Nuremberg: Secretariat of the Military Tribunal, 1949.

Newspapers and Magazines

Die Deutsche Polizei.
Der Deutsche Polizeibeamte.
Der märkische Adler (Berlin).
Völkischer Beobachter (Berlin).
Vossische Zeitung (Berlin).

Books and Articles

Allen, Michael Thad. *The Business of Genocide: The SS, Slave Labor, and the Concentration Camps*. Chapel Hill: University of North Carolina Press, 2002.
Anderson, Truman. "Incident at Baranivka: German Reprisals and the Soviet Partisan Movement in Ukraine, October–December 1941." *Journal of Modern History* 71 (September 1999): 585–621.
Andreas-Friederich, Ruth. *Berlin Underground, 1938–1945*. Translated by Barrows Mussey. New York: Paragon, 1947.
Angrick, Andrej. *Besatzungspolitik und Massenmord: Die Einsatzgruppe D in der südlichen Sowjetunion, 1941–1943*. Hamburg: Hamburger Edition, 2003.
Angrick, Andrej, Martina Voigt, Silke Ammerschubert, and Peter Klein. "Da hätte man schon Tagebuch führen müssen." In *Die Normalität des Verbrechens: Bilanz und Perspektiven der Forschung zu den nationalsozialistischen Gewaltverbrechen*, ed. Helge Grabitz, Klaus Bästlein, and Johannes Tuchel, 325–385. Berlin: Druckhaus Hentrich, 1994.
Baird, Jay W. *To Die for Germany: Heroes in the Nazi Pantheon*. Bloomington: Indiana University Press, 1990.
Bar-On, Dan. *Legacy of Silence: Encounters with Children of the Third Reich*. Cambridge, Mass.: Harvard University Press, 1989.

Bartov, Omer. *The Eastern Front, 1941–1945: German Troops and the Barbarisation of Warfare.* New York: Macmillan, 1986.

————. *Hitler's Army: Soldiers, Nazis, and War in the Third Reich.* Oxford: Oxford University Press, 1992.

Bathe, Rolf. *Der Feldzug der 18 Tage: Chronik des Polnischen Dramas.* Berlin: Gerhard Stalling, 1939.

Benz, Wolfgang. "Der Rückfall in die Barbarei: Bericht über den Pogrom." In *Der Judenpogrom 1938: Von der "Reichskristallnacht" zum Völkermord,* ed. Walter Pehle, 13–51. Frankfurt a.M.: Fischer Taschenbuch, 1988.

Bessel, Richard. *Political Violence and the Rise of Nazism: The Storm Troopers in Eastern Germany, 1925–1934.* New Haven, Conn.: Yale University Press, 1984.

————. "Militarisierung und Modernisierung: Polizeiliches Handeln in der Weimarer Republik." In *"Sicherheit" und "Wohlfahrt": Polizei, Gesellschaft und Herrschaft im 19. und 20. Jahrhundert,* ed. Alf Lüdtke, 323–343. Frankfurt a.M.: Suhrkamp, 1992.

————. "Die 'Modernisierung' der Polizei im Nationalsozialismus." In *Norddeutschland im Nationalsozialismus,* ed. Frank Bajohr, 371–386. Hamburg: Ergebnisse, 1993.

Best, Werner. *Die Deutsche Polizei.* Darmstadt: L. C. Wittich, 1940.

Bevans, Charles I., ed. *Treaties and Other International Agreements of the United States of America, 1776–1949.* Washington, D.C.: U.S. Government Printing Office, 1969.

Birn, Ruth Bettina. *Die Höheren SS- und Polizeiführer: Himmlers Vertreter im Reich und in den besetzten Gebieten.* Düsseldorf: Droste, 1986.

————. " 'Zaunkönig' an 'Uhrmacher': Große Partisanenaktionen 1942/43 am Beispiel des 'Unternehmens Winterzauber.' " *Militärgeschichtliche Zeitschrift* 60 (2001): 99–118.

Blachly, Frederick E., and Miriam E. Oatman. *The Government and Administration of Germany.* Baltimore: Johns Hopkins University Press, 1928.

The Black Book of Poland. New York: G. P. Putnam's Sons, 1942.

Blackburn, Gilmer W. *Education in the Third Reich: A Study of Race and History in Nazi Textbooks.* Albany: State University of New York Press, 1985.

Borodziej, Włodzimierz. *Terror und Politik: Die Deutsche Polizei und die Polnische Widerstandsbewegung im Generalgouvernement, 1939–1944.* Mainz: Philipp von Zabern, 1999.

Bracher, Karl D., Wolfgang Sauer, and Gerhard Schulz. *Die nationalsozialistische Machtergreifung.* Cologne: Westdeutscher, 1960.

Breitman, Richard. *The Architect of Genocide: Himmler and the Final Solution.* New York: Knopf, 1991.

————. *Official Secrets: What the Nazis Planned, What the British and Americans Knew.* New York: Hill & Wang, 1998.

Broszat, Martin. *Nationalsozialistische Polenpolitik, 1939–1945.* Stuttgart: Deutsche Verlags–Anstalt, 1961.

————. *The Hitler State: The Foundation and Development of the Internal Structure of the Third Reich.* Translated by John W. Hiden. London: Longman, 1981.

Browder, George C. *Foundations of the Nazi Police State: The Formation of SIPO and SD.* Lexington: University Press of Kentucky, 1990.

Browning, Christopher R. *The Final Solution and the German Foreign Office: A Study of Referat D III of Abteilung Deutschland, 1940–43.* New York: Holmes & Meier, 1978.

————. *Ordinary Men: Reserve Police Battalion 101 and the Final Solution in Poland*. New York: Harper Collins, 1992.

————. *The Origins of the Final Solution: The Evolution of Nazi Jewish Policy, September 1939–March 1942*. Lincoln: University of Nebraska Press, 2004.

Buchheim, Hans. "Die Höheren SS- und Polizeiführer." *Vierteljahrshefte für Zeitgeschichte* 11 (October 1963): 362–391.

Büchler, Yehoshua. "Kommandostab Reichsführer-SS: Himmler's Personal Murder Brigades in 1941." *Holocaust and Genocide Studies* 1 (1986): 11–25.

Buhlan, Harald, and Werner Jung, eds. *Wessen Freund und wessen Helfer? Die Kölner Polizei im Nationalsozialismus*. Cologne: Emons, 2000.

Burdick, Charles, and Hans-Adolf Jacobsen. *The Halder War Diary, 1939–1942*. Novato, Calif.: Presidio, 1988.

Burleigh, Michael. *Germany Turns Eastwards: A Study of Ostforschung in the Third Reich*. Cambridge: Cambridge University Press, 1988.

————. *The Third Reich: A New History*. New York: Hill & Wang, 2000.

Campbell, Bruce. *The SA Generals and the Rise of Nazism*. Lexington: University Press of Kentucky, 1998.

Chapman, Brian. *Police State*. New York: Praeger, 1970.

Combs, William L. *The Voice of the SS: A History of the SS Journal "Das Schwarze Korps."* New York: Peter Lang, 1986.

Daenekas, Bernhard. "Verbrechen deutscher Polizeieinheiten im Zweiten Weltkrieg— aus der Sicht eines Ermittlungsbeamten." *Archiv für Polizeigeschichte* 4 (1993): 21–24.

Dallin, Alexander. *German Rule in Russia, 1941–1945: A Study of Occupation Policies*. Boulder, Colo.: Westview, 1981.

Danner, Lothar. *Ordnungspolizei Hamburg: Betrachtungen zu ihrer Geschichte 1918 bis 1933*. Hamburg: Deutsche Polizei, 1958.

Dean, Martin. "The German Gendarmerie, the Ukrainian Schutzmannschaft, and the 'Second Wave' of Jewish Killings in Occupied Ukraine: German Policing at the Local Level in the Zhitomir Region, 1941–1944." *German History* 14 (1996): 168–192.

de Bruyn, Günter. *Zwischenbilanz: Eine Jugend in Berlin*. Frankfurt a.M.: Fischer Taschenbuch, 1992.

Deist, Wilhelm, Manfred Messerschmidt, Hans-Erich Volkmann, and Wolfram Wette. *Ursachen und Voraussetzungen des Zweiten Weltkrieges*. Frankfurt a.M.: Fischer Taschenbuch, 1989.

"Deutsche Polizei im besetzten Polen—ein Leserbrief aus dem Jahr 1939." *Archiv für Polizeigeschichte* 10 (1999): 28–29.

de Zayas, Alfred M. *The Wehrmacht War Crimes Bureau, 1939–1945*. Lincoln: University of Nebraska Press, 1989.

Diembach, Thomas. "Vom Spazierstock zur Automatikpistole: Die Bewaffnung der Kriminalpolizei im Kaisserreich." *Archiv für Polizeigeschichte* 14 (2003): 46–48.

DiNardo, Richard L. *Mechanized Juggernaut or Military Anachronism? Horses and the German Army of World War II*. New York: Greenwood, 1991.

Dodd, William E. *Ambassador Dodd's Diary, 1933–1938*. Edited by William E. Dodd Jr. and Martha Dodd. New York: Harcourt, Brace, 1941.

Domarus, Max, ed. *Hitler: Reden und Proklamationen, 1932–1945*. 2 vols. Wiesbaden: R. Löwit, 1973.

————, ed. *Hitler: Speeches and Proclamations, 1932–1945: The Chronicle of a Dic-*

tatorship. Vol. 1, *The Years 1932–1934.* Translated by Mary Fran Gilbert. Wauconda, Ill.: Bolchazy-Carducci, 1990.

————, ed. *Hitler: Speeches and Proclamations, 1932–1945: The Chronicle of a Dictatorship.* Vol. 3, *The Years 1939–1940.* Translated by Mary Fran Gilbert. Wauconda, Ill.: Bolchazy-Carducci, 1997.

Dower, John. *War without Mercy: Race and Power in the Pacific War.* New York: Pantheon, 1986.

Engelmann, Bernt. *In Hitler's Germany: Everyday Life in the Third Reich.* New York: Schocken, 1986.

Falter, Jürgen W. *Hitlers Wähler.* Munich: C. H. Beck, 1991.

Förster, Jürgen. "Operation Barbarossa as a War of Conquest and Annihilation." In *The Attack on the Soviet Union,* ed. Research Institute for Military History, trans. Dean S. McMurry, Ewald Osers, and Louise Wilmot, 481–521. Oxford: Clarendon, 1998.

Fosdick, Raymond. *European Police Systems.* Montclair, N.J.: Patterson Smith, 1969.

Frank, Hans. *Hans Frank's Diary.* Edited and translated by Stanisław Piotrowski. Warsaw: Drukarnia Uniwersytetu im A. Mickiewicza, 1961.

Franz, Hermann. *Gebirgsjäger der Polizei: Polizei-Gebirgsjäger-Regiment 18 und Polizei-Gebirgsartillerieabteilung 1942 bis 1945.* Bad Nauheim: Hans-Henning Podzun, 1963.

Friedman, Tuviah, ed. *Schupo-Kriegsverbrecher in Kolomea.* Vienna: Jewish Historical Documentation Center, 1990.

Friedrich, Horst. "Eine bewegte Gedenkstätte: Das 'Ehrenmal der gefallenen Gendarmen' der ehemaligen Gendarmerieschule Bad Ems." *Archiv für Polizeigeschichte* 8 (1997): 58–60.

Friedrich, Jörg. *Der Brand: Deutschland im Bombenkrieg, 1940–1945.* Berlin: Propyläen, 2002.

Fröhlich, Elke. *Die Tagebücher von Joseph Goebbels: Sämtliche Fragmente.* Part 1. Vol. 2. Munich: K. G. Saur, 1987.

Gellately, Robert. *The Gestapo and German Society: Enforcing Racial Policy, 1933–1945.* Oxford: Clarendon, 1990.

————. *Backing Hitler: Consent and Coercion in Nazi Germany.* New York: Oxford University Press, 2001.

Gerlach, Christian. *Kalkulierte Morde: Die deutsche Wirtschafts- und Vernichtungspolitik in Weißrußland 1941 bis 1944.* Hamburg: Hamburger Edition, 1999.

————. "Kontextualisierung der Aktionen eines Mordkommandos—die Einsatzgruppe B." In *Täter im Vernichtungskrieg: Der Überfall auf die Sowjetunion und der Völkermord an den Juden,* ed. Wolf Kaiser, 85–95. Berlin: Propyläen, 2002.

Giesen, Rolf. *Nazi Propaganda Films: A History and Filmography.* Jefferson, N.C.: McFarland, 2003.

Glantz, David. *Barbarossa: Hitler's Invasion of Russia, 1941.* Stroud: Tempus, 2001.

Goda, Norman. *Tomorrow the World: Hitler, Northwest Africa, and the Path toward America.* College Station: Texas A&M University Press, 1998.

Goldhagen, Daniel J. *Hitler's Willing Executioners: Ordinary Germans and the Holocaust.* New York: Knopf, 1996.

Gordon, Harold, Jr. "Police Careers in the Weimar Republic." In *Proceedings of the Citadel Symposium on Hitler and the National Socialist Era, 24–25 April 1980,* ed. Michael B. Barrett, 160–169. Charleston, S.C.: Citadel Development Foundation, 1982.

Graml, Hermann. *Reichskristallnacht: Antisemitismus und Judenverfolgung im Dritten Reich*. Munich: Deutscher Taschenbuch, 1988.

———. "Die Wehrmacht im Dritten Reich." *Vierteljahrshefte für Zeitgeschichte* 45 (July 1997): 365–384.

Grenkevich, Leonid D. *The Soviet Partisan Movement, 1941–1944*. London: Frank Cass, 1999.

Gritzbach, Erich, ed. *Hermann Göring: Reden und Aufsätze*. Munich: Zentralverlag der NSDAP, 1939.

Hansen, Willy. "Zwischen Selbstdarstellung und Propaganda-Aktion: 'Verkehrserziehungswochen' und 'Tag der Deutschen Polizei' als Beispiele der polizeilichen Öffentlichkeitsarbeit im NS-Staat." In *Wessen Freund und wessen Helfer? Die Kölner Polizei im Nationalsozialismus*, ed. Harald Buhlan and Werner Jung, 230–262. Cologne: Emons, 2000.

Harrison, Stephen J. "Police Organizational Culture: Using Ingrained Values to Build Positive Organizational Improvement." *Public Administration and Management: An Interactive Journal* 3, no. 2 (1998), http://www.pamij.com/harrison.html (accessed October 28, 2004).

Hartewig, Karin. " 'Eine sogenannte Neutralität der Beamten gibt es nicht': Sozialer Protest, bürgerliche Gesellschaft und Polizei im Ruhrgebiet, 1918–1924." In *"Sicherheit" und "Wohlfahrt": Polizei, Gesellschaft und Herrschaft im 19. und 20. Jahrhundert*, ed. Alf Lüdtke, 297–322. Frankfurt a.M.: Suhrkamp, 1992.

Hartmann, Christian. *Halder Generalstabschef Hitlers, 1938–1942*. Paderborn: Ferdinand Schöningh, 1991.

Harvey, Elizabeth. *Women and the Nazi East: Agents and Witnesses of Germanization*. New Haven, Conn.: Yale University Press, 2003.

Hayes, Peter. *Industry and Ideology: IG Farben and the Nazi Era*. Cambridge: Cambridge University Press, 2001.

Headland, Ronald. *Messages of Murder: A Study of the Reports of the Einsatzgruppen of the Security Police and the Security Service, 1941–1943*. Rutherford, N.J.: Fairleigh Dickinson University Press, 1992.

Heinemann, Isabel. *"Rasse, Siedlung, deutsches Blut": Das Rasse- und Siedlungshauptamt der SS und die rassenpolitische Neuordnung Europas*. Göttingen: Wallenstein, 2003.

Heller, Karl-Heinz. *The Reshaping and Political Conditioning of the German Ordnungspolizei, 1933–1945: A Study of Techniques Used in the Nazi State to Conform Local Police Units to National Socialist Theory and Practice*. Ann Arbor, Mich.: University Microfilms, 1971.

———. "The Remodeled Praetorians: The German Ordnungspolizei as Guardians of the 'New Order.' " In *Nazism and the Common Man: Essays in German History (1929–1939)*, ed. Otis Mitchell, 43–64. Lanham, Md.: University Press of America, 1981.

Henkys, Reinhard. *Die nationalsozialistischen Gewaltverbrechen: Geschichte und Gericht*. Stuttgart: Kreuz, 1964.

Herbert, Ulrich. *Best: Biographische Studien über Radikalismus, Weltanschauung und Vernunft, 1903–1989*. Bonn: J. H. W. Dietz, 1996.

———. "Ideological Legitimization and Political Practice of the Leadership of the National Socialist Secret Police." Translated by Maike Bohn. In *The Third Reich between Vision and Reality*, ed. Hans Mommsen, 95–108. Oxford: Berg, 2001.

Hilberg, Raul. *The Destruction of the European Jews.* 3 vols. Rev. ed. New York: Holmes & Meier, 1985.

Hitler, Adolf. *Mein Kampf.* Translated by Ralph Manheim. Boston: Houghton Mifflin, 1962.

Höhne, Heinz. *The Order of the Death's Head: The Story of Hitler's SS.* Translated by Richard Barry. New York: Coward-McCann, 1969.

Holborn, Hajo. *A History of Modern Germany, 1840–1945.* Princeton, N.J.: Princeton University Press, 1969.

Horne, John, and Alan Kramer, "German 'Atrocities' and Franco-German Opinion, 1914: The Evidence of German Soldiers' Diaries." *Journal of Modern History* 66 (March 1994): 1–33.

Höss, Rudolf. *Commandant of Auschwitz: The Autobiography of Rudolf Höss.* Translated by Constantine Fitz Gibbon. Cleveland: World, 1959.

Howard, Michael. *The Franco-Prussian War: The German Invasion of France, 1870–1871.* New York: Dorset, 1961.

Huck, Jürgen. "Ausweichstellen und Aktenschicksal des Hauptamtes Ordnungspolizei im 2. Weltkrieg." In *Zur Geschichte der Ordnungspolizei,* by Hans-Joachim Neufeldt, Jürgen Huck, and Georg Tessin, pt. 1, pp. 119–144. Koblenz: Schriftenreihe des Bundesarchivs, 1957.

Hunold, Tonis. *Polizei in der Reform: Was Staatsbürger und Polizei voneinander erwarten könnten.* Düsseldorf: Econ, 1968.

Jones, Nigel H. *Hitler's Heralds: The Story of the Freikorps, 1918–1923.* New York: Dorset, 1987.

Kater, Michael H. *The Nazi Party: A Social Profile of Members and Leaders, 1919–1945.* Cambridge, Mass.: Harvard University Press, 1983.

Kehrl, Hans, ed. *Jahrbuch der deutschen Polizei, 1936.* Leipzig: Breitkopf & Härtel, 1936.

———. *Die Polizei.* Berlin: Industrieverlag Spaeth & Linde, 1939.

Kenkmann, Alfons, and Christoph Spieker, eds. *Im Auftrag: Polizei, Verwaltung, und Verantwortung.* Essen: Klartext, 2001.

Kershaw, Ian. *Hitler, 1889–1936: Hubris.* New York: Norton, 1998.

———. *Hitler, 1936–1945: Nemesis.* New York: Norton, 2000.

Kitterman, David H. "Those Who Said 'No!': Germans Who Refused to Execute Civilians during World War II." *German Studies Review* 11 (May 1988): 241–254.

Klee, Ernst, Willi Dreßen, and Volker Rieß, eds., *"The Good Old Days": The Holocaust as Seen by Its Perpetrators and Bystanders.* Translated by Deborah Burnstone. New York: Free Press, 1991.

Klein, Peter, ed. *Die Einsatzgruppen in der besetzten Sowjetunion, 1941/42: Die Tätigkeits- und Lageberichte des Chefs der Sicherheitspolizei und des SD.* Berlin: Druckhaus Hentrich, 1997.

Klemp, Stefan. *Freispruch für das "Mord-Bataillon": Die NS-Ordnungspolizei und die Nachkriegsjustiz.* Münster: Lit, 1998.

Klemperer, Victor. *I Will Bear Witness: A Diary of the Nazi Years, 1933–1941.* Translated by Martin Chalmers. New York: Random House, 1998.

———. *I Will Bear Witness: A Diary of the Nazi Years, 1942–1945.* Translated by Martin Chalmers. New York: Random House, 1999.

Koch, H. W. *The Hitler Youth: Origins and Development, 1922–1945.* New York: Dorset, 1975.

Koehl, Robert Lewis. *The Black Corps: The Structure and Power Struggles of the Nazi SS.* Madison: University of Wisconsin Press, 1983.

Kohl, Paul. *Der Krieg der Wehrmacht und der deutschen Polizei, 1941–1944.* Frankfurt a.M.: Fischer Taschenbuch, 1995.

Kohler, Eric D. "The Crisis in the Prussian Schutzpolizei, 1930–32." In *Police Forces in History,* ed. George L. Mosse, 131–150. London: Sage, 1975.

Köhler, Thomas. "Anstiftung zur Versklavung und Völkermord." In *Im Auftrag: Polizei, Verwaltung, und Verantwortung,* ed. Alfons Kenkmann and Christoph Spieker, 130–158. Essen: Klartext, 2001.

———. "Helmuth Koschorke: 'Wenn ich an die letzten beiden Tage denke, packt mich der Ekel. Juden, Juden und nochmals Juden.'" In *Im Auftrag: Polizei, Verwaltung, und Verantwortung,* ed. Alfons Kenkman and Christoph Spieker, 130–158. Essen: Klartext, 2001.

Koonz, Claudia. *Mothers in the Fatherland: Women, the Family, and Nazi Politics.* New York: St. Martin's, 1987.

———. *The Nazi Conscience.* Cambridge, Mass.: Harvard University Press, 2003.

Kopitzsch, Wolfgang. "Polizeieinheiten in Hamburg in der Weimarer Republik und im Dritten Reich." In *Die Deutsche Polizei und ihre Geschichte: Beiträge zu einem distanzierten Verhältnis,* ed. Peter Nitschke, 139–161. Hilden: Deutsche Polizeiliteratur, 1996.

Koschorke, Helmuth. "Von der 'Knüppelgarde' zur Volkspolizei!" In *Jahrbuch der deutschen Polizei, 1936,* ed. Hans Kehrl, 29–43. Leipzig: Breitkopf & Härtel, 1936.

———, ed. *Die Polizei—einmal anders!* Munich: Zentralverlag der NSDAP, 1937.

———. *Polizeireiter in Polen.* Berlin: Franz Schneider, 1940.

———. *Polizei greift ein! Kriegsberichte aus Ost, West und Nord.* Berlin: Franz Schneider, 1941.

Krausnick, Helmut. *Hitlers Einsatzgruppen: Die Truppen des Weltanschauungskrieges, 1938–1942.* Frankfurt a.M.: Fischer Taschenbuch, 1981.

Krausnick, Helmut, Hans Buchheim, Martin Broszat, and Hans-Adolf Jacobsen. *Anatomy of the SS State.* Translated by Richard Barry, Marian Jackson, and Dorothy Long. New York: Walker, 1968.

Kwiet, Konrad. "Auftakt zum Holocaust: Ein Polizeibataillon im Osteinsatz." In *Der Nationalsozialismus: Studien zur Ideologie und Herrschaft,* ed. Wolfgang Benz, Hans Buchheim, and Hans Mommsen, 191–208. Frankfurt a.M.: Fischer Taschenbuch, 1993.

Lankenau, Heinrich, ed. *Polizei im Einsatz während des Krieges in Rheinland-Westfalen.* Bremen: H. M. Haunschild, 1957.

Leßmann, Peter. *Die preußische Schutzpolizei in der Weimarer Republik: Streifendienst und Straßenkampf.* Düsseldorf: Droste, 1989.

Liang, Hsi-Huey. *The Berlin Police Force in the Weimarer Republic.* Berkeley: University of California Press, 1970.

Lichtenstein, Heiner. *Himmler's grüne Helfer: Die Schutz- und Ordnungspolizei im "Dritten Reich."* Cologne: Bund, 1990.

Linck, Stephan. "'. . . schon allein wegen des Schmutzes . . .' Wie Polizisten über ihren Einsatz schreiben: Das Mitteilungsblatt der Schutzpolizei Flensburg, 1944/45." *Archiv für Polizeigeschichte* 9 (1998): 51–55.

———. *Der Ordnung verpflichtet: Deutsche Polizei 1933–1949, der Fall Flensburg.* Paderborn: Ferdinand Schöningh, 2000.

Lissance, Arnold, ed. *The Halder Diaries: The Private War Journals of Colonel General Franz Halder*. 2 vols. Boulder, Colo.: Westview, 1976.

Löhken, Ingo. *Die Polizei-Uniformen in Preussen, 1866–1945*. Freidberg: Podzun-Pallas, 1986.

Longerich, Peter. *Politik der Vernichtung: Eine Gesamtdarstellung der nationalsozialistischen Judenverfolgung*. Munich: Piper, 1998.

Lower, Wendy. "Der 'reibungslose' Holocaust? Nazi Implementation of the Holocaust in Ukraine, 1941–1944." In *Networks of Nazi Persecution: Bureaucracy, Business, and the Organization of the Holocaust*, ed. Gerald Feldman and Wolfgang Seibel, 238–258. New York: Berghahn, 2004.

Lozowick, Yaacov. *Hitler's Bureaucrats: The Nazi Security Police and the Banality of Evil*, Translated by Haim Watzman. London: Continuum, 2000.

Lüdtke, Alf. *Police and State in Prussia, 1815–1850*. New York: Cambridge University Press, 1989.

———, ed. *"Sicherheit" und "Wohlfahrt": Polizei, Gesellschaft und Herrschaft im 19. und 20. Jahrhundert*. Frankfurt a.M.: Suhrkamp, 1992.

MacDonogh, Giles. *Berlin: A Portrait of Its History, Politics, Architecture, and Society*. New York: St. Martin's, 1997.

MacLean, French L. *The Field Men: The SS Officers Who Led the Einsatzkommandos—the Nazi Mobile Killing Units*. Atglen, Pa.: Schiffer Military History, 1999.

Madajczyk, Czelaw. *Die Okkupationspolitik Nazideutschlands in Polen, 1939–1945*. Cologne: Pahl-Rugenstein, 1988.

Mallmann, Klaus-Michael. "Vom Fußvolk der 'Endlösung': Ordnungspolizei, Ostkrieg und Judenmord." *Tel Aviver Jahrbuch für deutsche Geschichte* 26 (1997): 355–391.

———. "Der Einstieg in den Genozid: Das Lübecker Polizeibataillon 307 und das Massaker in Brest-Litowsk Anfang Juli 1941." *Archiv für Polizeigeschichte* 10 (1999): 82–88.

———. "Der qualitative Sprung im Vernichtungsprozeß: Das Massaker von Kamenez-Podolsk Ende August 1941." *Jahrbuch für Antisemitismusforschung* 10 (2001): 239–264.

———. " '. . . Mißgeburten, die nicht auf diese Welt gehören': Die deutsche Ordnungspolizei in Polen, 1939–1941." In *Genesis des Genozids: Polen 1939–1941*, ed. Klaus-Michael Mallmann and Bogdan Musial, 71–89. Darmstadt: Wissenschaftliche Buchgesellschaft, 2004.

Mallmann, Klaus-Michael, Volker Rieß, and Wolfram Pyta, eds. *Deutscher Osten, 1939–1945: Der Weltanschauungskrieg in Photos und Texten*. Darmstadt: Wissenschaftliche Buchgesellschaft, 2003.

Mann, Michael. "Were the Perpetrators of Genocide 'Ordinary Men' or 'Real Nazis'? Results from Fifteen Hundred Biographies." *Holocaust and Genocide Studies* 14 (winter 2000): 331–366.

Manoschek, Walter. "Kriegsverbrechen und Judenvernichtung in Serbien, 1941–1942." In *Kriegsverbrechen im 20. Jahrhundert*, ed. Wolfram Wette and Gerd R. Ueberschär, 123–136. Darmstadt: Primus, 2001.

Martin, Lawrence, ed. *The Treaties of Peace, 1919–1923*. Vol. 1. New York: Carnegie Endowment for International Peace, 1924.

Maschmann, Melita. *Fazit: Kein Rechtfertigungsversuch*. Stuttgart: Deutsche Verlags–Anstalt, 1963.

Matthäus, Jürgen. "What about the 'Ordinary Men'? The German Order Police and the Holocaust in the Occupied Soviet Union." *Holocaust and Genocide Studies* 10 (fall 1996): 134–150.

————. "Ausbildungsziel Judenmord? Zum Stellenwert der 'weltanschaulichen Erziehung' von SS und Polizei im Rahmen der 'Endlösung.'" *Zeitschrift für Geschichtswissenschaft* 47 (1999): 673–699.

————. "'Warum wird über das Judentum geschult?'" In *Die Gestapo im Zweiten Weltkrieg: "Heimatfront" und besetztes Europa,* ed. Gerhard Paul and Klaus-Michael Mallmann, 100–124. Darmstadt: Primus, 2000.

Matthäus, Jürgen, Konrad Kwiet, Jürgen Förster, and Richard Breitman. *Ausbildungsziel Judenmord? "Weltanschauliche Erziehung" von SS, Polizei und Waffen-SS im Rahmen der "Endlösung."* Frankfurt a.M.: Fischer Taschenbuch, 2003.

McKale, Donald M. *Hitler's Shadow War: The Holocaust and World War II.* New York: Cooper Square, 2002.

Mehner, Kurt, ed. *Die Waffen-SS und Polizei, 1939–1945: Führung und Truppe.* Norderstedt: K. D. Patzwall, 1995.

Merkl, Peter. *The Making of a Stormtrooper.* Princeton, N.J.: Princeton University Press, 1980.

Meyer, Ahlrich. *Die deutsche Besatzung in Frankreich, 1940–1944: Widerstandsbekämpfung und Judenverfolgung.* Darmstadt: Wissenschaftliche Buchgesellschaft, 2000.

Michaelis, Herbert, and Ernst Schraepler, eds. *Das Dritte Reich: Die Zertrümmerung des Parteienstaates und die Grundlegung der Diktatur.* Vol. 9 of *Ursachen und Folgen vom deutschen Zusammenbruch 1918 und 1945 bis zur staatlichen Neuordnung Deutschlands in der Gegenwart.* Berlin: Dokumenten Verlag Dr. Herbert Wendler, 1964.

Mierzejewski, Alfred. "A Public Enterprise in the Service of Mass Murder: The Deutsche Reichsbahn and the Holocaust." *Holocaust and Genocide Studies* 15 (spring 2001): 33–46.

Milgram, Stanley. *Obedience to Authority: An Experimental View.* New York: Harper & Row, 1974.

Moczarski, Kazimierz. *Conversations with an Executioner.* Edited by Mariana Fitzpatrick. Englewood Cliffs, N.J.: Prentice-Hall, 1981.

Mommsen, Hans, ed. *The Third Reich between Vision and Reality: New Perspectives on German History, 1918–1945.* Oxford: Berg, 2001.

Mommsen, Wolfgang J. *Imperial Germany, 1867–1918: Politics, Culture, and Society in an Authoritarian State.* Translated by Richard Deveson. London: Arnold, 1995.

Müller, Norbert, ed. *Die faschistische Okkupationspolitik in den zeitweilig besetzten Gebieten der Sowjetunion (1941–1944).* Berlin: Deutscher Verlag der Wissenschaften, 1991.

Neufeldt, Hans-Joachim. "Entstehung und Organisation des Hauptamtes Ordnungspolizei." In *Zur Geschichte der Ordnungspolizei,* by Hans-Joachim Neufeldt, Jürgen Huck, and Georg Tessin, pt. 1, pp. 5–118. Koblenz: Schriftenreihe des Bundesarchivs, 1957.

Neufeldt, Hans, Jürgen Huck, and Georg Tessin. *Zur Geschichte der Ordnungspolizei.* Koblenz: Schriftenreihe des Bundesarchivs, 1957.

Nipperdey, Thomas. *Deutsche Geschichte, 1866–1918.* Vol. 2, *Machtstaat vor der Demokratie.* Munich: C. H. Beck, 1992.

Noakes, Jeremy. "The Development of Nazi Policy Towards the German-Jewish 'Mischlinge,' 1933–1945." In *Holocaust: Critical Concepts in Historical Studies*, vol. 1, *Hitler, Nazism, and the 'Racial State'*, ed. David Cesarani, 239–311. London: Routledge, 2004.

Office of U.S. Chief of Counsel for Prosecution of Axis Criminality. *Nazi Conspiracy and Aggression*. Vol. 1. Washington, D.C.: U.S. Government Printing Office, 1946.

Okroy, Michael. " 'Man will unserem Batl. was tun . . .': Der Wuppertaler Bialystok-Prozeß 1967/68 und die Ermittlungen gegen Angehörige des Polizeibataillons 309." In *Im Auftrag: Polizei, Verwaltung und Verantwortung*, ed. Alfons Kenkmann and Christoph Spieker, 301–317. Essen: Klartext, 2001.

Overy, Richard J. *Goering: The "Iron Man."* London: Routledge & Kegan Paul, 1984.

Padfield, Peter. *Himmler: Reichsführer SS*. New York: Henry Holt, 1990.

Pannbacker, Heiko M. "Die Polizei im Bild der 'Polizei'—die Preußische Schutzpolizei zwischen Weimarer Republik und Drittem Reich in Selbstdarstellungen." *Archiv für Polizeigeschichte* 7 (1996): 21–29.

Peukert, Detlev. *Inside Nazi Germany: Conformity, Opposition, and Racism in Everyday Life*. Translated by Richard Deveson. New Haven, Conn.: Yale University Press, 1987.

Picker, Henry. *Hitlers Tischgespräche im Führerhauptquartier*. Frankfurt a.M.: Ullstein, 1993.

Pohl, Dieter. "Die Einsatzgruppe C." In *Die Einsatzgruppen in der besetzten Sowjetunion, 1941/42: Die Tätigkeits- und Lageberichte des Chefs der Sicherheitspolizei und des SD*, ed. Peter Klein, 71–87. Berlin: Druckhaus Hentrich, 1997.

———. *Nationalsozialistische Judenverfolgung in Ostgalizien, 1941–1944: Organisation und Durchführung eines staatlichen Massenverbrechens*. Munich: R. Oldenbourg, 1997.

———. "Ukrainische Hilfskräfte beim Mord an den Juden." In *Die Täter der Shoah: Fanatische Nationalsozialisten oder ganz normale Deutsche?* ed. Gerhard Paul, 205–234. Göttingen: Wallstein, 2002.

Die Polizei: Dein Freund, dein Helfer: Ein Leseheft für die deutsche Jugend. Breslau: Ferdinand Hirt, 1936.

Das Polizeibataillon 307 (Lübeck) "im Osteinsatz," 1940–1945. Essen: Schmidt-Römhild, 2002.

Querner, Rudolf. "Schutzpolizei einst und jetzt!" In *Jahrbuch der deutschen Polizei, 1936*, ed. Hans Kehrl, 55–60. Leipzig: Breitkopf & Härtel, 1936.

Radecke, Erich. "Die Landespolizei als Kadertruppe für die Wehrmacht." *Archiv für Polizeigeschichte* 2 (1991): 41–43.

Read, Anthony, and David Fisher. *Kristallnacht: The Unleashing of the Holocaust*. New York: Peter Bedrick, 1989.

Das Recht des Generalgouvernements. Krakau: Burgverlag, 1940.

Richter, Hans. *Einsatz der Polizei: Bei den Polizeibataillonen in Ost, Nord, West*. 2d ed. Berlin: Zentralverlag der NSDAP, 1942.

———. *Ordnungspolizei auf den Rollbahnen des Ostens: Bildbericht von den Einsätzen der Ordnungspolizei im Sommer 1941 im Osten, ergänzt durch kurze Erlebnisberichte*. Berlin: Zentralverlag der NSDAP, 1943.

Riechert, Hansjörg. "Die Polizei des Dritten Reiches im Dienst der Rassenhygiene." *Archiv für Polizeigeschichte* 5 (1994): 70–74.

Rigg, Bryan Mark. *Hitler's Jewish Soldiers: The Untold Story of Nazi Racial Laws and Men of Jewish Descent in the German Military.* Lawrence: University Press of Kansas, 2002.

Roediger, Werner. "Welche Bedeutung hat der neue Eid für den Offizier der Schutzpolizei?" In *Jahrbuch der deutschen Polizei, 1936,* ed. Hans Kehrl, 51–54. Leipzig: Breitkopf & Härtel, 1936.

Roehr, Werner. *Nacht über Europa: Die Faschistische Okkupationspolitik in Polen.* Cologne: Pahl-Rugenstein, 1989.

Roeseling, Severin. "Konkurrenz, Arbeitsteilung, Kollegialität—Zum Verhältnis von Polizei und Gestapo in Köln." In *Wessen Freund und wessen Helfer? Die Kölner Polizei im Nationalsozialismus,* ed. Harald Buhlan and Werner Jung, 198–229. Cologne: Emons, 2000.

Rossino, Alexander B. "Nazi Anti-Jewish Policy during the Polish Campaign: The Case of Einsatzgruppe von Woyrsch." *German Studies Review* 24 (February 2001): 35–53.

———. *Hitler Strikes Poland: Blitzkrieg, Ideology, and Atrocity.* Lawrence: University Press of Kansas, 2003.

Rühle, Gerd. *Das Dritte Reich: Dokumentarische Darstellung des Aufbaues der Nation.* Berlin: Hummelverlag, 1934.

———. *Das Dritte Reich: Dokumentarische Darstellung des Aufbaues der Nation, das vierte Jahr.* Berlin: Hummelverlag, 1937.

———. *Das Dritte Reich: Das fünfte Jahr.* Berlin: Hummelverlag, 1938.

Rürup, Reinhard, ed. *Topography of Terror: Gestapo, SS, and Reichssicherheitshauptamt on the "Prince Albrecht Terrain."* Berlin: Willmuth Arenhövel, 1989.

———. *Der Krieg gegen die Sowjetunion, 1941–1945.* Berlin: Argon, 1991.

Sandkühler, Thomas. *"Endlösung" in Galizien: Der Judenmord in Ostpolen und die Rettungsinitiativen von Berthold Beitz, 1941–1944.* Bonn: J. H. W. Dietz, 1996.

Schein, Edgar H. *Organizational Culture and Leadership.* San Francisco: Jossey-Bass, 1985.

Schenk, Dieter. *Auf dem rechten Auge blind: Die braunen Wurzeln des BKA.* Cologne: Kiepenheuer & Witsch, 2001.

Schoenberner, Gerhard. *Der gelbe Stern: Die Judenverfolgung in Europa, 1933–1945.* Frankfurt a.M.: Fischer Taschenbuch, 1992.

Schoenfelder, Roland, Karl Kasper, and Erwin Bindewald. *Vom Werden der deutschen Polizei.* Leipzig: Breitkopf & Härtel, 1937.

Segev, Tom. *Soldiers of Evil: The Commandants of the Nazi Concentration Camps.* Translated by Haim Watzman. New York: McGraw-Hill, 1987.

Severing, Carl. *Mein Lebensweg.* Vol. 2. Cologne: Greven, 1950.

Sheperd, Ben. "Hawks, Doves, and Tote Zonen: A Wehrmacht Security Division in Central Russia, 1943." *Journal of Contemporary History* 37 (July 2002): 349–369.

Shirer, William L. *Berlin Diary: The Journal of a Foreign Correspondent, 1934–1941.* New York: Knopf, 1942.

Siggemann, Jürgen. *Die kasernierte Polizei und das Problem der inneren Sicherheit in der Weimarer Republik.* Frankfurt a.M.: Rita G. Fischer, 1980.

Sperber, Jonathan. *Rhineland Radicals: The Democratic Movement and the Revolution of 1848–1849.* Princeton, N.J.: Princeton University Press, 1991.

Spieker, Christoph. "Export von Münster nach Den Haag: BdO Dr. Heinrich Lankenau (1891–1983)." In *Im Auftrag: Polizei, Verwaltung und Verantwortung,* ed. Alfons Kenkmann and Christoph Spieker, 176–191. Essen: Klartext, 2001.

SS: Unter Sigrune und Adler. Krakau: Buchverlag Ost, 1940.

Steinhoff, Johannes, Peter Pechel, and Dennis Showalter. *Voices from the Third Reich: An Oral History.* Washington, D.C.: Regnery Gateway, 1989.

Strasser, Robert B., ed. *The Landmark Thucydides: A Comprehensive Guide to the Peloponnesian War.* New York: Free Press, 1996.

Streit, Christian. *Keine Kameraden: Die Wehrmacht und die sowjetischen Kriegsgefangenen, 1941–1945.* Bonn: J. H. W. Dietz, 1991.

Sydnor, Charles W., Jr. *Soldiers of Destruction: The SS Death's Head Division, 1933–1945.* Princeton, N.J.: Princeton University Press, 1977.

Tec, Nechama. *In the Lion's Den: The Life of Oswald Rufeisen.* Oxford: Oxford University Press, 1990.

Tessin, Georg. "Die Stäbe und Truppeneinheiten der Ordnungspolizei." In *Zur Geschichte der Ordnungspolizei,* by Hans-Joachim Neufeldt, Jürgen Huck, and Georg Tessin, pt. 2, pp. 1–110. Koblenz: Schriften des Bundesarchivs, 1957.

Tucker, Spencer, ed. *The Encyclopedia of the Vietnam War: A Political, Social, and Military History.* Oxford: Oxford University Press, 1998.

von Heydebreck, Peter. *Wir Wehr-Wölfe: Erinnerungen eines Freikorpsführers.* Leipzig: K. F. Koehler, 1931.

Wagner, Elisabeth, ed. *Der General Quartiermeister: Briefe und Tagebuchaufzeichnungen des Generalquartiermeisters des Heeres General der Artillerie Eduard Wagner.* Munich: Günter Olzog, 1963.

Wagner, Heinz. "Die Polizei im Faschismus." In *Strafjustiz und Polizei,* ed. Udo Reifner and Bernd-Rüdeger Sonnen. Frankfurt a.M.: Campus, 1984.

Waite, Robert G. L. *The Vanguard of Nazism: The Free Corps Movement in Postwar Germany, 1918–1923.* Cambridge, Mass.: Harvard University Press, 1952.

Wegner, Bernd. *Hitlers politische Soldaten: Die Waffen-SS, 1933–1945.* 4th ed. Paderborn: Ferdinand Schöningh, 1982.

Wegner, Gregory. *Anti-Semitism and Schooling under the Third Reich.* New York: Routledge Falmer, 2002.

Wehler, Hans-Ulrich. *The German Empire, 1871–1918.* Translated by Kim Traynor. Oxford: Berg, 1985.

Weinberg, Gerhard. *World in the Balance: Behind the Scenes of World War II.* Hanover, N.H.: University Press of New England, 1981.

———. *A World at Arms: A Global History of World War II.* Cambridge: Cambridge University Press, 1994.

———. *Germany, Hitler, and World War II: Essays in Modern German and World History.* Cambridge: Cambridge University Press, 1995.

———, ed. *Hitler's Second Book: The Unpublished Sequel to Mein Kampf by Adolf Hitler.* Translated by Krista Smith. New York: Enigma, 2003.

Weisbrod, Bernd. "Violence and Sacrifice: Imagining the Nation in Weimar Germany." In *The Third Reich between Vision and Reality,* ed. Hans Mommsen, 5–21. Oxford: Berg, 2001.

Westermann, Edward B. " 'Friend and Helper': German Uniformed Police Operations in Poland and the General Government, 1939–1941." *Journal of Military History* 58 (October 1994): 643–661.

———. "Himmler's Uniformed Police on the Eastern Front: The Reich's Secret Soldiers, 1941–1942." *War in History* 3 (1996): 309–329.

———. " 'Ordinary Men' or 'Ideological Soldiers'? Police Battalion 310 in Russia, 1942." *German Studies Review* 21 (February 1998): 41–68.

————. "Shaping the Police Soldier as an Instrument for Annihilation." In *The Impact of Nazism: New Perspectives on the Third Reich and Its Legacy,* ed. Alan Steinweis and Daniel Rogers, 129–150. Lincoln: University of Nebraska Press, 2003.

Wette, Wolfram. "NS-Propaganda und Kriegsbereitschaft der Deutschen bis 1936," In *Francia: Forschungen zur westeuropäischen Geschichte,* ed. Institut Historique Allemand, 567–590. Munich: Artemis, 1978.

Wildt, Michael. *Generation des Unbedingten: Das Führungskorps des Reichssicherheitshauptamtes.* Hamburg: Hamburger Edition, 2003.

Wilhelm, Friedrich. *Die Polizei im NS-Staat: Die Geschichte ihrer Organisation im Überblick.* Paderborn: Ferdinand Schöningh, 1997.

Wirth, Hans, and Fritz Göhler. *Schutzpolizei im Kampfeinsatz: Handbuch der Taktik des Polizeibataillons.* 2d ed. Berlin: E. S. Mittler & Sohn, 1942.

Witte, Peter, Michael Wildt, Martina Voigt, Dieter Pohl, Peter Klein, Christian Gerlach, Christoph Dieckmann, and Andrej Angrick, eds. *Der Dienstkalender Heinrich Himmlers, 1941/42.* Hamburg: Christians, 1999.

Zaika, Siegfried. *Polizeigeschichte: Die Executive im Lichte der historischen Konfliktforschung-Untersuchungen über die Theorie und Praxis der preußischen Schutzpolizei in der Weimarer Republik zur Verhinderung und Bekämpfung innerer Unruhen.* Lübeck: Verlag für polizeiliches Fachschrifttum Georg Schmidt-Römhild, 1979.

Zeller, Friederic. *When Time Ran Out: Coming of Age in the Third Reich.* Sag Harbor, N.Y.: Permanent, 1989.

Zentner, Christian, and Friedemann Bedürftig, eds. *The Encyclopedia of the Third Reich.* Translated by Amy Hackett. New York: Macmillan, 1991.

Zwingelberg, Werner. "Die Erziehung des Polizeibeamten zum Nationalsozialisten." In *Jahrbuch der deutschen Polizei, 1936,* ed. Hans Kehrl, 15–28. Leipzig: Breitkopf & Härtel, 1936.

Zyśko, Wojciech, ed. *Zeszyty Majdanka.* Vol. 5, *Z Dziakalnósci Niemieckies Policji w Dystrykcie Lubelskim w Pierwszym Okresie Okupacji.* Lublin: Wydawnictwo Lubelskie, 1971.

————, ed. *Zeszyty Majdanka.* Vol. 6, *Eksterminacyjna Działalność Truppenpolizei w Dystrykcie Lubelskim w Latach, 1943.* Lublin: Wydawnictwo Lubelskie, 1972.

INDEX